ALSO BY PATRICIA A. TAYLOR

Easy Care Shade Flowers

Easy Care Perennials

The Weekender's Gardening Manual

Easy Care
Native Plants

Easy Care Native Plants

*A Guide to Selecting and Using Beautiful
American Flowers, Shrubs, and Trees
in Gardens and Landscapes*

Patricia A. Taylor

Henry Holt and Company
New York

Henry Holt and Company, Inc.
Publishers since 1866
115 West 18th Street
New York, New York 10011

Henry Holt® is a registered
trademark of Henry Holt and Company, Inc.

Published in Canada by Fitzhenry & Whiteside Ltd.,
195 Allstate Parkway, Markham, Ontario L3R 4T8

Library of Congress Cataloging-in-Publication Data
Taylor, Patricia A., 1938–
Easy care native plants : a guide to selecting and using beautiful
American flowers, shrubs, and trees in gardens and
landscapes / Patricia A. Taylor.—1st Henry Holt ed.
p.   cm.
Includes index.
1. Native plant gardening—United States.   2. Native plants for
cultivation—United States.   3. Native plant gardens—United States.
4. Native plant gardening—Canada.   5. Native plants for
cultivation—Canada.   6. Native plant gardens—Canada.   I. Title.
SB439.T32   1996   96-11758
635.9'517—dc20   CIP

ISBN 0-8050-3861-2

Henry Holt books are available for special promotions
and premiums. For details contact: Director, Special Markets.

First Edition—1996

Designed by Betty Lew

Printed in the United States of America
All first editions are printed on acid-free paper.

1   3   5   7   9   10   8   6   4   2

Half-title page: *Golden columbine* (Aquilegia Chrysantha).

Title page: *White sprays of flowering spurge* (Euphorbia corollata) *add airy
grace to an August border filled with colorful, carefree flowers from throughout
the North American continent. Included here are red and orange cosmos*
(C. sulphureus), *blue salvia* (S. farinacea *'Victoria'*), *pink lobelia* (L. X hybrida
'Rose Beacon'), *orange butterfly weed* (Asclepias tuberosa), *and yellow
Moonbeam coreopsis* (C. *'Moonbeam'*).

CONTENTS

❈

SPECIAL PLANT LISTS

SECTION I

The Basics

Welcome to the incredibly beautiful and diverse subject of American flora. In the following pages, you will meet plants ranging from tiny annuals to towering trees—wonderful, often little known, plants that can be incorporated into a wide variety of gardens and landscapes. For most readers there will be dozens of new plants to try, since many of the over five hundred described here have just entered commerce. All, however, have ancestors that were growing on the North American continent when Columbus set forth from Spain.

What is really remarkable about these plants is that they are to be enjoyed rather than fussed over. That is, you should be able to grow them without using pesticides and with little or no fertilizers if you provide the kind of growing conditions in which they evolved naturally. Thus, there are some plants you will not be able to grow easily because there is no single part of the country that encompasses all growing conditions within its area. But do not despair—there are literally hundreds of other easy care, truly rewarding plants to take their place.

Plants do not exist as independent entities. They are all part of a broad environment. In the case of American plants, this environment extends beyond weather and location to encompass history, politics, and economics. That's what much of this first section is about. It explains why so few of the beautiful flowers we see in fields, meadows, and woods are found in our beds and borders, shows why this is about to change in the near future, and then describes the work and gardens of two major national native plant organizations. Finally, it presents some basic design principles.

Lists of easy care plants, all selected for gardens today, illustrate many of the points and are scattered throughout the discussion. In every case, the first word describing the plant—tree, shrub, perennial, and so on—refers to the chapter in the last section of this book in which detailed information on appearance and growing requirements is presented.

Chapter 1

Native Plants at Home and Abroad: A Brief Historical Review

American flowers have a peculiar history in that they have traditionally been neglected in their native haunts while being honored and treasured abroad. Time and time again, American travelers have visited European gardens and been struck by an exceptionally exquisite plant, only to learn that the unknown beauty grows naturally in the woods or meadows near their stateside homes. Even if you haven't become acquainted with gorgeous native plants on overseas tours, there are probably still many in your area that are excellent yet overlooked candidates for cultivation.

This chapter first explains just what is meant by "native plants" and then briefly reviews how our prejudices against them developed. It is hoped that this historical background will allow you to take a second look at our native flora and to see them not as weeds or wildflowers but rather as handsome plants deserving of honor and pride of position in your beds and borders.

Cultivars of American perennials star at Hall's Croft in Stratford-upon-Avon, England. These flowers are grown for their attractiveness and ease of care rather than for their historical accuracy—the Pilgrims had yet to settle in Plymouth when the Halls first inhabited their home (Mrs. Hall was Shakespeare's daughter). Pictured here in late September are bronze red heleniums, purple blue New England asters, and the long-blooming bright yellow blossoms of Herbsonne (Rudbeckia nitida 'Herbsonne').

THE TRICKY TASK OF DEFINITION

In the beginning, there was no abroad. Our planet featured just one large land mass, now called Pangaea. Its surface unity, however, was misleading because it was actually composed of many parts on top of movable "plates" crammed together much as is a completed jigsaw puzzle. Eventually these "plates" began to shift ever so slightly and as they did so, ocean waters rushed in to fill the resulting rifts. Shortly thereafter, about 100 million years ago, flowering plants made their appearance.

While the process of continental separation must have been spectacular—fiery volcanic eruptions and cataclysmic earthquakes were integral components—it nevertheless occurred at an extremely minute pace. As plants evolved over the next 75 million years, Greenland served as a floral stepping stone between the slowly drifting North American and Eurasian land masses.

A few of our native plants reflect this ancient heritage. Among the more beautiful is the marsh marigold *(Caltha palustris)*, a groundcover with bright yellow spring blossoms and glossy green foliage, which is native throughout moist areas in Eurasia and from Newfoundland and Alaska south to North Carolina and Tennessee.

And then there are the straddlers. These are plant groups—each called a genus in botanical terms because they share many similar characteristics—that acclimated themselves to more than one land mass; in the evolutionary process that followed, their members developed special traits that led to their being characterized as species or distinct life forms. Rhododendrons, for example, are a far-flung genus with individual species located in both North America and Asia.

Occasionally there would be a quirky development among all the plant movement. Astilbes, for example, represent East Asia's elegant gift to American shade gardens. Unknown to most gardeners is the existence of an American species, *A. biternata*, which can be found in the mountains of Kentucky, Virginia, North Carolina, and Georgia. Popularly called false goatsbeard and decked with large white summer plumes, it has just recently entered commercial trade.

While wind, water, and animals all contributed to plant migration throughout the northern hemisphere in this time period, little floral contact occurred with distant land masses in the southern hemisphere. Finally, about 3 million years ago, the Isthmus of Panama directly linked North and South America, allowing the first overland exchange of flowering plants between these two large continents. That's why we have so many plants in common with Eurasia but so little with South America: in geological terms, the floral movement between the southern and northern continents is playing catch-up.

Many plants, however, didn't move. They stayed put and became unique to just one continent. Poppy mallows *(Callirhoe)* and alumroots *(Heuchera)* are two that are native only to North America. Different members of each genus spread about so that species of both plants can be found throughout much of our land.

Other plants refused to take advantage of the wide open spaces of America. They settled in just one place and became known as regional natives. The lovely golden-flowered fremontia shrubs, for example, are native to California, Arizona, and Baja California. In South Carolina, they are as alien as English bluebells.

Franklin tree *(Franklinia alatamaha)* is perhaps the most extreme example of a plant existing in one specific locality. It was found growing in Georgia in 1765 by the Philadelphia botanist John Bartram and his son, William. Had William not returned later to collect seed and introduce it to ornamental gardens it would have disappeared, because this lovely tree, with its glossy green leaves and lustrous white summer flowers, has never been found again in the wild.

Obviously, the term "native American plant" can have many mean-

In early spring, wet deciduous woods throughout the northern hemisphere are home to the sunny yellow flowers of marsh marigolds (Caltha palustris). They are pictured here in their late April splendor at the Pettoranello Gardens in Princeton, New Jersey.

ings. In this book, it covers all plants whose ancestry can be traced to any part of the North American continent prior to the arrival of Columbus in 1492. Using this definition, popular wildflowers such as Queen Anne's lace and field daisies are not natives because they were brought to North America by European colonists. On the other hand, the Alma Potchke aster, a cultivar bred in Germany, is a native because it is a direct descendant of the New England aster *(A. novae-angliae)*.

THE ARRIVAL OF EUROPEANS

The discovery of the Americas and the consequent looting of the gold and silver in the Aztec and Inca civilizations led to a great increase of wealth and financial liquidity in Europe. Among the many activities funded during this prosperous time were the acquisition and study of plants.

Heretofore, plants had been chiefly viewed as food or medicinal sources. Now there was enough money to create new categories of plantspeople: the scientists, who were interested in plants for their botanical aspects, and the ornamentalists, who grew them solely for their beauty. Often, these two new groups would work together with wealthy patrons funding expeditions that led to novelties for their gardens as well as to scientific advances. Such partnerships laid the foundation for the coming centuries of worldwide plant exploration. The first focus of this great endeavor was the North American continent.

Given the frequent political turmoil in Europe, however, scientific collaboration with aristocrats did have its dangerous aspects. John Tradescant the Younger, for example, was a royal servant of Charles I. When civil war broke out in 1642, he thought it expedient to leave England for Virginia, where he spent at least two years collecting plants in relative safety. As a result of this sojourn, Tradescant introduced trumpet honeysuckles *(Lonicera sempervirens)*, red maples *(Acer rubrum)*, and tulip trees to England *(Liriodendron tulipifera)*. Neither he nor his father, however, discovered the native spiderwort *(Tradescantia virginiana)* that Linnaeus named in their

While most astilbes hail from East Asia, false goatsbeard (A. biternata) is at home in moist woodlands in the southeastern United States. They are easy care plants well beyond their native range, however, and are pictured here at Susan Sawicki's late June display gardens in Berlin, Connecticut.

honor; this plant reached mainland Europe sometime in the mid–1500s.

Literally boatloads of plants crossed the ocean. Those that survived the salt air, the pirate raids, and the sinkings were hardy and adaptable. They were also profitable. A new type of business, called a plant nursery, came into being and was instrumental in both acquiring and spreading new plants throughout the European continent. In 1737, for example, the Englishman Christopher Gray published a bilingual catalog to sell American plants in both Great Britain and on the European continent.

While enriching gardens and landscapes, the tremendous volume of American flora overwhelmed the existing methods of naming and classifying plants. Herbalists, horticulturists, and botanists were increasingly frustrated by the fact that they did not speak a common language in describing the fabulous trees, shrubs, bulbs, and perennials crossing the oceans.

In his book detailing the botanical discovery of North America, James Reveal suggests that Linnaeus was spurred to complete the work that became the basis for our current nomenclature system when his student, Pehr Kalm, returned to Sweden in 1751 with a wealth of plants collected during three years of botanizing in our northeast. Kalm was desperate for acknowledged plant names so that he could

Fremontia flowers, pictured here in a late September garden west of London, are native to California. As such, they are aliens not only in England but also throughout the remainder of the North American continent.

write up his work. Linnaeus created them, with each name beginning with the genus (similar to our last name) and then followed by a species name (similar to our first name).

To ensure the universal acceptance of his plant names, Linnaeus drew upon the only common language existing among scholars at the time: Latin. In the process, he created a new language, called Botanical Latin, which remains in use to this day.

There are benefits to being first with a system; in the case of Lin-

---

❋

A BRITISH SELECTION OF CLASSIC NATIVES

The following American flowers appear in CLASSIC GARDEN PLANTS by Will Ingwersen, a preeminent plantsman and holder of Great Britain's highest horticultural award. Published by Collingridge, the book was written in 1975 for British gardeners and represents the author's selection of plants that are of the highest excellence. When this book first appeared, most American gardeners were unaware of the existence of these plants.

Swamp Milkweed *(Asclepias incarnata)*. Perennial with pink or white flowers in early summer.

White Wood Aster *(A. divaricatus)*. Perennial with white flowers late summer into fall.

Dutchman's Breeches *(Dicentra cucullaria)*. Tuber with white flowers in spring.

Mexican Daisy *(Erigeron karvinskianus)*. Annual with white flowers aging to pink, spring through frost.

Pagoda Trout Lily *(Erythronium tuolumnense 'Pagoda')*. Corm with soft yellow flowers in spring.

Fremontia *(Fremontodendron californicum* X *F. mexicanum* 'California Glory')*. Climber with golden yellow flowers all summer.

Bowman's Root *(Gillenia trifoliata)*. Perennial with white flowers on reddish stems in summer.

Box Sandmyrtle *(Leiophyllum buxifolium)*. Shrub with pink buds opening to white flowers in spring.

Missouri Primrose *(Oenothera missouriensis)*. Perennial with yellow flowers in summer.

Mountain Andromeda *(Pieris floribunda)*. Shrub with white flowers in spring.

Snowberry *(Symphoricarpos albus)*. Shrub with small pink flowers in spring and white berries late summer into fall.

Culver's Root *(Veronicastrum virginica)*. Perennial with spires of white or light blue flowers mid- to late summer.

naeus it meant he got to create the new plant names. That's why the nomenclature for so many of our native plants honors his friends and family. Rudbeckias, or black-eyed Susans, for example, commemorate his University of Uppsala professor Olaf Rudbeck. Naming such a prolific group of flowers in honor of this man was most apt: Rudbeck himself had twenty-four children. Linnaeus's regard for Kalm was exemplified in using the name *Kalmia latifolia* for our beautiful mountain laurel, which had been brought to Europe in 1734.

Now properly named and part of a growing distribution system, American plants were welcomed throughout Europe, particularly in England, which had physically escaped the eighteenth- and nineteenth-century ravages of revolutions and wars. Twentieth-century American gardeners besotted with English borders might be amazed to learn that the situation was reversed two hundred years ago. At the end of the eighteenth century, the concept of an "American garden" was the rage in England. The noted English landscape architect Humphry Repton, for example, included such plantings in his park designs.

Of course then, as now, those with the newest and most exotic flora were considered the most fashionable and interesting. Accordingly, the Duke of Wellington installed an American garden at Stratfield Saye outside of Reading. Other such gardens were to be found at Milburn Tower near Edinburgh and at Woburn Abbey near London.

And just as many an English flower border has melted in our humid weather, so too did the American gardens struggle in the climate and lime soil of England. The English, ultimately practical with their long borders, eventually championed only those American plants that were suited to British growing conditions.

They also had something new to occupy their fancies. A great flood of beautiful Asian plants began to enter European commerce in the early 1800s, and with that the novelty of American plants—many of which had then been in British gardens for almost two centuries—began to disappear. Our native plants became so settled in the British border that they became viewed as staples rather than as exotics.

UNDERUTILIZATION BY AMERICAN GARDENERS

It is ironic that such a large number of American plants have been grown longer in European gardens than in ours. In 1975, for example, the noted British plantsman Will Ingwersen published a book titled CLASSIC GARDEN PLANTS. Almost one-fourth of his selections were American natives, plants that only a few American gardeners had probably ever heard of, then or now.

What caused such ignorance? For one thing, the first colonists had neither the time nor the money to indulge in ornamental gardening. According to U. P. Hendrick's A HISTORY OF HORTICULTURE IN AMERICA TO 1860, our forebears were for the most part a scruffy lot that lived in shacks and scorned to add adornment to their properties. Hendrick quotes what can only be described as a particularly snotty British visitor to Long Island in the early 1800s as follows: "This want of attention is hereditary from the first settlers," the Englishman wrote. "They found land so plenty, that they treated small plots with contempt."

Those who did engage in ornamental gardening tended to stick with what they knew best. And what they knew were European flowers: tulips, carnations, feverfew, hollyhocks, and snapdragons were popular plants. There were exceptions, of course, and Thomas Jefferson is an outstanding example. About one-fourth of the plants on his estate were native to America. He not only grew these plants, he also championed them abroad—particularly during his tenure as minister to France from 1785 to 1789.

Jefferson raised and promoted native plants not necessarily because they were American but rather because they were beautiful. Our willow oak *(Quercus phellos)*, according to Peter J. Hatch, Monticello's director of gardens and grounds, was Jefferson's favorite tree. He placed this ideal shade plant, with its majestic shape and tidy yellow fall foliage, around Monticello and also lined it along the streets of Washington, D.C.

A keen plantsperson, Jefferson was always seeking new flowers. Indeed, one of the primary purposes he assigned to the Lewis and Clark expedition was the search for new plants. It is said that if he had not been elected president in 1800, he would have led the expedition himself. As it was, he did get to grow some of plants brought back from the west. In 1812, the Philadelphia nurseryman Bernard McMahon—himself an ardent admirer of American plants—sent Jefferson "a beautiful shrub brought by C. Lewis from the River Columbia, the flower is small but neat, the berries hang in large clusters are of a snow white colour . . . retaining their beauty all the winter. . . . I have given it the trivial English name of Snowberry-bush."

✳

NATIVES GROWN BY THOMAS JEFFERSON

The following, planted by Jefferson and still grown at Monticello today, have been selected for both their garden attractiveness and ease of care by Peter J. Hatch, director of gardens and grounds. For further information on Jefferson's horticultural endeavors, see THOMAS JEFFERSON'S FLOWER GARDEN AT MONTICELLO by Edwin M. Betts and Hazelhurst Bolton Perkins, revised and enlarged by Peter J. Hatch (published for the Thomas Jefferson Memorial Foundation, Inc., by the University Press of Virginia).

American Columbine *(Aquilegia canadensis)*. Perennial with red and yellow flowers in spring.
Sweet Shrub *(Calycanthus floridus)*. Shrub with highly fragrant, brownish maroon flowers in spring.
Carolina Silverbell *(Halesia carolina)*. Small tree with white bell-shaped flowers in spring and lemon yellow fall foliage.
Virginia Bluebell *(Mertensia virginica)*. Perennial with pink buds opening to sky blue flowers in early spring.
Cherokee Plum *(Prunus angustifolia)*. Shrub with white flowers in spring, edible reddish yellow fruits in summer, and yellow fall foliage.
Willow Oak *(Quercus phellos)*. Shade tree with neat foliage turning yellow in fall.
Pinxterbloom *(Rhododendron periclymenoides)*. Shrub with white to light pink flowers in late spring.
Blue-eyed Grass *(Sisyrinchium angustifolium)*. Groundcover with blue flowers in spring.
Snowberry *(Symphoricarpos albus)*. Shrub with small pink flowers in spring and white berries late summer into fall.
Black Haw *(Viburnum prunifolium)*. Shrub with white flowers in late spring, dark blue berries late summer through fall, and wine red fall foliage.

For all his originality in designing and planting his Monticello landscape, however, Jefferson was still guided by European precepts. The natural look, as most prominently espoused by Lancelot "Capability" Brown, was in vogue when Jefferson had toured British gardens in 1786. This style did away with the formal, geometric garden layouts that Jefferson had seen copied in Williamsburg and expanded the garden vision to include all the landscape that the eye could see.

*Two centuries ago, Thomas Jefferson championed American plants for both their beauty and their ease of care. Cherokee plum (*Prunus angustifolia) *provided an additional bonus: edible fruits. It is pictured here in early spring at Monticello and is recommended for today's gardeners by Peter J. Hatch, Monticello's director of gardens and grounds. [Photo by Skip Johns]*

This aping of European fashion—particularly as espoused by the British—is a constant aspect of our garden history. Despite our political independence from England, culturally we have long remained in its thrall. In those days, however, fashion news crossed the Atlantic slowly. When Jefferson died in 1826, the natural landscape concept was flourishing in our country—particularly in the development of our public parks—but was on its way out overseas.

The Europeans were becoming enamored of flowers, cascades of exotic blossoms in gaudy reds, oranges, yellows, blues, and purples. These were the profuse blooms on the sun-loving annuals being shipped from Africa and South America. With the development of greenhouses, it was possible to propagate masses of these plants and to sell them at reasonable prices. The Victorian craze for "bedding out" set in, and has remained popular to this day Gas stations, golf courses, fast food outlets, public buildings, and real estate developments across our country continue to feature colorful petunias, geraniums, and impatiens.

In the European case, this love of cheerful summer annuals was placed on top of a long foundation of growing native American plants. We had no such history in our country. The large number of middle-class households were just beginning to garden when the bedding craze reached our shores. And since that was the fashion, that was how we gardened. Thus, another reason for our ignorance about the beauty of our native flora is that culturally we never had the opportunity to appreciate it.

Andrew Downing, often called the father of American horticulture, bemoaned this situation in an article he wrote for the May 1851 HORTICULTURIST. After noting that American gardens consisted of plants from Africa, South America, Europe, and northern Asia, he wrote that "the rarest spectacle in an American country place is to find . . . any of our native wildflowers." And yet throughout Europe, Downing wrote, American plants were extremely popular. "The Germans make avenues of our tulip-trees," he stated, "and in the South of France one finds more planted magnolias . . . than there are . . . in all the United States."

There is one last reason concerning our historic neglect of American plants that needs to be mentioned. In our garden hearts, many of us are snobs. When we walk through our late summer forests and see the profuse blooms of the white wood aster *(A. divaricatus)*, we look at a mangy weed. Gertrude Jekyll saw it as a perfect late season plant and routinely incorporated it into her borders. Similarly, may apple *(Podophyllum peltatum)* is only a common woodland wildflower here but is a carefully chosen spring groundcover situated under rhododendrons on the grounds of Windsor Castle.

In summary then, three major factors contributed to the majority of American gardens being filled with plants from every corner of the world except that of the surrounding areas: an initial lack of opportunity, the resulting lost opportunity, and the snobbism (or, perhaps, inferiority complex) that decreed "foreign is better."

THE GRADUAL APPRECIATION OF OUR FLORAL HERITAGE

Frederick Law Olmsted, Sr., incorporated a new feature in his landscape design for New York City's Central Park, begun in 1863. He included an American Garden, an idea developed in Europe a half century or so earlier. Of particular note, however, is that there were citizens who felt that Olmsted was not devoting enough attention to native plants.

Their pressure was such that Olmsted felt it necessary to write a rebuttal, entitled "Foreign Plants and American Scenery." In this piece, he argued strenuously that there were many perfectly worthy foreign plants that were quite suited to the American climate in terms of both good looks and ease of maintenance. Obviously, native plant lovers have been around a long time, and from early on they have been a bit vociferous in espousing their cause!

Certainly their beliefs received a tremendous boost with the arrival of O. C. Simonds and Jens Jensen on the landscape architecture scene. Simonds had grown up on a Michigan farm in the decade before the Civil War and Jensen was a Danish immigrant who settled in Chicago in 1886. The two are generally credited with creating the "prairie style" of design. This borrowed from the British natural landscape movement in its respect for the contours and conditions of an area; it then went one step further by keeping plants native to the region in the design.

Both men practiced in the Midwest around the turn of this century. The location and the timing were significant. The Midwest, an area roughly defined as having not only its geographical but also its intellectual and cultural heart anchored in Chicago, was not as beholden to European styles as the East. The immigrants who had trekked there had come to create a new life and to shuck off the old. And while they soon destroyed the land they saw—the prairie was ripped out to make way for farming—they nevertheless appreciated its expansive beauty. Much of the great wealth extracted from the region's natural resources was banked in Chicago, creating ample money for both public institutions and private individuals to fund landscape work.

With Simonds and then Jensen leading the way, regional plants were gorgeously displayed in many of the area's parks and estates. Simonds, for example, combined the scarlet orange foliage of sumacs *(Rhus)*, the purple blues of New England asters, and the rich yellow of goldenrods *(Solidago)* to create spectacular fall displays. His goal was to use these "weeds" not to duplicate the randomness of nature but rather to capture its essence in an artistic arrangement.

Jensen, for his part, favored native trees that branched out rather than up, a pattern that reflected the vast stretches of the prairie. He became a leading booster of the white-flowered Washington hawthorn (grown, incidentally, over a century earlier by Jefferson at Monticello) and other *Crataegus* species. He would often combine these with additional low, horizontally branched trees such as eastern redbud *(Cercis canadensis)* and pagoda dogwood *(Cornus alternifolia)* and

place them in groupings at the edge of meadows, in the process creating an effect in which the extended branches would guide a viewer's eye down the vista.

By incorporating what was then thought of as common weeds into low-maintenance design schemes (Jensen hated trees that needed to be pruned), these two men did much to establish a strong native plant ethic. To this day, the Midwest remains a leader in championing the beauty and diversity of our native flora.

It is one thing, however, for landscape architects to advocate the use of native plants. It is another to find them. Plant nurseries saw no need to propagate native flora when it was easier and more profitable to sell the colorful annuals that were still the rage. Indeed, it was just as easy and perhaps even more profitable to loot nearby woods and meadows to fill orders for indigenous plants.

New Englanders, another bastion of native plant lovers, were among the first to become alarmed over the situation and in 1900 founded the New England Wild Flower Society, the nation's oldest native plant conservation organization. Originally called the Society for the Pro-

*The pagoda dogwood (*Cornus alternifolia*), photographed in mid May at Bowman's Hill Wildflower Preserve in Pennsylvania, was heavily utilized by Jens Jensen in his early twentieth-century Midwest landscape designs. He believed the tree's lateral branches, grouped along meadow edges, not only guided viewers' eyes down the vista but also evoked the expansiveness of the prairie.*

tection of Native Plants, the name was changed to emphasize wild-flowers in hopes of broadening the society's image. (In those days, the term "wild flower" consisted of two words; now, of course, it is just one word—causing much headache for garden writers and editors).

Though the New England Wild Flower Society preached, there were few who practiced. With so much undeveloped land around them, it was difficult for individual gardeners as well as those in the nurseries to realize that freely helping themselves to wild natives was harmful. Research among the archives at Winterthur by garden writer Marnie Flook illustrates this point. She found that Henry Francis du Pont, a highly sophisticated gardener, incorporated many regional flowers in his garden, but not as many as he wanted to. A 1931 note from a New Jersey native plant nursery explains why he was unable to obtain rue anemones *(Anemonella thalictroides)*, walking ferns *(Camptosorus rhizophyllus)*, and miterworts *(Mitella diphylla)*: "These are rare varieties—supply exhausted—found the territory where they grow to be entirely denuded."

With his great wealth, Henry Francis du Pont was able to garden continuously at his own pace. For just about everyone else, however, two world wars, the depression, and a sociological shift in which cheap garden laborers metamorphosed into higher paid factory workers literally changed the landscape.

Following World War II, our country—in garden terms—found itself in a situation similar to that which had existed a century earlier: there was a large group of middle-class home owners seeking to plant newly acquired properties. This time, however, there were long-established organizations and societies devoted to our native flora and eager to wean the American gardening public from its total reliance on tulips, begonias, impatiens, and petunias. Two factors helped to draw attention to the message emanating from these societies: the expansion of the environmental movement and the failure of English-style perennial borders.

In 1962, Rachel Carson published her seminal work, SILENT SPRING. Her warnings that the indiscriminate use of pesticides was harming not only the environment but also human lives reached a large audience. People such as Jerome Rodale, who had been dismissed as a fringe fanatic when his book THE ORGANIC FRONT was published in 1948, began to acquire respectability.

At the same time, many of those who had planted a geranium or two decided it might be fun to expand their garden palettes. Their best examples were gardens created overseas. Native plant societies offered black-and-white pamphlets; British publishers produced books filled with stunning pictures of colorful English borders. The latter were far more tempting, and names such as Gertrude Jekyll and Vita Sackville-West became part of an American gardener's social conversations.

In trying to duplicate the lush romanticism of English gardens, however, many Americans found spikes of delphiniums difficult if not impossible to grow. Not only did they require fertilizers and pesticides, they also demanded staking and pampering. Somehow the British publishers had never emphasized that the romantic, picturesque gardens in their books were extremely labor-intensive. Busy Americans wanted to spend more time admiring rather than working in their gardens.

The news in the black-and-white pamphlets became appealing. They told of thousands of underutilized native plants and how these beautiful creations grew without either fertilizers or pesticides throughout woods and meadows across the country. And, my goodness, they were even to be found in British borders! Gertrude Jekyll, for example, had placed the silver gray foliage of our western sage (*Artemisia ludoviciana*) next to delphiniums to emphasize their rich blues. In admiring the latter, we had neglected to note the former.

Many factors essential to the horticultural success and popularity of our natural flora were now in place. There were isolated but stunning examples of native plant gardens. There were numerous societies. And there was a small but growing number of nurseries offering these plants.

Nevertheless, despite the fact that these flowers had been growing unobtrusively on our continent for centuries, their widespread artistic placement in beds and borders gave rise not only to some truly spectacular gardens but also to passion, politics, and—to some extent—fraud. These more recent aspects of gardening with native plants are discussed in the next chapter.

FOR FURTHER INFORMATION on the origin, discovery, and early use of native American plants start with the following four books.

❀ FLORA OF NORTH AMERICA NORTH OF MEXICO, Volume I, introduction edited by Flora of North America Editorial Committee

(Oxford University Press), describes the physical and geological factors affecting the evolution and distribution of our plants.

❀ A HISTORY OF HORTICULTURE IN AMERICA TO 1860 by U. P. Hedrick, with an addendum to 1920 by Elisabeth Woodburn (Timber Press), is one of the most comprehensive books on this subject. While Hedricks felt compelled to name what seems like every apple cultivar ever grown in our country, he also provides many wonderful stories detailing our sometimes futile, sometimes successful involvements with plants.

❀ GENTLE CONQUEST: THE BOTANICAL DISCOVERY OF NORTH AMERICA by James L. Reveal, with illustrations from the Library of Congress (Starwood Publishing), is a beautifully illustrated, anecdote-filled history of plant exploration on our continent.

❀ JENS JENSEN, MAKER OF NATURAL PARKS AND GARDENS by Robert E. Grese (Johns Hopkins University Press) describes landscape architecture developments and the rise of the native plant ethic in the period from the Civil War to the Depression.

Chapter 2

Native Plants Today: A Primer
on Their Controversies and Charms

When Lady Bird Johnson said she was interested in beautifying America and promoting native plants, few people realized the implications of having a politically connected individual provide a national forum for this subject. At the time (the early 1960s) it seemed to be just another do-gooder cause for a presidential wife to espouse.

Today, the term "native plants" represents an emotionally charged issue that involves billions of dollars and the conflicting opinions and interests of business owners, politicians, environmentalists, government bureaucrats, and conservationists. And yet, at the same time, the term also represents a very narrow scope of gardening, one too often associated with natural settings, such as prairie restorations or spring woodlands. Rarely is the emphasis on beautiful, low-maintenance plants that are as elegant as any to be found elsewhere in the world.

Consider, for example, meadow blazingstar *(Liatris ligulistylus)*. This sun-loving prairie plant, native from Wisconsin and Alberta south to

Many visitors to the National Wildflower Research Center in Texas are amazed to learn that this formal garden consists solely of plants native to the region. Because they are "naturals" little maintenance is required to ensure their attractiveness. Plants in this setting include a lawn of buffalo grass (Buchloe dactyloides) *bordered by wiry sprays of red yucca* (Hesperaloe parviflora)*, a drift of rosy pink prairie verbena* (V. binpinnatifida)*, and—in the back border—a large planting of intensely red autumn sage* (Salvia greggii)*. [Photo: J. C. Blumenfeld]*

Colorado and New Mexico, has crimson red buds that open to brilliant purple flowers in July and August. Monarch butterflies swarm about its blossoms and goldfinches devour its seed. This gorgeous flower is a natural for a prairie landscape, and would be a fabulous addition to a formal garden.

It is this multiuse aspect of native plants that has led to controversy. They are both public and private adornments, decorating thousands of acres of meadows and woods and enriching countless artfully constructed private gardens. They are both part of our natural heritage and the artificial creation of plant breeders here and overseas. In the former case they are often regarded as weeds, and in the latter as exotic as any Asian or European plant. American flora are unique among all plant categorizations in that they are discussed and argued about in patriotic and ethical as well as horticultural terms.

This chapter presents a brief primer on the charms and controversies associated with utilizing native species in gardens today. It also offers suggestions to horticultural pacifists on how to stay clear of some of the highly emotional issues and, in the process, highlights great plants for both public and private settings.

THE INJECTION OF POLITICS

For the first time in our nation's history, federal regulations and, perhaps even more important, federal funds are profoundly influencing our horticultural practices. The crucial 1965 Highway Beautification Act, passed largely through Mrs. Johnson's influence, served to clear the ground. It set a new precedent for the appearance of federally funded roadways by eliminating billboards, screening junkyards, and enhancing landscapes.

In 1987, political involvement in promoting native flora took a regulatory leap forward with the passage of STURAA, the Surface Transportation and Uniform Relocation Assistance Act. It mandated that one-fourth of one percent of every landscape budget using federal transportation funds had to use native plants. Funds emanating from its regulations nudged many seed producers and plant wholesalers to increase facilities devoted to native flora.

In 1994, native plants fully blossomed on the political landscape when President Clinton signed an executive memorandum (which is one step below legally binding regulation) that stipulated the practical use of regional plants on all federal grounds and in all federally funded landscaping projects. This action represented federal involvement on a scale unheard of in our nation's horticultural history. It affects millions of acres and millions of landscaping dollars, as well as the production and distribution of all ornamental plants.

Even before the passage of the Highway Beautification Act, however, several state governments had been busy promoting wildflowers as attractive, easy care candidates for public plantings. In 1973, this work received a considerable boost with the initiation of Operation Wildflower by the National Council of State Garden Clubs. A public/private partnership, Operation Wildflower promotes roadway plantings of native wildflowers and grasses by having clubs financially support and work with state Departments of Transportation (DOTs).

Collaboration in this program varies from state to state. One of the most successful is the partnership formed by the Michigan DOT and the Federated Garden Clubs of Michigan. In this program, the state prepares the site and provides the seed (obtained through a program of supporting Michigan seed growers) while the clubs hire contractors to carry out the planting.

Because it is so well established, the Michigan program provides some proof as to what can be expected from the recent federal commitment to native plants. Two examples represent great news for home gardeners.

In the first place, there are wonderful, easy care American flowers that flourish despite the stress of automotive fumes, the vagaries of weather, and the condition of soil that has been improved but still leaves much to be desired. Perennials native to Michigan and elsewhere that meet these criteria include lavender wild bergamots *(Monarda fistulosa),* golden black-eyed Susans *(Rudbeckia hirta),* yellow prairie coneflowers *(Ratibida pinnata),* and bluish purple New England

Recent federal regulations ensure that native trees such as black tupelo (Nyssa sylvatica) *will be more widely planted in highway and governmental landscaping projects. Only a hint of its exceptionally colorful fall foliage is shown here in early October at the Scott Aboretum, which is located on the campus of Swarthmore College in Pennsylvania.*

asters *(A. novae-angliae)*. The colorful roadway display created by these flowers has been heightened by Michigan DOT personnel with the addition of the equally tough, summer-long white sprays of flowering spurges *(Euphorbia corollata)*.

In the second place, programs using regional native flowers uncover little-known plant gems. One really "special surprise" of the Michigan program, according to DOT personnel, is the performance of round-leaf ragwort *(Senecio obovatus)*. Native from Massachusetts to Michigan, south to Florida and Texas, it has 3-inch green foliage rosettes and lovely yellow spring flowers on 18-inch stems. It's an "exciting little plant" that is now grown not only on Michigan's highways but also in the home gardens of both DOT personnel and Federated Garden Club members.

THE SEARCH FOR SUPPLIES

One unintended result of President Clinton's 1994 executive memorandum was the creation of a supply bottleneck. Simply put, there were not enough native plants to go around. Behind the scenes, private nurseries and government agencies are still scrambling to develop the planting stock—both seedlings and seeds—for the thousands of public acres to be converted to wildflower displays each year as well as to meet the increased demand of home gardeners.

The subject is controversial for many reasons. Chief among these are: (1) the impact of government actions on the nursery business; (2) the destruction of native plant habitats; and (3) the suitability of non-regional seed.

Impact of Government Actions on the Nursery Business

The American Association of Nurserymen (AAN) has not been overly enthusiastic about the federal government's role in stimulating demand for regional natives. Its unhappiness, in large part, is based on the bottom line (that is, possible adverse effects on profits).

Take the beautiful black tupelo *(Nyssa sylvatica)*, for example. A small canopy tree, it resists disease, insects, wind and ice damage, and salt spraying. It has greenish white clusters of spring flowers and glossy green leaves that turn a brilliant scarlet red in fall. Native to the eastern half of the United States from the Atlantic coast to Michigan and

Texas, it can be marketed widely under regional native criteria and is a perfect candidate for city streets as well as suburban properties. Alas, because of its deep taproot, the black tupelo can be difficult to transplant. It needs to be raised in containers and transplanted as a young tree in early spring. If a nursery does not sell all its stock at that time, the trees could well be too difficult to plant the following year and would go on the books as an inventory loss.

Other native trees present different problems. The elegant sourwood *(Oxydendron arboreum)*, for example, is native from Pennsylvania to Florida and Louisiana. Natural stands of this beautiful tree decorate highways throughout its native range with summer sprays of slightly fragrant white flower clusters and fall showings of brilliant red foliage. Is the landscaping potential of this tree too good to be true? Not in the wild, obviously. However, sourwoods only grow 8 to 10 inches a year. It would take a nursery over a decade to have a 10-foot tree ready for market; few can afford such a time investment for selling their stock.

It is simply easier, and more profitable, for nurseries to sell tried-and-true (and award-winning) nonnative performers such as the handsome paperbark maple *(Acer griseum)* or the beautiful flowering cherry *(Prunus* X 'Okame'). Nevertheless, the federal government represents such a huge market that nurseries cannot ignore it. While many AAN members will continue to grumble and while plant devotees will continue to point out the undisputed merits of flora from other continents, political forces ensure that there will be a sustained, steady increase in the volume and variety of native plants offered in the marketplace.

Destruction of Native Plant Habitats

A second supply factor, one long predating government promotion of native flora, is that some individuals view the interest in American plants as a free lunch to be exploited. These people simply go into nearby woods and meadows, dig up whatever they see, and profitably ship the plants around the country.

In her November 19, 1991, column in the WALL STREET JOURNAL, Patti Hagan brought this situation to national attention. Not only were these people depleting natural sources of many species, she noted, they were also carefully concealing their actions. Under Federal Trade Commission guidelines, sources for collected plants did not have to be named if the plants were subsequently grown in a nursery row for at least one growing season before being marketed.

Thus suppliers can, and quite a few do, state that they are offering nursery-grown plants when, in effect, the true source is from a wild population. That's why there is such emphasis in many catalogs today on the fact that the plants are nursery propagated as opposed to nursery grown. In the former case, the business has grown the plant from seed or cuttings and has not ripped it from its natural habitat.

Many feel that rampant development is equally as destructive—if not more so—of native habitats. In 1994, plant conservationists both in and out of government joined forces under a new umbrella organization, the Federal Interagency Native Plant Conservation Committee. The goal is to conserve and protect native plant species by maintaining, restoring, or establishing them on both public and private lands. The work involves not only encouraging commercial propagation of native plant flora but also publicizing the dangers of nonnative plants, such as kudzu and purple loosestrife, which destroy both animal and plant habitats as they run rampant through countrysides.

To carry out the committee's goal, the resources of all native plant enthusiasts—societies, garden clubs, academic experts, amateur botanists, and individual gardeners—are being mobilized throughout the United States, Canada, Mexico, and the Caribbean. Their basic messages to home gardeners are: (1) purchase only nursery-propagated plants; (2) never dig flowers in the wild; and (3) stay away from invasive, nonnative plants.

Suitability of Nonregional Seed

Controversies over the protection of and sources for natives have been further heightened by purists. Is it right, these people ask, to use purple coneflower seed in Texas that was collected from stock plants in California? Actually, the question is not quite as silly as it sounds.

Purple coneflowers *(Echinacea purpurea)* are wide ranging, easy care perennials that are native from Ohio and Iowa south to Georgia and Louisiana. They can be successfully grown, however, from Maine to Alaska and from Florida to California. Generally, these 2- to 5-foot-tall meadow plants bear flowers all summer long that appear as copper-burnished cones surrounded by purple petals. Breeders, however, have been able to encourage traits resulting in greenish cones and cream petals (Alba), maroon cones and rosy pink petals (Bright Star), and bronze cones and white petals (White Lustre). Obviously, this is a plant with a lot of genetic variation.

✳

AN IDAHO SEEDMAN'S SELECTIONS

Loring M. Jones is proprietor of Northplan, a seed company specializing in native plants from throughout North America. Since 1974, his firm has been supplying seed for erosion control, mined-land reclamation, wetlands, and xeriscaping for homes and ranches. Seed is obtained from designated collectors who gather—in a sustainable manner—tree cones, fleshy berries, and dried seed capsules from wildland stands in several western as well as a few midwestern and eastern states. To the extent known, customers are provided with information on seed source and quality. After processing, seed is packaged in quantities ranging from one-quarter ounce to several pounds. Jones reports that the following easy care natives are among his best sellers. To obtain his firm's native species seed list, send a long self-addressed envelope to Northplan, P.O. Box 9107, Moscow, Idaho 83843-1607.

Vine Maple *(Acer circinatum)*. Tree with yellow to vibrant red fall foliage.

Western Serviceberry *(Amelanchier alnifolia)*. Shrub with white spring flowers and edible blue berries in summer.

Bearberry *(Arctostaphylos uva-ursi)*. Evergreen groundcover bearing white flowers tipped with pink in spring and red berries late summer through fall.

Curl-leaf Mountain Mahogany *(Cercocarpus ledifolius)*. Evergreen shrub with white bark and dark green leaves.

Ocean Spray *(Holodiscus discolor)*. Shrub with creamy white flower clusters in summer and orange fall foliage.

Creeping Holly Grape *(Mahonia repens)*. Groundcover with yellow flowers in late spring and dark blue berries in late September.

Wild Mock Orange *(Philadelphus lewisii)*. Shrub with fragrant white flowers in early summer and yellow fall foliage.

Ponderosa Pine *(Pinus ponderosa)*. Conifer with dark green horizontal branches.

Douglas Fir *(Pseudotsuga menziesii)*. Conifer with dark green needles.

Antelope Bitterbush *(Purshia tridentata)*. Shrub with yellow flowers in spring and year-round gray foliage.

Golden Currant *(Ribes aureum)*. Shrub with scented yellow flowers in spring and yellow, red, or purple fruits in late summer.

Snowberry *(Symphoricarpos albus)*. Shrub with small pink flowers in spring and white berries late summer into fall.

✳
A DANISH PLANTSWOMAN'S PREFERENCES

As do plantspeople throughout Europe, Grethe B. Petersen propagates an extensive list of native Americans for sale at Lynge Staudegartneri, the perennial nursery she owns and operates in Denmark. Her business is described by an admiring American nurseryman as "an absolute gem, almost all organic, and always with something new and exciting." Though it was "much more difficult than I imagined" to select only twelve, she submitted the following as being both attractive and easy to grow.

Windflower *(Anemone multifida)*. Perennial with white flowers in early summer.

Black Cohosh *(Cimicifuga racemosa)*. Perennial with candlelike spires of white flowers in summer.

Fairy Candles *(Cimicifuga racemosa* var. *cordifolia)*. Perennial with fragrant, creamy white flowers in late summer.

Fringed Bleeding Heart *(Dicentra eximia)*. Perennial with pink flowers late spring into fall.

Purple Coneflower *(Echinacea purpurea)*. Perennial with purple, rose pink, or white flowers all summer.

Bowman's Root *(Gillenia trifoliata)*. Perennial with white flowers on reddish stems in summer.

Lewisia *(L. cotyledon* hybrids)*. Perennial with white, orange, salmon, or pink flowers in late spring.

Gayfeather *(Liatris spicata)*. Corm with lavender pink flower spikes in summer.

Streamside Lupine *(Lupinus polyphyllus* hybrids)*. Perennial with yellow, white, blue through red, or pink flowers late spring into summer.

Evening Primrose *(Oenothera biennis)*. Biennial with yellow flowers all summer.

Goldsturm Black-eyed Susan *(Rudbeckia fulgida* var. *sullivantii* 'Goldsturm')*. Perennial with black-centered yellow flowers summer into fall.

Fringe Cups *(Tellima grandiflora)*. Groundcover with small, greenish white bell flowers on wiry stems in late spring.

It stands to reason, then, that purple coneflowers raised on acreage in California will exhibit adaptations suited to that growing climate and not necessarily to environmental conditions elsewhere. It is this rationale that underlies the concept and promotion of ecotype seed: seed harvested in the locality where it is to be planted.

The Iowa Ecotype Project, for example, is a special program based at the University of Northern Iowa. Under it, about twenty Iowa-based seed dealers are encouraged to carry locally collected and produced ecotype seed for use in highway plantings. The project reduces state reliance on seed from western varieties, many of which often lack resistance to local diseases, pests, and even weather.

Thus, the increased demand for locally produced seed resulting from federal and state government actions has proven to be a great bonus for many businesses. As with any major change, some people are benefiting handsomely from political promotion of native plants and others are having to undergo shifts in both their operations and outlooks.

THE DEBATE ABOUT DIVERSITY

Several years ago, Kim Hawks, proprietor of Niche Gardens in Chapel Hill, North Carolina, collected the seed of a giant sunflower *(Helianthus giganteus)* growing wild in fields near her nursery. She was attracted to its blossoms, which were a soft pastel as opposed to the usual warm yellow. When Hawks's customers saw its beautiful late summer display of flowers on top of 7-foot stems, they urged her to put the plant into production.

A superb local gardener named Sheila Goff was politely persistent about this, Hawks explains, and in honor of both her efforts and expertise, Hawks called the plant Sheila's Sunshine. With its lovely color and light, airy form, this is an easy care garden giant that adds grace rather than bulk to borders.

According to guidelines issued in 1995, however, Sheila's Sunshine is not a favored plant in any public landscaping project funded with federal money. Even though it is a naturally occurring native American flower, it is still a cultivar—a term used to describe plants that must be propagated vegetatively or through careful monitoring of seed production to ensure that the desired trait (pastel yellow in this case) remains dominant.

So, once again, the question of genetics pops up. Those who wish to preserve diversity feel that plant selections should not be made; that variation in plant forms and colors is to be appreciated and admired. Perhaps most important, variation is necessary for survival of any species. Plant

Under guidelines issued in 1995, cultivars and hybrids such as the stately Ruby Slippers lobelia are not favored in landscaping projects funded with federal money. The two flowers in the background— white boltonia and yellow helenium—can be included because they are species plants.

breeders and most horticulturists will have none of this. They feel that superior plants—whether found occurring naturally in the wild or bred in a laboratory—should be treated as such. If cultivars or hybrids better resist disease and if they are more beautiful, then these forms—and not the common wild plant—should adorn beds and borders.

Well, yes, say those who seek a middle ground. Put your cultivars and your hybrids in your cultivated gardens and place your common species, with their great genetic variation, in the large plantings required for public areas such as roadways. This makes not only common but also economic sense. Due to the extra cost associated with creating and preserving a desired trait, cultivars and hybrids tend to be more expensive than species plants. Large public works projects cannot afford such additional costs; gardeners working with one or two exquisite plants feel they are well worth a higher price tag.

No one knows this better than savvy overseas plant breeders. For well over a century, European nurseries have been creating stunning cultivars and hybrids from American flora, plants that are widely grown in public and private gardens throughout Europe and which are just now being snapped up on our side of the Atlantic Ocean. More recently, Japanese breeders have become entranced with the beauty of our plants. Their work, for example, started the transformation of lisianthus *(Eustoma grandiflorum)* from a pesty prairie plant, roaming about from Colorado and Nebraska south to Texas, into an elegant cut flower and pot plant found in chic settings from coast to coast.

Gardeners, in the final analysis, are as individual and as idiosyncratic as the thousands of plants they admire and grow. Thought police could never take over the garden. Catchy magazine titles—such as "Against Nativism"—could, however, deter many from exploring the great diversity and splendor of American flora.

Try some of these plants in your gardens. Whether you take either the national or the regional approach described below, you will find your beds and borders considerably enriched with their presence.

A NATIONAL APPROACH: GARDEN IN THE WOODS, FRAMINGHAM, MASSACHUSETTS

The Garden in the Woods in Framingham, Massachusetts, is a premier showcase for the horticultural display of North American plants. Here you will find Northwest natives such as the spring blooming Oregon grapes *(Mahonia aquifolium)* with clusters of yellow flowers; Midwest charmers such as prairie blazingstars *(Liatris pycnostachya)* with purple spikes in summer; and Southeast flowers such as pink turtleheads *(Chelone lyonii)*, which bloom around Labor Day.

These and the garden's primary collection of Northeast natives can coexist in a 45-acre setting located 25 miles west of Boston because they are each placed in a habitat carefully created to mimic their natural growing conditions. Using this strategy, the garden beautifully demonstrates how easy it is to grow a broad range of wonderful plants.

Indeed, many of the displays on the garden's grounds had previously been deemed unsuitable for a New England setting. Most literature, for example, states that the fiery red flowers of the southeastern plumleaf azalea *(Rhododendron prunifolium)* are not hardy north of Washington, D.C. At Garden in the Woods, they bloom in a filtered shade location in late summer and have done so for a decade at this writing.

What is perhaps even more amazing about this horticultural treasure trove—over 1,500 native flowers, trees, shrubs, and grasses are on display—is that it is an exceptionally low-maintenance creation. Absolutely no pesticides are used on the property. If a plant requires extra care to survive, it is not grown. There are simply too many other beautiful natives to take its place.

The garden's exquisite presentation of plants from throughout our

At Garden in the Woods in Massachusetts, visitors can see beautiful displays exemplifying the horticultural potential of native plants from throughout the North American continent. Pictured here in early June, for example, are the wispy silver pink seedheads of prairie smoke (Geum triflorum), *the pale blue flowers on a large clump of amsonia* (A. tabernaemontana var. salicifolia), *and rose verbena* (V. canadensis). *In the background, the creamy white buds on a majestic spire of prairie indigo* (Baptisia leucantha) *rise behind a planting of prickly pears* (Opuntia humifusa).

✳

A NORTH AMERICAN ARRANGEMENT

This list of exceptionally easy care plants, representing natives from throughout North America, was complied by Heather McCargo, propagator at Garden in the Woods. If she had to select just one, she reports, it would be the heartleaf alexander.

Nodding Onion *(Allium cernuum)*. Bulb with sprays of white, pink, rose, or lilac flowers in summer.

Swamp Milkweed *(Asclepias incarnata)*. Perennial with pink or white flowers in early summer.

Smooth Aster *(A. laevis)*. Perennial with white through lavender flowers late summer into fall.

Pink Turtlehead *(Chelone lyonii)*. Perennial with pink or rosy purple flowers in late summer.

Wild Geranium *(G. maculatum)*. Perennial with blue violet flowers in spring.

Bowman's Root *(Gillenia trifoliata)*. Perennial with white flowers on reddish stems in summer.

Horsemint *(Monarda punctata)*. Perennial with purple-spotted yellow flowers in summer.

Beard Tongue *(Penstemon smallii)*. Perennial with pink and white flowers late spring into summer.

Blue Woodland Phlox *(P. divaricata)*. Groundcover with fragrant light blue flowers in spring.

Seaside Goldenrod *(Solidago sempervirens)*. Perennial with golden flowerheads in fall.

Labrador Violet *(Viola labridorica)*. Groundcover with purple flowers in spring and purple-tinged foliage throughout growing season.

Heartleaf Alexander *(Zizia aptera)*. Perennial with golden yellow flowers clustered like Queen Anne's lace in spring.

country is a direct reflection of its history. It was created by two men—Will C. Curtis, a landscape architect with a passion for plants, and Howard Stiles, who started as an assistant and became equally passionate and knowledgeable about native flora.

Curtis bought the property, which included an overgrown, abandoned quarry, in 1930. Then, as now, the acreage consisted of a glacially sculpted terrain of rolling hills, ponds, and streams. He set about transforming it into a landscape masterpiece. At first he was interested in pairing closely related Asian and New England plants. This work is reflected in the garden's woodland section. With increasing concern over the depletion of American plants in the wild, however, he began to concentrate on native flora. Given his initial international scope, it is not surprising that he opted to include plants from throughout North America in his subsequent designs. The emphasis on low maintenance never changed, however. With only a landscape architectural practice to support him, Curtis had neither the money nor the time to coddle plants.

By 1965, Curtis's goal of creating a "big wildflower sanctuary in which plants will be grown [and] their likes and dislikes discovered" was realized. He recognized, however, that suburban encroachment and his increasing age threatened its survival. Thus, that year, he donated the garden to the New England Wild Flower Society, a longtime champion of the beauty of native flora and the need for their conservation.

Today, Garden in the Woods serves not only as the physical headquarters for the society but also as a botanical garden and sanctuary. More than two miles of landscaped trails wind through the property. While retaining Curtis's naturalistic style, the society has expanded

Heartleaf alexander (Zizia aptera), an easy care recommendation from Garden in the Woods in Massachusetts, is an elegant little perennial. Its spring blossoms linger on as dried flower heads long into summer and its exquisitely scalloped green leaves are thinly edged with a hint of gold. [Photo: Dorothy S. Long]

both the number of landscaped habitats and the variety of plants. The Western Garden, for example, contains over 100 plants from plateau areas west of the Mississippi.

The society is, however, selective in the kinds of plants it recommends for different groups. When approached by the Massachusetts DOT, for example, it named only regional natives for highway plantings. It feels these are best suited for large, unbounded public areas because they are naturally adapted to such sites and are thus low-maintenance and noninvasive.

In contained settings, such as its own property, the possibilities for working with native flora from throughout the continent are literally unlimited. New plants are continually added to test their garden worthiness or to provide a safe refuge from their destruction in the wild; approximately 200 flowers at Garden in the Woods are rare or endangered species.

The society has also expanded propagation research, which is conducted in outdoor nursery beds and in a 1,000-square-foot passive solar greenhouse. It supports this work because it wants to obviate the need for wild collection by demonstrating the feasibility and profitability of commercially propagating native flora. And the society practices what it preaches by raising thousands of plants for sale at its museum shop throughout the growing season. For those too far away to be tempted by its varied and wonderful plant offerings, it sells seeds through the mail.

From April 15 through October 31, visitors to the garden can take the equivalent of a botanical tour of the North American continent while seeing a sumptuous, ever-changing, landscaped display of carefully labeled flower and foliage combinations. Thanks to the garden's research, propagation, and extensive education programs, gardeners across the country can learn how to transform their beds and borders into similar horticultural settings.

A REGIONAL APPROACH: NATIONAL WILDFLOWER RESEARCH CENTER, AUSTIN, TEXAS

Though there are Texas flowers at Garden in the Woods, there is not one regional northeastern native at the stunning new headquarters for the National Wildflower Research Center in Austin, Texas. In con-

trast to the garden's continent-wide horticultural focus, the center takes a regional, holistic approach. Both the buildings and the landscaping on the 42-acre property in the heart of Texas Hill Country are site-specific, carefully designed, and constructed to honor the integrity of the land.

The center was founded by Lady Bird Johnson in 1982 as an education and research institution to champion the beauties and landscape potential of regional flora. There was a bit of radicalism in its agenda as well, for Mrs. Johnson was dismayed at what she perceived to be the horticultural homogenization of America. She wanted Texas to look like Texas, blanketed with its famous bluebonnets *(Lupinus texensis)* in spring, and New England to look like New England, ablaze with sugar maples *(Acer saccharum)* in fall. Bluebonnets do not do well in New England and sugar maples are not suited to the many dry, open areas of Texas. That was Mrs. Johnson's point and has been the credo of the center since its founding.

There are, literally, thousands of indigenous plants in each region of

The colorful flowers of pavonia (P. lasiopetala) bloom from late spring to frost at the National Wildflower Research Center in Texas. [Photo: J. C. Blumenfeld]

❋

A SOUTHWEST SAMPLER

Selected by Denise R. Delaney, horticulturist at the National Wildflower Research Center, the following plants provide year-long interest in a garden or landscape. While these Southwest natives are all quite beautiful, ease of care was the primary selection criterion.

Northern Sea Oats *(Chasmanthium latifolium)*. Grass with green foliage and arching flower heads that turn copper in fall and then tan in winter.

Purple Coneflower *(Echinacea purpurea)*. Perennial with purple, rose pink, or white flowers all summer.

Red Yucca *(Hesperaloe parviflora)*. Perennial with coral to salmon pink flowers on pinkish stems from spring into early summer.

Possumhaw *(Ilex decidua)*. Shrub with orange to scarlet red berries lasting through winter.

Cardinal Flower *(Lobelia cardinalis)*. Perennial with scarlet flowers in late summer.

Trumpet Honeysuckle *(Lonicera sempervirens)*. Vine with red, orange, or yellow flowers through-out summer.

Agarito *(Mahonia trifoliata)*. Evergreen shrub with yellow flowers in early spring and bright red berries in summer.

Turk's Cap *(Malvaviscus arboreus* var. *drummondii)*. Hardy annual with red flowers late summer into fall.

Lindheimer Muhly *(Muhlenbergia lindheimeri)*. Grass with fountainlike form and silvery plumes in fall.

Pavonia *(P. lasiopetala)*. Annual with pink flowers from late spring to frost.

Autumn Sage *(Salvia greggii)*. Hardy annual with red, coral, pink, or white flowers spring to frost.

our country. Tap your artistic imagination, the center tells us all, and create beds and borders with these plants. To help spread the message, the center distributes fact sheets and kits giving recommended native species for each state, regional sources for native plants and seeds, and propagation and seed collection tips.

Of course, gardening with regionally native plants translates to little or no use of pesticides or fertilizers. There is one area of the center's complex, however, where chemicals are used. This is located in the demonstration gardens, where three plots of the same size feature (1) a formal setting with a lush green lawn and foreign plants, (2) a similar formal setting with regional flowers and a mowed lawn of buffalo grass *(Buchloe dactyloides)*, and (3) an elegant natural setting with regional plants and a very small turf area.

The first plot requires heavy use of both fertilizers and pesticides. Data are being collected on the dollar costs and work hours needed to maintain this setting as opposed to its two companions. It is hoped that this dramatic example, an ongoing project begun in 1995 with the center's move to its new headquarters, will be persuasive in convincing individual home owners to try native plants.

Although not quite as blatant as the above three research plots, the center's entire landscape is a demonstration project of ways to work with native plants in both natural and created settings. There are, for example, a butterfly garden, a wildflower meadow, and a children's garden. The whole represents the successful collaboration between Overland Partners, Inc., of San Antonio; master site planner Darrel Morrison of the University of Georgia; and landscape architect J. Robert Anderson of Austin.

One of the more dramatic plantings—"different from anything seen before," according to Morrison—is the seed court, located smack in the middle of the complex and surrounded by buildings and the wooded shade garden. In this court, ribbons of color have been been created with swaths of grasses and wildflowers. There is a silver, blue, purple, and pink ribbon; an orange and copper band; and a yellow strip with purple accents. It represents a highly stylized version of a prairie landscape and no one—not even Anderson or Morrison—knows what it will evolve into. The consensus is that the ribbons will eventually become feathered at the edges as some plants at the color borders intermingle. Beyond that, nature holds its own secrets.

What was discovered in the planning stages, however, is that several of the more than eighty species initially chosen for the ribbon plantings in the seed court were not commercially available. And since they were not being propagated, they were not included in the final planting.

Though regional in scope, the center remains national in stature as it collaborates with institutions throughout the country—including Garden in the Woods—in promoting native flora and respect for the environment. Thanks in large part to the leadership provided by these two organizations, the crucial grass-roots support of numerous other local, regional, and national horticultural institutions, and now the significant involvement of federal and state governments, more American flowers are being cultivated than ever before. And in introducing and growing a stunning variety of native plants, both institutions and individuals are discovering—as did those involved in beautifying Michigan's highways—that there are many "truly delightful," simply lovely, absolutely easy care plants waiting to grace beds and borders. What a great time to be gardening!

FOR FURTHER INFORMATION:

❀ about Operation Wildflower, contact The National Council of State Garden Clubs, Inc., 4401 Magnolia Avenue, St. Louis, Missouri 63110-3492 (314/776-7574).

❀ about groups involved in conserving and protecting native plant species, contact Center for Plant Conservation, c/o Missouri Botanical Garden, P.O. Box 299, St. Louis, Missouri 63166 (314/577-9450).

❀ about The Iowa Ecotype Project, contact Office for Integrated Roadside Vegetation Management, 113 CEEE, University of Northern Iowa, Cedar Falls, Iowa 50614-0293.

❀ about mail-order seed and the many other programs of Garden in the Woods, send a self-addressed stamped envelope to the New England Wild Flower Society, 180 Hemenway Road, Framingham, Massachusetts 01701-2699 (617/237-4924 or 508/877-7630).

❀ about recommended natives specific to geographical regions, information kits, and the many programs of the National Wildflower Research Center, send a self-addressed, stamped envelope to the center at 4801 La Crosse Boulevard, Austin, Texas 78739 (512/292-4200).

Chapter 3

Native Plant Gardens: A Professional and a Novice Approach to Design

In very basic terms, native plant gardens are no different from any other gardens in that they are a group of plants artistically placed in a site. Thus, while their plant selection is constrained by specific criteria, their placement still follows general design principles.

This chapter briefly describes these principles and then tells how they were applied in the creation of two native plant gardens: one within the National Garden in Washington, D.C., and the other in my front yard in Princeton, New Jersey. Roger G. Courtenay, a member of the American Society of Landscape Architects, principal in EDAW, Inc., in Alexandria, Virginia, and chief landscape architect for the National Garden, utilized a carefully thought-out strategy to bring about a garden that serves as a national demonstration of conservation, ecological, and environmental issues. While I certainly can't claim my approach was well thought out (my mistakes were far too numerous for that), I nevertheless did do some prior planning and successfully

Great care needs to be taken in selecting trees and large shrubs because their demise results in very visible garden disasters. The Pennsylvania Horticultural Society's Gold Medal Award seeks to obviate such problems by singling out woody ornamentals that are of exceptional merit with regard to both appearance and low maintenance. Florida silverbell (Halesia diptera var. magniflora), pictured here in an early May setting in a Philadelphia suburb, is one such winner. "It has everything going for it except fame," commented a plant evaluator. [Photo: Larry Albee] met my goal of showing all who pass by that it's easy to have a color-ful flower display without the use of pesticides or fertilizers.

GENERAL DESIGN PRINCIPLES

As befits the gap between a professional and an amateur, Courtenay and I use different terms to describe our projects. To my pleasant sur-prise, however, we each employed the same three phases in our design work. Courtenay refers to the first as the program and site analysis phase and I call it determining the garden's purpose and location. We are both talking in terms of three components: the garden's function, its site, and how the two match.

The purpose can be as simple as wanting some flowers blooming in front of a house and as complex as expressing an ethical belief such as an artistic homage to plants native to a region. Choosing a site can be a complicated issue. While some people have a wide range of options as to where they want to establish their gardens, others are severely constrained. City gardeners, for example, are often restricted to a small balcony or roof. That's why it is so important to match the site with the purpose. While city gardeners, as shown in the list on page 39, can grow a wide array of native plants, they can't have a prairie landscape on a blacktop roof.

It is essential that the site and purpose of the garden—or the pro-gram, as Courtenay would say—are harmonious. Every other step fol-lows from such unity. Disaster or, at a minimum, a series of errors are inevitable with a mismatch. Constructing a bog garden, for example, in an area without ready access to water is a recipe for horticultural tragedy or unending work.

Courtenay describes the second phase as conceptual design and I think of it as analyzing the garden's structure and growing conditions. The two key components are the physical layout of the garden and a review of light, drainage, and soil composition.

It is in the physical layout of the garden, I believe, that the talents of landscape architects truly come to the fore. These are people trained to look at an entire setting and then to create a composition of plants and structures that enhances the scene, rather than one that stands alone. Only after sketching a design that complements the landscape do they then review the layout of the proposed garden. This last activ-

✳

NATIVES FOR CITY ROOFTOPS, BALCONIES, AND PATIOS

While city gardeners are severely restricted in their site selections, they can still choose numerous native plants that thrive under what are essentially alien conditions. The following are among the many recommended by Manhattan gardener and NEW YORK TIMES writer Linda Yang in THE CITY AND TOWN GARDEN: A HANDBOOK FOR PLANTING SMALL SPACES AND CONTAINERS (Random House). She writes from personal experience that all can be grown in either containers or the ground and are both beautiful and easy care.

Ageratum *(A. houstonianum).* Annual with fuzzy summer-long flowers in blue, purple, pink, or white.

Fringed Bleeding Heart *(Dicentra eximia).* Perennial with pink flowers late spring into fall.

Oakleaf Hydrangea *(H. quercifolia).* Shrub with cones of creamy white summer flowers aging to pink and rich wine red fall foliage.

Inkberry *(Ilex glabra).* Shrub with handsome jet black berries that often persist through winter.

Trumpet Honeysuckle *(Lonicera sempervirens).* Vine with red, orange, or yellow flowers throughout summer.

Christmas Fern *(Polystichum acrostichoides).* Fern with dark, evergreen fronds.

Celandine Poppy *(Stylophorum diphyllum).* Perennial with yellow flowers in spring and sometimes into midsummer.

American Arborvitae *(Thuja occidentalis).* Conifer with fine-textured yellow green foliage.

Mexican Shell Flower *(Tigridia pavonia).* Bulb with white, yellow, orange, or red petals and densely spotted, usually purplish centers in summer.

Blueberry *(Vaccinium corymbosum).* Shrub with white spring flowers, edible blue summer fruit, and crimson fall foliage.

ity is often called constructing the "bones" of the garden—it's what you see when the area is naked, a time that usually occurs in winter for most gardeners.

Questions that are reviewed at this stage include the organization of the garden (will it be round, square, or abstract); the use of paths and the direction in which they will guide visitors; and the placement of large structures, such as walls of manmade materials or of trees and shrubs. Landscape architects will then step back and see how their initial

GOLD MEDAL AWARD PROGRAM

The Pennsylvania Horticultural Society's Gold Medal Award Program is a boon for home gardeners and landscape architects because it singles out little-known plants that are not only superb candidates for gardens but also commercially available. Each year, the program cites four to six woody ornamentals that are hardy, handsome, and low maintenance. Up to fourteen ardent horticulturists serve on the award committee; they not only personally inspect mature nominees but also scrutinize all recommendation papers. At this writing, the following native Americans have received Gold Medal Awards. For further information on the program and on retail and wholesale sources for these plants, send a self-addressed, stamped envelope to: Gold Medal Award Program, PHS, 100 North 20th Street, Philadelphia, Pennsylvania 19103-1495.

Red Buckeye *(Aesculus pavia)*. Shrub with bright red flowers in spring.

Heritage River Birch *(Betula nigra* 'Heritage'*)*. Tree with creamy white bark that exfoliates to reveal a salmon pink to reddish brown inner bark.

American Yellowwood *(Cladrastis lutea)*. Tree with fragrant white spring flowers and yellow fall foliage.

Hummingbird *(Clethra alnifolia* 'Hummingbird'*)*. Dwarf shrub with fragrant white or pink flowers in summer.

Silver and Gold Dogwood *(Cornus sericea* 'Silver and Gold'*)*. Shrub with creamy white flowers in spring, variegated foliage all growing season, and colorful bare red bark in winter.

Winter King *(Crataegus viridis* 'Winter King'*)*. Disease resistant, almost thornless tree with white spring flowers, purple fall foliage, and orange red winter fruit.

Blue Mist Fothergilla *(F. gardenii* 'Blue Mist'*)*. Shrub with white flowers in spring, blue green foliage spring through summer, and flashy orange red foliage in fall.

Florida Silverbell *(Halesia diptera* var. *magniflora)*. Tree with large white bell-shaped flowers in spring and yellow fall foliage.

Snow Queen Hydrangea *(H. quercifolia* 'Snow Queen'*)*. Shrub with upright cones of creamy white summer flowers aging to pink and rich wine red fall foliage.

Densa *(Ilex glabra* 'Densa'*)*. Thick, dense shrub with handsome jet black berries that often persist through winter.

Scarlett O'Hara *(Ilex verticillata* 'Scarlett O'Hara'*)*. Shrub with small, clear red berries through much of winter.

Winter Red *(Ilex verticillata* 'Winter Red'*)*. Shrub with long-lasting scarlet red berries persisting through March.

Henry's Garnet *(Itea virginica* 'Henry's Garnet'*)*. Shrub with fragrant white flowers late spring to early summer and scarlet to purple red fall foliage.

Edith Bogue Magnolia *(M. grandiflora* 'Edith Bogue'*)*. Extra-hardy tree with large, fragrant, creamy white flowers in June and July.

Winterthur Viburnum *(V. nudum* 'Winterthur'*)*. Shrub with creamy white flowers in early summer, dusty blue berries in early fall, and red to purple fall foliage.

overall sketches of the garden—now filled in with structures—fit in with the surrounding area. I suspect few home gardeners take this step. Landscape architects, on the other hand, will often go back and forth several times to ensure that the garden is not only harmonious within its own borders but also within the setting in which it is located.

Growing conditions are, of course, crucial to the success of any garden. If the proposed area is part of a dense woodland, trees may need to be limbed (lower branches cut off) to let in more light. Additionally, since the numerous roots in such a setting compete for water, flowers and shrubs amenable to dry shade may be called for even though rainfall is usually adequate every year. On the other hand, woodlands inhabit wet areas also and here bog plants would definitely be suitable, as long as they are bog plants that tolerate shade.

It is at this stage of the garden's creation that lists are constructed of plants suitable to the growing conditions. This, of course, is one bedrock of an easy care gardening philosophy: in choosing hardy plants that are suited to an area's growing conditions, you can dispense with fertilizers, pesticides, and other forms of plant coddling. (Another bedrock, one which I confess to ignoring, is to keep the garden small.)

Great care needs to be taken in acquiring trees and shrubs, or woody ornamentals as they are called by horticulturists. These are not only expensive but also relatively large; their demise results in very noticeable garden disasters. Gardeners east of the Mississippi are fortunate in having the Pennsylvania Horticultural Society's Gold Medal Award program as a resource. This singles out underutilized woody ornamentals that are hardy, handsome, low maintenance, and commercially available. North American natives that have been honored through this program are presented in the list on pages 40–41 and may well be perfect candidates for many gardens in the Pacific Northwest and in surburban settings in the Midwest.

Landscape architects call the last phase of creating a garden design development and I call it the fun part—selecting and then arranging materials, including plants and structures. At this point, the physical components of the garden have been created and a list of plants compiled. Now it's time to look at both and match the two.

A landscape architect, for example, has specified a tree of a certain size and shape. In this last phase, plant lists are scrutinized to determine which ones match the conceptual design. Actually, the plants more than match the concept; they bring it to life as they are selected for their flower color and size, foliage form and shape, and overall size and bloom period. These attributes are then grouped in a four-dimensional arrangement that balances height, width, depth, and time (or season).

THE REGIONAL GARDEN AT THE NATIONAL GARDEN, WASHINGTON, D.C.

The National Garden is located in the shadow of the U.S. Capitol and occupies three acres immediately adjacent to the U.S. Botanic Conservatory on the National Mall. Envisioned by Congress as a commemoration of its bicentennial, the garden has four major components: the rose garden, which celebrates our country's national flower; the environmental learning center, which provides classroom and meeting space for educational programs; water and water features, which fluidly unite the entire setting; and the regional garden, which occupies a central position. The following describes the design work used in creating the last garden.

Phase I: Program and Site Analysis
In one sense, Courtenay was relieved of a major planning component in that he had nothing to do with the basic program of the regional plant garden. When he was awarded his assignment, Congress had already stated its wishes that the National Garden beautifully demonstrate the value of an environmentally responsible approach to an urban American garden. The site—smack in the heart of Washington, D.C.—was certainly appropriate to one part of the program. And, of

✳

A CAPITOL COLLECTION

The following natives are among the many on display at the foot of the U.S. Capitol as part of the U.S. Botanic Garden's National Garden. They were cited for their ease of care ("it was extremely difficult to choose only a representative dozen") by Ann Anderson, Shelley Rentsch, and Celia Radek, EDAW landscape architects who worked with U.S. Botanic Garden staff on plant selection for the project.

Bottlebrush Buckeye *(Aesculus parviflora)*. Shrub with cones of creamy white flowers in mid-summer.

American Beautyberry *(Callicarpa americana)*. Shrub with tiny blush pink flowers in spring and purple berries late summer through winter, depending on geographical location.

Trumpet Creeper *(Campsis radicans)*. Vine with orange to scarlet flowers all summer.

Red Osier Dogwood *(Cornus sericea)*. Shrub with creamy white flowers in spring and colorful bare red bark in winter.

Dwarf Fothergilla *(F. gardenii)*. Shrub with white flowers in spring and flashy orange red foliage in fall.

Rose Mallow *(Hibiscus moscheutos)*. Perennial with dark-eyed red, pink, or white flowers late summer to midfall.

Winterberry *(Ilex verticillata)*. Shrub with scarlet red berries persisting through January.

Bee Balm *(Monarda didyma)*. Perennial with purple, red, pink, or white flowers in summer.

Virginia Creeper *(Parthenocissus quinquefolia)*. Vine with pinkish to crimson red fall foliage.

Staghorn Sumac *(Rhus typhina)*. Small tree with yellowish green flower clusters in early summer; bright red berries late summer through winter; and yellow, orange, or bright red fall foliage.

Bloodroot *(Sanguinaria canadensis)*. Perennial with white flowers in early spring.

Allegheny Foamflower *(Tiarella cordifolia)*. Groundcover with white flowers in spring.

---

course, the choice of an American designer at an American landscape architecture firm was crucial to meeting another criterion.

Courtenay's initial work, then, focused on environmental aspects and on creating an aesthetically pleasing setting. That's where the first alteration came into play. The Congressional concept had been that of a truly American garden, one incorporating styles and plants from throughout the country. Site analysis soon revealed that this was impractical; plants thriving in the cool Northwest, for example, would be prostrated by the notorious heat and humidity of Washington's summers.

The decision was reached to make the garden a regional one, an approach gaining great credence because it emphasizes growing plants suited to an area rather than spending untold hours, expense, and chemicals in maintenance. In electing to go regional, however, the question immediately arose as to what constitutes a regional plant. In a response that makes many a pure native plant enthusiast shudder, introduced plants that had naturalized throughout the capital area were included in the criteria of being regional. However, because of the richness and diversity of native flora available (Washington, D.C., straddles two floristic areas, the Piedmont and the Tidewater), only one or two introduced plants ultimately appeared in the garden.

Phase II: Conceptual Design

Here, Courtenay had to transform an underused plot of land into one that seamlessly fit in with the adjacent conservatory on one side, the Mall on the other, and the Capitol above. He also had to take into account the fact that hundreds of thousands of people would be visiting the garden. Pathways needed to move these along and they had to be constructed of both attractive and durable materials.

The garden's goal of illustrating an environmental approach determined both the arrangement of plants and the shape of the beds. Rather than highlighting individual plant species, Courtenay emphasized plant associations because most species naturally group themselves in communities of trees, shrubs, and groundplane plants, creating their own microclimate and growing conditions over time.

The reliance on curved garden beds and restful shapes was deliberate. "Nature abhors a straight line," he explains, "and thus in dealing with native plants I usually prefer not to group them in formal arrangements." And though most visitors will probably not recognize the extent of planning behind the design, Courtenay spent a lot of time examining the viewing relationship between visitor and plant. "The relative position of the viewer with respect to that being viewed is extremely important to understand in order to make the most of any plant presentation," he says.

Because the garden is a regional one, it was necessary to illustrate regional landscapes. Courtenay chose three distinct habitats: woodland forest, floodplain, and wet meadow. In the garden, he notes, they are presented as abstractions rather than as replicas of actual ecological habitats. Their placement follows the gradient along the slopes within the garden and the moisture levels maintained in each area.

Phase III: Design Development

Once the overall structure was approved, plant selection began in earnest. The EDAW design team drew up a preliminary list of plant candidates, indicated their preferences, and forwarded the document to the U.S. Botanic Garden staff for their comments. The two met to discuss their choices and jointly prepared a "short list" for Courtenay. With this list, Courtenay then examined the relationship of the recommended plants to each other in the wild, their bloom period, and their composition in a replicated setting. He also took into account the spatial structure of each plant and its texture and scale of foliage and habit.

And because this is a very visible public garden with very visible opening ceremonies, it was necessary to go for the instant effect. This, Courtenay explains, entails overplanting in order to make the garden appear as a mature setting. In making that decision, he recognized that it would be necessary to thin out the garden in a major way within four or five years. Home gardeners, he adds, can benefit from such an approach as the eventual overgrowth of an instant landscape installation means that a great deal of material could be available for the next phase of garden development.

THE AUTHOR'S FRONT YARD GARDEN, PRINCETON, NEW JERSEY

As a writer, I like to know the history and background of any subject I deal with. And in conducting research on numerous easy care plants, I was soon struck by how many were native to North America. If these plants could grow on their own in fields and forests across the continent, I reasoned, why couldn't they do likewise on my property? And so was born my creation of an all-season, all-American garden to celebrate the great beauty and diversity of our native plants. The following describes how I designed this garden and how it has fared in its first seven years.

Phase I: Determining the Garden's Purpose and Location

From the very beginning, I wanted my garden to be more than a native plant garden. I wanted it to be one that would show people (1) how easy it is to garden and (2) how you don't have to use fertilizers or pesticides to do so. In order to be a demonstration garden, it had to be a public one and the only suitable space on my small Princeton, New Jersey, property was the front yard. Note that I do not use the word "lawn" to describe this area; though my husband had repeatedly tried to grow grass on the packed clay soil, weeds such as plantains, dandelions, and crab grass dominated.

Not being one to settle for small goals, I wanted everyone to become enthusiastic about gardening. That meant I had to have plants for both sun and shade settings. Fortunately, there was one part of the property that was shaded by a neighbor's tree and then drifted out to open sun. It was close to the street and was ideal for viewing by people either walking or driving by.

To further generate gardening enthusiasm, I knew I had to have something in flower from spring through fall. I bravely proposed to accomplish this in an area approximately 19 feet long and 4½ feet wide. Obviously, I had not at the time come across the tenets of garden design that decree my size is too small to accomplish such a goal in an aesthetically pleasing manner.

Phase II: Analyzing the Garden's Structure and Growing Conditions

One aspect of garden design that had been drummed into my head is that gardens should have some sort of structure to them. A look at the soil in the proposed area led to my interpretation of this tenet. As I already knew, the heavily packed clay was impossible to deal with. And when I looked at my husband with a view to his double-digging and amending it, I knew that was impossible. I leafed through the yellow pages in the phone book and found a supplier listed under "topsoil." I called and was told that the minimum order was a truckload. Eureka! A load of dirt would become the "bones" of my garden by being transformed into a curved mound, one that would additionally ensure good drainage and reasonable fertility.

Further structure would be provided by the plants themselves. Since the area was so small, large woody ornamentals were ruled out. The shape and form of perennials, bulbs, and annuals would have to do. I devised a

❋

UNRECOGNIZED GARDEN GEMS

The following plants represent a cross section of little known natives found throughout the North American continent. They are elegant additions to my gardens and easy care ones as well, for they flourish without pesticides or fertilizers. I call them garden gems and I believe you will too once you become acquainted with them.

Arkansas Amsonia *(A. hubrectii)*. Perennial with light blue flowers in spring and striking golden tan fall foliage.

Rue Anemone *(Anemonella thalictroides)*. Perennial with white or pale pink flowers early to mid-spring.

Umbellatus Aster *(A. umbellatus)*. Perennial with white flowers mid August to mid October.

White Brodiaea *(B. lactea)*. Corm with white flowers in spring.

Spring Beauty *(Claytonia virginica)*. Corm with blush pink flowers veined with dark pink in spring.

Montrose Ruby *(Heuchera americana* X *H.* 'Palace Purple'). Perennial with reddish maroon foliage and blush pink flowers on reddish maroon stems late spring to early summer.

Ruby Slippers *(Lobelia* X *hybrida* 'Ruby Slippers'). Perennial with spikes of ruby red flowers late summer into early fall.

Mina *(M. lobata)*. Vine with banana-shaped red, orange, yellow, and white flowers late summer to frost.

American Jacob's Ladder *(Polemonium reptans)*. Perennial with blue flowers early to midspring.

Pearlberry *(Symphoricarpos* 'Mother of Pearl' Doorenbos hybrid). Shrub with tiny pink flowers in early summer and iridescent blush pink berries in fall.

American Alpine Speedwell *(Veronica wormskjoldii)*. Perennial with blue flowers in midsummer.

Appalachian Violet *(Viola appalachiensis)*. Groundcover with purple flowers in spring.

scheme in which the garden was divided into five sections: shade at one end, sun at the other, a front border facing the street, a rear border facing the house, and a fringe on top. The last I envisioned as a series of tall plants that would crown my mound of dirt in much the same way a mohawk hairdo arches across the head of a punk rocker. This wall of greenery would form a backdrop for the plants on either side.

Phase III: Selecting and Arranging Plants

Transplants or divisions of seven easy care natives already growing in my back gardens formed the core of my front garden. Three bloom in early spring: blue Jacob's ladders *(Polemonium reptans)*, pink bleeding hearts *(Dicentra eximia)*, and yellow celandine poppies *(Stylophorum diphyllum)*. They were followed by coral bells *(Heuchera sanguinea)* with light pink flowers from mid May to August; sundrops *(Oenothera tetragona)* for a month of bright yellow blossoms beginning in early June; purple coneflowers *(Echinacea purpurea)* for tall, stately, large-petaled blossoms from July into September; and boltonias *(B. asteroides)* for the freshness of their asterlike white flowers that start blooming after Labor Day.

Many plants were to be new ones. My selections were made in winter, a dangerous time for gardeners with a pile of nursery catalogs for reading material. I slowly turned page after page and devoured descriptions of enticing plants. I did, however, have some resistance guidelines. For example, I chose only plants with wide geographical native ranges. My reasoning was that if they could survive under many geographical and climatic conditions, they could survive in Princeton, New Jersey. Frankly, the concept of a regional planting never entered my head. My guiding light to this day has been the search for beautiful plants that require neither pesticides nor fertilizers to decorate my gardens.

I also checked each plant with regard to light needs and bloom period. Candidates were then temporarily assigned to one of the designated garden areas. My first review of possible plants led to the elimination of some in areas that were overrepresented. A totaling of the costs led to a further pruning. In the end, I ordered about two dozen previously untried perennials through the mail.

The First Year

On a sunny March day, a truck drove down our street, backed up on our front lawn, raised its hinges, and let loose 3.5 cubic yards of dirt. The dirt had been scraped off one of the many New Jersey farms being converted to housing developments and had been screened; that is, it had been through a mesh that cleaned out large debris such as rocks and sticks. My neighbors, naturally, were quite curious. I told them that they were witnessing the first stage in the creation of an all-season, all-American garden. One man could not resist retorting that it looked like I had created a burial mound.

There was some truth to his observation. I felt that I had to get something green on it quickly and transferred clumps of my early spring bloomers to the front border facing the street. Wherever I planted, I added buckets of sand and peat moss to lighten and enrich the soil. By the end of April, there were blue, yellow, and pink flowers blooming in the street side of the garden.

Soon, mail order plants arrived and annuals were tucked in to fill blatantly bare spots. By the end of May, it was obvious that the pile in the front yard was indeed a flower garden. It was also obvious why flowers are usually not grown on unfenced front lawns: children, cats, dogs, and other creatures do not think of a garden as being off-limits.

The children were the easiest to handle. I explained to the older ones on our street that this was going to be a special garden and they respected that. I repeated this story to the parents of the younger ones.

To date, the garden has not attracted the neighborhood cats. This may be due to the vigilance of our neurotic border collie, Fergus, who watches our property from the dining room window and starts a ferocious barking when any living thing so much as touches one blade of our grass. While highly embarrassing when guests come by, this behavior does convey a message to cats that they are not welcome (occasionally, we let her charge out the front door to reinforce the message).

The dogs, however, are another matter. They have long since realized there is no bite to Fergus's bark and they ignore her with impunity. Furthermore, the leash laws in Princeton allow dogs to roam free from 7 P.M. to 7 A.M. and roam they do. Thus it was that at 7:15 one early June evening I ran screaming out of the house, waving my arms and shrieking at a large golden retriever acting most unbecomingly on the top of my garden. The dog almost shrugged as he sauntered off, leaving behind a mess to be cleaned.

This scene reconfirmed for me the wisdom in having only tough plants in a front bed. Despite several more dog invasions and an occasional soccer ball trespass, the flowers have performed magnificently. And as they have grown and filled out, the area has become less inviting to both animals and children.

I had no idea what weeds or insects might sprout from the topsoil. To guard against the former, I mulched heavily with grass clippings throughout the growing season. These smothered potential weeds, conserved moisture, and added their own nutrients to the soil as they decomposed. Insect attacks were almost nonexistent.

This picture shows my garden in August in its first year. While it was colorful and certainly more attractive than the clover and dandelions that previously grew on the spot, it was also terribly jumbled. It does illustrate, however, the flowering display that can be had just four months after planting small, potted seedlings. Annuals include white salvia (S. farinacea 'Victoria White'), pinkish blue ageratums, and red cosmos (C. sulphureus). Perennials—all of which were eventually moved to other borders—include, from left to right, yellow threadleaf coreopsis (C. verticillata) and black-eyed Susans (Rudbeckia fulgida var. sullivantii 'Goldsturm'), purple coneflowers (Echinacea purpurea), and golden ox-eye sunflower (Heliopsis helianthoides 'Summer Sun'). The dramatic, way-out-of-proportion foliage of wild senna (Cassia marilandica) waves in the background and to the right of it are the yellow flowers of prairie coneflower (Ratibida pinnata).

The street border, thank goodness, was the most successful of all. Blue ageratums were tucked among the dark green foliage of the Jacob's ladders and sun yellow heliopsis flowers glowed above. In between, flashing orange cosmos put on a firecracker display and blossoms of pink bee balm *(Monarda didyma)* sprayed forth profusely in July and August.

In September, the garden put on a grand finale. I had planted clumps of boltonia and two different asters as part of the top fringe. These now exploded with color. Through sheer happenstance, the aster nearest the sun section was Harrington's Pink. This outdid itself in blossoms that tumbled about, perfectly complementing the color of the still-blooming purple coneflower. Behind it, white boltonia flowers separated Harrington's Pink from the reddish pink Alma Potchke asters. This, in turn, was backed by a clump of blue hardy ageratums *(Eupatorium coelestinum).*

My goal of creating a colorful garden with flowers all season long was certainly achieved. Neighbors came over to learn about the different flowers and to thank me for adding the garden to the street. Drivers would inevitably slow their cars as they passed our house.

I also met my second objective: the garden was the epitome of an easy care endeavor. The continuing rains that first summer eliminated any need for watering. The mulch and crowded plantings kept weeds at a minimum, and there were no fertilizer applications or insecticidal sprayings.

The Fifth Year

By the fifth year, it is a pleasure to report, there were four more front gardens on my small street. There were also major changes in the plant composition of my all-American display and some major regrets on my part that I had not done a better job in what Courtenay calls site analysis.

As an amateur, I had assumed that site analysis meant looking at the spot where you want to have a garden. To a landscape architect, it means looking at the garden in relation to the entire area in which it is located. My garden, I had to admit, was a lump on the front lawn— a colorful lump, but a lump nevertheless. I debated extending the narrow border abutting our front steps and deck to better join the two planted areas but inertia and expense restrained me from doing so.

The first wet year was followed by dry years and I quickly learned that water does not seep through a mound of dry dirt; it runs off. And when it did rain, the slightly downward slope of the yard (another factor neglected in site analysis) led to a lot of the house-side border being washed away with the flow.

I had also learned that invasive, as well as fast-spreading, plants are not suitable in a small space. Threadleaf coreopsis *(C. verticillata)* was dug out before it had a chance to settle in permanently; so too were black-eyed Susans *(Rudbeckia fulgida)* and white physostegia *(P. virginiana* 'Summer Snow'). I'm still working on the hardy ageratum.

Two months later, on June 22, the white flowers of New Jersey Tea (Ceanothus americanus) *are in full bloom. They serve as a color break between Homestead Purple* (Verbena canadensis 'Homestead Purple') *on the right and coral bells* (Heuchera sanguinea) *and yellow sundrops* (Oenothera fruticosa) *on the left.*

The wonderful combination formed by the purple coneflower and Harrington's Pink aster went. The plants were simply too big and formed thick clumps totally out of proportion for such a small garden space. Indeed, a lot of tall plants were sent to the backyard. Wild senna *(Cassia marilandica)* and yellow coneflower *(Ratibida pinnata)* look much better now in different settings. The Alma Potchke aster and boltonia, on the other hand, stayed; I simply whack them back in late June so that their blooming height is more in keeping with the rest of the garden.

New easy care plants were added. Camassias, wonderful stately bulbs, add dramatic form and soft color in spring. Three perennial workhorses—pale yellow Moonbeam coreopsis, purplish blue stokesia *(S. laevis)*, and gleaming white flowering spurge *(Euphorbia corollata)*—provide color all summer. The latter, whacked back with the asters in June to keep its height under control, contributes a bonus after Labor Day when its foliage turns an orange red. All-season foliage color is provided by the cream-splashed leaves of Virginia tovara *(T. virginianum* 'Variegata'*)* and the rich reddish purple Royal Red heuchera *(H. villosa* 'Royal Red'*)*.

All these plants have flourished without any application of fertilizers. Nor have I used pesticides. As a result of the latter action, chewing insects have appeared among the plants but have not liked them enough to do significant damage.

And then disaster struck in September. While planting some West Coast bulbs in the garden, I noticed a funny smell and called my gas company. Sure enough, there was a gas leak and it was located right under my front garden. "You can't dig there," I wailed. "I just planted some bulbs."

"Don't worry, lady," I was told as the backhoe roared into action, "we'll put everything back."

The Sixth and Seventh Years

Things were put back, but not quite in the order in which they had originally been placed, as I discovered the following spring. In addition, there were depressions in the ground in some areas and mounds in others. Something had to be done with the now undulating lawn and I knew I did not have the background to do it. I called in a landscape architect.

Alan Goodheart is not just any landscape architect. He is a personal friend and he agreed to come over and consult on an hourly basis. Most landscape architects do not like to do this; they much prefer—their whole training prepares them for this—to carry out a project from start to finish.

I wanted Goodheart to give me some ideas on how to unify the entire front yard; to make it seem all of one piece. I also wanted to solve the rushing water problem during heavy rains. He sauntered over, took one look at the stones holding a small raised garden my husband had built on the narrow strip of land on one side of our driveway, and suggested that we pair this with another stone wall setting in our main front yard. The height of this new wall would be determined by the level of the ground at the base of our front deck. Thus, this absolutely wonderful design solution also took care of the

On August 16, white flowering spurge (Euphorbia corollata) assumes the role previously held by New Jersey Tea. Other flowers included cosmos (C. bipinnatus 'Sonata White' and C. sulphureus 'Ladybird Scarlet'), blue salvia (S. farinacea 'Victoria'), pink lobelia (L. X hybrida 'Rose Beacon'), orange butterfly weed (Asclepias tuberosa), yellow Moonbeam coreopsis (C. 'Moonbeam'), and, lower right, a lavender ruellia (R. humilis). Note the brown grass—a result of the drought conditions that just about killed the lawn but did not faze the easy care native plants!

drainage problem. It was also quite fortuitous that the walls on both sides of the driveway were eventually the same height.

As Goodheart roughly sketched out the proposed stone wall and the level area that would flow back from it, I asked, "What about the garden?"

"Oh," he said casually, "the garden goes."

"The garden stays," I immediately replied.

"That's what being a landscape architect is all about," he responded without missing a beat. "We always consult with our clients and take into account their wishes."

The garden then became part of the wall. Instead of a mound in the front of our property, we now had a raised, level area ending in a garden–stone wall combination. With Goodheart's crucial design contribution, I set about incorporating the garden as a part—rather than an unrelated component—of our front yard. My initial results, the seventh year of my native plant garden, are shown in the pictures on pages 51–53.

As with any garden, this is not a static one. Since I keep experimenting with new plants and new combinations, it is becoming clear to me that I must sharpen my concept of the garden's purpose. Do I want an area that is beautifully planted throughout the growing season, or a floral laboratory with the inevitable gaps and failures that accompany the search for new plants? Either way I go, the plantings will be easy care, educational, and fun. Learning about native plants has been a very rewarding experience for me and I know it will be so for you.

The next section of this book describes public and private gardens throughout the United States. These examples provide further guidance on the design and maintenance of native plant gardens. The last section describes over five hundred easy care native plants, and they are but a representative sample of the thousands that are available! Thus with the general design precepts discussed here, the concrete examples in the following gardens, and the recommended plants in the last section, you now have all the ingredients you need to create your own beautiful, easy care, native plant garden.

FOR FURTHER INFORMATION on large-scale, nonresidential landscaping projects utilizing native plants, contact Roger G. Courtenay, EDAW, Inc., 601 Prince Street, Alexandria, Virginia 22314 (703/836-1414).

SECTION II

The Gardens

*G*arden tours are fun. They provide you with the opportunity not only to meet interesting people but also to become acquainted with new plants and design possibilities. That's what this section is all about. It introduces you to selected institutions and individuals and tells how they went about creating gardens and landscapes filled with native plants. I think you will enjoy reading their stories as much as I have enjoyed writing about them.

And I think you will also be impressed, both with the gardens and with the dedication of so many to beautifying and enriching our environment. Read about the vital role of garden clubs in donating time and money to support plantings in public areas. Praise the nameless, unsung individuals who have voluntarily worked to preserve open spaces and to introduce wonderful new plants to all our gardens. And give a rousing cheer for the horticulturists and staff members of gardens and arboreta across the continent who broaden the meaning of their employment to encompass service to and stewardship of our planet.

Each organization or gardener has provided a list of native plants of exceptional merit. As is true of the lists presented in Section I, the first designation in each plant description (shrub, bulb, annual, and so on) refers to the chapter in which more detailed information is contained.

Chapter 4

Public Gardens

A public garden is one that can be viewed without invitation. As you will read on the following pages, this broad definition is as large as the 600,000 acres of highway rights-of-way in Iowa and as small as the 3-acre quarry hole that has been transformed into the Mary Howard Gilbert Memorial Garden in Atlanta, Georgia.

Fourteen public gardens are described in this chapter; of these, three are profiled in depth. All serve as wonderful horticultural stewards and, as such, have been extremely generous in contributing lists of native plants best suited for their growing areas (indeed, most chafed at restricting their list to only twelve). As you find your gardens enriched with one or more of these plants, you may wish to express your appreciation by becoming actively involved in the work undertaken by these organizations. All you have to do is to call and ask how you can help.

*On a foggy morning in early August, a fantasyland is created at the Shaw Arboretum in Missouri with the sculptural forms of Kansas gayfeather (*Liatris pychnostachya*) weaving about a spread of sweet black-eyed Susans (*Rudbeckia subtomentosa*) and purple coneflowers (*Echinacea purpurea*). A magnificent stand of yellow cup plants (*Silphium perfoliatum*) backs up the scene. [Photo: Mary Ann Kressig]*

ATLANTA HISTORY CENTER, ATLANTA, GEORGIA

The Atlanta History Center is a unique complex in that it honors the environmental as well as the political and cultural history of its area. Situated among its 32 acres are Atlanta's newest history museum (1993) and one of its oldest surviving farm houses, the Tullie Smith House (about 1840). Seven named gardens and landscapes are located on the property as well. Filled with color from spring through fall and displaying beautiful contrasts in form and texture, these gardens exhibit plants that Georgians have viewed and used at different periods in history.

Indeed, the innovative landscape designed by Darrel Morrison for the newly constructed museum illustrates the natural history of Georgia from presettlement days to the present. It also demonstrates, Morrison notes, "that an aesthetically pleasing, functional landscape can be created using only plants native to a specific region."

From the property's roadway border, through the entrance gates, and along the drive to the museum building itself, Morrison has grouped over eighty native species into five zones. Each zone represents a different stage of vegetational succession common throughout the Georgia Piedmont.

The roadside area—filled with yellow coreopsis species, orange butterfly weed *(Asclepias tuberosa)*, golden black-eyed Susans *(Rudbeckia hirta)*, and grasses with blue and purple tints—presents nature's first steps at reclaiming property either abandoned as farmland or inadvertently cleared by natural phenomena such as tornadoes or lightning-ignited fires. This roadside planting leads to the entryway, which is landscaped to represent the second stage of succession in this region. Here, a young pine forest includes split beard bluestem *(Andropogon ternarius)* and other taller grasses, and loblolly pines *(Pinus taeda)*.

The upland forest area, located on the north side of the museum, features mature woodland species and includes trees such as white oaks *(Quercus alba)* and American beeches *(Fagus grandifolia)*. Additional color and contrast in this setting is provided by the flowers, berries, and foliage of smaller, ornamental trees such as eastern redbud *(Cercis canadensis)* and downy serviceberry *(Amelanchier arborea)*, and shrubs such as Carolina allspice *(Calycanthus floridus)*.

A streamside forest setting was created for an area periodically swamped during heavy runoff. The "stream" is actually a swath of flood-tolerant northern sea oats grass *(Chasmanthium latifolium)*, bordered by exuberant fall-flowering natives such as intense rose purple ironweed *(Vernonia noveboracensis)* and golden yellow swamp sunflower *(Helianthus angustifolius)*.

The centerpiece of Morrison's landscape design is located in front of the museum and is called the Granite Outcrop. It is a stylized version of a naturally occurring phenomenon throughout the Piedmont: the emergence of underlying granite as flat rocks or domelike monadnocks. The hot, sunny site here is decorated with outcrop plants such as dwarf liatris *(L. microcephala)* and broom sedge *(Andropogon virginicus)*.

The entire landscape reflects not only Georgia's environmental history but also its current concerns: it has an extremely low maintenance budget. Because plant groupings are matched to each area's soil, light, and moisture conditions, they are able to sustain themselves without the need for fertilizers or pesticides. Watering was required only for the plant establishment period and the open areas are mowed just once a year.

Ironically, the biggest problem—and major chunk of the maintenance budget—is combatting the aggressiveness of nonnative species such as common privet and Japanese wisteria. Constant surveillance is needed to keep these plants from establishing themselves in the landscape and smothering the native flora.

After seeing this stylized landscape history, visitors to the Atlanta History Center complex can experience part of the "real thing" in a walk along the Swan Woods Trail. This 10-acre woodland, developed and supported by the Peachtree Garden Club, has remnants of a presettlement hardwood forest as well as an ecological demonstration of a succession forest evolving from an abandoned farm field in one section.

In another part of the property, Georgia's early agricultural history is displayed in the grounds

In mid September, the profuse yellow blossoms of wingstems (Verbesina alternifolia) *and the thick purple berries of American beautyberry* (Callicarpa americana) *provide rich color in the dappled shade of the Atlanta History Center's Quarry Garden. [Photo: Sue Vrooman]*

surrounding the Tullie Smith House. Here several garden clubs support work in the vegetable and field crop gardens and roadside beds.

Thus, history buffs, environmentalists, ecologists, and vegetable gardeners all have much to learn from the grounds of the Atlanta History Center. Perhaps the biggest treat, however, is reserved for ornamental gardeners, particularly those looking for beautiful easy care plants adapted to shaded surroundings. More often than not, you will find these people gravitating toward the Quarry Garden.

This too has historical interest as its gravel—some of it possibly produced by convict labor—was once used throughout the area. Abandoned at the beginning of this century, the quarry was an overgrown mess of brambles and vines when the center acquired the property in 1966. Indeed, given its central location, some thought the sunken, pit-like area should be filled in and converted to a parking lot.

Mrs. Ivan Allen, Jr., wife of the then-mayor of Atlanta, felt otherwise. She convinced her fellow members of the Mimosa Garden Club to develop the site as a Georgia native plant garden. This was truly visionary thinking. American horticulturists had just barely begun to appreciate the charms of all-season garden borders and here was Mrs. Allen leading the way in the creation of a 3-acre ornamental landscape decorated only with regionally native flora.

The Mimosa Garden Club thought it was a wonderful idea and has remained a crucial supporter to this day. At the time, however, they recognized that the large expense needed to clear the quarry was beyond their means and obtained a significant financial contribution from the Gilbert Foundation to do so. The official name of the area, the Mary Howard Gilbert Memorial Quarry Garden, honors this contribution.

Visitors do not walk into this garden; they walk down it. Shaded paths are enclosed by granite walls and massive rocks protrude from woodland soils. Soaring tree trunks provide a cathedrallike canopy.

The equivalent of a stained-glass mosaic is created by the brilliant, varied color of over three hundred species of native trees, shrubs, bulbs, perennials, ferns, and selfseeding annuals. These are placed in physical settings ranging from the woodlands bordering the granite outcrop to the bog area in the garden's core.

As with Morrison's entryway landscape, budget constraints dictate that the garden be a low-maintenance one. Sue Vrooman, the horticulturist, has only an occasional volunteer to help her keep its three main pathways cleared, autumn leaves raked, introductions planted, and invading nonnatives weeded out.

For both fiscal and environmental reasons, poisonous chemicals are not used. Pests, particularly black vine weevils, do make some inroads but are not serious problems. The vine weevil population in particular appears to have been significantly reduced with the introduction of parasitic nematodes in 1993.

While the garden is lovely throughout the year, late summer may well be the most inspiring time to visit. This hot, humid season is brutal in the Southeast. Gardens tend to wilt or go dormant when August arrives and hide until the refreshing coolness of late September brings them out again. The splendidly colorful native plants in the Quarry Garden show that this need not be the case. On even the most smog-smothered days, for example, Vrooman has ensured constant pools of sunlight yellow with groupings of the orange and gold tones of brown-eyed Susans *(Rudbeckia triloba)* and the fragrant, bee-drenched blossoms of yellow wingstems *(Verbesina alternifolia).*

Along another garden path, Vrooman has installed a cooling combination of blue hardy ageratum *(Eupatorium coelestinum)*, pink obedient plant *(Physostegia virginiana)*, and the purple fruits of American beautyberry *(Callicarpa americana).* While readily admitting that the first two plants are invasive, Vrooman quickly adds that "they are not that hard to pull out and have such wonderful, late-season color."

Fragrance permeates the sultry air, emanating from the lemon yellow flowers of stoneroot *(Collinsonia canadensis)*, the white blossoms of sweet pepperbush *(Clethra alnifolia)*, and the blush pink flower clusters of climbing hempweed *(Mikania scandens).* The last is one of Vrooman's favorite plants. "It's just beautiful and blooms from late summer into fall," she says. "It's a well-behaved, 10-foot vine that loosely twines itself around the trunks and stems of shrubs in the Quarry Garden. I think it would be equally stunning on a fence or trellis."

She laments the paucity of horticultural information about this native, which is found from Maine and Ontario south to Florida and Texas. "Indeed, how climbing hempweed arrived in the Quarry Garden is somewhat of a mystery, though I suspect it was a selection of Eugene Cline, who designed the original garden. It has thrived for two decades here with minimal care and would be a lovely, beautifully fragrant addition to home gardens."

Climbing hempweed and all the other plants mentioned in this

❋

LATE SUMMER SHADE PLANTS

Sue Vrooman, horticulturist at the Atlanta History Center's Quarry Garden, thinks all her plants are great. To help narrow her focus, she was asked to limit her easy care recommendations to those with late summer interest. The following are her choices.

White Wood Aster *(A. divaricatus)*. Perennial with white flowers late summer into fall.

American Beautyberry *(Callicarpa americana)*. Shrub with tiny blush pink flowers in spring and purple berries late summer through winter, depending on geographical location.

Sweet Pepperbush *(Clethra alnifolia)*. Shrub with fragrant white or pink flowers in summer.

Stoneroot *(Collinsonia canadensis)*. Perennial with yellow flowers in late summer.

Hardy Ageratum *(Eupatorium coelestinum)*. Perennial with blue flowers midsummer to early fall.

White Snakeroot *(Eupatorium rugosum)*. Perennial with white flowers late summer to early fall.

Turk's Cap *(Malvaviscus arboreus* var. *drummondii)*. Hardy annual with red flowers late summer into fall.

Climbing Hempweed *(Mikania scandens)*. Vine with fragrant, blush pink flowers late summer into fall.

Obedient Plant *(Physostegia virginiana)*. Perennial with rose, pink, or white flowers and with bloom times ranging from midsummer to early fall.

Cutleaf Coneflower *(Rudbeckia laciniata)*. Perennial with yellow flowers late summer into fall.

Brown-eyed Susan *(Rudbeckia triloba)*. Biennial with golden yellow flowers late July through September.

Wingstem *(Verbesina alternifolia)*. Perennial with yellow daisylike flowers throughout summer.

brief profile represent just a small sample of the hundreds of gorgeous natives on display at the Atlanta History Center. In providing such a wonderful showcase for these flora, the center serves not only as a national model for an environmental museum but also as an inspiring resource for landscape designers and individual gardeners throughout the Piedmont area and beyond.

FOR FURTHER INFORMATION about the center and its programs and gardens, write or call Atlanta History Center, 130 West Paces Ferry Road N.W., Atlanta, Georgia 30305-1366 (404/814-4000).

IOWA DEPARTMENT OF TRANSPORTATION

Iowa was literally ripped bare when its rolling fields of soybeans and wheat were created. The tall prairie grass that once blanketed the state was replaced not only with highly productive farms but also with European grasses and other plants familiar to the first settlers. The pioneers' physical and horticultural takeover of Iowa was so complete that less than 1 percent of the original vegetative cover remains and there are now more public lands in highway rights-of-way than in parks.

These two aspects of the state's history—600,000 acres of publicly maintained roadsides and an almost vanished natural heritage—have led to the creation of one of our country's foremost highway native plant programs.

The program began inauspiciously in the late 1950s when the Iowa Department of Transportation (DOT) began to use switch grass *(Panicum virgatum)* in its roadside plantings. Though this widespread native with dark red to purple spikelets was just beginning to enter a few gardens as an ornamental, DOT personnel chose it for its ease of maintenance. Unlike the so-called cool season European grasses, which go dormant in Iowa's blistering, often dry, summer heat, switch grass blossoms naturally at this time of year. Its beautiful vegetative cover during July and August not only guards against soil erosion but also prevents noxious weeds from seeding.

Farmers along the rights-of-way are highly concerned about these weeds. It is but a short leap from roadways to their fields, where the weeds grab not only space but also soil nutrients. To prevent such spread, all Iowa road departments—state, county, and city—invest heavily in spraying and mowing operations.

The success with switch grass in the late 1950s prompted the inclusion of other natives in highway plantings starting in the 1960s. Trees such as the pollution-tolerant hackberry *(Celtis occidentalis)* and the majestic bur oak *(Quercus macrocarpa)* began to provide shade along busy highways.

The number of such plantings was limited by a crucial factor—supply. The idea of using native plants was a novelty in those days and nursery sources couldn't afford to grow plants that had limited appeal. The Iowa Department of Transportation, for example, puts out bid orders in fall for spring plantings. A nursery will already have to have in stock hundreds—and sometimes thousands—of specified trees or shrubs in order to fulfill an order. Not unreasonably, most are reluctant to gamble that a relatively unrecognized plant that takes two to four years to nurture could be profitably sold in large quantities.

To surmount this problem, DOT personnel embarked on a long-term strategy in which they would place a limited order for a heretofore untried native for use on a small project and then, after a successful installation, reorder the same plant the following year. As the nurseries came to recognize that there was a market for such plants, they increased their production of them.

While the Iowa Department of Transportation was undoubtedly the largest single purchaser of native plants in the state, it was not alone in advocating them. A citizen's group using the acronym REAP (Resources Enhancement and Protection) became active in promoting the preservation of the remaining bits of unspoiled land and the enhancement of all public properties. Their efforts came to fruition in 1988, when the Iowa legislature passed a series of measures establish-

Black-eyed Susans (Rudbeckia hirta) *and pale purple coneflowers* (Echinacea pallida) *add color to highway plantings along Iowa roads in July. [Photo: Iowa Department of Transportation]*

ing trust funds and administrative entities to further such work. Since highway rights-of-way constitute such a large chunk of public land, the legislature designated the Department of Transportation as one center for REAP activity and mandated that it involve all levels of government. Mechanisms were set up for roadside personnel in city, county, and state government to work together in highway plantings—a system that sounds eminently sensible but which is unique in our country at this writing.

With both monetary and administrative support, the scope of native plantings throughout Iowa sprouted dramatically. In the first five years alone, $2.8 million was dispersed through a special trust fund to support over 300 roadside planting and native plant management projects. Other state funds supported the installation of over 600,000 native trees and shrubs on highway rights-of-way and the annual seeding of 1,000 roadside acres with native grasses and wildflowers.

This is planting on a major scale. It is, however, all fine-tuned. Research, for example, has indicated that the prairie was never as colorful as popular literature would have it. Rather, tall grasses dominated and shaded out or overran many wildflowers. These last flourished in little niches, environments that did not admit tall grasses.

DOT has mimicked this history in its landscape strategy. Tall grasses predominate in large plantings, such as the 40- to 150-foot-deep right-of-way along a 5-mile stretch of Highway 61 near Muscatine. Here dominant plantings of switch grass, big bluestem *(Andropogon gerardii)*, and Indian grass *(Sorghastrum nutans)*—all of which turn a warm red in early fall—are supplemented with a limited number of flowers. These include liatris species, purple prairie clover *(Petalostemon purpureum)*, and a trio of coneflowers—yellow *(Ratibida pinnata)*, purple *(Echinacea purpurea)*, and pale *(E. pallida)*—which add color and contrast spring through summer.

The tall grasses, however, are deliberately omitted at intersections and overpasses containing small plots of less than one acre. Here intensified wildflower plantings reflect those previously found in prairie niches and are packed in to provide spectacular all-season color. A typical setting includes the golden yellows of spring blooming coreopsis plants *(C. tinctoria, C. lanceolata,* and *C. palmata)*, a summer rainbow of lavender leadplant *(Amorpha canescens)*, orange butterfly weed *(Asclepias tuberosa)*, red and yellow cultivars of Mexican hat *(Ratibida columnifera)*, and purple spikes of several liatris species as well as flowers planted in tall-grass landscapes. The floral parade ends in late September with the rich blues and lavenders of New England asters *(A. novae-angliae)*. Low-growing native grasses such as little bluestem *(Schizachyrium sco-parium)* and sideoats grama *(Bouteloua curtipendula)* create textural contrasts and winter interests.

One of the marvelous aspects of the above two examples is that the plants are all easy care. Once established—generally within two to four years—their deep roots allow them to withstand drought, fire, and flood. They require minimal mowing, need neither fertilizers nor spraying, and crowd out most if not all weeds.

Taxpayers benefit significantly from the lower maintenance costs of such displays. Gardeners also benefit, but indirectly. With state purchases prodding commercial sellers of plant material, the supply and variety of native plants coming into the market has increased steadily over the years. In 1995, for example, over 780 nannyberries *(Viburnum lentago)* were planted in one roadway project. These versatile, extremely low-maintenance small trees bear profuse clusters of creamy white flowers in midspring and have glossy leaves that turn purple red in the fall. They provide a long-season visual delight for all motorists driving by. And the quantity in which they were planted was simply not available three decades ago.

The key players in the Iowa DOT planting program enjoy telling people about their work. Talk to one or all—to Jim Carpenter, Steve Holland, Mark Masteller, Evelyn O'Loughlin, or Ole Skaar—and it is quickly apparent that they constitute one of our country's most experienced groups of native plant advocates.

They'll readily explain that there are problems—that farmers sometimes find it hard to believe roadsides don't need to be mowed when there are native plantings, that highway maintenance crews find it difficult to believe that native plants should *not* be mowed, and that there are extra short-term costs required to produce substantial long-term savings. And they'll say that they continue to experiment with planting methods, that they see nothing wrong with using superior cultivars over species, and that they still use adapted nonnatives, although in ever diminishing numbers. They particularly like to cite that chemical usage has plummeted 80 percent since their integrated roadside vegetation program was begun in earnest.

Being low-key midwesterners, however, they need to be prodded to admit openly that when they see their handiwork on their drives

✳

PLANTS FOR HIGHWAYS AND ROADS

The following easy care natives are planted along highways and roads throughout Iowa and survive beautifully. Indeed, reports Iowa Department of Transportation Chief Landscape Architect Mark D. Masteller, "it was extremely difficult to choose only twelve such plants."

Big Bluestem *(Andropogon gerardii)*. Grass with statuesque blue green leaves that turn a rich bronze in fall.

Butterfly Weed *(Asclepias tuberosa)*. Perennial with bright orange flowers in summer and striking seed pods in September.

Red Osier Dogwood *(Cornus sericea)*. Shrub with creamy white flowers in spring and colorful bare red bark in winter.

Purple Coneflower *(Echinacea purpurea)*. Perennial with purple, rose pink, or white flowers all summer.

Green Ash *(Fraxinus pennsylvanica)*. Shade tree with golden yellow to orange fall foliage.

Kansas Gayfeather *(Liatris pychnostachya)*. Corm with spikes of purple flowers in midsummer.

Bur Oak *(Quercus macrocarpa)*. Massive tree with ridged bark and yellow brown fall foliage.

Prairie Coneflower *(Ratibida pinnata)*. Perennial with yellow flowers in midsummer.

Black-eyed Susan *(Rudbeckia hirta)*. Annual with golden yellow flowers all summer.

Little Bluestem *(Schizachyrium scoparium)*. Grass with stalks in blue to green hues that turn brilliant red to orange in fall.

Indian Grass *(Sorghastrum nutans)*. Tall grass with soft, golden brown seedheads in fall.

Nannyberry Viburnum *(V. lentago)*. Small tree with creamy white flower clusters in spring and purple red fall foliage.

home—miles of roadside tapestries not only shimmering with native color but also benefiting the environment, reflecting their state's natural heritage, and saving taxpayer dollars—they can't help but feel their jobs are among the most satisfying to be found.

FOR FURTHER INFORMATION about Iowa's Integrated Roadside Vegetation Management program, write or call the Iowa Department of Transportation, 800 Lincoln Way, Ames, Iowa 50010 (515/239-1768; FAX 515/239-1873).

SHAW ARBORETUM OF THE MISSOURI BOTANICAL GARDEN, GRAY SUMMIT, MISSOURI

In St. Louis, the decade of the roaring twenties was also that of the deadly twenties as booming factories and plants belched forth streams of pollutants. Black soot swirled within the humid air and plastered plant and human alike. It was too much for many of the exotic flora growing on the 79 acres of the city's Missouri Botanical Garden. The plants had been collected from throughout the world and had never experienced such industrial pollution; many were showing signs of stress and others were dying.

The institution's trustees embarked on a long-term plan to move the collection to a more pristine location. The first step, taken in 1925, was the purchase of five abandoned farm properties at Gray Summit, an area situated on the northern edge of the Ozarks and located 40 miles west of the city. The acquisition was named in honor of Henry Shaw, who had founded the garden in 1859.

It is somewhat ironic, then, that an arboretum created to preserve

In early June, the Shaw Arboretum's magnificent woodland planting of pale pink sundrops (Oenothera speciosa), deep rose Ozark phlox (P. pilosa var. ozarkana), and violet pygmaeus penstemon (P. hirsutus 'Pygmaeus') enchant all who walk by. [Photo: Scott Woodbury]

exotic plants has become an institution containing superb displays of native flora. For a long time, it attained this stature through default. The arboretum's 2,400 acres were rich in many habitats—upland forest, bottomland forest, glades, meadows, 1½ miles of the Meramec River, streams, and gravel bars—and contained a trove of native plants despite the years of farming and clearing. The Missouri Botanical Garden trustees did little to disturb this natural habitat. Rather, they concentrated on building an infrastructure that would allow public access. Fourteen miles of hiking trails were eventually constructed, as well as service roads and parking areas.

With the arrival of the Depression, however, money for any kind of activity became scarce. Thus, while plans to move the garden were put into abeyance, so too were the pollution-producing factories. That slowdown plus the switch to cleaner-burning fuel led to a great improvement in St. Louis's air quality. At the close of the 1930s, the garden's trustees decided to remain within the city.

While the decision certainly made horticultural life easier for many people, it did raise the question as to what should be done with the large property outside the city. The temporary answer: let it sit. Greenhouses had been erected on the property for propagation purposes and they continued their work of supplying many of the plants for the garden's displays.

The extensive trail system, open to the public from its inception, was used by nature lovers and native plant enthusiasts. Among their favorite destinations—then and now—were outcrop areas of thinbedded rocks called glades. The combination of dolomitic rocks and steep western- or southern-facing slopes that comprise the glades produces a hot, extremely dry setting and a thin, rocky soil that does not support the growth of trees. The resulting environment is wide open to a breathtakingly beautiful collection of wildflowers. Bright yellow Missouri primroses *(Oenothera missouriensis)* and pale purple coneflowers *(Echinacea pallida)* are among the many colorful plants that decorate these areas.

In the period following World War II, it became increasingly obvious that the garden in the city and the arboretum in the countryside formed a complementary partnership. While both work to discover and share knowledge of plants and their environments, the former serves as an international research and display center for the collection and study of all plants, both domestic and foreign, and the latter concentrates on native flora and fauna. As part of its mission, the arboretum also serves as a regional laboratory for developing and testing outdoor programs and as a center for training teachers in environmental education.

In the late 1970s, the arboretum initiated a major program that significantly affected the scope of its activities. Under the direction of William Davit and with the assistance of staff and many volunteers, an experimental prairie was constructed. The goal was not to duplicate the habitat that had once existed long ago but rather to study the plant communities within it and to observe how they evolve and interact. Utilizing both direct seeding and greenhouse-grown transplants, 40 acres were covered with grasses and wildflowers that had once flourished in the area. And that was just the beginning. The prairie, never envisioned as static setting, continues to expand and now extends over 80 acres. Visitors from throughout the country come to admire its beauty and to examine its evolving plant composition.

When James Trager joined the arboretum as naturalist, he teamed up with Superintendent John Behrer in 1991 to construct another major project, known as the wetlands. Today, 25 acres of what was once hayed meadow have been converted into three distinct plantings. Running on a north-to-south gradient, there is an area always under water, a seasonally flooded section, and a wet prairie habitat. The before-and-after contrast is particularly dramatic at the end of summer: where once there was the brown stubble of a flat field there is now movement, life, and striking color such as that provided by scarlet spikes of cardinal flowers *(Lobelia cardinalis)* weaving in and out of the rustling grasses.

This contrast provides a deep inner satisfaction to both Behrer and Trager, who have spent untold hours working on the conversion. "While we know that wetlands existed here in presettlement days, we haven't duplicated them," Behrer explains. "That would be impossible. What we have done is to build new ones, make them accessible through trails and a boardwalk, and use the entire setting for educational purposes."

It was around the beginning of this second major project that the arboretum became blessed with two guardian angels, Blanton and Peg Whitmire. With their encouragement and financial leadership, an entirely new kind of setting was created—a wildflower garden. Heretofore, all areas had been open, natural ones. Now the arboretum moved into the forefront of showing home owners the great possibilities of gardening and landscaping with native flora.

The 5-acre planting is in its fourth year at this writing and under the purview of staff horticulturist Scott Woodbury. Designed by Environmental Planting and Design in Pittsburgh as a seamless setting where one area naturally leads into another, the Whitmire Wildflower Garden consists of five major components: a prairie area, which gives ideas to those with one or more acres to landscape; a savanna setting, which demonstrates plants that do well in areas where prairies meet woodlands; a woodland area for shade gardeners; a sandy pine savanna, where acid-loving plants such as roseshell azalea *(Rhododendron prinophyllum)* flourish; and the home landscaping area.

This last is where Woodbury concentrates his showiest and most carefree native plants and consists of three 20- to 30-foot-deep formal beds along a curving path. The most challenging display, and thus perhaps the most successful, is in the bed dominated by a magnificent hackberry *(Celtis occidentalis)*. Here the shade and soil surface roots have created a setting that many would equate with that of a moonscape.

Using easy care natives, Woodbury has transformed it into a colorful pastoral that includes the tubular, purple-flushed white flowers of pygmaeus penstemon *(P. hirsutus* 'Pygmaeus'*)*, pinkish rose verbena *(V. canadensis)*, and pale pink sundrops *(Oenothera speciosa)*. While the pink sundrops are beautiful terrors in most gardening settings, spreading rampantly through underground stolons, the dry shade, root-infested environment under the hackberry keeps them well behaved. Native spiderworts *(Tradescantia virginiana)* also do well and appear in a range of blues, purples, and pinks. The spring centerpiece and one of the nicest plants, according to Woodbury, is a rose-colored local phlox variety *(P. pilosa* var. *ozarkana)*.

The color scheme in this dry, shady area shifts with the arrival of summer. While purple coneflower *(Echinacea purpurea)* and airy, green bottlebrush grass *(Elymus hystrix)* continue the cool color theme, golden threadleaf coreopsis *(C. verticillata)*, another normally rampant spreader, and orange butterfly weed *(Asclepias tuberosa)* fire up the display. Though butterfly weeds are usually recommended for full sun, they flower under the hackberry with less than two hours of direct sunlight.

In this and all his home landscape plantings, Woodbury has taken a

❋

GARDEN JEWELS FOR JUNE

The following selection of natives is used by Scott Woodbury in his June home landscapes. They provide color and interest in gardens adjusting to the transition from balmy spring weather to summer heat.

Purple Milkweed *(Asclepias purpurascens)*. Perennial with deep rose to purple flowers in late spring.

Poppy Mallow *(Callirhoe involucrata)*. Perennial with wine red flowers late spring well into summer.

Tussock Sedge *(Carex stricta)*. Grass with arching, light green foliage spring through summer and rustling tan sprays fall through winter.

Copper Iris *(I. fulva)*. Perennial with reddish brick petals and apricot centers late May to early June.

Contraband Girl *(Iris virginica* 'Contraband Girl'*)*. Perennial with blue purple flowers late May to early June.

Smooth Phlox *(P. glaberrima)*. Perennial with reddish purple to pink flowers spring well into summer.

Ozark Phlox *(P. pilosa* var. *ozarkana)*. Groundcover with deep rose-colored flowers in late spring.

Prairie Dropseed *(Sporobalus heterolepis)*. Grass with spraying mounds of emerald green leaves that turn orange gold in fall and a rich rust brown in winter.

Broad Beech Fern *(Thelypteris hexagonoptera)*. Fern with crisp green leaves in summer and yellow and bronze fall color.

Rose Verbena *(V. canadensis)*. Hardy annual with purple, red, or pink flowers all summer and often into fall.

Count Pulaski Viburnum *(V. nudum* 'Count Pulaski'*)*. Shrub with creamy white flowers in early summer, salmon pink berries in early fall, and russet orange to earthy red fall foliage.

Heartleaf Alexander *(Zizia aptera)*. Perennial with golden yellow flowers clustered like Queen Anne's lace in spring.

stance not always found in major public gardens: he uses only commercially available plants. If he discovers a wonderful plant that is not offered, he collects its seed and distributes it to other botanical gardens, nurseries, and native plant enthusiasts. In so doing, he not only furthers the arboretum's educational mission but also enriches many gardens.

With its vast natural habitats, magnificent recreated plantings, stunning home landscapes, and—perhaps most important of all—dedicated staff and volunteers, the Shaw Arboretum serves as both a regional leader and a national example in the stewardship and horticultural exploration of native plants. Who would ever have imagined such a wonderful silver lining in the black clouds swirling through St. Louis so long ago?

FOR FURTHER INFORMATION about the arboretum and its programs, write or call Shaw Arboretum, P.O. Box 38, Gray Summit, Missouri 63039 (314/451-0850).

A POTPOURRI OF PUBLIC GARDENS

To broaden the geographical representation covered in the garden profiles, I asked additional institutions throughout the continent to name plants that were grown on their properties and were considered to be of exceptional merit. The following presents—in alphabetical order by geographical location—brief descriptions of the institutions and the plants they selected. Each institution is a wonderful source for native plant information, as well as a great place to visit to see the recommended plants in landscaped or natural settings.

British Columbia
Native Plant Gardens
Royal British Columbia Museum
675 Belleville Street
Victoria, British Columbia
Canada V8V 1X4

The Native Plant Gardens at the Royal British Columbia Museum are spread throughout the grounds and serve as settings for interpretive programs in plant identification, ecology, and aboriginal use; these programs, in turn, complement the natural history exhibits indoors. Established in 1968, the collection now consists of mature specimens of about 350 species indigenous to British Columbia, grouped in seven meticulously labeled plantings: sand dune bed, dry interior garden, alpine garden, wetland garden, Oregon grape bed, camass bed, and coast forest garden. Regularly scheduled guided tours are offered in summer and special-interest tours can be arranged. The following list of easily grown plants was submitted by Robert T. Ogilvie, curator of botany. "While they do not require pesticides or fertilizers," he notes, "they do need natural leaf mold or leaf compost for annual nutrient input."

Great Camass *(Camassia leichtlinii).* Bulb with tall spikes of violet or dark blue flowers in late spring.

Male Fern *(Dryopteris filix-mas).* Stately fern with large, dark green, twice-pinnate fronds.

Golden Yarrow *(Eriophyllum lanatum).* Groundcover with mats of yellow flowers throughout summer.

Giant Fawn Lily *(Erythronium oregonum).* Corm with large white flowers and strongly mottled leaves in early spring.

Salal *(Gaultheria shallon).* Evergreen groundcover with pale pink flower clusters in June and edible purple fruit in August.

Ocean Spray *(Holodiscus discolor).* Shrub with creamy white flower clusters in summer and orange fall foliage.

Longleaf Oregon Grape *(Mahonia nervosa).* Evergreen shrub with yellow flowers in late spring and edible dark blue berries in late summer.

Bush Penstemon *(P. fruticosus).* Groundcover with mats of large purple or lavender blue flowers in summer.

Wild Mock Orange *(Philadelphus lewisii).* Shrub with fragrant white flowers in early summer and yellow fall foliage.

Western Sword Fern *(Polystichum munitum).* Fern with large, once-pinnate evergreen fronds.

Red Flowering Currant *(Ribes sanguineum).* Shrub with crimson red flowers in spring and bluish black fall berries.

Evergreen Huckleberry *(Vaccinium ovatum).* Evergreen shrub with blush pink flowers in spring and edible dark purple berries in fall.

California
C. M. Goethe Arboretum
California State University, Sacramento
6000 J Street
Sacramento, California 95819-2694
916/454-6494

The Goethe Arboretum (named after its benefactor, not the German author) is located on the campus of California State University at Sacramento and is open to the public all year. Its 3-acre collection features plants suitable to the greater Sacramento area and includes plantings of native flowers. The following thrive in the arboretum's displays and were selected for their low-maintenance qualities by Dr. Michael Baad, professor of ecology and systematics in the Department of Biological Sciences. "All but the spicebush," he says, "are adapted to well-drained soils and a climate that consists of hot, dry summers and moisture from late fall to early spring. The spicebush, on the other hand, is riparian and can thus take wetter growing conditions."

California Allspice *(Calycanthus occidentalis)*. Shrub with fragrant, reddish brown flowers spring into summer.

Bush Anemone *(Carpenteria californica)*. Evergreen shrub with fragrant, glistening white flowers in the first half of summer.

Mountain Mahogany *(Cercocarpus betuloides)*. Evergreen shrub covered with sprays of silvery seed and fruit in fall.

Sulfur Flower *(Eriogonum umbellatum* var. *polyanthum)*. Groundcover with pale yellow flowers late spring through summer.

Apache Plume *(Fallugia paradoxa)*. Shrub with white roselike flowers in May and feathery plumes of purple fruits late summer into fall.

Golden Currant *(Ribes aureum)*. Shrub with scented yellow flowers in spring and yellow, red, or purple fruits in late summer.

Matilija Poppy *(Romneya coulteri)*. Perennial with large, fragrant white flowers all summer.

Creeping Sage *(Salvia sonomensis)*. Groundcover with blue violet flowers in spring.

The beautiful but invasive matilija poppy (Romneya coulteri) *is an exceptionally easy care plant as long as it is kept within a confined setting. Its flowers open throughout summer—it is pictured here in mid July on the grounds of California State University at Sacramento—and emit a sweet fragrance. [Photo: Judy Jakobsen]*

Hummingbird Sage *(Salvia spathacea)*. Hardy annual with spikes of deep magenta flowers in summer.

Snowdrop Bush *(Styrax officinalis* var. *californica)*. Shrub with pendulant white flowers in spring.

Delaware

Mt. Cuba Center for the Study of Piedmont Flora
Box 3570
Barley Mill Road
Greenville, Delaware 19807-0570
302/239-4244

In 1983, Mrs. Lammot du Pont Copeland established the Mt. Cuba center on her 230-acre estate. Containing spectacular garden and naturalistic displays of wildflowers, the center concentrates on cultivating and introducing plants native to the Piedmont region, an area extending a thousand miles from the Hudson River south to central Alabama. While currently open only by appointment, the Mt. Cuba Center is formulating plans to welcome the public on a regular basis. The following are recommended by Jeanne Frett, assistant to the director. "Once established," she writes, "these are remarkably durable and also easy to control. They don't wilt, defoliate, or become invasive once you turn your back!"

Red Sunset Maple *(Acer rubrum* 'Red Sunset')*. Tree with brilliant red fall foliage.

Heart Leaf Ginger *(Asarum arifolium)*. Groundcover with attractive evergreen leaves.

Wild Blue Indigo *(Baptisia australis)*. Perennial with indigo blue flowers in early summer.

Hummingbird *(Clethra alnifolia* 'Hummingbird')*. Dwarf shrub with fragrant white flowers in summer.

Dwarf Fothergilla *(F. gardenii)*. Shrub with white flowers in spring and flashy orange red foliage in fall.

Carolina Silverbell *(Halesia carolina)*. Beautiful small tree with white bell-shaped flowers in spring and lemon yellow fall foliage.

Snow Queen Hydrangea *(H. quercifolia* 'Snow Queen')*. Shrub with upright cones of creamy white summer flowers aging to pink and rich wine red fall foliage.

Winter Red *(Ilex verticillata* 'Winter Red'*)*. Shrub with scarlet red fall
   berries persisting through January.
Edith Bogue Magnolia *(M. grandiflora* 'Edith Bogue'*)*. Tree with large,
   fragrant, creamy white flowers in June and July.
Bayberry *(Myrica pensylvanica)*. Shrub with neat, dark green foliage and
   grayish white berries over winter.
Allegheny Pachysandra *(P. procumbens)*. Groundcover with mottled
   purple spring foliage.
Christmas Fern *(Polystichum acrostichoides)*. Fern with dark, evergreen
   fronds.

Kansas
Dyck Arboretum of the Plains
Hesston College
P.O. Box 3000
Hesston, Kansas 67062
316/327-8127

In late spring, pale lavender shell-leaf penstemon (P. gran-diflorus) *and red and yellow American columbine* (Aquilegia canadensis), *both seen in the rear, and white cobaea penstemon* (P. cobaea) *and rosy Ozark phlox* (P. pilosa var. ozarkana) *greet visitors at the entrance to the Dyck Arboretum of the Plains in Kansas. [Photo: Larry G. Vickerman]*

The Dyck Arboretum of the Plains is a 12-acre outdoor education facility created in 1981 to foster an appreciation of the natural beauty of Kansas. Both woody and herbaceous plants native to Kansas and the Great Plains, as well as nonnatives suited to south-central Kansas, are displayed in naturalistic settings and formal borders. A special propagation and cultural program covering mixed-grass and shortgrass species seeks to persuade more nurseries to offer these native plants to the public. The following are recommended by Larry G. Vickerman, director of the arboretum. "They are all native to Kansas," he writes, "drought- and heat-resistant, and tolerant of alkaline soils."

American Columbine *(Aquilegia canadensis)*. Perennial with red and yellow flowers in spring.

Leadplant *(Amorpha canescens)*. Shrub with purple and orange flowers in summer.

Heath Aster *(A. ericoides)*. Perennial with sprays of white flowers late summer into fall.

Sideoats Grama *(Bouteloua curtipendula)*. Grass with purple and orange flower parts in summer.

Western Coneflower *(Echinacea angustifolia)*. Perennial with rose purple or white flowers in summer.

Rattlesnake Master *(Eryngium yuccifolium)*. Perennial with white buttonlike flowers in summer.

Willowleaf Sunflower *(Helianthus salicifolius)*. Perennial with yellow flowers late summer into fall.

Cobaea Penstemon *(P. cobaea)*. Perennial with purple, lavender, or white flowers in late spring.

Shell-leaf Penstemon *(P. grandiflorus)*. Perennial with lavender flowers in late spring.

Mexican Hat *(Ratibida columnifera)*. Perennial with red and yellow flowers in summer.

Blue Sage *(Salvia azurea)*. Perennial with blue flowers late summer into fall.

Little Bluestem *(Schizachyrium scoparium)*. Grass with stalks in blue to green hues that turn brilliant bronze red to orange in fall.

Kentucky

Bernheim Arboretum and Research Forest
Clermont, Kentucky 40110
502/955-8512

The Bernheim Arboretum is a 14,000-acre arboretum and forest dedicated to the preservation, study, and enjoyment of the biodiversity of Kentucky's knob lands. Located about 25 miles from Louisville, the Arboretum was established in 1929 by Isaac W. Bernheim as a gift for the people of Kentucky and their friends. Approximately 2,000 acres are open to the public and include a landscape arboretum, a nature center, picnic areas, hiking trails, and lakes. The remaining 12,000 acres are closed to the general public and serve as a botanical and ecological research laboratory. The following plants, all native to Kentucky, are recommended by Horticultural Information Specialist Clarence "Buddy" Hubbuch, who served as the arboretum's chief horticulturist for thirty-two years.

Eastern Redbud *(Cercis canadensis)*. Small tree with purple pink flowers in spring.

American Yellowwood *(Cladrastis lutea)*. Tree with fragrant white spring flowers and yellow fall foliage.

Flowering Dogwood *(Cornus florida)*. Tree with white to pink flowers in spring and brilliant red late summer foliage.

Eastern Wahoo *(Euonymus atropurpureus)*. Tree with reddish purple flowers in early summer and carmine pink to bright red fall foliage.

American Beech *(Fagus grandifolia)*. Magnificent tree with slate gray bark and yellow fall foliage.

Trumpet Honeysuckle *(Lonicera sempervirens)*. Vine with red, orange, or yellow flowers through summer.

Black Tupelo *(Nyssa sylvatica)*. Tree with scarlet red fall foliage.

Carolina Buckthorn *(Rhamnus caroliniana)*. Tree with red berries in summer and golden yellow fall foliage.

Hoary Skullcap *(Scutellaria incana)*. Perennial with blue flowers all summer.

Rusty Black Haw *(Viburnum rufidulum)*. Tree with creamy white flowers in late spring and red to purple fall foliage.

Yellowroot *(Xanthoriza simplicissima)*. Groundcover with delicate purple flowers in spring and yellow to reddish purple fall foliage.

Louisiana

Briarwood, The Caroline Dormon Nature Preserve
216 Caroline Dormon Road
Saline, Louisiana 71070
318/576-3379

Briarwood is a horticultural and botanical feast for those interested in studying, propagating, and preserving native plants, especially those from the southeast. This 130-acre estate in the sandhills of northwestern Louisiana was transformed from a family summer home into a renowned botanical garden by Caroline Dormon (1888–1971). Her work is now carried on by the nonprofit Foundation for the Preservation of the Caroline Dormon Nature Preserve, which opens the garden every weekend in April, May, August, and November. Curator Richard Johnson, a personal friend of Miss Dormon's, recommends the following, noting that "limiting a plant nut to twelve favorite ones is difficult—impossible!"

Red Buckeye *(Aesculus pavia)*. Shrub with bright red flowers in spring.

Sweet Pepperbush *(Clethra alnifolia)*. Shrub with fragrant white or pink flowers in summer.

Swamp Sunflower *(Helianthus angustifolius)*. Perennial with golden yellow flowers late summer to early fall.

Yaupon Holly *(Ilex vomitoria)*. Evergreen shrub decorated with numerous bright red berries in fall.

Florida Anise *(Illicium floridanum)*. Shrub with red flowers in spring.

Crested Iris *(I. cristata)*. Groundcover with light blue, lilac, purple, or white flowers in spring

Louisiana Iris *(I. X 'Louisiana', a group of native species that interbreed)*. Stunning perennial group with spring to summer flowers in every color of the spectrum, plus white.

Mountain Laurel *(Kalmia latifolia)*. Evergreen shrub with large, beautiful, white to blush pink blossoms in spring.

Bigleaf Magnolia *(M. macrophylla)*. Tree with fragrant, creamy white flowers in early summer.

Wax Myrtle *(Myrica cerifera)*. Willowy evergreen shrub with numerous, waxy, pale gray berries.

Golden Club *(Orontium aquaticum)*. Aquatic perennial with golden yellow flowers in early spring.

Florida Flame Azalea *(Rhododendron austrinum)*. Shrub with fragrant yellow to orange red flowers in spring and reddish to golden yellow fall foliage.

New York
New York Botanical Garden
200th Street and Southern Boulevard
Bronx, New York 10458-5126
718/817-8700

One of the world's major horticultural institutions, the New York Botanical Garden is located on 450 acres in the Bronx, New York City's northernmost borough. There, one can visit the only remaining natural forest in the city, the beautiful and renowned Enid A. Haupt Conservatory, and numerous collections and display gardens. Among the latter is the Native Plant Garden, a 2½-acre setting containing ferns, perennials, shrubs, and trees native to eastern North America and suitable for gardens and landscapes within a 100-mile radius of the city. Though the garden looks most glorious in mid August when its central wet meadow bristles with statuesque color, there are plantings for many habitats and seasons. The following selection encompasses these various conditions and flowering times and has been compiled by the garden's curator, Robert Bartolomei.

Canadian Wild Ginger *(Asarum canadense).* Groundcover with large, velvety green leaves.

Pink Turtlehead *(Chelone lyonii).* Perennial with pink or rosy purple flowers in late summer.

Wild Geranium *(G. maculatum).* Perennial with blue violet flowers in spring.

Bowman's Root *(Gillenia trifoliata).* Perennial with white flowers on reddish stems in summer.

Downy Sunflower *(Helianthus mollis).* Perennial with butter yellow flowers in summer.

Willowleaf Sunflower *(Helianthus salicifolius).* Perennial with yellow flowers late summer into fall.

Sweetbay Magnolia *(M. virginiana).* Tree with large creamy white flowers in late spring and sporadic bloom through summer.

Allegheny Pachysandra *(P. procumbens).* Groundcover with mottled purple spring foliage.

Prairie Dock *(Silphium terebinthinaceum).* Perennial with yellow flowers in late summer.

Allegheny Foamflower *(Tiarella cordifolia).* Groundcover with white flowers in spring.

This grouping of two clethra species at the Greensboro Arboretum in North Carolina provides all-season interest. In mid July, when this photograph was taken, the more floriferous sweet pepperbushes (C. alnifolia) emit a delightful fragrance. In fall, both species have colorful foliage. In winter, the exfoliating, rich brown stems of cinnamon clethra (C. acuminata) are particularly handsome against a snow-covered background. And in spring, both produce clean, rich green foliage.

North Carolina
The Greensboro Arboretum
c/o Greensboro Beautiful, Inc.
P.O. Box 3136
Greensboro, North Carolina 27402-3136
919/373-2558

The Greensboro Arboretum is a national model for what can be accomplished with private-public partnerships. Opened in 1991, the 17-acre, beautifully landscaped and labeled site was developed through the cooperative efforts of the City of Greensboro Parks & Recreation Department and Greensboro Beautiful, Inc., a nonprofit organization. The arboretum is both an educational and recreational attraction for all interested in the cultural characteristics and use of plants in landscapes. Nine permanent plant collections and special displays feature herbaceous and woody species that are hardy to the Piedmont region of North Carolina. The following easy care natives were selected by Irene McIver and Charles Bell, assisted by Irma F. Lyday.

Bottlebrush Buckeye *(Aesculus parviflora)*. Shrub with cones of creamy white flowers in midsummer.

Red Chokeberry *(Aronia arbutifolia)*. Shrub with white flowers in spring, orange to red fall foliage, and bright red berries persisting into December.

Eastern Redbud *(Cercis canadensis* 'Forest Pansy'*)*. Small tree with purple pink flowers and plum purple foliage in spring.

Sweet Pepperbush *(Clethra alnifolia)*. Shrub with fragrant white or pink flowers in summer.

Dwarf Fothergilla *(F. gardenii)*. Shrub with white flowers in spring and flashy orange red foliage in fall.

Large Fothergilla *(F. major)*. Shrub with white flowers in spring and fall foliage blended with orange, yellow, red, and purple tints.

Possumhaw *(Ilex decidua* 'Warren's Red'*)*. Shrub with orange to scarlet red berries lasting through winter.

Inkberry *(Ilex glabra* 'Compacta'*)*. Shrub with handsome jet black berries that often persist through winter.

Drooping Leucothoe *(L. fontanesiana* 'Rainbow'*)*. Shrub with white flowers in spring and glossy green leaves variegated with pink, cream, and yellow tints.

Southern Magnolia *(M. grandiflora* 'Little Gem'*)*. Dwarf tree with large, fragrant, creamy white flowers in June and July.

Sweetbay Magnolia *(M. virginiana)*. Tree with large creamy white flowers in late spring and sporadic bloom through summer.

Sourwood *(Oxydendron arboreum)*. Tree with sprays of creamy white flowers in July and scarlet red fall foliage.

Ohio

The Dawes Arboretum
7770 Jacksontown Road SE
Newark, Ohio 43056-9380
614/323-2990 or 800/44-DAWES

The Dawes Arboretum, located in the heart of Ohio, was founded by Beman and Bertie Dawes in 1929 to encourage the research and planting of trees and shrubs and thereby to increase the public's knowledge, love, and horticultural uses of these plants. Today, the arboretum is a private foundation that oversees 1,149 acres of horticulture collections, natural areas, farmland, and research plots. A 4-mile auto tour and over 9 miles of trails—all open free to the public—traverse collections of hollies, crab apples, rare trees, and rhododendrons as well as a 4½-acre wildflower field, woodlands, and a cypress swamp. The following, all native to central Ohio, are easy care stalwarts at the arboretum and were selected by Luke E. Messinger, public information officer.

Butterfly Weed *(Asclepias tuberosa)*. Perennial with bright orange flowers throughout summer and striking seedpods in September.

Wild Blue Indigo *(Baptisia australis)*. Perennial with indigo blue flowers in early summer.

American Hornbeam *(Carpinus caroliniana)*. Tree with ash gray bark and orange to deep red fall foliage.

Eastern Redbud *(Cercis canadensis)*. Small tree with purple pink flowers in spring.

Purple Coneflower *(Echinacea purpurea)*. Perennial with purple, rose pink, or white flowers all summer.

Common Witch Hazel *(Hamamelis virginiana)*. Tree with yellow ribbon-like flowers appearing immediately after yellow foliage drop in fall.

Spicebush *(Lindera benzoin)*. Shrub with fragrant yellow flowers in spring; scarlet red berries in September, and bright yellow fall foliage.

Cardinal Flower *(Lobelia cardinalis)*. Perennial with scarlet flowers in late summer.

American Hop Hornbeam *(Ostrya virginiana)*. Tree with yellow fall foliage.

Switch Grass *(Panicum virgatum)*. Grass with gray to blue green leaves and airy panicles with dark red to purple tones that mature first to yellows and then to warm beiges.

Allegheny Foamflower *(Tiarella cordifolia)*. Groundcover with white flowers in spring.

Canadian Hemlock *(Tsuga canadensis)*. Conifer with dark green foliage.

Ontario
Royal Botanical Gardens
P.O. Box 399
Hamilton, Ontario
Canada L8N 3H8
905/527-1158

The Royal Botanical Gardens is dedicated to the development of public understanding and appreciation of the relationship between the plant world, humanity, and the rest of nature. Located at the western tip of Lake Ontario, its 2,800 acres cover a wide range of habitats:

woodlands, meadows, shallow lake, escarpment face, marsh, and agricultural land. The nearly fifty documented collections of herbaceous and woody plants include the world's largest collection of lilacs, a native tree and shrub collection, New World Species Orchid Collection, and Living Library of Interior Landscape Plants. The following North American natives are recommended by Chris Graham, manager of horticultural services.

Bottlebrush Buckeye *(Aesculus parviflora)*. Shrub with cones of creamy white flowers in midsummer.

American Hornbeam *(Carpinus caroliniana)*. Tree with ash gray bark and orange to deep red fall foliage.

American Bittersweet *(Celastrus scandens)*. Vine with bright orange fruits in fall.

Eastern Redbud *(Cercis canadensis)*. Small tree with purple pink flowers in spring.

Fringetree *(Chionanthus virginicus)*. Tree with feathery white late spring flowers and bright yellow fall foliage.

Black Cohosh *(Cimicifuga racemosa)*. Perennial with candlelike spires of white flowers in summer.

Pagoda Dogwood *(Cornus alternifolia)*. Tree with creamy white spring flowers and maroon purple fall foliage.

Dwarf Fothergilla *(F. gardenii)*. Shrub with white flowers in spring and flashy orange red foliage in fall.

Fragrant Sumac *(Rhus aromatica)*. Shrub with clusters of yellow flowers in early spring, bright red berries summer into winter, and orange to intense scarlet red fall foliage.

Allegheny Foamflower *(Tiarella cordifolia)*. Groundcover with white flowers in spring.

Culver's Root *(Veronicastrum virginica)*. Perennial with spires of white or light blue flowers mid to late summer.

American Cranberry Bush *(Viburnum trilobum)*. Shrub with white spring flowers, red to orange berries late summer to late winter, and purplish red fall foliage.

Oregon
Leach Botanical Garden
6704 S. E. 122nd Avenue
Portland, Oregon 97236
503/761-9503

Just twenty minutes from downtown Portland, the Leach Botanical Garden is situated in a woodland hollow carved by Johnson Creek. More than a mile of public trails wind through its 9 acres, where over 1,500 plant species and cultivars—the great majority native to the Northwest—grow in woodland, rock garden, xeric, bog, and riparian habitats. Named for the Leaches, who donated the original garden and land to the city, the garden is now operated as a cooperative effort by the City of Portland Bureau of Parks and the Leach Garden Friends, a nonprofit group. In recommending the following as wonderful, easy care natives, curator Bonnie Brunkow and gardener Scotty Fairchild commented, "It was hard to shorten the list to a dozen."

Vine Maple *(Acer circinatum)*. Tree with yellow to vibrant red fall foliage.

Western Maidenhair Fern *(Adiantum aleuticum)*. Fern with graceful green fronds.

Western Wild Ginger *(Asarum caudatum)*. Groundcover with shiny, dark green, heart-shaped leaves.

Deer Fern *(Blechnum spicant)*. Evergreen fern with neat, compact growth.

Giant Fawn Lily *(Erythronium oregonum)*. Corm with large white flowers and strongly mottled leaves in early spring.

Coast Fawn Lily *(Erythronium revolutum)*. Corm with deep pink flowers and mottled leaves in early spring.

Oregon Grape *(Mahonia aquifolium)*. Shrub with yellow flowers in spring and edible blue berries in summer.

Redwood Sorrel *(Oxalis oregana)*. Groundcover with cloverlike leaves and white or rose spring flowers.

Western Sword Fern *(Polystichum munitum)*. Fern with large, once-pinnate evergreen fronds.

Western Azalea *(Rhododendron occidentale)*. Shrub with fragrant white to blush pink flowers in spring and orange red fall foliage.

Red Flowering Currant *(Ribes sanguineum)*. Shrub with crimson red flowers in spring and bluish black fall berries.

Western Solomon's Seal *(Smilacina racemosa* var. *amplexicaulis)*. Perennial with white flowers in spring and red berries in late summer.

Chapter 5

Private Gardens

This chapter gives you the opportunity to visit four private gardens. They are personal creations that express the individuality of each designer, and range from a woodland setting in which native flora mix with exotics to a drought garden that uses plants native to the site. They demonstrate that the possibilities of gardening with native plants are wide open; that there is, in fact, no one, rigid way to garden with American flora. What they share—and perhaps what is most appropriate for this book—is that every garden is ultimately a low-maintenance creation. There are times, of course, when you have to work for what you get and the profiles in this chapter illustrate this truism also. Fortunately, the gardeners on the following pages offer tips on how to reduce such prior efforts. I think that when you finish reading these four personable and inspiring stories, you will want to go right out and create your own very special, very attractive native plant garden.

The white form of pinkshell azalea (Rhododendron vaseyi) glistens by a pool of blue woodland phlox (P. divaricata) in early May in David Benner's Pennsylvania garden.

BERT AND CELESTE WILSON'S DROUGHT GARDENS, SANTA MARGARITA, CALIFORNIA

How does a California drought garden survive a flood? That was the question repeatedly asked during the torrential rains of winter 1995. For some Californians, the answer was: easily.

Their gardens and landscapes were decorated with regional natives, plants that flourish despite California's frequent years-long drought periods, constant dry summers, and sporadic, drenching wet winters. Among these are trees, such as western redbud *(Cercis occidentalis)* with magenta flowers in February and reddish purple seedpods throughout fall; shrubs, such as fuchsia flowered gooseberry *(Ribes speciosum)* with red jewellike flowers and glossy green leaves; and perennials, such as blue flax *(Linum perenne* var. *lewisii)* with lovely morning flowers all spring and well into summer.

These are the kinds of plants that Bert and Celeste Wilson have grown for over twenty years at their Las Pilitas Nursery and use in their garden design and ecological restoration projects. Since they only work with plants native to California, the scope of their selection may seem limited. But a look at their extensive catalog quickly negates this notion, for California has the most diverse native flora in the continental United States, a flora ten times richer than a comparable-sized area in the northeast.

While California's plant palette is extensive, so too are the adverse conditions under which it exists. Temperatures within the state swing from 130°F to -54°F. Fog blankets some areas over 150 days a year and other areas less than 10. Soil varies from thick adobe clay to dry desert sand and from highly acidic to very alkaline contents.

To most home owners, however, the truly exasperating aspect of gardening in California is the periodic droughts, dry periods that last for years and even, in the distant past, decades. Many of these people—particularly those with an East Coast heritage—spend extravagant amounts of money and countless hours watering their gardens in an attempt to keep them green and colorful. The Wilsons say this expensive effort is not necessary and their work proves their contention.

One of their most daunting—and ultimately most satisfying—projects involved a 1½-acre property on a windswept shoreline south of Cambria. The salty, alkaline ground water in the area was fit for neither plant nor animal. Humans rely on purified water; the plants have only the vagaries of rainfall. The Wilsons spent eight months analyzing the site and selecting plants. The benefit, indeed the necessity, of such careful planning was ultimately demonstrated: though there was no rain for thirty days after the landscaping was installed completely without water, the project was a success.

This is an amazing accomplishment. It is also one that illustrates the practicality of following the Wilsons' tenet that beautiful landscapes can be created under just about any condition when native plants that naturally grow in such a site are used. In this case, two groups of plants were outstanding. The first was as site-specific as possible. The Wilsons had collected seed and cuttings from plants already on the property, propagated them at their nursery, and then replanted the results in a designed setting. Success was 99 percent with this material.

To increase the floral variety, the Wilsons propagated another group of plants, those that naturally grow in similar situations. About three-fourths survived the unusually harsh conditions of the initial planting. Among these was a lovely dark green groundcover known as coyote bush *(Baccharis pilularis)*. Native to the central California coast, this is not only drought tolerant but also deer-proof. The Wilsons highly recommend the Pigeon Point cultivar. "I use this plant to cover large areas of ground when we landscape rural estates," Bert says. "I break up the plots with walks or colorful plants, such as the similarly drought-tolerant ceanothus shrubs."

While strongly emphasizing that "the best plants for your site are ones that are native on your site," the Wilsons also recognize that for many gardeners there is no native site. These are the people who live in towns and developments, which are inherently unnatural settings. A look at a landscape project for a new home in San Luis Obispo illustrates their work in these situations. They began, as always, with a study of light patterns, temperature variation, and soil composition and drainage. Because the property was in town, prevailing winds were not as important a factor as they are in coastal work. Animal life, in the form of deer, was also negligible but insect pests were not. At the time, a periodic drought was raging. A drainage analysis, however, indicated that using just drought-tolerant plants would not be satisfactory. "The plot of land is right above creek level," Bert says, "and in wet years water has stood on the site for as long as three months."

"I hate the concept of berms and fake creeks," he admits, "but this

This San Luis Obispo street corner had survived five years of drought and one winter of torrential rain when photographed in early March. Its easy care California natives include (from top to bottom) pale blue maritime ceanothus (C. maritimus) and lavender pink seaside daisy (Erigeron glaucus 'Wayne Roderick'). To the right are the blue flowers and glossy green leaves of Yankee Point (Ceanothus griseus horizontalis 'Yankee Point'). The latter contrast with the grayish green foliage of red buckwheat (Eriogonum grande var. rubescens). [Photo: Bert Wilson]

site needed such protection." Small berms were used to raise the front corner of the lot, providing a 2-foot barrier against flood water. The detested fake stream was installed on the inside to act as a drainage ditch for any water spilling over the berm. This strategy proved an exceedingly wise one during the winter of 1995.

City regulations stipulated not only that new homes had to be landscaped but also that legal approval had to be obtained for all plant material and placements. The Wilsons are of two minds about such regulations. They agree that guidelines on plants should be given because there are economic and environmental consequences in selecting the wrong ones. They feel, however, that statutes should be exclusionary (that is, no invasive plants, no plants requiring excessive waterings) rather than inclusionary (such as the mandated use of London plane trees, which are not all that suitable to California). After several talks with local officials (London planes were a contentious subject), the Wilsons' plant selection was approved. Though not native to the site, they all claimed a California heritage and flourished under similar stresses elsewhere in the state.

A well-designed, low-maintenance landscape is more than just a grouping of easy care plants. It is an aesthetically pleasing arrangement that ensures all-season color as well as contrast in foliage form and texture. And here again, the use of native plants more than meets such a goal.

Given the small, in-town setting, the Wilsons opted for a formal approach. Two handsome western redbuds were placed as 12-foot guards of honor, one on each side of the entrance. Though their lovely magenta flowers quickly disappear in the San Luis Obispo heat, their bluish green leaves stand out for months against the warm stucco walls of the building. Groundcovers were chosen for neatness and foliage contrast. These include maritime ceanothus *(C. maritimus)* with dark green, hollylike leaves. "It looks like a prostrate cotoneaster," Bert explains. "Though it likes coastal areas best, it is astonishingly good inland. It's great outside California, too. I would have no hesitation using this plant in coastal Washington or even on much of the East Coast."

To remedy the lack of privacy in the backyard, a 12-foot-tall evergreen hedge of alderleaf mountain mahogany *(Cercocarpus betuloides* var. *blancheae)* was placed on the rear edge. "Its narrow habit makes it an excellent screen," Bert says. "We sell a lot of these to people who don't want to see their neighbors but only have a 3- or 4-foot border for planting." A 4-foot-tall row of fuchsia-flowered gooseberry was placed in front of the alderleaf. From January through May, the red flowers and the hummingbirds they attract can be seen from the kitchen window.

A small number of drought-tolerant, easy care groundcovers and perennials were added for further color. Lavender blue seaside daisies *(Erigeron glaucus* 'Wayne Roderick') look particularly smashing next to the feathery silver foliage of David's Choice sandhill sage *(Artemisia pycnocephala)*. Despite its popular name, red buckwheat *(Eriogonum grande rubescens)* actually has pink flowers, which bloom from June into October.

The above are but a few of the many native plants that give this intown property color and structure from January through December. Now into its fifth year, it relies solely on rainfall for water and only requires a semiannual check for any weeding or pruning. Clearly, as the Wilsons demonstrate, neither drought nor flood are obstacles when lovely, site-specific natives are used in garden and landscape settings.

✳

COLORFUL DRY WEST NATIVES

A junior in high school at this writing, Penny A. Wilson plans to be a landscape architect. Having grown up at her parents' Las Pilitas Nursery in Santa Margarita, California, she already has more plant knowledge than many practitioners in her chosen field. While some designers emphasize foliage color, texture, and form for dry California landscapes, Wilson feels flower color and fragrance are equally important. She has compiled the following list of easy care natives for those who agree with her philosophy.

Mountain Yarrow *(Achillea millefolium* var. *lanuosa).* Perennial with lacy white blooms in summer.

Western Columbine *(Aquilegia formosa).* Perennial with red and yellow flowers May to August.

Western Redbud *(Cercis occidentalis).* Small tree with brilliant magenta flowers late winter to spring, reddish purple seed pods throughout fall, and yellow or red fall foliage.

Desert Willow *(Chilopsis linearis).* Small tree with fragrant lilac flowers all summer.

Seaside Daisy *(Erigeron glaucus* 'Wayne Roderick').* Groundcover with lavender flowers in spring.

Blue Flax *(Linum perenne* var. *lewisii).* Perennial with petite blue flowers for almost three months, starting when snow melts.

Purple Butterfly Mint *(Monardella antonina).* Hardy annual with pale purple flower balls from July to December.

Blue Bedder *(Penstemon heterophyllus* var. *purdyi).* Groundcover with rich blue or striking purple flowers spring well into summer.

Pozo Blue Sage *(Salvia clevelandii* X *S. leucophylla).* Evergreen shrub with violet blue flowers in summer.

Hummingbird Sage *(Salvia spathacea).* Hardy annual with spikes of deep magenta flowers in summer.

FOR FURTHER INFORMATION on the variety and garden potential of California plants (many of them suitable for gardens across the country), consult A MANUAL OF CALIFORNIA NATIVE PLANTS by Bert Wilson. This is available for $10 from Las Pilitas Nursery, Las Pilitas Road, Santa Margarita, California 93453. All plants mentioned in this profile, plus hundreds more, are included in the Las Pilitas price and nursery list, which can be obtained by sending a self-addressed, stamped envelope.

BONNIE HARPER-LORE'S FRONT YARD GARDEN, MINNETONKA, MINNESOTA

"Native plants are my life," Bonnie Harper-Lore says and she means it. Ever since she was a little girl walking through the nearby woods and meadows of her rural Wisconsin home, she has been enchanted with the beauty and diversity of regional flora. She has channeled this enchantment into a twenty-year career of working with and promoting native plants. This has included stints as an assistant professor of landscape architecture at the University of Minnesota, director of the National Wildflower Research Center's Midwest office, freelance landscape designer, and currently national Roadside Vegetation Coordinator for the Federal Highway Administration.

It was not until 1990, however, that her moment of truth came. She and her husband bought a house on a tree-lined street in a Minneapolis suburb. She had, as she admits, "talked the talk" and now it was time to "walk the walk." In clearer English, that meant Harper-Lore wanted to install a front yard prairie garden in a green lawn neighborhood.

She had been around long enough to realize that this approach clashes with the widespread belief that properties in front of houses should be mowed expanses of green. While the resulting lawns require a lot of time, money, and pesticides, they do have the neighborly attribute of being predictably neat—an adjective rarely used to describe prairies. Thus, Harper-Lore's first step was to give her neighbors a year's advance notice and, in doing so, to describe the concept behind this new kind of suburban landscaped setting.

She explained that she would be creating rather than restoring a prairie on her quarter-acre front yard. There is an important difference between the two approaches. The latter, as demonstrated in the Diboll landscape described on pages 103–7, allows nature free rein in the evolution of the plants and their composition. In a created prairie, the designer's hand is ever present.

In Harper-Lore's case, she sketched out a plan in which wildflower blooms would splash distinctly against a background of native grasses, rather than mixing with them as in a natural setting. In further contrast to a real prairie, plant height was limited to no more than 24 inches so that the landscape would not clash too dramatically with the rest of the neighborhood.

And then it was time to get to work. In a perfect world—the kind that rarely exists—Harper-Lore would have allowed herself at least three months for site preparation, performing a cyclical series of spraying glyphyosate on existing sod and weeds and then raking off the dead turf. Since this would have created an ugly brown area for an extended time, she allowed herself only two weeks for just one clearing.

Then she and her husband lightly raked the soil (deep tilling brings weed seeds to the surface) and broadcast seed. She started with short grasses: June grass *(Koeleria macrantha)*, with silvery green seedheads in early summer; sideoats grama *(Bouteloua curtipendula)*, featuring fine-textured foliage and summer flowers tinged with purple; and little bluestem *(Schizachyrium scoparium)*, chosen for its warm red fall stems. Last, as a neighborhood pleaser, she and her husband scattered 4 ounces of yellow coneflower *(Ratibida pinnata)*, a beautiful prairie perennial that flowers naturally among grasses.

Next, using a time-honored instruction option, she called in her students. First, she reviewed elements of her design: (1) a 4-foot lawn grass border about the landscape provides continuity with the rest of the front yards on the street; (2) inside this green mowed ribbon, the prairie component wraps around the corner of the property and forms a transition into the back oak woodland; and (3) the use of colorful forbs (the scientific word botanists use for wildflowers) brightens up the highest-visibility areas in the front yard. Each of the last, she added, was matched to the microclimate of the site.

With Harper-Lore leading the way, the students were put to work planting thirty different wildflower species in this last component. These were not just any wildflower seedlings; they were Minnesota natives propagated by local seed firms. Harper-Lore feels quite strongly—"passionate" is an adjective often applied to her—that using plants that once grew naturally in an area is the most ethical and practical approach to landscaping and gardening. It is ethical because it respects the integrity of the land and practical because minimal time and money are required for maintenance.

Two star performers from this initial planting are prairie smoke *(Geum triflorum)* and Ohio spiderwort *(Tradescantia ohiensis)*. The former, covered with demure pink flowers that dramatically change into feathery silver or rose seedheads, is a distinctive early spring plant. The Ohio spiderwort has deep blue flowers that start their months-long bloom period shortly afterward. These two plants are especially important in a suburban prairie setting because of their flowering time—prairies are not known for spring splendor.

"Then came the hard part," Harper-Lore relates. "Patience!" While she had routinely told clients that it takes a perennial stand of native forbs and grasses three to five years to become established, she had never fully comprehended how long this was until she planted her own prairie. What made it particularly difficult for her was that her front yard represented a public display of her private credo. She wanted it to be absolutely wonderful and it was not.

One hurdle to early beauty was Harper-Lore's strict adherence to her stance of using only regional native plants. "There's just one annual native to eastern Minnesota," she explains. "It's called partridge pea *(Cassia fasciculata)* and its deep yellow flowers are in bloom from July to frost. While it would have been absolutely great in my front yard, I could not find a commercial source." (Prairie Moon, whose address is given in the Appendix, now offers this plant.)

And then there were the grasses, her major design component. "For some reason," she admits, "they did not establish themselves as anticipated. I planted at the standard rate of 7 to 10 pounds per acre in the month of June, a perfect time for a Midwest prairie planting." It is the only instance in her years of prairie plantings that they did not become quickly established. Had they done so, they would have quickly crowded out any annual weeds. As it was, the weeds won.

She and her husband got down on their knees and started pulling them out. Though they were keeping the garden neat for neighborhood appearance, they were not demonstrating that it required low

In creating her front yard prairie garden, Bonnie Harper-Lore strove for all-season interest. Prairie smoke (Geum triflorum), one of the few prairie plants to bloom in spring, bursts into color shortly after the sculptural forms of the overwintering grasses have been burned or mowed. This carefree perennial gets its name from its wispy seedheads rather than its attractive flowers. [Photo: Bonnie Harper-Lore]

maintenance. And, in a vicious circle, the hand weeding only loos-
ened the soil enough for perennial weeds to gain a foothold. High
mowings can often discourage this and Harper-Lore thinks she should
have used this maintenance tool more often.

To remedy the sparseness of seed-sprouting grass, Harper-Lore
bought flats of little bluestem and prairie dropseed *(Sporobolus heterolepis)*, an elegant grass with thick sprays of summer green that
mature in beautiful fountains of rich rust brown in autumn. These
seedling grasses have settled in without any problems.

When asked how others might profit from her experience in creating a prairie front yard, Harper-Lore offers the following advice:

1. Start small. Large failures, such as the grasses on her property,
   stand out. The prairie setting can be expanded each year and
   filled with plants that have established success records in the particular site.
2. Know your soil. Harper-Lore had assumed her planting area
   contained the sandy loam found on the rest of her property.
   Only after she had seeded plants suitable for such soil did she discover that past construction had unearthed the heavy clay that
   makes up most of the front garden. The mismatch of plant and
   soil contributed to many of her initial problems.
3. Plant annuals to fill in bare spots. Eastern Minnesota is unusual in
   having only one such native.
4. Use seedlings for instant effect. While this does increase the initial expense, it also guarantees greater initial success. Here again,
   the benefits of starting small are apparent. As the seedlings spread
   or even reseed, they can be transplanted to newly cleared areas.
5. Mulch between plantings. Indeed, effective use of mulch can
   eliminate weeds in a year or two and prepare the way for wider
   use of direct seeding. Harper-Lore recommends prairie hay or
   weed-free straw, both of which decompose into the soil.

And, of course, should Harper-Lore inspect such a creation, she
would never be as critical of the results as she initally was of hers. Even
that first year when she wanted—unreasonably, as she inwardly
knew—a full-grown prairie to appear, there was color, variety, and all-
season interest. By the third year, her neighbors had started asking for
a transplant or two to decorate their own monochromatic green

✳

PRAIRIE PLANTS FOR FRONT YARDS

The following is an easy care selection of plants that Bonnie Harper-Lore used in her front yard. "In terms of ease of establishment, relatively long bloom, and wonderful colorful splashes," she writes, "these are among my favorites." With these plants, you can have color and interest from spring through fall.

Butterfly Weed *(Asclepias tuberosa)*. Perennial with bright orange flowers in summer and striking seedpods in September.

Smooth Aster *(A. laevis)*. Perennial with white through lavender flowers late summer into fall.

Flowering Spurge *(Euphorbia corollata)*. Perennial with sprays of white flowers summer into fall.

Prairie Smoke *(Geum triflorum)*. Perennial with rose red flowers and silver pink seed plumes in spring.

Kansas Gayfeather *(Liatris pychnostachya)*. Corm with spikes of purple flowers in midsummer.

Wild Lupine *(Lupinus perennis)*. Perennial with spires of blue flowers in spring.

Prairie Phlox *(P. pilosa)*. Groundcover with reddish purple flowers in late spring.

Prairie Coneflower *(Ratibida pinnata)*. Perennial with yellow flowers in midsummer.

Little Bluestem *(Schizachyrium scoparium)*. Grass with stalks in blue to green hues that turn brilliant bronze red to orange in fall.

Stiff Goldenrod *(Solidago rigida)*. Perennial with yellow flowers late summer into fall.

Prairie Dropseed *(Sporobalus heterolepis)*. Grass with spraying mounds of emerald green leaves that turn orange gold in fall and a rich rust brown in winter.

Golden Alexander *(Zizea aurea)*. Perennial with yellow flowers in spring.

lawns. And now, in its fifth year, Bonnie Harper-Lore has finally "walked the walk"—she has a front yard filled with the beauty, color, and foliage form and contrast of her beloved native plants.

FOR FURTHER INFORMATION on regional native plants for your area, send for an Introductory Fact Pack from the National Wildflower Research Center. Include the name of your state and a $10 check ($5 for members) made out to NWRC-Clearing House and mail your request to: Clearing House, NWRC, 4801 La Crosse Boulevard, Austin, Texas 78739.

DAVID BENNER'S ONE-SEASON GARDEN, NEW HOPE, PENNSYLVANIA

During the first three weeks of May, there is probably no finer home woodland garden on the East Coast than that of David Benner's. It is a fragrant sea of spectacularly colorful groundcovers washing through flowering shrubs and towering trees. Pictures of this paean to spring beauty grace the cover of a major horticultural book and have been prominently featured in many national magazines.

By June, however, the woods comprising Benner's sloping, 2-acre hill property have settled into their basically green existence and Benner can usually be found hiking and fishing in Maine. It is precisely because he is often not around to enjoy a summer floral display that he decided to concentrate all his flower power into one ravishing moment of glory.

It also made life a lot easier for him. And Benner is a man who says he enjoys an easy existence despite the fact that as soon as he comes up with yet another labor-saving device he quickly uses any increase in

Luxuriant groundcovers and perennials stream through David Benner's woods in May. Pictured here are white foam-flowers (Tiarella cordifolia), *pink creeping phlox* (P. stoloni-fera), *and yellow celandine poppies* (Stylophorum diphyllum).

free time to delve into another activity. A botanist and a former college professor, Benner's current schedule includes lecturing, hosting tours, consulting, participating in his garden information and product business, and trying to enjoy semiretirement.

When he and his wife bought their home in 1962, he was working at the nearby Bowman's Hill Wildflower Preserve, a state park featuring native Pennsylvania plants. Since he dealt with lovely easy care flowers all day, it was only natural that he wanted to have some decorating his home grounds as well. A few were already in place. Clumps of Christmas fern, for example, were scattered about the property. "The best fern there is, no doubt about it," he says. "They complement any garden and can be placed anywhere. Their evergreen fronds can even survive in sun and the plant is never invasive."

There were also a limited number of flowering shrubs, including a stand of pinxterbloom *(Rhododendron periclymenoides)*, whose rosy pink flowers have continued to burst forth every spring, and a huge summer blooming rosebay rhododendron *(R. maximum)*, "which has probably been growing here for two hundred years and is one of the most magnificent that I've ever seen." And there was a lot of overgrown, unwanted brush.

As a botanist, he knew this brush would ultimately overwhelm any plantings. Therefore, rather than rushing out and installing plants, he spent the first year clearing the overgrowth. Then, as now, he did not use pesticides (he is fortunate in not being one of those people highly susceptible to poison ivy). His position on this subject is both personal and universal: he didn't want the poisonous runoff from the pesticides entering his well system, and he believes that the environment as a whole could do without such chemicals.

He also took out all maples, a task that eliminated weeding of any selfsown seedlings. The remaining trees, already dominant on the property, were all natives and include oaks, tulip trees, and beeches. These were limbed; that is, their lower branches were cut off to create a high canopy that provides bright rather than dense shade.

With preparation work out of the way, planting began in earnest. It should be noted that Benner did not concentrate on natives; rather, he emphasized spring bloom, beauty, and ease of care. Because so many natives meet these criteria—particularly the latter two—they constitute the great majority of plants in the garden.

Four, indeed, form the backbone of Benner's May woodland show:

goldenstar *(Chrysogonum virginianum)* with bright yellow flowers; blue woodland phlox *(P. divaricata)* with fragrant flowers that range from rich blue to white; creeping phlox *(P. stolonifera)* with predominantly pink flowers but random, selfsown white, lavender, or blue ones as well; and foamflower *(Tiarella cordifolia)* with foamy white to pink spikes. These all were planted in 1963 and have since spread robustly throughout the property.

Though Benner added many more May-blooming plants, he did so without any garden plans. "Plotting on paper is useless," he comments. "You have to know your plants and know the right place to put them so that they will flourish on their own. I would sometimes walk around for days before placing a plant."

And he does admit, "Of course, I made mistakes. I put in several cute little things that went on to become way too big for their spots. Most people do that. I just cut them out or learned to live with them." Even though he sometimes ignores his own advice, he feels it is extremely important to know the mature size of a shrub before planting it. Such knowledge eliminates both mistakes and time spent rectifying them.

Benner's garden is, and was always intended to be, a one-man show and maintenance operation. His initial thought was to keep the size to one-half acre. Since he was doing a lot of walking about initially to place many unusual shrubs—a red-flowered Florida anise *(Illicium floridanum)* has flourished on his zone 6 property for ten years now—and to transplant some of the many selfsown azaleas, it quickly grew to an acre and, at this writing, is fast approaching an acre and a half. The expansion led to an increase in the work needed to maintain the garden. While Benner wanted the extra flower power he had neither the time nor the inclination for the additional upkeep hours.

He then came up with two ingenious labor-saving approaches. The first eliminated the lawn area and, with such a disappearance, the need for any mowing or grass upkeep. In its place, he put in paths and swaths of moss and became one of the country's leading experts on creating moss gardens. The second did away with leaf raking. He purchased vinyl netting and placed it loosely on top of all evergreen groundcovers. In a yearly ritual that he considers essential, he spreads these about at the beginning of September and rolls them up with their leaf catch at the end of October. The leaves are deposited in a big compost pile and returned to the garden as humus the following spring. This is the only fertilizer that the entire setting receives.

Because his woodland habitat is so natural, Benner is able to raise and display many uncommon natives. His growing conditions, for example, are responsible for what he calls "the largest partridge berry patch in the United States." This 18-by-25-foot area is literally blanketed with the dark green foliage of the diminutive groundcover *(Mitchella repens)*. Its red berries sparkle amidst the leaves throughout winter and come June are replaced with tiny but exquisitely fragrant white flowers. "A patch like that is just terrific," Benner can't help commenting.

Over time, however, there was one aspect of the garden that was becoming decidedly unnatural: the increasing presence of deer herds. Benner hated the thought of erecting a fence, since he believed this would detract from the lovely naturalness of his woodland setting. Once again, he hit upon an ingenious solution, one that has gained him the thanks of gardeners across the country. He turned to nets once more, but this time he converted them to fences. Using a dark vinyl import from Italy, he tacked the 7½-foot-high material to trees around his property. The netting usually cannot be seen and is completely effective in keeping the deer out of the garden.

With all deer at bay and with ideal growing conditions, Benner's garden remains a spectacular demonstration of May flowers. By early June the native groundcovers and perennials have assumed their cool green summer appearance. So too have the many flowering exotics—primroses, honesty plant, epimediums, daffodils, and tulips.

Nature then takes over where Benner has deliberately left off. In early July, the rosebay rhododendron opens up its blush pink blossoms and the clove-scented fragrance of the white to light pink flowers of swamp azaleas *(Rhododendron viscosum)* wafts through warm summer air. In the background, white spires of black cohosh *(Cimicifuga racemosa)* shoot up and join the pinkish magenta blossoms of flowering raspberry *(Rubus odoratus)*.

When fall comes, the foliage on many of the azaleas turns purple, red, or orange. Spicebush *(Lindera benzoin)*, according to Benner, is particularly attractive, with bright yellow foliage profusely decorated with cheery red berries. "Birds love it," he adds.

All of this demonstrates that though Benner has constructed a one-

✳

NATIVES FOR WOODLANDS

David Benner has selected the following plants for their ease of care, beauty, and broad adaptability. With them, you can have something of interest in a wooded setting from spring through fall.

Goldenstar *(Chrysogonum virginianum)*. Groundcover with yellow flowers spring into early summer and often reblooming in fall.

Fringed Bleeding Heart *(Dicentra eximia)*. Perennial with pink flowers late spring into fall.

Twinleaf *(Jeffersonia diphylla)*. Perennial with white flowers in early spring.

Spicebush *(Lindera benzoin)*. Shrub with fragrant yellow flowers in spring, scarlet red berries in September, and bright yellow fall foliage.

Blue Woodland Phlox *(P. divaricata)*. Groundcover with fragrant light blue flowers in spring.

Creeping Phlox *(P. stolonifera)*. Groundcover with blue, pink, white, or purple violet flowers in spring.

Rosebay Rhododendron *(Rhododendron maximum)*. Tall, evergreen shrub with purplish pink to white blossoms in early summer.

Roseshell Azalea *(Rhododendron prinophyllum)*. Shrub with fragrant rosy pink or purple flowers in May.

Swamp Azalea *(Rhododendron viscosum)*. Shrub with clove-scented white to light pink flowers in early summer and orange to purple fall foliage.

Celandine Poppy *(Stylophorum diphyllum)*. Perennial with yellow flowers in spring and sometimes into midsummer.

Allegheny Foamflower *(Tiarella cordifolia)*. Groundcover with white flowers in spring.

Blueberry *(Vaccinium corymbosum)*. Shrub with white spring flowers, edible blue summer fruit, and crimson fall foliage.

season garden, easy care native plants see to it that his setting is one with some color and variety throughout the year.

FOR FURTHER INFORMATION on how to obtain deer-proof netting or a video describing Benner's low-maintenance approach to shade gardening and how he created his moss garden, call Benner's Gardens at 800/753-4660.

NEIL DIBOLL'S PRAIRIE LANDSCAPE, WESTFIELD, WISCONSIN

The prairie landscape concept represents a unique American contribution to garden design. It is chaos theory let loose in the horticultural world: a setting is created and then random, unpredictable events determine its future. "After all," says Neil Diboll, one of its leading practitioners, "what fun is there if you know exactly what's going to happen?"

It is the deliberate randomness that sets apart the prairie approach as a landscape tool. In very broad terms, one can say that Western (that is, European and American) gardens are conscientiously constructed to serve specific purposes, whether these are the informalism of the natural look or the geometric structure of a room garden. They are appreciated both for the thought behind their construction and for the choice of plant material. While Asian—particularly Japanese—gardens are just as carefully constructed, there is an added dimension: the unconscious is invited to seep through and is expected to respond to the design. They are, in short, contemplative gardens. The position and the balance of the components, rather than the components themselves, are of greater importance in these settings.

Randomness is not a major factor in either of these great garden traditions. It is essential to American prairie landscape creation. "If you're a control freak," Diboll warns, "don't attempt a prairie landscape. You'll be disappointed." If, however, you want less work, less expense, and sublimely gorgeous results in the planted areas on your property, grow a prairie and you'll be amply rewarded.

That last statement is what Diboll has been repeating since 1982 to convince both corporate and residential landscapers throughout the Midwest and along the eastern seaboard that they should take a second look at the inherent, season-long beauty of prairie plants. He is both a businessman—his Prairie Nursery sells seeds, plants, and consulting services—and a proselytizer. This is a man who truly loves the prairie, one who can't contain a feeling of awe when he talks about it.

He explains that it is a uniquely midwestern ecosystem that once ranged from Canada to Texas and from Ohio to Kansas. He tells of early explorers crossing Illinois and having to stand on the backs of their horses in order to see over the exuberant waves of bluestem (*Andropogon gerardii*) grasses. Less than one-tenth of one percent of that

Though purple coneflowers (Echinacea purpurea) still dominate the color scheme in Neil Diboll's late August prairie landscape, the yellow flowers of stiff goldenrod (Sol-idago rigida) presage the shift to a fall vista of tan, orange, and reddish brown grasses intermingled with many other goldenrod species.

original prairie remains and the few patches—called remnants—today constitute the rarest of all plant communities in North America.

Diboll chooses the word "community" carefully, one that embraces relationships not only among plants but with animals as well. He cites, for example, how the white flowers of New Jersey Tea *(Ceanothus americanus)* act as protein suppliers for hummingbirds. "Hummingbirds can't survive on nectar alone," he explains. "They need protein and get it by swooping down and devouring the teeny flies that are attracted to the New Jersey Tea flowers." He promotes New Jersey Tea and other prairie plants because "they are not out to take over the world." These plants are better behaved than rampant European invaders such as loosestrife and thus require less work in the garden. They are, literally, naturals.

It is only appropriate, Diboll feels, that this naturalness spill over into landscaped areas. In such settings, prairie plants should be allowed to seed and intermingle—creating shifting color and texture scenes—not only through the seasons but from year to year as well. From this viewpoint, a prairie is a chaotic environment, one that is never static. Indeed, those who love and work with our native midwestern plants often eschew the use of the word "garden." A garden is a controlled environment; a prairie landscape is a freewheeling adventure.

And yet, Diboll's love of the beauty and variety of these native flowers and grasses is such that he doesn't limit his practice to large plantings. Among his designs are numerous small gardens in confined spaces. In a long, 3-foot-deep border, for example, he placed a variety of plants with a height limit ranging from 12 to 30 inches. The stars in front are orange butterfly weeds *(Asclepias tuberosa)* and small fountains of deep green prairie dropseed *(Sporobalus heterolepis)*, one of Diboll's favorite grasses. Behind and intermingled with these plants, Diboll placed blue spiderworts *(Tradescantia ohiensis)*, purple prairie clovers *(Petalostemon purpureum)*, blue lupines *(Lupinus perennis)*, lavender pink blazing stars *(Liatris* species*)*, and—for the grand fall finale—showy goldenrods *(Solidago speciosa)* and sky blue asters *(A. azureus)*. The front plantings provide color and structure throughout the season, while the other flowers contribute a shifting pattern of hues, tints, and shapes.

And this is only one of the lovely, easy care gardens Diboll has designed with prairie plants. Though rightly proud of these works, however, he wanted no such creation on his own property. He wanted his very own prairie landscape. He got it, but it was not easy.

When he bought the land in 1988, he looked out his front door and saw a quarter-acre rocky slope choked by junk weeds and woods. The latter were particularly ominous, because prairies thrive in full sun and air circulation—open areas in which there are few if any trees or shrubs. The density of a prairie planting, plus an annual burning or mowing, retards the invasion of woody plant materials. Place a tree or a shrub in such a setting and you have the beginning of structure and perhaps even the start of a full-scale woody infiltration.

"Death to the invaders," Diboll proclaimed. (Prairie devotees are rather selective in their love of nature.) It took him two years, spending a lot of quality time with a chain saw, to carry out his declaration and properly clear his property. Herbicides—the big "no-no" among environmentalists—were selectively used. Diboll says these are seldom required in a restored prairie but are often a measure of last resort in clearing particularly difficult sites, such as his, prior to planting.

In fall 1990, the time had come to transform the "big, ugly brown spot" of cleared land. He collected the sweepings from his seed-sorting operation and threw them on the ground. For all his talk of chaos, however, there was a method in his randomness. Grass seed was concentrated in the back part of the property and flower seed in the area nearest the house.

This strategy lets him have it all. He revels in the summer closeness of the showy purples of coneflowers *(Echinacea purpurea)* and blazing stars and the rich yellows of cup plants *(Silphium perfoliatum)* and black-eyed Susans *(Rudbeckia* species*)*. This is the kind of prairie scene endlessly photographed and promoted and he personally likes to look at it from his front steps rather than in a book.

The prairie season extends well beyond summer. In the fall there is an exquisite subtleness when the grasses combine to form mosaics of red, purple, brown, and orange tints that rustle with undulating streams of soft colors on cloudy days or brilliant glory when backlit by setting suns. Seedheads, ranging from fluffy whites to spiky rust reds, contribute further interest to the scene. This is the kind of distant prairie scene that emerges behind Diboll's summer-long display of gaudy flowers.

In late fall, fogs often roll across the open space and their moisture is captured and frozen on the grasses. The landscape is magically crystalized and the morning picture is that of a sparkling extravaganza with brilliant rainbow gleams of light bouncing everywhere. Before repeated heavy snow buries the view for winter, the tallest of the grasses—particularly the warm golden brown of the big bluestem—bend their seedheads down and create delicate etchings in the white, windswept snowfield.

While Diboll selected the seed for this landscape and directed its placement to some degree, the prairie is now beginning to assume a life of its own. Flower patterns change, grasses intermingle. It is creating itself. Diboll no longer knows what the details of his beautiful landscape will be from year to year and finds this exciting.

There is basically only one chore needed to maintain an established prairie and it is one that Diboll loves. Scratch a prairie fan and more often than not you'll find a person with pyromaniacal tendencies; Diboll certainly has his fair share of such a trait. While admitting that a spring mowing is a perfectly adequate substitute, he rejoices in the fact that there are no laws in his area restricting the use of a spring prairie burn as a maintenance tool.

In his work and on his own property, Diboll seeks to return to the

✳

LATE SEASON PRAIRIE PLANTS

Prairies are known and depicted for their blaze of summer color. Not as widely recognized is that they add structure and interest to late-season garden settings as well. With this in mind, Neil Diboll has assembled the following list of some of his favorite easy care prairie flowers and grasses.

Butterfly Weed *(Asclepias tuberosa)*. Perennial with bright orange flowers in summer and striking seedpods in September.

Heath Aster *(A. ericoides)*. Perennial with sprays of white flowers late summer into fall.

Smooth Aster *(A. laevis)*. Perennial with white through lavender flowers late summer into fall.

Prairie Indigo *(Baptisia leucantha)*. Perennial with creamy white flowers in summer and striking black seed pods fall into winter.

Bottle Gentian *(Gentiana andrewsii)*. Perennial with blue flowers late summer into fall.

Meadow Blazingstar *(Liatris ligulistylus)*. Corm with crimson red buds that open to purple flowers midsummer through Labor Day.

Sweet Black-eyed Susan *(Rudbeckia subtomentosa)*. Perennial with golden yellow flowers in late summer.

Little Bluestem *(Schizachyrium scoparium)*. Grass with stalks in blue to green hues that turn brilliant bronze red to orange in fall.

Showy Goldenrod *(Solidago speciosa)*. Perennial with blazing yellow flower clusters in fall.

Indian grass *(Sorghastrum nutans)*. Tall grass with soft, golden brown seedheads in fall.

Prairie Dropseed *(Sporobalus heterolepis)*. Grass with spraying mounds of emerald green leaves that turn orange gold in fall and a rich rust brown in winter.

---

land some of the environment that was destroyed during our westward expansion. And, to be honest about it, less maintenance for others is also less maintenance for him. "You come home at the end of a day to admire a prairie landscape," he says, "not to work in it."

FOR FURTHER INFORMATION about gardening with prairie plants, contact Prairie Nursery at P.O. Box 306, Westfield, Wisconsin 53964 (608/296-3679). The firm's catalog, filled with extensive information on working with seeds or plants, is available for $3.

SECTION III

The Plants

Page 109: Native plants in this book are not only beautiful and easy care but also commercially available. This grouping of recommended plants—pictured in early May at Fairweather Gardens, a mail-order nursery in New Jersey—illustrates the kinds of materials you can purchase through the mail. The cart contains—clockwise from bottom left—the small, flat white flowers of Red Wing cranberry bush (Viburnum trilobum 'Red Wing'), the white, brush-like flowers of large fothergilla (F. major), a creamy white flowered form of Florida anise (Illicium floridanum 'Semmes'), the profuse white flowered branches of red choke-berry (Aronia arbutifolia), an upright bud of red buckeye (Aesculus pavia), a double white form of flowering dog-wood (Cornus florida 'Pluri-bracteata'), and the bright red flowers of trumpet honeysuckle (Lonicera sempervirens 'Alabama Crimson'). Tucked in the middle of this arrange-ment are the vivid purple red flowers of Oklahoma redbud (Cercis canadensis subsp. tex-ensis 'Oklahoma') and the soft yellow blossoms of Sulphurea

*T*his section presents detailed descriptions of over five hundred easy care native plants. All are either recommended by contrib-utors to this book, grown in my gardens, or mentioned in the text descriptions in the first two sections. What I find truly astonishing is that they represent but a sample of the wonderful easy-to-grow natives suitable for gardens and landscapes.

In order to ensure that all recommendations were truly low main-tenance, contributors were told that they could name no more than twelve plants. This caused great difficulty for many contributors because of the large number of candidates—and led to carefully cho-sen selections for readers of this book. I thought I was home free—as author, I could include every native plant I've grown and liked. Not so. The list of easy care plants became too long. As with the contrib-utors, I had to go over my plants and winnow down my choices. Thus, many readers will be acquainted with some terrific native plants and wonder why they weren't included in this book; there simply was not enough room. What you will find are superb candidates for a wide range of garden styles and designs, from formal to informal, from mixed to solely native plantings. Gardens everywhere will be enriched with the wonderful plants described in the following pages.

Since this book is primarily about plant selection and not about gar-den maintenance, there is little information provided about the latter. Ask your supplier for any specific planting instructions. And for a gen-eral, all-purpose reference book on designing and maintaining a gar-den, consult the book CHARLES CRESSON ON THE AMERICAN FLOWER GARDEN (Macmillan).

I feel quite strongly that it makes no sense to describe plants that are extremely difficult to locate. Some plants that were initially recom-mended could only be obtained through detailed searches among seed exchanges; this was deemed too time-consuming and frustrating; these plants were ultimately dropped. I also feel strongly that it is wrong to deplete wild stands of native flora; thus, plants named in this book are not only commercially propagated but also produced in such economical and sufficient quantities that it is not necessary or profitable to destroy stands in the wild.

And just what does "named" mean? Plant nomenclature has always been a nightmare—botanists keep changing their minds about correct classification. The nursery industry is slow to accept many of the new names because this entails educating customers who generally could care less about the proper botanical name just as long as they have a great plant. In an attempt to make it as easy as possible to track down plants, I have often presented two botanical names, as in *(Gillenia [Porteranthus] trifoliata)*. That conglomeration of words stands for bowman's root, one of the most highly recommended perennials in this book. Years ago, it was classified as *Porteranthus* and some nurseries still sell it under that name; that's why the *Porteranthus* is bracketed—it gives you another name option to track down the plant. Meanwhile, purple praire clover is listed as *Petalostemon purpureum [Dalea purpurea]*. While the second name is the correct one, the change is so new that it has yet to appear in nursery catalogs; there, the first name is cited. Hence, when two botanical names appear, the first is the one that is generally used in the trade.

The summary information accompanying each plant description provides key data as to whether or not a plant will be suitable for your area. Though the information varies somewhat by category, the following are common to all.

Light. In general, when a listing is given of sun to part shade, the plant should be placed in a sunnier rather than a shadier setting. Similarly, part shade to shade means to lean toward the shade side or to situate a plant so that it receives only morning sun.

Height. Growing conditions—both in natural habitats and in garden borders—have a tremendous effect on the ultimate height of a plant. While the information provided here gives you some general idea, it will not always match what you experience in your own garden.

Bloom Period. This often varies by geographical region; where known, this is noted. For example, American beautybush *(Callicarpa americana)* is evergreen in Florida, retaining its colorful berries through winter, but at the northern edge of its range it is a bare, deciduous

honeysuckle (Lonicera sempervirens 'Sulphurea'). The container outside the cart contains Blue Ice cypress (Cupressus glabra 'Blue Ice') and the handsome conifers in the background are Emerald Green (Thuja occidentalis 'Emerald Green').

shrub by late September. Note that in many cases, bloom period is based on a plant's performance in Princeton, New Jersey. If you live in a warmer area, the plant will often flower sooner, and vice versa.

Zones. This information is based on climate zones constructed by the U.S. Department of Agriculture. The range of average annual minimum temperatures (in degrees Fahrenheit) for each zone is as follows:

> Zone 3. -40° to -30°
> Zone 4. -30° to -20°
> Zone 5. -20° to -10°
> Zone 6. -10° to　0°
> Zone 7.　0° to　10°
> Zone 8.　10° to　20°
> Zone 9.　20° to　30°
> Zone 10. 30° to　40°
> Zone 11. Above 40°

Occasionally, a plant will have a mixed zone designation, such as 5/6. That means it should be hardy to the warmer areas of zone 5 (-15°) but not the colder parts.

Native to. This information appears at the end of each plant's text description. As there is no authoritative listing of the native range of all North American plants, the locations provided here are often suggestive only. I relied primarily on four sources: GARDENING WITH NATIVE WILD FLOWERS (Timber Press), HORTUS THIRD (Macmillan), A MANUAL OF CALIFORNIA NATIVE PLANTS (Las Pilitas Nursery), and NATIVE TREES, SHRUBS, AND VINES FOR URBAN AND RURAL AMERICA (Van Nostrand Reinhold). While the range of some plants extends beyond the North American continent, only areas within the continent were named.

Enough of this. Time to read about the wonderful plants on the following pages. Have fun exploring their beauty and charms, and enjoy them in your garden or landscape.

Chapter 6

Trees and Conifers

While botanists probably have the definition of the word "tree" down pat, the rest of the world does not. Generally, it refers to a woody plant that has one main stem and is at least 12 to 15 feet tall. In horticultural circles, however, the Franklin tree *(Franklinia alatamaha)* is grouped in this category even though it is multistemmed and sometimes only reaches 10 feet in height. The red buckeye *(Aesculus pavia)*, on the other hand, is usually called a shrub even though it is often trained to one main stem and has a mature height of 20 to 35 feet. Classification, thus, is often in the hand of the writer and in this and the following chapter, the placement of a plant in the tree or the shrub category was often done through this author's guess as to what popular consensus deems appropriate.

Whether classified as tree or shrub, however, the variety of woody plant species in North America is exceedingly rich and diverse. Two

In the polluted, exhaust-infested air of Manhattan, the delicate white flowers of shadblow (Amelanchier canadensis) *bloom in mid April on the grounds of Rockefeller University. This tree, planted decades ago and surviving with only minimal maintenance, exemplifies the suitability of shadblows for city plantings.*

major groups dominate: the eastern deciduous forest, which occupies about 11 percent of the continent, and the western conifer forest, which covers about 10 percent.

The composition of a forest and its spread are governed first by the length of the growing season and second by the amount of water and its ratio to warm temperatures. For example, few deciduous trees evolved in the northern part of Canada because the growing season is not long enough to allow a tree to produce new leaves for food and energy; evergreen conifers—so named because their fruits are called cones—predominate in this part of the world. Grasslands, on the other hand, begin to take over the natural landscape in the flat, central part of the North American continent because there is not enough rainfall to support either a deciduous or a coniferous forest. And though water supply in Minnesota is not that drastically different from that in Texas, you will find more trees in the former state because cooler temperatures lead to less water evaporation from leaves. Indeed, due solely to temperature differences, a Texas deciduous forest grove requires 50 percent more water than a similar planting in Minnesota.

While the eastern deciduous forest covers a broad contiguous area bordered on one side by the northern Atlantic Ocean and the southeastern coastal plain and on the other side by the prairie lands that sweep through the center of our continent, the western conifer forest is found in two distinct areas. In the Pacific coast section, a narrow coastal strip from Alaska's Cook Inlet to California's Monterey shores, conifers enjoy a 1,000 to 1 advantage over hardwood trees. In the Western Montane, conifers coexist with many other trees and are found in a large area that includes the coastal range from British Columbia to northern California and the Rocky Mountains and their extensions into Mexico and southern California.

All of these factors are important in determining whether or not a native tree will be easy care in your area. Thus, if you live in Texas you need to give serious thought to water requirements before planting a tree. Similarly, your chances of a successful planting will tend to be greater with a conifer than with a deciduous tree if you garden in San Francisco. Still, no matter where you reside, there are lovely, easy care native trees that are suited to your property. You will find them in the following descriptions.

DECIDUOUS TREES

Deciduous trees are often selected for seasonal characteristics. Some are noted primarily for spring flowers, others for brilliantly colored fall foliage. Smaller property owners might well want to select trees with interest in at least two seasons; for example, both lovely spring blossoms and colorful fall foliage. Note that trees in cultivation tend to be shorter than those growing in the wild; this accounts for some of the tremendous height variations in the information presented below.

Maple *(Acer)*

Found throughout the northern hemisphere, maples are reliable shade trees that bear tiny flower clusters in spring and feature brilliantly colored fall foliage.

Vine Maple *(A. circinatum).* This lovely, undeservedly neglected Northwest native is a recommendation of the Leach Botanical Garden in Portland, Oregon. It was cited as a wonderful plant to use in pots on patios and decks, as a single specimen, or in Oriental landscapes. Indeed, it is a close relative of the much overused Japanese maple. In addition to its many horticultural uses, the vine maple also features fabulous fall foliage, picturesque trunks and stems that twist into interesting architectural shapes, and a high shade tolerance. Though its native range is limited, its hardiness range is not. Native to: British Columbia to northern California.

Red Maple *(A. rubrum).* The red maple—sometimes called the swamp maple because of its natural affinity for wet places—has one of the largest ranges of our native trees. As is true of other trees covering broad territories, different varieties have evolved to adapt to local conditions. Thus, southern red maples freeze in the North and northern red maples wilt in southern heat. When not subject to road salt in winter, red maples make excellent street trees. Among the many cultivars that have been developed, two are of special note. The foliage on Red Sunset turns orange to red early in the season. October Glory was bred to provide brilliant red fall color no matter where it is planted and holds its leaves for a long time after all other trees have shed theirs.

Vine Maple

Light: Sun to part shade
Height: 25 to 35 feet
Bloom Period: White and purple flower clusters in spring
Fall Foliage Color: Yellow to vibrant red
Zones: 5–9

Red Maple

Light: Sun to shade
Height: 40 to 100 feet
Bloom Period: Tiny red flower clusters in early spring
Fall Foliage Color: Yellow to red
Zones: 3–10

Sugar Maple

Light: Sun to part shade
Height: 50 to 100 feet
Bloom Period: Insignificant
yellowish flower clusters
in spring
Fall Foliage Color: Brilliant
yellow, orange, and red
Zones: 3–7

Downy Serviceberry

Light: Sun to part shade
Height: 15 to 25 feet
Bloom Period: White flow-
ers in early spring
Fall Foliage Color: Orange
to red
Zones: 4–9

Native to: Newfoundland to Florida Keys, west to Minnesota, Iowa, Oklahoma, and Texas.

Sugar Maple (*A. saccharum*). Look at a New England fall picture and you are bound to see this tree in it. Though it too covers a wide area of the continent, its reddish orange fall color seems particularly brilliant in this area. The New England winter pattern also stimulates the production of sap, from which the famous maple syrup is made. Green Mountain has an extra thick waxy protective coating on its dark green leaves and this enables it to survive in dry, windy areas. Native to: Newfoundland to Minnesota, south to northern Georgia and Missouri.

Shadblow (*Amelanchier*)

Shadblows are treasured for their early spring flowers. Indeed, their popular name reflects their bloom time in New England in the unpolluted days when shad returned to spawning grounds in the region. Another common name, serviceberry, describes the beautiful, edible fruits that appear on the trees in mid to late summer. Unfortunately, birds usually devour them before gardeners can! Brilliant orange to red fall foliage and a sleek, slate gray bark are further attributes of shadblows. When allowed to grow in a clump form, these small trees make handsome sculptural displays in winter.

Of the twenty-five or so species in the wild, only three are commonly found in landscapes: downy serviceberry (*A. arborea*), shadblow (*A. canadensis*), and Allegheny serviceberry (*A. laevis*). Generally, only botanists can distinguish between the first two and both, in the wild, hybridize with the third. This has encouraged plant breeders to do the same and the results form a group usually designated as either *A. grandiflora* or *A. X grandiflora*. Nomenclature, in other words, is a bit messy when it comes to shadblows. In every other respect, however, they are very tidy and handsome trees. Cultivars possess the additional attribute of bearing consistently disease-resistant foliage.

Downy Serviceberry (*A. arborea*). Alone among the often clumpish serviceberries, this one tends to naturally form one trunk. Its gray bark is handsomely flecked with red. Note that its natural range is further south than the other species cited here. Native to: New Brunswick to Ontario and Minnesota, south to Florida, Louisiana, and Oklahoma.

Shadblow (A. canadensis). Recognized by the Royal Horticultural Society with an Award of Merit in 1938, this has been a very popular tree in Europe and, as is not uncommon, a relatively neglected native here. This particular shadblow is noteworthy in that it resists road salt and is thus a good candidate for a street tree as long as it is watered in drought periods. Native to: swamps from Quebec to eastern Minnesota, south to Georgia and Oklahoma. *(Pictured on page 113)*

Apple Serviceberry (A. X grandiflora). This hybrid has a more spreading habit in its branches and tolerates a wide variety of soils and drought. Its flowers are generally larger than the species; in addition, several cultivars—most notably Robin Hill Pink—have been developed with pale pink buds. Cumulus, another cultivar, has a columnar form and is taller than most. Imbued with hybrid vigor, all apple serviceberries are highly resistant to insect attacks and disease. Native to: A hybrid created in 1870; parents some combination of either *A. arborea, A. canadensis,* or *A. laevis.*

Allegheny Serviceberry (A. laevis). Very similar to the shadblow, the distinguishing characteristic of Allegheny serviceberry is its young leaves, which have a red or amber color when they first come out. Where springs are cold, the new leaves and flowers often appear at the same time, creating memorable displays. Native to: Newfoundland to Manitoba, south to Georgia mountains, Ohio, and Missouri.

River Birch *(Betula nigra)*

As indicated by its common name, river birch grows on water banks and does not mind being inundated for a month or two. It is thus a perfect tree for swamp areas in the Southeast. This tree is so adaptable, however, that it thrives in drier situations as well. River birch is further valued for its resistance to the birch borer, which so disfigures other birches. It is most treasured for its beautiful bark; probably no other tree can match it in this respect. The reddish brown to light tan covering exfoliates to reveal pink and salmon layers underneath and is

Shadblow

Light: Sun to part shade
Height: 15 to 30 feet
Bloom Period: White flowers in early spring
Fall Foliage Color: Yellow through orange to maroon red
Zones: 4–8

Apple Serviceberry

Light: Sun to part shade
Height: 25 feet
Bloom Period: White or pink flowers in early spring
Fall Foliage Color: Orange to red
Zones: 4–8

Allegheny Serviceberry

Light: Sun to part shade
Height: 10 to 15 feet
Bloom Period: White flowers in early spring
Fall Foliage Color: Orange to red
Zones: 4–8

River Birch

Light: Sun
Height: 30 to 75 feet; cultivar, 20 feet
Bloom Period: Insignificant yellow green catkins in spring
Fall Foliage Color: Yellow
Zones: 4–9

American Hornbeam

Light: Sun to shade
Height: 20 to 40 feet
Bloom Period: Insignificant reddish brown catkins in spring
Fall Foliage Color: Orange to deep red
Zones: 3–9

Hackberry

Light: Sun to part shade
Height: 50 to 100 feet
Bloom Period: Insignificant yellow green flower clusters in spring
Fall Foliage Color: Pale yellow
Zones: 2–9

Eastern Redbud

Light: Sun to part shade
Height: 25 to 40 feet
Bloom Period: Purple, pink, or white flowers in early spring
Fall Foliage Color: Golden yellow
Zones: 4–9

Western Redbud

Light: Sun to part shade
Height: 15 feet
Bloom Period: Magenta flowers late winter to spring; reddish purple seedpods throughout fall
Fall Foliage Color: Yellow or red
Zones: 6–9

absolutely stunning in winter months; Heritage, a 1990 Gold Medal Award winner, has an outer layer of creamy white bark. Little King, a recent introduction of the Chicago Botanic Garden, represents good news for those with small spaces: it only reaches 20 feet at maturity. As an added bonus, Little King remains resplendent in heavy clay soils as well as in extreme summer heat. Native to: Massachusetts to Florida, west to Wisconsin, Iowa, and Texas. *(Pictured on page 148)*

American Hornbeam *(Carpinus caroliniana)*

With ash gray bark and colorful fall foliage, this handsome tree thrives under any light conditions and adapts either to clay or loam soils. Long-lived, it is perfect as either an understory or a specimen tree. As further evidence of its easy care credentials, it is seldom if ever bothered by insects or diseases. And, as Luke Messinger of the Dawes Arboretum reports, while it does best in slightly moist acid soils, it will tolerate drier sites as well. Native to: eastern North America.

Hackberry *(Celtis occidentalis)*

Hackberry is a tough, low-maintenance tree that does well in the polluted atmosphere of city streets and in the alkaline soil of the Midwest. Plant it only in its native range, however, as it is susceptible to several diseases in warmer areas. Native to: New Hampshire to North Dakota, south to Tennessee and Oklahoma.

Redbud *(Cercis)*

An early spring treasure, redbuds burst forth with thick clusters of flowers just as the first hint of green is beginning to sprout on other trees. These plants are best bought as container-grown stock rather than as transplants from nursery beds.

Eastern Redbud *(C. canadensis).* Eastern redbuds, as indicated below, are found growing wild over a large geographical area. As often happens, the trees have adapted to local conditions and many of the beautiful cultivars in the trade reflect this. The gorgeous double-flowered Flame, for example, was discovered growing wild near Fort Adams, Mississippi in 1905; it is probably only marginally hardy in zone

5. Forest Pansy, with deep purple leaves, was originally found in Tennessee and is not suitable for zone 9. Indeed, speciation is either occurring or just being recognized; the Texas redbud, which is usually sold as *C. canadensis* subsp. *texensis*, is known as *C. reniformis* in botanical circles. It has a bold, glossy foliage that is almost tropical in appearance. A cultivar, Oklahoma, features extremely vivid purple red flowers; alas for northern gardeners, it is only fully hardy through zone 6. Native to: dry uplands to moist bottomlands from New Jersey to Michigan and Nebraska, south to Florida and Texas. *(Oklahoma cultivar pictured on page 109)*

Western Redbud *(C. occidentalis).* This plant makes an excellent case for using regional natives. It thrives in its home area's bone-dry summers and periodic wet winters and does not do well elsewhere. Growing in either lime or acid soils, this elegant small tree needs protection in zones 6 and 7 until reaching maturity. Native to: dry slopes in Utah west to coast ranges and Sierra foothills in California.

Western redbud (Cercis occidentalis), shown here in a July setting in Sacramento, evokes the following praise from Californian Judy Jakobsen: "This is a favorite of mine. It has wonderful pink blossoms in spring, gorgeous heart-shaped leaves in summer, and nice fall color." [Photo: Judy Jakobsen]

Desert Willow *(Chilopsis linearis)*

Though WYMAN'S GARDENING ENCYCLOPEDIA dismisses this plant as an unimportant ornamental, Penny A. Wilson of Las Pilitas Nursery in California springs to its defense and describes it as "a small tree with an elegance that few can match." She likes it not only for its form—which can be pruned to create a weeping willow effect—but also for its slightly fragrant, long-blooming, lilac flowers. Mid Atlantic gardeners take note: this tree does well in your area as well as throughout its native range. Native to: Texas to southern California, south to Mexico.

Fringetree *(Chionanthus virginicus)*

Graham Stuart Thomas, one of England's leading plantspeople, calls this native tree a really good garden plant of exceptional beauty. It earns these accolades because of its ease of care and the spectacular shimmering white haze of its late spring flowers. In addition, unlike many other trees, the root pattern of this tree makes it suitable for

Desert Willow

Light: Sun
Height: 12 to 25 feet
Bloom Period: Lilac flowers throughout summer
Fall Foliage Color: Green
Zones: 6–9

Fringetree

Light: Sun to part shade
Height: 20 to 35 feet
Bloom Period: Feathery white flowers in late spring
Fall Foliage Color: Bright yellow
Zones: 4–9

American Yellowwood

Light: Most beautiful in full sun; will also grow well in part shade
Height: 50 to 75 feet
Bloom Period: Fragrant white flowers in late spring; Rosea has light pink blossoms
Fall Foliage Color: Clear yellow, often with orange tint
Zones: 4–8

American yellowwood (Cladrastris lutea) *was deemed "almost indestructible" when it was honored with a Gold Medal Award in 1994. Its thick clusters of May flowers, pictured here at Longwood Gardens in Pennsylvania, are delightfully fragrant and in fall its foliage turns a beautiful yellow. [Photo: Larry Albee]*

mixed borders. Native to: Pennsylvania to Florida, west to Oklahoma and Texas.

American Yellowwood *(Cladrastis lutea [kentukea])*

A 1994 "almost indestructible" Gold Medal Award winner, yellowwood is a fast grower that provides quick shade, fragrant white flower clusters in May, and golden fall foliage that pairs beautifully with its smooth, light gray bark. As one of the award evaluators commented, "How could any plant this attractive and known to gardeners since colonial days have missed becoming popular?" Native to: Smoky Mountains west to Missouri and Arkansas.

Dogwood *(Cornus)*

These are wonderful, multiseason trees with spring flowers, colorful summer fruits, and brilliant autumn foliage.

Pagoda Dogwood *(C. alternifolia).* The spreading, tiered, horizontal branches of this tree are responsible for its popular name. Supposedly more resistant to anthracnose, the fungal disease destroying so many stands of flowering dogwood, pagoda dogwood has lovely spring blooms and good fall foliage. Jens Jensen used it to edge his prairie landscapes at the turn of the century and Chris Graham of Ontario's Royal Botanic Gardens recommends it for winter landscapes today. Native to: Nova Scotia to Minnesota, south to Georgia and Alabama. *(Pictured on page 15)*

Flowering Dogwood *(C. florida).* Among the most popular and most beautiful trees in the eastern half of the continent, flowering dogwoods are wonderful additions to many landscapes. Unfortunately, they have recently become diseased additions and rumors spread that the plant was doomed almost to extinction from a fungal disease known as anthracnose. In a March–April 1993 article in FINE GARDENING, Rutgers University professor and world renowned dogwood authority Elwin R. Orton, Jr., gainsaid such talk and offered the following measures to ensure healthy trees: cut down and destroy any existing infected dogwoods; plant only disease-free dogwoods in areas with good air circulation; provide them with a wide ring of mulch; keep the soil moist but not soggy; and prune and burn dead branches or twigs. Native to: Massachusetts through Ontario to Michigan, south to Florida and Texas. *(Pictured on page 188)*

Hawthorn *(Crataegus)*

Hawthorns are attractive trees with lovely spring flowers and colorful fall foliage. They thrive in poor soils, whether alkaline or acid. Though often shunned because of their thorns and susceptibility to disease, the following two cultivars do much to alleviate these problems.

Princeton Sentry Hawthorn *(C. phaenopyrum* 'Princeton Sentry'). The species form of this small tree, popularly called Washington hawthorn, has lovely spring flowers, glossy green summer foliage, brilliantly colored fall foliage, and a striking winter display of red berries covering its slate gray bark. It serves as an excellent windbreak and with its sharp thorns is also a good hedge. Princeton Sentry has all but the last of these traits; almost thornless, it is perfect for city streets. Note, however, that it can be affected by fire blight and cedar apple

Pagoda Dogwood

Light: Sun to shade
Height: 20 to 35 feet
Bloom Period: Flat white flowers in late spring
Fall Foliage Color: Maroon purple
Zones: 3–8

Flowering Dogwood

Light: Sun to understory woodland shade
Height: 25 to 35 feet
Bloom Period: White or pink bracts in spring; scarlet red berries late summer into fall
Fall Foliage Color: Scarlet red
Zones: 5–8

Princeton Sentry Hawthorn

Light: Sun
Height: 20 to 35 feet
Bloom Period: White flowers in late spring; spectacular display of red berries all winter
Fall Foliage Color: Orange to scarlet red
Zones: 3–9

✿

SHADE TREES FOR CITIES AND TOWNS

William Flemer III of Princeton Nurseries recommends the following for both their handsome appearance and ease of maintenance in urban and small space settings. Flemer, who has bred and introduced more widely sold trees than any other nurseryman, is the winner of an American Horticultural Society award for extraordinary and dedicated efforts in the field of horticulture and is the author of NATURE'S GUIDE TO SUCCESSFUL GARDENING AND LANDSCAPING (University of South Carolina Press).

Red Maple *(Acer rubrum)*. Highly prized for both bright red early spring flower clusters and colorful yellow or red fall foliage; October Glory always has brilliant red fall foliage.

Green Mountain Maple *(Acer saccharum* 'Green Mountain'*)*. Waxy protective coating on dark green leaves enables this cultivar to survive in dry, windy areas; brilliantly colored fall foliage.

Shadblow *(Amelanchier canadensis)*. White flowers in early spring, handsome slate gray bark, colorful fall foliage, and resistance to road salt.

River Birch *(Betula nigra)*. Reddish brown to light tan bark exfoliates to reveal a salmon pink to reddish brown inner bark; resistant to borer that so disfigures other birches.

Hackberry *(Celtis occidentalis)*. Tough, low-maintenance tree with pale yellow fall foliage.

Princeton Sentry Hawthorn *(Crataegus phaenopyrum* 'Princeton Sentry'*)*. Almost thornless selection with billowing white spring flowers, orange to scarlet fall foliage, and striking winter display of red berries.

Winter King Hawthorn *(Crataegus viridis* 'Winter King'*)*. Disease resistant, almost thornless, white spring flowers, purple fall foliage, and orange red winter fruit.

White Ash *(Fraxinus americana)*. Strong, upright tree with rich purple or bronze fall foliage; Autumn Purple has deep purple fall foliage.

Green Ash *(Fraxinus pennsylvanica)*. Extremely tough and particularly suitable to northern Plains States, where few shade trees thrive; fast-growing Patmore is superb.

Kentucky Coffee Tree *(Gymnocladus dioicus)*. Bold tree, especially handsome in winter landscapes, with blue green foliage.

Carolina Silverbell *(Halesia carolina)*. Beautiful small tree with white bell-shaped flowers in spring and lemon yellow fall foliage.

Cucumbertree Magnolia *(M. acuminata)*. Majestic specimen tree with creamy yellow green flowers in late spring and pink to red berried conelike fruits in early fall.

Pin Oak *(Quercus palustris)*. Easy to transplant; colorful red fall foliage.

An excellent candidate for urban areas, the Gold Medal Award winner Winter King hawthorn (Crataegus viridis 'Winter King') resists both cedar apple rust and air pollution. What impresses most people, however, is that it is profusely covered with colorful fruit throughout dreary winter months. [Photo: Larry Albee]

Winter King Hawthorn

Light: Sun
Height: 30 to 40 feet
Bloom Period: Masses of white flowers in spring; orange red winter fruit
Fall Foliage Color: Purple
Zones: 5–9

Eastern Wahoo

Light: Sun to part shade
Height: 20 to 35 feet
Bloom Period: Small reddish purple flower clusters in early summer; glossy red seeds open from fuchsia pink capsules all fall
Fall Foliage Color: Carmine pink to bright red
Zones: 4–8

rust when these diseases are present. Native to: Pennsylvania to Florida, west to Missouri and Arkansas.

Winter King Hawthorn *(C. viridis* 'Winter King'). Introduced in 1955 and honored with a Gold Medal Award in 1992, this handsome tree resists both cedar apple rust and air pollution, has few thorns, and features a lovely silvery bark that contrasts beautifully with its orange red winter fruit. Native to: Virginia to Florida, west to Illinois, Missouri, and Texas.

Eastern Wahoo *(Euonymus atropurpureus)*

In the 1914 edition of his horticultural encyclopedia, L. H. Bailey recommended this tree as having a splendid fall coloring. Obviously not too many people took note because it is rarely found in cultivation today. It's an easy care recommendation from Buddy Hubbuch at Kentucky's Bernheim Arboretum and is an excellent candidate for an informal woodland planting. Native to: New Jersey to Georgia, west to Minnesota and Texas.

Franklin tree (Franklinia alatamaha), *pictured on July 11 at the Greensboro Arboretum in North Carolina, often blooms into fall. Even without late season flowers, the tree provides a magnificent autumn spectacle with its orange to scarlet red foliage.*

American Beech

Light: Sun to shade
Height: 50 to 100 feet
Bloom Period: Insignificant
   yellow green clusters in
   May
Fall Foliage Color: Yellow
Zones: 3–9

American Beech (*Fagus grandifolia*)

This magnificent specimen tree resists disease and pests but not city conditions. It is a perfect shade tree for a large area in a country setting, where its majestic shape and smooth silvery gray bark will be especially appreciated in winter. Native to: Newfoundland through Ontario to eastern Wisconsin, south to Florida and eastern Texas.

Franklin Tree (*Franklinia alatamaha*)

This beautiful plant dispels the notion that August gardens are tired, worn-out affairs. Named by John Bartram in honor of Benjamin Franklin, the tree is at the height of its long fragrant bloom period in this month. While it thrives in well-drained, moist, acidic soils, it will do well elsewhere if the growing site is regularly watered and the soil amended with peat and humus. Smaller, container-grown plants are easier to establish than larger, ball-and-burlapped trees. Native to: Last seen two hundred years ago at mouth of a Georgia river; no longer known in the wild.

Ash (*Fraxinus*)

Ashes are tall, upright trees that are excellent candidates for city streets and for suburban properties. Their deep taproots ensure that sidewalks stay unbuckled and that perennials and groundcovers can be planted underneath. The seeds, and subsequent seedlings, of these trees can be messy; to avoid this, choose cultivars bred to alleviate the problem. Note that a condition known as ash decline has surfaced in recent years, particularly among highly fertilized trees. If ashes in your area are so affected, do not plant this otherwise excellent tree.

White Ash (*Fraxinus americana*). The tallest of the native ashes, this is available in many forms. Autumn Purple is the most popular cultivar offered; it has a globular shape, no seeds, and deep purple fall foliage. Native to: Nova Scotia to Wisconsin, south to Florida and Texas.

Green Ash *(F. pennsylvanica [var. lanceolata]).* Among the hardiest of the ashes and able to tolerate drought, heat, and alkaline soil, this is an especially valued street tree in the north central states, where few shade trees do well. Patmore is recommended by nurseryman William Flemer III as a superb, fast-growing selection. Native to: stream banks and moist bottomlands from Nova Scotia to Alberta, south to Florida and Texas.

Kentucky Coffee Tree *(Gymnocladus dioica)*

After an admittedly awkward adolescence, this tough, almost inde-structible tree just gets better and more stately with each passing year. It is good looking and easy care from spring through fall and simply magnificent in winter as its bare, contorted limbs spread and become architecturally balanced on the central trunk. With the ability to tol-erate road salt, urban pollution, and drought, Kentucky coffee tree is an excellent candidate for city and suburban streets. And, yes, the hard seeds were once used as a coffee substitute; hence the popular name. Native to: New York to Tennessee, west to southern Minnesota, east-ern Nebraska, and Oklahoma.

Silverbell *(Halesia)*

Silverbells are small trees that look lovely in group arrangements or as specimen plants. While growing naturally in rich, moist, slightly acidic soil, they will also do well in other situations. Silverbells rarely need pruning and are almost never bothered by insects or pests.

Carolina Silverbell *(H. carolina [tetraptera]).* Called the snowdrop tree in England, where it is highly valued, this is yet another case of a beautiful, unappreciated native plant. It is hardier and earlier flowering than the Florida silverbell. Native to: West Virginia to Florida, west to Arkansas and Oklahoma.

Florida Silverbell *(H. diptera var. magniflora).* When it was desig-nated a Gold Medal Award winner in 1995, this magnificent tree was described as having "absolutely everything going for it except fame." It grows up to 3 feet a year; thrives in woodland settings as well as in full sun; has clean, dark green foliage; and is completely disease- and pest-

Franklin Tree

Light: Sun to part shade
Height: 10 to 35 feet
Bloom Period: Fragrant white flowers throughout last half of summer
Fall Foliage Color: Orange to scarlet red
Zones: 4–9

White Ash

Light: Sun to part shade
Height: 50 to 100 feet
Bloom Period: Tiny purple flowers in early spring
Fall Foliage Color: Rich purple or bronze
Zones: 4–9

Green Ash

Light: Sun
Height: 50 to 75 feet
Bloom Period: Tiny deep purple flowers in early spring
Fall Foliage Color: Golden yellow to orange
Zones: 3–9

Kentucky Coffee Tree

Light: Sun
Height: 50 to 100 feet
Bloom Period: Tiny, fra-grant greenish white flowers in late spring
Fall Foliage Color: Warm yellow
Zones: 4–8

Carolina Silverbell

Light: Sun to part shade
Height: 20 to 40 feet

Bloom Period: White, bell-shaped flowers in spring
Fall Foliage Color: Lemon yellow
Zones: 4–8

Florida Silverbell

Light: Sun to part shade
Height: 25 to 50 feet
Bloom Period: Large white flowers in spring
Fall Foliage Color: Yellow
Zones: Might be suitable for zone 5; definitely 6–9

Common Witch Hazel

Light: Sun to shade
Height: 15 to 25 feet
Bloom Period: Yellow ribbonlike flowers immediately after fall foliage drop
Fall Foliage Color: Yellow
Zones: 4–8

Tulip Tree

Light: Sun to part shade
Height: 50 to 100 feet
Bloom Period: Yellowish flowers splotched with orange in late spring
Fall Foliage Color: Lemon yellow
Zones: 4–9

Osage Orange

Light: Sun
Height: 35 to 60 feet
Bloom Period: Insignificant yellow green flowers in late June; large fall fruits resemble green oranges
Fall Foliage Color: Yellow
Zones: 5–8

resistant. Best of all, it produces a gorgeous flower display in mid May, when it is literally drenched in clusters of gleaming white blossoms. Native to: variety found in Florida panhandle; species found in moist loamy soil from South Carolina to Florida, west to Tennessee and Texas. *(Pictured on page 37)*

Common Witch Hazel *(Hamamelis virginiana)*

An easy care recommendation from the Dawes Arboretum in Ohio, this airy, open tree differs from other witch hazels in that it flowers in late fall. The yellow, ribbonlike blossoms are sweetly fragrant. Native to: eastern North America.

Tulip Tree *(Liriodendron tulipifera)*

This stately, beautiful tree can be best appreciated when situated on the edge of a clearing; because it grows so tall with age, its striking flowers are literally lost in the tree tops. Though resistant to insects and diseases, it needs to be placed outside of pedestrian traffic since it is somewhat weak-wooded and often loses limbs in wind and ice storms. Native to: Massachusetts to Michigan, south to Florida and Louisiana.

Osage Orange *(Maclura pomifera)*

City dwellers take note: the fruits of this tree are reputed to repel cockroaches. Just place one or two in each room of an apartment and you can banish the monthly exterminator. What's good for city slickers, however, is not advantageous for small property owners in the suburbs; the large fruits are messy when they fall to the ground. In areas where this would not be a problem—parks or large landscapes, for example—these trees have many fine attributes. They are completely trouble-free, and have interesting twisted thorny branches and a furrowed bark that glows with orange tints in winter sunshine. Native to: Arkansas, Oklahoma, and Texas.

Magnolia *(Magnolia)*

With the magnolia genus being found throughout the northern hemisphere, it is not surprising that individual members have adapted

❋

FAMOUS AND HISTORIC TREES

Famous and Historic Trees is an education project—sponsored by American Forests, the nation's oldest conservation organization—that seeks to encourage the preservation and planting of trees across the country. It does this by propagating seeds from trees associated with significant persons or events in American history and offering them with educational materials to individuals and groups. One of the project's strengths is that species seeds are collected from around the nation. Thus, white oak seeds have been obtained from designated trees in Georgia, Illinois, Ohio, Pennsylvania, and Virginia. All trees bought through the program are guaranteed for one year and staff members will advise purchasers as to which historic trees are best adapted to their areas. Further information may be obtained by calling 800/320-TREE(8733).

About half of the five dozen species offered through the program are native Americans. Of these, Education Director Susan Corbett recommends the following as requiring the least care.

Red Maple *(Acer rubrum)*. Highly prized for both bright red early spring flower clusters and colorful yellow or red fall foliage.

River Birch *(Betula nigra)*. Reddish brown to light tan bark exfoliates to reveal a salmon pink to reddish brown inner bark; resistant to borer that so disfigures other birches.

Franklin Tree *(Franklinia alatamaha)*. Fragrant white flowers through latter half of summer; orange to scarlet red fall foliage.

White Ash *(Fraxinus americana)*. Strong, upright tree with rich purple or bronze fall foliage.

Green Ash *(Fraxinus pennsylvanica)*. Extremely tough and particularly suitable to northern Plains States, where few shade trees thrive.

Kentucky Coffee Tree *(Gymnocladus dioicus)*. Bold tree, especially handsome in winter landscapes, with blue green foliage.

Tulip Tree *(Liriodendron tulipifera)*. Stately and long-lived, with large creamy flowers in late spring and lemon yellow fall foliage.

Osage Orange *(Maclura pomifera)*. Exceptionally tough; inedible, yellow green fruits resemble oranges.

White Oak *(Quercus alba)*. One of the largest native trees and the state tree of Illinois; burgundy fall foliage.

Live Oak *(Quercus virginiana)*. Great stress-tolerant urban tree for south and southwest.

Cucumbertree Magnolia

Light: Sun to part shade
Height: 50 to 90 feet
Bloom Period: Creamy yellow green flowers in late spring; pink to red berried fruits in early fall
Fall Foliage Color: Insignificant yellow green
Zones: 4–9

Southern Magnolia

Light: Sun to part shade
Height: 60 to 80 feet; Little Gem to 20 feet
Bloom Period: Fragrant, creamy white flowers in June and July
Fall Foliage Color: Evergreen in southern range; yellow and deciduous further north
Zones: 7–10; Edith Bogue cultivar to zone 6 and, with protection, warmer areas of zone 5

Bigleaf Magnolia

Light: Sun to part shade
Height: 50 feet
Bloom Period: Fragrant, creamy white flowers in spring
Fall Foliage Color: Pale yellow
Zones: 5–9

unique traits. Asian magnolias, for example, grow naturally in areas without late-season frosts and safely open their large lustrous flowers in early spring before their leaves emerge. Not so here; more often than not a gorgeous Asian magnolia blossom—welcomed as one of the first signs of spring—becomes a soggy brown mess and a reminder that frosts and cold weather are still the norm. American magnolias, on the other hand, do not bloom until after the leaves have emerged. The leaves and the later blooming time ensure that the flowers will not be damaged by frost, and thus that your garden will be filled with delicious summer scents and will remain neat, tidy, and low maintenance.

Cucumbertree Magnolia (*M. acuminata*). This majestic specimen tree is the largest and fastest-growing magnolia. It is rarely, if ever, troubled by pests or diseases and is an excellent candidate for suburban parks and golf courses. While it is pyramidal in shape when young, it assumes a towering, spreading form as it ages. Native to: New York south to Georgia, west to Missouri and Louisiana.

Southern Magnolia (*M. grandiflora*). Nurseryman William Flemer III once called this magnificent tree the glory of southern gardens and the envy of those in the North. With fragrant white flowers that open to a 12-inch spread and glossy, evergreen foliage, this had been an all-season star only for those with large amounts of land and warm temperatures. Recent breeding work, however, has diminished the mature size of the plant—thus making it suitable for smaller gardens—as well as extended its cold hardiness. Little Gem, as its name implies, only reaches 15 to 20 feet in height and blooms throughout summer. Edith Bogue, a 1992 Gold Medal Award winner, is hardy throughout zone 6 and even survives in zone 5 with protection. Blooming in June and July, its creamy 9- to 12-inch blossoms fill the air with a sweet, lemony fragrance. Native to: North Carolina to Florida and Texas.

Bigleaf Magnolia (*M. macrophylla*). If a contest was ever held as to the appropriateness of a popular name, bigleaf magnolia would win hands down. This tree has the largest leaves of any hardy native tree on our continent. It brings a tropical look to any setting, with leaves that can be as long as 3 feet and large creamy flowers that are over 1 foot in breadth. "The only way to describe this tree is magnificent!" wrote Richard Johnson, curator of the Caroline Dormon Nature Preserve, when he submitted his list of easy care native plants. "It provides year-round interest and only needs well-drained soil." Native to: Kentucky to Florida and Louisiana.

Sweetbay Magnolia *(M. virginiana).* Though introduced in England as early as 1688, this tree never acquired a following. To this day, it remains an uncommon plant abroad and plays second fiddle in this continent to many Asian magnolias and several native ones as well. It is, however, finally beginning to gather some fans, including the Greensboro Arboretum and the New York Botanical Garden, both of which not only recommend it but also appreciate its ability to grow in bog as well as ordinary garden conditions, its tolerance of shade, and its sweet fragrance. Perhaps one reason for the relative neglect of this elegant native is its variability. Indeed, it may well be in the process of speciation as southern members are now classified as *M. virginiana* var. *australis.* This variety is more evergreen and more treelike than its northern counterpart and is only hardy to zone 6. When buying a sweetbay magnolia for your property—and many more people should—check where it was propagated to make sure it is suitable for your climate. Native to: coastal areas from Massachusetts to Florida, west to Texas. *(Pictured on page 55)*

Black Tupelo *(Nyssa sylvatica)*

This outstanding tree features exceptionally colorful fall foliage and is an excellent choice for both naturalized landscapes and city streets. It has a handsome, pyramidal shape, resists insects and diseases, and can tolerate air pollution and salt spray. While it does transplant poorly when dug from a field, greater success has been obtained with container grown plants in up to 5 gallon pots. Native to: wetlands and bottomlands from Maine to Michigan, south to Florida and Texas. *(Pictured on page 21)*

American Hop Hornbeam *(Ostrya virginiana)*

This sturdy tree casts dense shade and is an excellent choice for city streets not exposed to salt spray. It is about as maintenance-free as a tree can get, resisting insects, diseases, harsh winds, and ice storms.

Sweetbay Magnolia

Light: Sun to part shade
Height: 15 to 25 feet at northern range; to 60 feet in South
Bloom Period: Lemon scented creamy white flowers in late spring; sporadic bloom throughout summer
Fall Foliage Color: Evergreen in South; bronze purple until dropped in North
Zones: 5–9

Black Tupelo

Light: Sun to part shade
Height: 30 to 75 feet
Bloom Period: Insignificant greenish white flowers in late spring
Fall Foliage Color: Brilliant scarlet red
Zones: 3–9

American Hop Hornbeam

Light: Sun to part shade
Height: 25 to 50 feet
Bloom Period: Insignificant reddish brown catkins in spring
Fall Foliage Color: Yellow
Zones: 3–9

Sourwood

Light: Sun to part shade
Height: 20 to 30 feet
Bloom Period: White pendulous flowers in July; seedpods persist through winter
Fall Foliage Color: Gorgeous scarlet red
Zones: 5–9

White Oak

Light: Sun to part shade
Height: 75 to 100 feet
Bloom Period: Insignificant yellow green catkins in May
Fall Foliage Color: Burgundy
Zones: 4–9

Bur Oak

Light: Sun
Height: 70 to 100 feet
Bloom Period: Insignificant yellow green catkins in May
Fall Foliage Color: Insignificant yellow brown
Zones: 2–8

Pin Oak

Light: Sun
Height: 50 to 90 feet
Bloom Period: Insignificant yellow green catkins in spring
Fall Foliage Color: Red
Zones: 4–8

Native to: Maine to Minnesota, south to Florida, Texas, and northern Mexico.

Sourwood *(Oxydendron arboreum)*

This beautiful tree provides multiseasonal interest. It is one of the few that bloom in summer, when it is decorated with profuse sprays of creamy white, slightly fragrant flowers that dangle. And then in fall it has almost unrivaled scarlet foliage. In winter, the pendulous seedpods from the flowers persist and delicately decorate bare branches. The only fault gardeners might find with this exceptionally easy care tree is that it is very slow growing. Native to: Pennsylvania to Florida panhandle, west to Louisiana.

Oak *(Quercus)*

Mighty is an adjective that is often applied to oaks. They can be found throughout the northern hemisphere and are major components of deciduous forests in well-watered regions. In addition to being a superb lumber source, they are also wonderful shade trees.

White Oak *(Q. alba).* The state tree of Illinois, white oak features cooling blue green summer foliage and a rich burgundy fall color. At maturity—around 30 years or so—it is one of the most majestic woody plants, with a graceful spreading crown of almost 100 feet. Native to: Maine to Minnesota, south to Florida and Texas.

Bur Oak *(Q. macrocarpa).* While it offers neither colorful flowers nor foliage, this magnificent tree resists both diseases and insects and is not noticeably bothered by air pollution or road salt. It is one of the trees recommended by the Iowa Department of Transportation for highway plantings. Native to: Nova Scotia to Manitoba, south through Pennsylvania, Tennessee, and northern Louisiana to Texas.

Pin Oak *(Q. palustris).* This is probably the most popular oak in the nursery trade. It is easy to propagate and transplant and quick to grow as well. While pin oak resists both road salt and urban pollution, it requires rich, moist, acidic soil to perform best. Native to: Massachusetts to North Carolina, west to Iowa, Kansas, and Oklahoma.

Willow Oak *(Q. phellos).* Thomas Jefferson's favorite tree, the willow oak has always ranked high with knowledgeable plantspeople. In contrast to many other oaks, it has a fine, easily raked foliage that turns a nice yellow in fall. Groundcovers or grasses thrive at its base, and its rapid growth rate provides plenty of cooling summer shade. Native to: New York to Missouri, south to Florida and Texas.

Live Oak *(Q. virginiana).* This southern tree is so tough it can take the hurricane winds and salt spray of South Carolina's barrier islands as well as the withering heat of central Texas. Rather than grow tall with age, it tends to spread and its strong, twisted limbs create fascinating sculptures; these are especially striking when festooned with strands of Spanish moss. Live oaks decorated many an antebellum plantation and will perform just as handsomely in today's urban surroundings. Native to: Virginia to Florida, west to Mexico.

Carolina Buckthorn *(Rhamnus caroliniana)*

Recommended by the Bernheim Arboretum, this easy care native is particularly striking in late summer as its sweet, edible fruits ripen and its foliage turns a golden yellow. Native to: New York to Florida and Texas.

Staghorn Sumac *(Rhus typhina)*

This small tree provides year-round interest in a garden setting. Furthermore, it's pest-free, not fussy about soil, and tolerant of heat and drought. Its only possible drawback is that it suckers and forms large colonies when left on its own. While these groupings can be attractive sculptural elements in a large landscape, they can overwhelm a small setting. Fortunately, the suckers can be easily controlled by mowing them or digging them out each spring. Laciniata is a handsome cultivar with heavily dissected, fernlike foliage. Native to: Nova Scotia through Ontario to eastern Minnesota, south to North Carolina and Tennessee.

Thomas Jefferson was far ahead of his time when he had his favorite tree, willow oak (Quercus phellos), planted throughout the streets of Washington, D.C. Pictured here in Princeton, New Jersey, this lovely easy care native is an underutilized street tree today.

Willow Oak

Light: Sun
Height: 40 to 60 feet
Bloom Period: Inconspicuous yellow green catkins in spring
Fall Foliage Color: Yellow
Zones: 5–8

Live Oak

Light: Sun

Height: 50 to 80 feet

Bloom Period: Insignificant yellow green catkins in spring

Fall Foliage Color: Evergreen in deep south; brownish yellow farther north

Zones: 7–10

Carolina Buckthorn

Light: Part shade

Height: 30 to 40 feet

Bloom Period: Small greenish flowers in spring; conspicuous red summer berries turn black in fall

Fall Foliage Color: Golden yellow

Zones: 6–9

Staghorn Sumac

Light: Sun to part shade

Height: 20 to 40 feet

Bloom Period: Yellowish green flower clusters in early summer; bright red berries late summer through winter

Fall Foliage Color: Yellow, orange, bright red

Zones: 3–9

Nannyberry Viburnum

Light: Sun to part shade

Height: 20 to 35 feet

Bloom Period: Flat, fragrant white clusters in spring; red berries ripen to blue black fruits that appear

Viburnum *(Viburnum)*

Viburnums are flowering woody ornamentals that often have colorful fall foliage. With their height and form, they straddle the definition of tree and shrub. The following are classified as trees because of their height and three others appear in the following chapter on shrubs.

Nannyberry Viburnum *(V. lentago).* A tough, beautiful tree with all-season interest, nannyberry viburnum is recommended as an easy care highway planting by the Iowa Department of Transportation. It is also a superb addition to private garden landscapes. Native to: New Brunswick to Alberta, south to Virginia and Iowa.

Rusty Black Haw *(V. rufidulum).* Though this plant is sometimes characterized as the southern version of the hardier black haw *(V. prunifolium)*, it can be successfully grown as far north as Boston. It is a beautiful tree that decorates gardens and landscapes over a long period: creamy white flowers in spring, lustrous dark green foliage in summer, and dark blue fruits and colorful foliage in fall. Native to: Virginia west to Kansas, south to Florida and Texas.

CONIFERS

Because they rarely lose their foliage and generally keep their form and appearance unchanged for years, conifers are often viewed as structures in garden design. They come in many shapes and colors and are particularly appreciated in winter, when the garden or landscape is at its barest. As with deciduous trees, conifers in cultivation tend to be much shorter than species plants in the wild.

Alaska Cedar *(Chamaecyparis nootkatensis)*

Widely acclaimed for its graceful beauty and dense, bluish green foliage, this sturdy tree thrives under many adverse conditions, including heat, high humidity, and urban pollution. Pendula is considered one of the best weeping conifers for a specimen plant. When used as a hedgerow, it makes everything look great in front of it. "Our clone," notes Buchholz & Buchholz Nursery, a wholesale firm in Gaston, Oregon, "was selected from seedlings grown in Holland over one hundred years ago. . . . [It is interesting] that many of the best garden cultivars of native American trees . . . come to us from the great horticultural heritage of Europe." Native to: species found from Alaska to Oregon.

Blue Ice Cypress *(Cupressus glabra [arizonica]* 'Blue Ice')

With its sleek column of icy blue foliage, this is an absolutely stunning plant. It is also an exceptionally hardy one as well, growing in almost any kind of soil, resisting insects and diseases, and able to withstand drought. It does not care for excessive moisture but, if given good drainage, will elegantly survive heavy rain periods and high summer humidity. Blue Ice was introduced in New Zealand in 1960 by Richard Ware and is often sold grafted on different roots. The relative newness of the plant and its grafted rootstock make it difficult to predict the extent of its hardiness range and its eventual height and spread. Native to: species found in central Arizona. *(Pictured on page 109)*

Eastern Red Cedar *(Juniperus virginiana)*

A tough, sturdy North American native that has been bred into many forms, shapes, and colors, the eastern red cedar is one of the first woody ornamentals to reclaim abandoned farmland. In the wild, its columnar shape and beautiful winter-long blue berries are handsome in the landscape. The many cultivars make it an attractive addition to home gardens as well. Two are recommended by the U.S. National Arboretum: Nova is upright and narrow, with bluish green foliage, and Silver Spreader—usually sold as a groundcover rather than as a tree—has low, greenish silver foliage. Give all these cedars lots of sunshine and air circulation to reduce the chance of their becoming host to cedar apple rust. While this disease is not harmful to the cedar, it is lethal to any nearby apple or hawthorn trees. Native to: Maine to South Dakota, south to Florida panhandle and Texas.

Colorado Blue Spruce *(Picea pungens)*

Though native to the Rocky Mountains, this beautiful tree with blue green foliage does very well in urban situations and has been a land-

on bright red stems all fall
Fall Foliage Color: Mottled with yellow, orange, and red and then turning purple
Zones: 2–8

Rusty Black Haw

Light: Sun to part shade
Height: 30 feet
Bloom Period: Creamy white flowers in late spring; dark blue berries late summer into fall
Fall Foliage Color: Scarlet red to purple
Zones: 5–8

Alaska Cedar

Light: Sun to part shade
Height: 20 to 65 feet, depending on cultivar
Foliage Color: Rich bluish green
Zones: 4–8

Blue Ice Cypress

Light: Sun
Height: 20 to 50 feet
Foliage Color: Icy blue gray
Zones: 6–9; when grafted on *C. glabra* rootstock, might be hardy to warmer areas of zone 5

Eastern Red Cedar

Light: Sun
Height: 2 to 90 feet, depending on cultivar

On a bleak, late February morning in Washington, D.C., the majestic Hoopsii Colorado blue spruce (Picea pungens 'Hoopsii') and the cream-flecked sculptural form of Wareana Lutescens arborvitae (Thuja occidentalis 'Wareana Lutescens') create a stunning scene among the plantings of the Gotelli Collection at the U.S. National Arboretum.

Foliage Color: Green with blue, yellow, or maroon tints
Zones: 3–9

Colorado Blue Spruce

Light: Sun to part shade
Height: 10 to 100 feet, depending on cultivar
Foliage Color: Bluish green to silvery gray, depending on cultivar
Zones: 2–8

Ponderosa Pine

Light: Sun
Height: 75 to 100 feet
Foliage Color: Dark green
Zones: 5–9

scape favorite ever since its introduction in 1861. Fat Albert (what a great name) is a very dense form, which is pyramidal and slow growing—less than 10 feet in a decade. Hoopsii, a tall, majestic plant, is widely regarded as having the most attractive blue foliage. R. H. Montgomery, or simply Montgomery, is probably the most commonly grown dwarf and has a beautiful, dense pyramidal form. Native to: Colorado and Rocky Mountains.

Pine *(Pinus)*

Pines are among our planet's most important plants, valued for their economic importance as a lumber source and their horticultural role in adding structure and beauty to garden and landscaped settings. Horticulturists usually group the ninety or more species by the number of needles in each cluster or sheath. Of the three species below, ponderosa and loblolly pines are in the three-needle group and eastern white pine in the five.

Ponderosa Pine *(P. ponderosa).* "This is one of the prettiest dark green trees and well behaved as well," reports Bert Wilson of California's Las Pilitas Nursery. "It made it through one dry, hot spell here that saw temperatures around 120° for five days and a yearly rainfall of four inches. That impressed me! While not smog-tolerant, it has suf-

✳

CHOICE CONIFERS

The Gotelli Collection of Dwarf and Slow-Growing Conifers at the U.S. National Arboretum in Washington, D.C., is one of the finest in the world and consists of approximately 1,500 specimens, representing 30 genera and many colorful shapes and forms. Displayed in attractive settings, all plants have been selected not only for their beauty and ease of maintenance but also for their tolerance to brutal summer humidity and heat. Further information about the arboretum and its collection may be obtained by calling 202/245–2726. In citing the following cultivars, all of which have thrived beautifully for at least five years, Curator Susan Martin notes that they do best in well-drained, slightly acid soil, rarely need to be pruned, are pest- and disease-resistant, and require only a yearly surface application of shredded bark or leaf mold as a fertilizer.

Alaska Cedar *(Chamaecyparis nootkatensis)*
'Pendula'—dense, drooping, bluish green foliage
Eastern Red Cedar *(Juniperus virginiana)*
'Nova'—upright and narrow, with bluish green foliage
'Silver Spreader'—low, greenish silver foliage; often used as a groundcover
Colorado Blue Spruce *(Picea pungens)*
'Fat Albert'—shorter and stouter than species
'Hoopsii'—majestic and with magnificent blue foliage
'R. H. Montgomery'—shortest of all
Eastern White Pine *(Pinus strobus)*
'Nana'—name applied to many dwarf forms with bluish green needles
American Arborvitae *(Thuja occidentalis)*
'Emerald Green'—holds green color throughout winter
'Sunkist'—bright gold splashes on tips of green foliage
'Wareana Lutescens'—dense, dark green column flecked with creamy white
Canadian Hemlock *(Tsuga canadensis)*
'Brandley'—dwarf; globose when young and matures into pyramidal form
'Jeddeloh'—dwarf; low spreader with spiraling branches

Eastern White Pine

Light: Sun
Height: 3 to 80 feet,
 depending on cultivar
Foliage Color: Bright
 green, sometimes with
 blue tints
Zones: 2–8

Loblolly Pine

Light: Sun
Height: 50 to 100 feet
Foliage Color: Dark green
Zones: 6–9

Douglas Fir

Light: Sun to afternoon
 shade
Height: 75 to 100 feet; cultivars from 1 foot up
Foliage Color: Dark green
 with blue tints
Zones: 5–8

American Arborvitae

Light: Sun to part shade
Height: 10 to 80 feet,
 depending on cultivar
Foliage Color: Many shades
 and tints of green, some
 with gold and white var-
 iegation
Zones: 2–7

fered just about every other abuse on our nursery grounds—including being run over with the tractor—and still looks good." Native to: western North America, from Canada to Mexico.

Eastern White Pine (*P. strobus*). WYMAN'S GARDENING ENCYCLOPEDIA calls this an essential landscape plant, citing its low maintenance, great beauty, and ease of transplanting. Obviously many agree with this assessment because the slender, dark green needles on these trees contribute a soft-textured appearance and beautiful backdrop to landscapes throughout eastern North America. The designation 'Nana' is applied to several dwarf forms that feature bluish green needles and slow growth; many of these forms are as wide as they are high. Native to: eastern North America.

Loblolly Pine (*P. taeda*). Darrel Morrison's use of this tree at the Atlanta History Center is quite daring, as it has rarely been planted as a landscape attraction. He chose it as a low-maintenance representative of the second succession stage in open fields transforming into woodlands. It is a statuesque tree with exceptionally long needles. Native to: New Jersey to Florida, west to Texas.

Douglas Fir *(Pseudotsuga menziesii)*

The popular and the botanical name of this major timber tree honor the two men who brought it to the attention of Western civilization: Archibald Menzies discovered it in 1792 and David Douglas introduced it into cultivation when he sent it to England in 1827. "It's very drought-tolerant," notes Bert Wilson of California's Las Pilitas Nursery. "In its natural element, it grows very fast. In other areas, it grows only a few inches a year." With some cultivars attaining a height of only 15 inches over a decade, Wilson believes this fir would be a good bonsai item in small containers. Native to: British Columbia to Texas, Mexico, and California.

American Arborvitae *(Thuja occidentalis)*

Given its native range, it is obvious that this easily grown American native does not like excessive heat or dryness. It does tolerate city conditions, however, and is one of the natives recommended for small space gardens by NEW YORK TIMES garden writer Linda Yang. Among the hundred-plus cultivars available, Sunkist is conical in shape and has bright gold splashes on the edge of its green stems and Wareana Lutescens forms a dense, dark green column flecked with creamy white. Emerald Green was discovered and introduced in Denmark, where it is known as Smaragd. It is perfect for those who dislike the fact that the edges of many American arborvitae turn brown in cold winter months; those on this cultivar hold their rich color all through snow and freezing temperatures. Native to: Nova Scotia to North Carolina and Illinois. *(Emerald Green pictured on page 109; Wareana Lutescens on page 134)*

Canadian Hemlock *(Tsuga canadensis)*

This slightly pendulous, pyramidal tree is a favorite of both Susan Martin, curator of the Gotelli Collection at the U.S. National Arboretum in Washington, D.C., and Luke Messinger of the Dawes Arboretum in Ohio. Both cite this conifer's good-looking dark green foliage and shade tolerance. Brandley is a dwarf form with dark green needles and a rounded, globose shape when young; it becomes more pyramidal with age. Jeddeloh is probably the most commonly grown spreading dwarf as well as the most unusual of all hemlock cultivars: its spiraling branches form a slight depression in the center of the plant and the whole resembles a bird's nest. The name, odd to English speakers, comes from the Jeddeloh Nursery in Oldenburg, Germany. Native to: Nova Scotia to Alabama.

FOR FURTHER INFORMATION on native trees see Gary L. Hightshoe's extremely comprehensive NATIVE TREES, SHRUBS, AND VINES FOR URBAN AND RURAL AMERICA: A PLANTING DESIGN MANUAL FOR ENVIRONMENTAL DESIGNERS (Van Nostrand Reinhold). While Robert A. Obrizok's A GARDEN OF CONIFERS (Capability's Books) is not devoted solely to natives, it does describe over 2,500 cultivars and provides detailed information on the form and hardiness rating for each.

SOURCES. Trees are relatively expensive investments compared to the purchase of other plant material. As such, they are best bought from a local garden center where you can inspect them before pur-

Canadian Hemlock

Light: Sun to part shade
Height: Species from 40 to 90 feet; cultivars often less than 3 feet
Foliage Color: Dark green
Zones: 3–7

chase and ask about their suitability for your site's growing conditions as well as about the extent of guarantees that are offered. If you can't purchase a tree locally, try the mail-order nursery Forestfarm, which offers over 90 percent of the above selections. Its address appears in the Appendix.

Chapter 7

Shrubs

The North American continent is rich in a wide variety of shrubs, which is a nonscientific term used to describe hardy plants with woody stems. They range in size from several inches to many feet; bear flowers in spring, summer, or even fall; and are deciduous or evergreen. The choice is exceptionally rich. Many also travel well, as evidenced by their popularity in Great Britain and other countries overseas. The following plants, many of which are little recognized, are all outstanding and easy care. Use one or more to add structure, color, and perhaps even fragrance to your garden or landscape.

In mid February, colorful branches of American beautyberry (Callicarpa americana) drape over the picket fence in front of the Audubon House in Key West, Florida. At the northern edge of its hardiness range, this shrub loses its leaves and berries by early October.

BUCKEYE (*Aesculus*)

Though buckeyes are the smaller, shrub members of the horsechestnut (*Aesculus*) genus, they are rather massive when compared with

Bottlebrush Buckeye

Light: Sun to shade
Height: 6 to 15 feet
Bloom Period: Brushlike
spikes of white flowers in
summer
Fall Foliage Color: Yellow
Zones: 5–8

Red Buckeye

Light: Sun to part shade
Height: 15 to 30 feet
Bloom Period: Bright red
flowers in spring
Fall Foliage Color: Yellow
green
Zones: 4–9

Western Serviceberry

Light: Sun to part shade
Height: 3 to 15 feet
Bloom Period: White flow-
ers in spring; edible blue
berries in summer
Fall Foliage Color: Orange
to red
Zones: 4–8

Leadplant

Light: Sun
Height: 3 feet
Bloom Period: Purple and
orange flowers in sum-
mer
Fall Foliage Color: Silvery
leaves turn dull yellow
Zones: 3–9

other shrubs. Wonderfully pest-free, the following recommended selections should be grown in large-scale landscapes.

Bottlebrush Buckeye (*A. parviflora*). This slowly but ever-expanding shrub makes a dramatic statement on hot July days when its large (up to 2-feet-tall) flowers poke up from dark green leaves. It is particularly effective in the landscape when used as a screen or as a shrub border on the edge of a clearing. Native to: rich moist woods from South Carolina to Florida and Alabama.

Red Buckeye (*A. pavia*). A Gold Medal Award winner, red buckeye is a marvelous hummingbird plant. "Blooms for us from late February through May," reports Richard Johnson, curator of the Caroline Dormon Nature Preserve in Louisiana. In full sun, its domed spread is almost equal to its height and its shiny green leaves show no evidence of sun scorch. Doing especially well in loamy, well-drained soil, this large shrub shines in open clearings or along woodland edges. Native to: Illinois and Missouri south to Florida and Texas. *(Flower bud pictured on page 109)*

Western Serviceberry *(Amelanchier alnifolia)*

This stoloniferous shrub is best suited for its native growing area. There, it provides multiseason interest with its profusion of white flowers in spring, edible blue berries in summer, and colorful fall foliage. Native to: western Ontario to Yukon, south to Nebraska, Colorado, Idaho, and California.

Leadplant *(Amorpha canescens)*

In early summer, the purple and orange flower spikes on this plant gleam among its silvery gray foliage and make a powerful presence in dry, sunny gardens. Because of its shortness and neat appearance, this shrub is often planted in perennial borders, where it looks particularly smashing when paired with orange butterfly weeds *(Asclepias tuberosa)* and lavender wild petunias *(Ruellia humilis)*. In such a setting, it's easy to see why leadplant has been called one of the most ornamental of the prairie natives. Just give it good drainage and a biennial pruning to keep it from becoming too leggy, and you will have a star attraction in your garden. Native to: prairies and open woodlands from southern Manitoba to Texas, and from Indiana west to Colorado and New Mexico.

Red Chokeberry *(Aronia arbutifolia)*

Especially suited for damp sites (although doing fine in dry ones as well), this shrub contributes a touch of red to garden settings throughout the year. Its bare winter bark is a reddish brown, its leaf buds are red to purplish, the anthers in its white flowers are red, and its fall foliage is red. The best red of all, however, is that of its berries, which are born in dense clusters along each stem. Native to: wetlands and wet woods from New England to Florida, west to Ohio, Arkansas, and Texas. *(Flowers pictured on page 109)*

Groundsel Bush *(Baccharis halimifolia)*

Groundsel bush is an undemanding plant that is especially appreciated by seashore gardeners because of its tolerance for salt air and spray. I like it in my inland garden because its neat and tidy green foliage serves as a nice background screen for a gray and white garden bed. And then I especially appreciate it at the end of summer when its fluffy white seedheads open, adding a new touch of interest at a time of year when most plants are quickly fading. Breeders have been busy working to enhance this last attribute and a new cultivar named White Caps has recently been introduced. Native to: salt marshes, bogs, and swamps from Massachusetts to Florida, west to Arkansas and Texas. *(Pictured on page 182)*

American Beautyberry *(Callicarpa americana)*

Since this shrub flowers on new wood, its branches can freeze to the ground in its northern range and still produce spring flowers and late summer purple berries. At its other climate extreme—Key West, Florida—it is evergreen and its purple berries look handsome against its dark green foliage as late as February. In Georgia, where it is one of the easy care plants recommended by Sue Vrooman of the Atlanta History Center, this shrub is deciduous but retains its berries for a long time. "They are bright, showy, and look wonderful with the yellow flowers so common in late summer," Vrooman says. "Though Amer-

---

Red Chokeberry

Light: Sun to part shade
Height: 6 to 10 feet
Bloom Period: White to reddish pink flowers in spring; bright red berries throughout fall
Fall Foliage Color: Orange to red
Zones: 4–9

Groundsel Bush

Light: Sun
Height: 6 to 12 feet
Bloom Period: Inconspicuous white flowers in summer; fluffy white seedheads late summer into fall
Fall Foliage Color: Purplish, grayish green
Zones: 4–10

American Beautyberry

Light: Sun to shade
Height: 4 to 10 feet
Bloom Period: Tiny blush pink flowers in spring; beautiful purple berries late summer through winter, depending on geographical location
Fall Foliage Color: Evergreen in southernmost areas; shriveled green and deciduous elsewhere
Zones: 6–11

Carolina Allspice

Light: Sun to shade
Height: 4 to 10 feet
Bloom Period: Fragrant,
  brownish maroon flowers
  spring into midsummer
Fall Foliage Color: Yellow
Zones: 4–9

California Allspice

Light: Sun to part shade
Height: 8 to 10 feet
Bloom Period: Fragrant,
  reddish brown flowers
  spring into summer
Fall Foliage Color: Green
Zones: 6/7–9

Bush Anemone

Light: Sun to part shade
Height: 6 to 8 feet
Bloom Period: Fragrant,
  glistening white flowers
  first half of summer
Fall Foliage Color: Ever-
  green
Zones: 7/8–9

ican beautyberry best appreciates good garden soil, it grows for me in soil that is wet and heavy." This remarkably insect-resistant plant (deer, however, do love it) can be grown in acid to slightly alkaline situations. Native to: Maryland to Oklahoma, south to West Indies and Texas. *(Pictured on pages 59 and 139)*

Calycanthus *(Calycanthus)*

The easily grown shrubs in this North American genus are noted for their aromatic flowers. For best results, choose the plant that is closest to you in its natural habitat.

Carolina Allspice *(C. floridus).* "Heavenly fragrance plus beautiful fall color," is how Richard Johnson of Louisiana's Caroline Dormon Nature Preserve describes this shrub. He adds that the plant does spread, a fact that makes it an excellent candidate for a large, informal setting and a poor one for a small, formal garden. Though it can be grown in just about any light condition, it is more compact and dense when placed in full sun. Native to: moist woods from Pennsylvania through the Appalachians to Florida panhandle and Mississippi.

California Allspice *(C. occidentalis).* British and California gardeners agree that the flowers on this West Coast species are larger and showier than those on its East Coast counterpart and that its large leaves are handsome. It offers further bonuses for North American gardens in that it is rarely eaten by deer and does well in either sandy or well-drained clay soils. Native to: mountains of central and northern California.

Bush Anemone *(Carpenteria californica)*

The fragrant, glistening white flowers on this evergreen shrub are valued by British gardeners and neglected by those in its home state. "We like it and don't know why it's not grown more," reports Bert Wilson of Las Pilitas Nursery. Dr. Mike Baad of California State University in Sacramento agrees, for he included this shrub in his list of recommended plants. According to Wilson, "Deer generally do not bother with this plant." Native to: foothills of Fresno County, California.

New Jersey Tea *(Ceanothus americanus)*

This shrub earned its popular name when colonists used its leaves as a tea substitute during the American Revolution. It is a completely undemanding shrub, one that has anchored my native plant garden for eight years now. Five feet wide and three feet tall, it is covered with white flowers the last three weeks in June. Most horticulturists tout the beautiful, blue-flowered California members of the genus in its place; unfortunately for many gardeners, these are not winter hardy beyond zone 8. Native to: Maine to Minnesota, south to Florida and Texas. *(Pictured on page 52)*

Cercocarpus *(Cercocarpus)*

Native to: the western half of North America, members of this genus are excellent easy care landscape plants.

Mountain Mahogany *(C. betuloides).* This evergreen shrub has a graceful shape and open structure. It is especially valued for its fall display of silvery seed and fruit and is an easy care recommendation of Dr. Mike Baad at California State University in Sacramento. Bert Wilson of Las Pilitas Nursery in Santa Margarita likes to use the *blancheae* variety—popularly known as alderleaf mountain mahogany—in his city landscapes because it creates an attractive screen in narrow planting areas. Native to: southern Oregon to Arizona and Baja California.

Curl-leaf Mountain Mahogany *(C. ledifolius).* This trouble-free shrub is frequently planted as a bushy screen or wind break. Its white bark and dark green leaves form a neat and tidy decoration in either gardens or landscapes. In addition to its ability to grow in a wide temperature range, it is also drought-tolerant. Native to: Montana to Arizona, west to Washington and California.

Clethra *(Clethra)*

Wonderful low-maintenance, medium-sized shrubs, clethras can be grown in many soil and light conditions and are handsome, summer-blooming components of either mixed or shrub borders.

New Jersey Tea

Light: Sun to part shade
Height: 36 to 40 inches
Bloom Period: White flowers late spring to early summer
Fall Foliage Color: Greenish yellow
Zones: 3–8

Mountain Mahogany

Light: Sun
Height: 8 to 15 feet
Bloom Period: Inconspicuous spring flowers; sprays of silvery seed and fruit in fall
Fall Foliage Color: Evergreen
Zones: 6–9

Curl-leaf Mountain Mahogany

Light: Sun to part shade
Height: 10 to 20 feet
Bloom Period: Insignificant
Fall Foliage Color: Evergreen
Zones: 4–9

✳
SHRUBS FOR WINTER INTEREST

When winter season comes early, as it often does in Hamilton, Ontario, shrubs with colorful berries, striking bark, or dried flowers extend the design aspects of the garden year. Chris Graham, manager of horticultural services at the Royal Botanical Gardens, recommends the following as being particularly attractive and easy care candidates for winter settings.

Cinnamon Clethra *(C. acuminata)*. Exfoliating, rich cinnamon brown stems.

Red Osier Dogwood *(Cornus sericea)*. Colorful red bark.

Yellowtwig Dogwood *(Cornus sericea* 'Flaviramea'*)*. Striking yellow bark. Graham says the winter combination of this cultivar and the species plant is one of the most effective to be had.

Wild Hydrangea *(H. arborescens)*. Large ball-shaped dried flower heads are lovely not only outdoors but also in arrangements indoors.

Oakleaf Hydrangea *(H. quercifolia)*. A double winter bonus: outstanding, exfoliating bark and cones of dried flower heads.

Possumhaw *(Ilex decidua)*. Orange to scarlet red berries lasting through winter.

Winterberry *(Ilex verticillata)*. Scarlet red fall berries persisting through January.

Yellow Winterberry *(Ilex verticillata* 'Winter Gold'*)*. Deep yellow berries lasting through the Christmas season. Graham suggests pairing this cultivar with either the species plant or the possumhaw for a colorful winter display.

Bayberry *(Myrica pensylvanica)*. Green foliage often lasts into winter and is beautiful when covered with a light dusting of snow; grayish white berries all winter.

Cinnamon Clethra

Light: Part shade to shade
Height: 12 to 20 feet
Bloom Period: White flowers late July through mid August
Fall Foliage Color: Yellow to orange
Zones: 5–8

Cinnamon Clethra *(C. acuminata)*. Much less well-known than the sweet pepperbush, the cinnamon clethra is valued by knowledgeable horticulturists for its exfoliating, rich cinnamon brown stems, which add color and interest to snow-covered winter settings. This shrub also contributes flowers to summer borders and though they are neither fragrant nor as large as those on the sweet pepperbush they are nevertheless profuse and an attraction in their own right. Native to: southwestern Pennsylvania to Tennessee and northwestern Georgia. *(Pictured on page 82)*

Sweet Pepperbush (*C. alnifolia*). This plant looks beautiful no matter how or where it is grown—from an informal shrub in seashore plantings to a clipped hedge in structured city gardens. In fall, its foliage turns a lovely yellow orange. And yet these are not the plant's major attributes. As Richard Johnson of the Caroline Dormon Nature Preserve in Louisiana writes, "The big bonus is that it flowers in the heat of summer here." It actually does so throughout its hardiness range and the lovely white or pink flower spikes are delightfully fragrant. Maintenance requirements depend on the moisture content of your soil: if it is dry, you should probably water twice a week; if it is boggy, you might want to pull out plants that spread rapidly through underground stems in moist situations. Native to: moist areas throughout the East Coast from Maine to Florida, west across the panhandle to eastern Texas. *(Pictured on page 82)*

Cumberland Rosemary *(Conradina verticillata)*

Now federally listed as an endangered species, this is one of the rarest shrubs on the North American continent. It was discovered in 1930 by University of Tennessee Professor H. M. Jennison, who found it growing along the river banks and sandbars of the Cumberland plateau. Fortunately, cuttings that were taken prior to its being designated endangered are now yielding a large supply of commercially offered plants. Its thin, needlelike leaves do indeed resemble those of the herb from which it gets its popular name; their aroma or taste is said to repel rabbits. The plant attracts gardeners, however, because of its lovely profuse flowers and delicate, tidy appearance. Note, however, that it is reputed to be a short-lived species outside its native area. Native to: Cumberland plateau of Kentucky and Tennessee.

Red Osier Dogwood *(Cornus sericea [stolonifera])*

In a way, it's odd. Here is a shrub that is simply stunning when all decked out: creamy white flowers over a long period and wonderfully colorful fall foliage (the Gold Medal Award winner Silver and Gold even has variegated foliage throughout the summer). And yet it is chiefly honored for its winter nakedness, when its bright red stems are handsome in leafless settings and look even more dramatic and color-

---

Sweet Pepperbush

Light: Sun to shade
Height: 6 to 10 feet; Hummingbird cultivar to 3 feet
Bloom Period: Fragrant white or pink flowers through much of summer
Fall Foliage Color: Yellow orange to gold
Zones: 3–9

Cumberland Rosemary

Light: Sun to part shade
Height: 10 to 15 inches
Bloom Period: Lavender pink to blush white flowers spring into summer (the further north, the later the bloom period)
Fall Foliage Color: Some leaves turn yellow and drop; others (generally at base of plant) remain evergreen with a purplish hue
Zones: 5–8

Red Osier Dogwood

Light: Sun
Height: 6 to 10 feet
Bloom Period: Creamy white flowers in late spring with some sporadic summer rebloom; white berries in September
Fall Foliage Color: Orange to red
Zones: 2–9

Apache Plume

Light: Sun

Height: 3 to 6 feet

Bloom Period: White rose-like flowers in May; feathery plumes of purple fruits late summer into fall

Fall Foliage Color: Evergreen but becomes deciduous under drought conditions

Zones: 6–9

Dwarf Fothergilla

Light: Sun to part shade

Height: 3 to 5 feet

Bloom Period: White flowers in spring

Fall Foliage Color: Brilliant yellow to orange red

Zones: 5–8

Large Fothergilla

Light: Sun to shade

Height: 6 to 12 feet

Bloom Period: Honey-scented white flowers in May

Fall Foliage Color: Combinations of yellow, orange, and scarlet red

Zones: 4–8

ful when paired with the yellow stems of the Flaviramea cultivar. Because of its ease of care and colorful appearance throughout the year, this shrub is becoming increasingly popular in commercial landscapes. Private gardeners might want to explore its beauty as well. Native to: across Canada south to Virginia, the Great Lakes region, Nebraska, scattered locations in Arizona and New Mexico, and northern California.

Apache Plume *(Fallugia paradoxa)*

This is a stunning plant, one that provides interest throughout the garden year with beautiful spring flowers and striking fall fruit. Bert Wilson of California's Las Pilitas Nursery suggests using Apache plume as a lacy screen and pairing it with the violet blue flowers on pozo blue sage *(Salvia clevelandii* X *S. leucophylla)*. Native to: desert areas from Utah to Texas, Mexico, and California.

Fothergilla *(Fothergilla)*

Classic multiseason shrubs, fothergillas are tidy, exceptionally low-maintenance plants with fragrant white spring flowers and spectacularly colored fall foliage. In both plants below, the sunnier the setting, the more the flowers and the more colorful the leaves. Gardeners who find it difficult to select just one should consider the possibility of having both these shrubs in their gardens.

Dwarf Fothergilla (*F. gardenii*). This is a perfect shrub for small gardens, particularly—though not exclusively—those that are naturally moist. Blue Mist, a Gold Medal Award winner, has been described as providing "one of the most delightful displays of any flowering shrub." It is valued above the species plant for its blue-toned leaves, which look especially cool in hot summer gardens. Native to: coastal plains and swamps in eastern North and South Carolina and scattered locations from Tennessee to Florida panhandle.

Large Fothergilla (*F. major [monticola]*). As befits its greater stature, large fothergilla has showier flowers than its dwarf counterpart. It is also hardier and more drought-tolerant. Native to: dry Appalachian woods from southern Virginia to northern Alabama. *(Pictured on page 109)*

Ocean Spray *(Holodiscus discolor)*

This beautiful shrub is an easy care selection of Robert T. Ogilvie of the Royal British Columbia Museum. As with many of our natives, it is deemed an outstanding plant in Great Britain and is little known outside the Northwest on our continent. In his GARDENING ENCYCLOPEDIA, Donald Wyman does comment that it is difficult to transplant and other gardeners in hot, humid areas have reported a black fungus on the foliage. Even with these negatives, I think more gardeners should give it a try—what other shrub gives you arching sprays of creamy white flowers in summer and beautiful orange fall foliage? I know I plan to place mine in a partial shaded location with good air circulation. And here's some good news for those plagued with deer: the creatures do not like this shrub. Native to: Montana to British Columbia, south to California.

Hydrangea *(Hydrangea)*

For far too long, native hydrangeas have taken a garden back seat to the ubiquitous blue hydrangeas from Asia. The following are superb, good-looking, trouble-free plants that you will most certainly want to incorporate in your landscape once you have read their descriptions.

Wild Hydrangea *(H. arborescens).* As easily grown on sunny seashores as in rocky gorges, this undemanding shrub is covered with white flowers during the height of summer heat. The Grandiflora cultivar, discovered growing over a century ago in a gorge near Yellow Springs, Ohio, has larger flowers than the species and, even more important to neat and tidy gardeners, is sterile—thus ensuring the absence of unwanted seedlings. Annabelle, a more recently introduced cultivar, was first found in Anna, Illinois, hence its popular name. This last has both its advocates and detractors, with the former praising its compact 4-foot height and foot-wide blossoms and the latter decrying the messy appearance of the shrub after a rain has knocked the top-heavy flowers to the ground. Native to: southern New York to Missouri, south to Florida panhandle and Mississippi. *(Pictured on page 148)*

Oakleaf Hydrangea *(H. quercifolia).* This is such an outstanding shrub: exfoliating bark; large, long-lasting cones of flowers; and color-

Ocean Spray

Light: Sun (in cool areas) to partial shade (in hot ones)
Height: 6 to 12 feet
Bloom Period: Large, pyramidal creamy white flowers in summer
Fall Foliage Color: Orange
Zones: 5–9

Wild Hydrangea

Light: Sun to shade
Height: 3 to 6 feet
Bloom Period: Creamy white flowers in summer; large, ball-shaped dried flower heads fall into winter
Fall Foliage Color: Brownish yellow
Zones: 4–9

Oakleaf Hydrangea

Light: Sun to shade
Height: 6 to 10 feet
Bloom Period: Cones of creamy white flowers in early summer fade to soft pink by August
Fall Foliage Color: Orange red to luscious wine red
Zones: 5–9

ful fall foliage. All it needs is average soil that it neither too wet nor bone dry. Deer tend to avoid it
until there is absolutely nothing else left to eat. I am
so biased in favor of the Snow Queen cultivar that it
is hard for me to moderate my enthusiasm for it. A
Gold Medal Award winner that was selected by
William Flemer III of Princeton Nurseries, it is
drenched in cones of goregous white flowers in June
and July. These age to a lovely pink and are usually
unaffected by heavy summer thunderstorms. By late
September, the now dried and light tan flowers hang
above foliage that has begun to turn orange red in
sunny locations and deep wine red in darker ones.
Because my Snow Queen is in a protected site, the
foliage lasts through much of winter; just a few
blocks away a Snow Queen planted in an open,
sunny spot loses its foliage by Christmas and displays
sculptured stems with exfoliating bark until new
foliage emerges in spring. Native to: southeastern
forests from Tennessee to Florida panhandle, west to
Louisiana.

Wild hydrangea (H. arborescens *'Grandiflora'*) *is so adaptable that it can be grown in
mountain shade or shoreline
sun, as shown here in an early
August Connecticut garden. Its
gleaming white summer flowers
dry to light tan and are handsome in winter arrangements.
The beautiful exfoliating bark
of a river birch* (Betula nigra)
frames this scene.

Holly *(Ilex)*

Hollies are wonderful staples of low-maintenance gardens. There's at
least one for your particular growing conditions in the following recommended selections. Note, however, that all species in this genus
consist of male and female plants. If you want good berry set on your
plants, you need to have one male within a several-hundred-yard
vicinity of up to twenty female plants.

Possumhaw *(I. decidua).* Among the largest of the cultivated species
in the *Ilex* genus, possumhaws are especially good choices for landscapes in the plains states because their attractive green foliage is not
damaged by strong winds. Down South, their ability to survive better
in drier situations than other hollies gives them a high rating from
Texas gardeners. Up North, they are recommended by the Royal
Botanical Gardens in Ontario for their orange to scarlet berries that

last through winter. Warren's Red, a favorite of the Greensboro Arboretum in North Carolina, has consistently red berries. Native to: Virginia to Illinois, south to Florida and Texas.

Inkberry *(I. glabra).* A great shrub for containers and city conditions and an excellent alternative to boxwood borders in suburban settings, this easy care plant tolerates heat, drought, sun, shade, wind, and transplanting without missing a beat. Compacta has a height of 5 to 7 feet and a width of 7 to 9 feet; its open, rounded appearance can be appreciated at the Greensboro Arboretum in North Carolina. Densa, a Gold Medal Award winner, is a thick shrub with consistently dark green foliage and a 4-foot height almost equal to its spread. Native to: Nova Scotia to Florida, west to Missouri.

Winterberry *(I. verticillata).* The popular name tells it all: this undemanding shrub is chiefly grown for its profuse, beautiful berries, which add color and drama to bare winter landscapes. If you like, prune young plants to five to seven strong stems to give the shrub a more graceful structure in its maturity. Scarlett O'Hara is tolerant of clay soils, Winter Gold has yellow berries, and Winter Red is laden with red fruit for a longer period than the species. Native to: moist areas from Maine to eastern Minnesota, south to Florida panhandle and Louisiana.

Possumhaw

Light: Sun to part shade
Height: 12 to 25 feet
Bloom Period: Inconspicuous clusters of cream white flowers in late spring; orange to scarlet red berries fall through winter.
Fall Foliage Color: Gold
Zones: 5–9

Inkberry

Light: Sun to shade
Height: 4 to 12 feet
Bloom Period: Inconspicuous white flowers in spring; jet black berries most of winter
Fall Foliage Color: Evergreen
Zones: 4–10

Winterberry

Light: Sun to part shade
Height: 8 to 10 feet
Bloom Period: Inconspicuous white flowers in late spring; scarlet red berries persisting through January

In late October, winterberry (Ilex verticillata) adds dramatic color to the pond area at Garden in the Woods in Massachusetts. Though found in moist situations such as that pictured here, winterberry thrives in a wide variety of garden settings throughout the continent.

Fall Foliage Color: Dull yellow
Zones: 3–8

Yaupon Holly

Light: Sun to shade
Height: 15 to 25 feet
Bloom Period: Insignificant white flowers in spring; beautiful red berries in fall
Fall Foliage Color: Evergreen
Zones: 7–10; 6 in sheltered locations

Florida Anise

Light: Sun to part shade
Height: 6 to 20 feet
Bloom Period: Red flowers in spring; cultivar with creamy white flowers
Fall Foliage Color: Evergreen in South
Zones: 6–9

Virginia Sweetspire

Light: Sun to shade
Height: 4 to 8 feet
Bloom Period: Fragrant, drooping clusters of white flowers in late spring in southern areas to early summer farther north
Fall Foliage Color: Crimson scarlet in full sun to deep purple red in full shade
Zones: 6–10; worth trying in protected locations in zone 5

Yaupon Holly *(I. vomitoria).* This plant's botanical name reflects the reaction most people get from drinking a brew made from its leaves. In every other aspect, however, it is most pleasing: drought and bog tolerant, happy in sun or shade, unaffected by salt spray in coastal areas or by humid heat in its native southeast, able to grow in moderately alkaline soils, handsome gray branches and trunks, evergreen foliage, and bright red berries. In formal settings, it makes a handsome clipped hedge. Native to: Virginia to Florida and Texas.

Florida Anise *(Illicium floridanum)*

This rhododendron look-alike bears exotic red flowers in spring and then dangles pale green star-shaped seedpods in summer. "It is a wonderful evergreen shrub for moist shady areas," writes Richard Johnson, curator of Louisiana's Caroline Dormon Nature Preserve, "and can also take drought when established." The plant is not always evergreen, however; it becomes deciduous in the northern sections of its hardiness range. The genus name is derived from the Latin word for allure and refers to the spicy fragrance of the crushed leaves and stems; perhaps this is why pests, including deer, leave them alone. Breeders, attracted to the plant's good looks and ease of care, are beginning to introduce cultivars: Halley's Comet is more floriferous than the species and Semmes is a creamy white flowered selection of Alabama plantsman Tom Dodd. Native to: Florida to Louisiana. *(Pictured on page 109)*

Virginia Sweetspire *(Itea virginica)*

Though inhabiting partially shaded, wet places in nature, this plant seems equally happy in garden soils that are sunny and dry. Henry's Garnet, one of the first six plants to receive a Gold Medal Award, has been described as "one of the finest shrubs to come along in a long time." In my garden its white, fragrant flowers appear in June and early July; farther south, these bloom as early as late April. In all areas in which it is cultivated, its foliage turns a brilliant red to purple crimson in the fall and clings to the stems well into winter. Native to: low, wet woods and swamps from the New Jersey Pine Barrens south to Florida, west to Missouri and Texas.

Mountain Laurel *(Kalmia latifolia)*

"This is by far our most beloved shrub," writes Richard Johnson, curator of the Caroline Dormon Nature Preserve. "Once established, it is maintenance-free but we try to only grow the ones native to Louisiana or from the same climate zone." This beautiful evergreen shrub with foliage that is poisonous to deer and other animals is also treasured farther north, where it is the state flower of both Pennsylvania and Connecticut. Breeders have been busy developing plants that thrive well beyond the native range; Ostbo Red does well on the West Coast. The British love this plant, though they do struggle with it because it must have well-drained, acidic, organic soil in order to thrive. Native to: moist woods in mountainous areas from Maine to Louisiana.

Box Sandmyrtle *(Leiophyllum buxifolium)*

The evolutionary history of this compact evergreen shrub would make a fascinating story: there are two distinct forms, each native to a different area on the North American continent. If you give either good drainage while ensuring that it never dries out you will have one of the most trouble-free plants on your property, a shrub that is covered for almost two months with either attractive buds or lovely flowers. Buy container-grown plants to ensure a successful transplanting. Native to: species, New Jersey; var. *prostratum*; sandy soils in mountains of North Carolina, Tennessee, and Georgia.

Drooping Leucothoe *(L. fontanesiana [catesbaei])*

This close *Andromeda* relative (it was once classified in the genus) has a graceful, spraying appearance and is very easy to transplant. It thrives best in cool shade settings and, with its handsome glossy foliage, is an excellent companion shrub to rhododendron and mountain laurel *(Kalmia)* plantings. Should any or all of its branches get messy looking, just cut them to the ground and fresh new ones will take their place. The Rainbow cultivar, recommended by the Greensboro Arboretum in North Carolina, has beautiful new leaves with cream, yellow, and pink markings. Native to: Virginia to Georgia and Tennessee.

Mountain Laurel

Light: Sun (in cool areas) to shade (in warm ones)
Height: 8 to 20 feet
Bloom Period: Large, rounded clusters of white to pink flowers in late spring
Fall Foliage Color: Evergreen
Zones: 4–9

Box Sandmyrtle

Light: Sun to part shade
Height: Species, 2 to 3 feet; var. *prostratum* to 1 foot
Bloom Period: Pink buds open to white flowers through much of spring
Fall Foliage Color: Evergreen; reddish tint in winter
Zones: 5–8

Drooping Leucothoe

Light: Part shade to shade
Height: 3 to 6 feet
Bloom Period: Fragrant clusters of white bell-shaped flowers late spring or early summer
Fall Foliage Color: Evergreen, with purple hues throughout winter
Zones: 4–8

Spicebush

Light: Sun to part shade
Height: 6 to 12 feet
Bloom Period: Fragrant yellow flowers in spring; scarlet red berries in September
Fall Foliage Color: Lemon yellow
Zones: 4–8

Oregon Grape

Light: Sun to shade
Height: 3 to 8 feet
Bloom Period: Fragrant yellow flowers late winter to spring (depending on location); clumps of edible, powder blue berries in summer
Fall Foliage Color: Rich maroon which persists through winter
Zones: 4–8

Longleaf Oregon Grape

Light: Sun to part shade
Height: 18 to 30 inches
Bloom Period: Bright yellow flowers in spring; edible dark blue berries in late summer
Fall Foliage Color: Evergreen, often with reddish tinge in winter
Zones: 5–8

Spicebush *(Lindera benzoin)*

This easy care recommendation from the Dawes Arboretum in Ohio is spicy in every way: its flowers add aroma and color to early spring woods, its lush green leaves have been used in herbal teas, and its dried berries were once crushed and used as allspice. All this plus good looks, especially at the end of summer when its red berries glow among its beautiful lemon yellow foliage. Native to: Maine through Ontario and Michigan south to Florida and Texas.

Mahonia *(Mahonia [Berberis])*

The name *Mahonia* honors Bernard McMahon, an Irish horticulturist who emigrated to Philadelphia in 1796 and became one of the first and leading promoters of American plants. It is said that the Lewis and Clark expedition, one of whose primary goals was the collection of native flora, was planned at his kitchen table. The plants that are now grouped in this genus reflect in many ways McMahon's qualities: tough, easily transplantable, and able to endure many growing conditions. They are also exceptionally good looking, exhibit all-season interest, and do not appeal to deer.

Oregon Grape *(M. aquifolium).* Widely grown in western gardens and quite suitable for eastern gardens as well, this evergreen shrub has lacquered, hollylike leaves, fragrant yellow flowers in spring, and clusters of plump, blue berries in summer. The last are edible and make a tart jam. Oregon's Leach Botanical Garden thinks highly of its early bloom and drought tolerance and recommends using this shrub as either a specimen plant or a hedge. Native to: British Columbia to northern California.

Longleaf Oregon Grape *(M. nervosa).* While British garden experts often cite this smaller version of the Oregon grape as being both handsome and striking, few North Americans are aware of its charms. Now that Robert T. Ogilvie of the Royal Columbia British Museum has brought it to the attention of readers of this book, its bright yellow flowers and long lustrous evergreen leaves might be seen in more gardens in its native continent. Native to: British Columbia south to Idaho and California.

Agarito *(M. trifoliolata).* Agarito is a Southwest shrub and recommended for gardeners in its native area by Denise Delaney, horticulturist at the National Wildflower Research Center. Delaney likes it for its bluish green foliage, which looks handsome throughout the year, the spicy fragrance of its lovely yellow flowers, and its bright, cheery red berries. Other gardeners like the prickly leaves on the plant, which form the basis for an attractive and effective security hedge. Native to: well-drained soils from Texas to Arizona, south to Mexico.

Myrica *(Myrica)*

Members of this genus are sometimes cited for their subtle beauty; this loosely translates as plants that are neat and provide a reliable green backdrop during the growing season. The chorus of praise increases when winter rolls around, however: the wax myrtle provides a good-looking evergreen appearance and the bare twigs of the bayberry are covered with grayish white berries that resemble fat buds. In addition, both plants described below can be grown in sandy soils, tolerate salt spray, and have foliage that is aromatic when crushed.

Wax Myrtle *(M. cerifera).* A shrub for southern gardens, this exceptionally carefree plant is tall enough to be classified as a tree by some and has a willowy appearance. It is often used as an attractive hedge or evergreen screening. Native to: New Jersey to Florida and Texas.

Bayberry *(M. pensylvanica).* The glossy green leaves of this attractive northern shrub not only decorate summer seashore gardens but swamp ones as well. It is also a plant for cold winter settings: early in the season its long-lasting green foliage looks particularly handsome when dusted with a light snow and later on a different effect is created when its thick, gray, waxy berries appear to float through the shrub's dark, bare twigs. These berries, by the way, are harvested to provide scent for candles. Native to: coastal sandflats and tidal marshlands from Maine to North Carolina and abutting Lake Erie.

Wild Mock Orange *(Philadelphus lewisii)*

This arching, elegant shrub is the state flower of Idaho, yet little known outside its natural range. It bears large, fragrant white flowers

Agarito

Light: Sun
Height: 3 to 7 feet
Bloom Period: Fragrant golden yellow flowers in early spring; bright red edible fruits late spring into summer
Fall Foliage Color: Evergreen
Zones: 8–10

Wax Myrtle

Light: Sun to partial shade
Height: 10 to 35 feet
Bloom Period: Insignificant grayish white flowers in spring; waxy pale gray berries in fall
Fall Foliage Color: Evergreen
Zones: 6–9

Bayberry

Light: Sun to part shade
Height: 9 feet
Bloom Period: Inconspicuous white early spring flowers become aromatic, grayish white berries persisting through winter
Fall Foliage Color: Dark green
Zones: 2–7

Wild Mock Orange

Light: Sun to part shade
Height: 6 feet
Bloom Period: Fragrant white flowers in early summer
Fall Foliage Color: Yellow
Zones: 5–8

Mountain Andromeda

Light: Part shade to shade
Height: 3 to 6 feet
Bloom Period: Erect, fragrant clusters of white flowers in early spring
Fall Foliage Color: Evergreen, with purple hue in winter
Zones: 4–8

Cherokee Plum

Light: Sun to part shade
Height: 10 to 16 feet
Bloom Period: White flowers in spring; edible reddish yellow fruits in summer
Fall Foliage Color: Yellow
Zones: 6–8

Growing over dry slopes throughout much of the western part of North America, antelope bitterbush (Purshia tridentata) keeps its gray foliage all year long. In early July, at the C. M. Goethe Arboretum on the campus of California State University at Sacramento, one last yellow flower is left from its heavy spring bloom. [Photo: Judy Jakobsen]

and is very drought-tolerant. And there's a winter bonus as well: the bark sheds in beautiful patterns. Native to: British Columbia to northwestern United States.

Mountain Andromeda *(Pieris floribunda)*

This "homegrown" shrub is much more resistant to disease and insects here than its Japanese counterpart. It is also shorter, neater, and earlier blooming. Just don't let it dry out, and mulch yearly with pine needles or chopped leaves and you'll find yourself with a constantly good-looking plant, one that annually blares forth the news of spring's arrival with upright clusters of creamy white flowers. Native to: mountains from Virginia to Georgia.

Cherokee Plum *(Prunus angustifolia)*

Peter J. Hatch, director of gardens and grounds at Monticello, praises this shrub as being one of the healthiest around in terms of pest and disease resistance. He also thinks it's an attractive one, with multi-season interest. At Monticello, it is used as a specimen plant in the orchard (Jefferson harvested the plums) as well as a deciduous, trimmed hedge. Native to: New Jersey to Missouri, south to Florida and Texas. *(Pictured on page 12)*

Antelope Bitterbush *(Purshia tridentata)*

"This is a nice shrub and I have no idea why it is not being used more often in formal or informal plantings," comments Bert Wilson of California's Las Pilitas Nursery. "It's drought-tolerant, good for erosion control, and perfect as a border shrub in desert gardens. What's more it's good-looking and really striking in spring when its yellow flowers bloom against its gray foliage." Native to: dry slopes from Montana to British Columbia, south to New Mexico and central California.

Rhododendron *(Rhododendron)*

While it is hard to generalize about a genus as large and diverse as rhododendrons, an attempt is nevertheless now going to be made. The genus contains approximately 850 species and is further fragmented by the existence of innumerable forms, varieties, subspecies, and hybrids. Amidst this welter of magnificent beauty, two popular names stand out: rhododendron and azalea. The former tend to be evergreen and found in eastern China and the latter tend to be deciduous and native to the southeastern United States. Botanically speaking, however, both are designated *Rhododendron.*

Most rhododendrons like some shade and highly organic acid soil that is moist but not boggy. To create the latter condition, mulch with chopped leaves in fall, grass clippings in summer, and pine needles or bark throughout the year; this serves to retain moisture, smother weeds, and increase the soil's organic content. Using just the following highly recommended easy care plants, you will have shrubs decked with colorful flowers from early spring well into summer and with either brilliant fall foliage or cool evergreen beauty.

Sweet Azalea *(R. arborescens).* This exceptionally hardy shrub is valued for its multiseason interest in the garden. From late spring to early summer, its white flowers, each with tiny reddish eyes, emit a pleasing fragrance that is especially beguiling in early evening. In fall, the foliage turns a rich red to purple and adds striking color to shaded settings. Native to: mountain forests and banks of streams and swamps throughout the Appalachians, especially the area encompassed by Pennsylvania and eastern Kentucky south to Georgia and Alabama.

Antelope Bitterbush
Light: Sun
Height: 4 to 10 feet
Bloom Period: Yellow, rose-like flowers in spring
Fall Foliage Color: Year-round gray
Zones: 5–8

Sweet Azalea
Light: Part shade to shade
Height: 9 to 20 feet
Bloom Period: Fragrant white flowers late spring to early summer
Fall Foliage Color: Red to purple
Zones: 4–9

In late spring, flame azalea blossoms (Rhododendron calendulaceum) burn among the dark greenery of woodlands. At Garden in the Woods in Massachusetts, they are paired with majestic fronds of ostrich fern (Matteuccia struthiopteris). [Photo: Hal Horowitz]

Coast Azalea

Light: Sun to part shade
Height: 2 to 4 feet
Bloom Period: Fragrant pale pink or white flowers in spring just before leaves break out
Fall Foliage Color: Yellow
Zones: 4–8

Coast Azalea *(R. atlanticum).* Covered with blooms in spring and beautiful bluish green leaves throughout summer, this compact shrub is perfect for small gardens. While it spreads by stolons or suckers, it does so at a slow pace. Indeed, if you separate the offshoots in early spring, trim the tops almost to the root crown, and then plant and thoroughly water them, you can cheaply increase your supply of these lovely azaleas. Native to: wet pine barrens and sandy open woods from New Jersey to Georgia, west to Alabama.

Florida Flame Azalea *(R. austrinum).* This stunning shrub, a favorite of Richard Johnson of the Caroline Dormon Nature Preserve in Louisiana, is valued not only for its ease of care but also for its spectacular color displays in both spring and fall. As further bonuses, it grows in sun or shade, bears delightfully fragrant flowers, and tolerates either dry or moist growing conditions. Though hardy as far north as Connecticut if planted in a protected site, it is best grown where its buds will not be killed by late April or early May frosts. Northern gardeners need not be too disappointed, however, as they can easily grow the flame azalea described next. Native to: Florida and adjacent Georgia and Alabama.

Flame Azalea *(R. calendulaceum).* The fiery flowers on this shrub appear just after the leaves open and look spectacular against the green foliage. They seem to consume the entire shrub, which is often as wide as it is high. Flame azaleas have long been striking in natural settings; two centuries ago, plant explorer William Bartram described the woods of northern Georgia as burning with the late spring glow of their flowers. Native to: dry woodlands in Appalachians from Pennsylvania to Ohio, south to Georgia and Alabama.

Rhodora *(R. canadense).* This small shrub is perfect for gardeners with bitterly cold winters. Its rose purple flowers reliably burst forth every spring, almost seeming to defy snows and frosts. Though best grown in moist situations, it can also thrive in dry areas if mulched and deeply watered at least once a week. Native to: bogs and wet or rocky hillsides: from Quebec and Newfoundland to New Jersey and Pennsylvania.

Carolina Rhododendron *(R. carolinianum [minus])*. This small, exceptional shrub has somehow been overlooked by both gardeners and landscapers. It tolerates many light conditions, resists pests, has a neat, compact habit, and bears a profusion of flowers among its handsome, glossy green foliage in spring. In a switch from most other members of the genus, the flowers are scentless and the leaves are fragrant when crushed. To ensure almost no care at all, give this plant good drainage and air circulation. Native to: rocky woodlands from North Carolina and Tennessee south to Florida panhandle.

Catawba Rhododendron *(R. catawbiense)*. The hills—especially those constituting Roan Mountain, which straddles the border between North Carolina and Tennessee—are alive with thousands of visitors in June when the catawba rhododendrons are in flower. These shrubs form exceptionally dense thickets and it appears as if a sea of magenta to purple flowers swarms above an undercurrent of dark green, glossy leaves. Breeders treasure this plant for more than its late spring glory, however; it is among the hardiest of rhododendrons and has been amenable to mixing its genes with many other species and varieties. Hybrids with a catawba parent are often called "ironclads" because of their ability to thrive in cold situations. Native to: southern Appalachians.

Rosebay Rhododendron *(R. maximum)*. This old-fashioned favorite should be a staple in deep shade gardens. It seems that no matter how dark the setting, it will be covered with blossoms in summer, a time when few shade shrubs are in flower. As the petals fall, they form a bright woodland carpet. Though this shrub can reach statuesque heights in the southern part of its natural range, it gets progressively shorter in colder climates. Native to: Maine through western New York, south throughout Appalachians.

Western Azalea *(R. occidentale)*. Both striking and unusual, the western azalea is a multiseason shrub that is probably the only member of its genus native to the West Coast (indeed, it is a close relative of the Japanese maple). And it is regionally native in that it does not do well elsewhere on the North American continent. Gardeners fortunate enough to live in the north

Florida Flame Azalea

Light: Sun to shade
Height: 5 to 12 feet
Bloom Period: Fragrant yellow to orange red flowers in spring
Fall Foliage Color: Reddish to golden yellow
Zones: 5–9

Flame Azalea

Light: Part shade to shade
Height: 6 to 12 feet
Bloom Period: Yellow to orange flowers in late spring

In mid July, blush pink blossoms of rosebay rhododendron (R. maximum) lighten a cool, dark mountain setting in Cashiers, North Carolina.

✳

REWARDING RHODODENDRONS

The American Rhododendron Society (ARS) is an organization of rhododendron and azalea enthusiasts that sponsors plant sales and exchanges as well as a scholarly journal describing new varieties and species. While the great majority of its chapters are located in the United States and Canada, there are several overseas as well. For membership information, write Barbara Hall, Executive Director ARS, P.O. Box 1380, Gloucester, Virginia 23061. A. Richard Brooks, ARS president at the time of this writing, says, "The following are my personal candidates for the twelve best *easy care* native rhododendrons and azaleas."

Sweet Azalea *(R. arborescens)*. Unusually fragrant white flowers in spring and rich red fall foliage.

Coast Azalea *(R. atlanticum)*. Fragrant pale pink or white flowers in spring and yellow fall foliage.

Florida Flame Azalea *(R. austrinum)*. Fragrant yellow to orange red flowers in spring and reddish to golden yellow fall foliage.

Flame Azalea *(R. calendulaceum)*. Yellow orange to reddish orange flowers in late spring and bright yellow fall foliage.

Rhodora *(R. canadense)*. Dwarf shrub with rose purple or white flowers in spring.

Carolina Rhododendron *(R. carolinianum)*. Compact, evergreen shrub with a profusion of white, blush pink, or rosy purple flowers in spring.

Catawba Rhododendron *(R. catawbiense)*. Hardy evergreen shrub with magenta, lilac, or purple flowers in late spring.

Rosebay Rhododendron *(R. maximum)*. Tall, evergreen shrub with purplish pink to white blossoms in early summer.

Western Azalea *(R. occidentale)*. Fragrant white to blush pink flowers in spring and orange red fall foliage.

Roseshell Azalea *(R. prinophyllum)*. Fragrant rosy pink or purple flowers in May.

Pinkshell Azalea *(R. vaseyi)*. Rose or white flowers in early May and crimson to purple fall foliage.

Swamp Azalea *(R. viscosum)*. Clove-scented white to light pink flowers in early summer and orange to purple fall foliage.

Pacific area enjoy beautiful spring flowers and gorgeous fall foliage. Native to: Southern Oregon to southern California.

Pinxterbloom (*R. pericylmenoides [nudiflorum]*). The popular name for this tough, deciduous shrub comes from the Dutch settlers that first populated the greater New York area. The plant blooms at "pinkster"—the Dutch word for Whitsuntide, the religious season following Easter. Another popular name is honeysuckle azalea, which reflects the fact that the fragrant flowers resemble honeysuckles. Gardeners with a lack of consistent moisture will enjoy this species because it can tolerate dry situations. Native to: dry open woods and along stream banks throughout the Appalachians from New England to the Florida panhandle and west to Mississippi.

Roseshell Azalea (*R. prinophyllum [roseum]*). Another old-fashioned stalwart, this easily transplanted shrub is covered with large, fragrant pink flowers just as its leaves appear in May. While it requires good drainage, it is extremely adaptable in that it can be grown in moist to dry soils that are moderately acid to even a bit on the alkaline side. Native to: woods and slopes from southern Quebec and Maine to southwest Virginia, west to Ohio and Illinois, and then south to Missouri, Arkansas, and Oklahoma.

Plumleaf Azalea (*R. prunifolium*). A relative newcomer to gardens (it was only discovered in this century), plumleaf azalea is now near to being an endangered species in the wild. Happily, it is easy to propagate and news of its beauty, resistance to heat and powdery mildew, and ease of care is beginning to spread. In 1995, it became the first winner of the Montine McDaniel Freeman Horticulture Medal, an award established by the Garden Club of America to recognize underused North American native plants. In protected situations, it is hardy well beyond its native range, thus giving northern gardeners the opportunity to enjoy its crimson red flowers, which glow exquisitely at a time when few other shrubs bloom. Native to: Georgia and Alabama.

Pinkshell Azalea (*R. vaseyi*). Another American azalea with an extremely limited native range, this shrub is so adaptable that it is now in the process of naturalizing in New England. Discovered in 1878

Fall Foliage Color: Bright yellow
Zones: 4/5–8

Rhodora

Light: Sun to shade
Height: 2 to 3 feet
Bloom Period: Rose purple or white flowers in spring
Fall Foliage Color: Greenish yellow
Zones: 2–6

Carolina Rhododendron

Light: Sun to shade
Height: 3 to 8 feet
Bloom Period: White, blush pink, or rosy purple flowers in spring
Fall Foliage Color: New foliage evergreen and often tinged with purple in northern hardiness range; older foliage frequently turns yellow, orange, or red before dropping
Zones: 4–8

Catawba Rhododendron

Light: Shade
Height: 6 to 15 feet
Bloom Period: Magenta, lilac, or purple flowers in late spring.
Fall Foliage Color: Evergreen
Zones: 4–8

Rosebay Rhododendron

Light: Part shade to shade
Height: 12 to 36 feet
Bloom Period: Purplish
  pink to white flowers in
  early summer
Fall Foliage Color: Ever-
  green
Zones: 3–8

Western Azalea

Light: Sun to part shade
Height: 10 feet
Bloom Period: White to
  blush pink flowers in
  spring
Fall Foliage Color: Orange
  red
Zones: 7–9

Pinxterbloom

Light: Part shade to shade
Height: 6 to 12 feet
Bloom Period: Fragrant
  white to light pink flow-
  ers in late spring
Fall Foliage Color: Yellow
Zones: 4–8

Roseshell Azalea

Light: Part shade
Height: 5 to 10 feet
Bloom Period: Fragrant
  rosy pink or purple flow-
  ers in May
Fall Foliage Color: Dark
  green with purple hue
Zones: 4–8

Plumleaf Azalea

Light: Part shade
Height: 8 to 12 feet

and honored just fifty years later with an Award of Garden Merit by the Royal Horticultural Society, it is a perfect candidate for both informal and formal settings. In either situation, it provides multisea-son interest with its spring flowers and its colorful fall foliage. Native to: moist, acid soils of western North Carolina. *(Pictured on page 87)*

Swamp Azalea (R. viscosum). Among the first native azaleas sent to Great Britain, this shrub is unusual in that it can grow in poorly drained soil—a fact reflected in its popular name and native habitats. It tolerates many light conditions, provides wonderful fragrance as well as lovely flowers in summer, and then tops off the garden year with colorful fall foliage. Native to: stream banks and swampy woods from Maine to Florida, west to Texas.

Fragrant Sumac (Rhus aromatica)

Chris Graham of Ontario's Royal Botanical Gardens feels that this is "a much maligned plant." It is probably disparaged by many precisely because there is no challenge involved in having a shrub of almost year-round interest. If this is what you are seeking and if you happen to have exposed banks or slopes on which nothing appears to grow, this is the plant for you. Those with smaller, more contained gardens might want to explore the merits of Gro-Low, a 3-foot cultivar origi-nating in Chicago. Native to: open, rocky areas from Vermont through Ontario to Minnesota, south to Florida and Texas.

Ornamental Currant (Ribes)

Our native ornamental currants hail from the west coast and are beau-tiful, drought-tolerant plants that host a disease fatal to eastern white pines *(Pinus strobus)*. Gardeners with these conifers on or near their properties should not attempt to grow currants. All others, however, will be enchanted by the ease of care and all-season beauty of these shrubs. Best of all, to many, is that they attract hummingbirds, which can be constantly seen hovering about the long-blooming, nectar-laden spring flowers.

Golden Currant (R. aureum). One of the many western plants brought back east by the Lewis and Clark Expedition, this shrub is exceptionally easy to grow. British gardeners love its scented spring flowers. California gardeners appreciate its ability to survive both drought and several days of standing in water. Native to: Montana to Washington, south to California.

Red Flowering Currant (*R. sanguineum*). In 1828, just two years after British plant explorer David Douglas had sent seeds, this shrub flowered in England and has remained a favorite there ever since. Indeed, the sponsors of Douglas's three-year expedition felt that this plant alone justified all his expenses. Here in our country, the Leach Botanical Garden in Oregon recommends this easy care plant for its early spring bloom, drought tolerance, and attraction for humming-birds. Native to: British Columbia to northern California.

Fuchsia Flowering Gooseberry (*R. speciosum*). When British plant explorer David Douglas arrived in California for a second visit in December 1830, he found this shrub blooming and noted that it was "remarkable for the length and crimson splendor of its stamens, a flower not surpassed in beauty by the finest fuchsia." Today, Bert Wilson of California's Las Pilitas Nursery reminds his customers there's even more to this plant: glossy dark green leaves and late summer fruits that nestle among the foliage like red jewels. Wilson admits there is one drawback: thorns. "Do not plant these in a narrow flower bed or along a walk next to a patio," he advises. Though hardy to zone 6, British gardeners who have long grown this plant suggest that it should be placed in a protected spot where frosts won't blast its buds. Native to: California.

Flowering Raspberry (*Rubus odoratus*)

In England, the flowering raspberry earns plaudits such as "splendid" and "magnificent." In North America more often than not it draws a complete blank. I have grown it for over five years now and appreciate its ability to bloom for up to two months with little or no sun. The flowers are a pinkish magenta and look lovely among the large, pale green, maplelike leaves. Indeed, I always recommend this shrub to shade gardeners with wooded settings. I hesitate to do so to those with more open or small shade areas, however, because this plant's almost invasive suckering habit could well lead to it becoming a nuisance

Bloom Period: Red flowers open over several weeks from early summer in the far south to Labor Day at the edge of its northern hardiness
Fall Foliage Color: Yellow green
Zones: 5–9

Pinkshell Azalea

Light: Sun to part shade
Height: 6 to 10 feet
Bloom Period: Rose or white flowers in early May
Fall Foliage Color: Crimson to purple
Zones: 4–9

Swamp Azalea

Light: Sun to shade
Height: 6 to 12 feet
Bloom Period: Fragrant, clove-scented white to light pink flowers in early summer
Fall Foliage Color: Orange to purple
Zones: 4–9

Fragrant Sumac

Light: Sun
Height: 3 to 10 feet
Bloom Period: Yellow flower clusters in spring; bright red berries, summer into winter
Fall Foliage Color: Orange to intense scarlet red
Zones: 4–8

Golden Currant

Light: Sun to part shade
Height: 3 to 6 feet
Bloom Period: Spice-
scented yellow flowers
in spring; yellow, red,
or purple fruits in late
September
Fall Foliage Color: Gold
Zones: 2–8

Red Flowering Currant

Light: Sun to part shade
Height: 6 to 12 feet
Bloom Period: Early spring
crimson red flowers (cul-
tivars offered with white,
pale pink, or rose flowers)
followed by blue black
fruits
Fall Foliage Color: Orange
Zones: 5–8

Fuchsia Flowering Gooseberry

Light: Sun to part shade
Height: 4 to 10 feet
Bloom Period: Red flowers
through most of winter
and well into spring
Fall Foliage Color: Glossy
dark green leaves
Zones: 6–9

Flowering Raspberry

Light: Part shade to shade
Height: 3 to 9 feet
Bloom Period: Pinkish
magenta flowers most of
summer
Fall Foliage Color: Brown-
ish yellow
Zones: 4–8

rather than a "splendid" presence. Native to: shaded ravines and rocky woodlands from Maine to Michigan, south to North Carolina, Georgia, and Tennessee.

Pozo Blue Sage *(Salvia clevelandii X S. leucophylla)*

"This lovely shrub," reports Penny A. Wilson of Las Pilitas Nursery in California, "gives off an alluring aroma and a wondrous show of flowers. Its leaves are edible and, when used sparingly, are tasty additions to chicken salads." Blooming up to six weeks in drought conditions, this tough little plant can also take salt spray and frost to 5° F. Native to: hybrid; parents California natives.

Snowdrop Bush *(Styrax officinalis* var. *californica)*

This shrub is one of the mysteries of the plant world. While the species plant is found throughout the Mediterranean, this variety is found only in California. How such a distant relative evolved is beyond guessing at this point. What is quite obvious, however, is that snowdrop bush is a beautiful member of spring gardens. Native to: San Luis Obispo to San Diego counties in California.

Snowberry *(Symphoricarpos)*

Snowberries are suckering shrubs that can be found throughout the North American continent. While they are exceptionally adaptable, growing in just about any soil or light condition, they are chiefly valued for their thick clusters of handsome berries.

Eastern Snowberry *(S. albus)*. Though native throughout much of eastern North America, this was not introduced into cultivation until Lewis and Clark brought it back from their 1804–6 expedition. Thomas Jefferson thought it was especially "singular and beautiful" with its white berries in winter. Somehow it took another seven decades before it was introduced to Great Britain, but once in that country it showed its tough mettle and is now so naturalized that many think of it as a native there. Native to: North America east of Continental Divide, excluding Southeast and Midwest.

Western Snowberry *(S. albus var. laevigatus [rivularis]).* This is a shorter, less hardy, and more heat-tolerant relative of the eastern snowberry. Its deep root system makes it an excellent candidate for erosion control and its tolerance of dry (but not drought) conditions and shade also make it a useful shrub to place under trees. Native to: Alaska to Wyoming and California.

Pearlberry ('Mother of Pearl' Doorenbos hybrid). Dutch breeders evaluated at least four American *Symphoricarpos* species and decided they could come up with something better—and they sure did. The resulting crosses are called the Doorenbos hybrids and the most beautiful, in my opinion, is the Mother of Pearl. It has a dense, bushy growth (making it an excellent hedge) and simply stunning lustrous pink berries in fall. Because one of its parents is a Mexican native, this shrub is not as hardy as the above two species. Native to: hybrid with parentage from throughout North American continent.

Blueberry *(Vaccinium)*

Most people are familiar with this genus because of its economic value; blueberries, cranberries, and huckleberries are members. Gardeners should become familiar with it because of its ornamental qualities: pretty flowers, neat and attractive fruit, and brilliant fall foliage. Just give any member highly acidic, moist soil and then relax and enjoy its beauty and produce.

Highbush Blueberry *(V. corymbusum).* I have grown this shrub for twenty years and can personally vouch for its attractiveness and ease of care. While my husband and I were advised to fertilize our three bushes every spring, we stopped doing so about ten years ago and they have continued to bear flowers, fruit, and fabulous fall color. We do, however, always put branches from our stripped Christmas tree around the plants in January so that the dried needles will keep the soil acidic. In the past year or two, the birds have become more aggressive and have managed to sneak under the loosely tossed vinyl black netting that I throw over the top of the plants in July. While I still have fresh blueberries for breakfast many mornings, I no longer have enough to make jam or to freeze. Personally, I don't miss the extra work this

---

Pozo Blue Sage

Light: Sun
Height: 3 to 4 feet
Bloom Period: Violet blue flowers in summer
Fall Foliage Color: Evergreen grayish green
Zones: 7–10

Snowdrop Bush

Light: Sun to part shade
Height: 4 to 8 feet
Bloom Period: Pendulant white flowers in spring
Fall Foliage Color: Green
Zones: 8–10

Eastern Snowberry

Light: Sun to shade
Height: 2 to 5 feet
Bloom Period: Tiny summer pink flowers; lustrous white fall berries, which often persist through much of winter
Fall Foliage Color: Green
Zones: 2–7

Western Snowberry

Light: Sun to shade
Height: 2 to 4 feet
Bloom Period: Tiny pink summer flowers; lustrous white fall berries, which often persist through winter
Fall Foliage Color: Green
Zones: 4–8

Pearlberry

Light: Sun to part shade
Height: 5 to 6 feet

Bloom Period: Tiny pink flowers in early summer; iridescent blush pink berries resembling pearls in fall
Fall Foliage Color: Green
Zones: 5–7

Highbush Blueberry

Light: Sun to bright shade
Height: 6 to 12 feet
Bloom Period: Small, white bell-shaped flowers in spring; edible blue berries in summer
Fall Foliage Color: Fiery red, sometimes dappled with yellow, orange, or purple
Zones: 3–8

Evergreen Huckleberry

Light: Part shade to shade
Height: 3 to 10 feet
Bloom Period: Blush pink flowers in spring; edible dark purple berries in fall
Fall Foliage Color: Evergreen
Zones: 6–9

Arrowwood Viburnum

Light: Sun to part shade
Height: 10 to 20 feet; Winterthur cultivar to 6 feet
Bloom Period: Flat clusters of creamy white flowers in early summer; colorful berries in fall
Fall Foliage Color: Red to purple
Zones: 5–9

involved. Native to: highly acidic soils from Maine to Florida and Louisiana. *(Pictured on page 188)*

Evergreen Huckleberry (*V. ovatum*). Recommended for its use as an excellent hedge by Robert T. Ogilvie, curator of botany at the Royal British Columbia Museum in Victoria, this shrub provides year-round interest: lovely flowers, compact habit, edible berries, and handsome foliage. Florists throughout the country, however, concentrate chiefly on the last attribute; when you receive a commercial floral arrangement, in all probability it contains the small, rich green, and long-lasting boxlike leaves of this shrub. Native to: British Columbia to California.

Viburnum *(Viburnum)*

Viburnums are treasured for their long season of interest: spring flowers, summer berries, and colorful fall foliage. The following add a further bonus: they are exceptionally low-maintenance, particularly when planted in moist but well-drained soil.

Arrowwood Viburnum (*V. nudum*). This shrub has many virtues: large clusters of creamy white flowers in late spring to early summer, shiny dark green leaves throughout summer, and a memorable foliage and fruit display in fall. Two cultivars are deemed to have even more wonderful traits. Winterthur, shorter (only 6 feet) and more compact than the species, was discovered in 1961 in southern Delaware by the late Hal Bruce, curator of plants at Winterthur. Dr. Richard Lighty, one of the evaluators responsible for selecting this plant as a Gold Medal Award winner, wrote: "All you have to do to covet [this plant] is to see it on a crisp autumn morning with its mix of pink and dusty blue berries set against its rich purple foliage." Gardeners in the middle and Deep South will want to explore the beauties of Count Pulaski, which was found in Pulaski County, Arkansas. Horticulturists are particularly excited about the fruit on this shrub: over a month-long period, it evolves from green to an exotic salmon pink through shades of lavender and finally purplish black. Native to: Nova Scotia to Florida and Louisiana. *(Species pictured on page 55)*

Black Haw (*V. prunifolium*). Among the native plants grown at Monticello today and utilized by Thomas Jefferson two centuries ago, this large shrub is not only exceptionally ornamental but also easy care. Its fruits have long been used in preserves. Native to: Connecticut south to Florida and Texas.

American Cranberry Bush *(V. trilobum).* An easy care recommendation from the Royal Botanical Gardens in Ontario, this shrub is best suited for northern landscapes. In fall gardens, its thick clusters of colorful fruits look especially attractive when paired with the bright red berries of jack-in-the-pulpits *(Arisaema triphyllum).* Native to: southern Canada and northern United States. *(Cultivar seedling pictured on page 109)*

FOR FURTHER INFORMATION on native shrubs see Gary L. Hightshoe's extremely comprehensive NATIVE TREES, SHRUBS, AND VINES FOR URBAN AND RURAL AMERICA: A PLANTING DESIGN MANUAL FOR ENVIRONMENTAL DESIGNERS (Van Nostrand Reinhold) and Graham Stuart Thomas's ORNAMENTAL SHRUBS, CLIMBERS AND BAMBOOS (Timber Press). Though the latter book surveys woody plant materials from around the world, it is so comprehensive that its American flora descriptions are not duplicated in any other popular horticultural publication.

SOURCES. Though not as expensive as trees, shrubs are still relatively costly investments and are best bought from a local garden center where you can inspect them before purchase. All shrubs native to your area should be offered locally; if not, find a better garden center. Gardeners who wish to try shrubs from outside their region may have to resort to mail-order nurseries. Forestfarm is an excellent resource, offering a superb variety of woody plant materials. Other mail order firms offfering good selections of native woody ornamentals include Fairweather Gardens, Lamtree Farm, Las Pilitas Nursery, Woodlanders, and Yucca Do Nursery. Addresses for all are presented in the Appendix.

Black Haw

Light: Sun to part shade
Height: 15 feet
Bloom Period: White flowers in late spring; dark blue berries in fall
Fall Foliage Color: Wine red
Zones: 3–9

American Cranberry Bush

Light: Sun to shade
Height: 6 to 12 feet
Bloom Period: White flowers in spring; red to orange berries late summer to late winter
Fall Foliage Color: Purplish red
Zones: 2–6

Chapter 8

Groundcovers and Wall Climbers

May woods at the Shaw Arboretum in Missouri are colored with streaks of golden ragwort (Senecio aureus) and a large planting of blue Jacob's ladders (Polemonium reptans). [Photo: Scott Woodbury]

Plants in this chapter have been grouped by their function rather than by their classification as a shrub, annual, or perennial. I like to refer to them as the carpets and curtains of the garden or landscape, and I think you will find your property beautifully furnished with one or more of the following.

GROUNDCOVERS

The definition of a groundcover is often in the eye of the beholder. In this book, it consists of plants that flood over large areas or that are mat-forming and solidly cover small areas. Because they do function as carpets, information on foliage is provided under each description.

Bearberry *(Arctostaphylos uva-ursi)*

To me, plant distribution is a fascinating subject and the *Arctostaphylos* genus is a good example of why this is so. All but two of its fifty or more species are native to California and the northwest. Generally called manzanitas, they are drought-tolerant and very popular plants in West Coast gardens. The two exceptions, however, are extraordinary in that they are found throughout the cooler parts of the northern hemisphere. Bearberry is one of these world travelers and is equally at home in Sweden, where its leaves were once used for tanning leather, and in British Columbia, where they were sometimes used as a tobacco substitute. Given this wide geographical distribution, it is not surprising that there are many forms and cultivars. All require good drainage and are thus perfect for sandy soils. Though not considered drought-tolerant by California standards, they can survive beautifully with only one weekly watering. I grow two: Massachusetts, an East Coast selection that is supposed to be more tolerant of wet conditions, and Wood's Red, perhaps the most adaptable of all and my favorite because its leaves are a bit wider and have more red in them through winter. Both are elegant, low-growing plants that offer all-season interest in a garden setting. Native to: Newfoundland to New Jersey, west through Michigan, Canada, and Alaska, south to New Mexico and California.

Wild Ginger *(Asarum)*

Wild gingers are an acquired taste, but once acquired they are treasured for their handsome, low-growing green foliage. Thriving in the dappled light of deciduous woods filled with slightly acidic soil and organic matter, the various species differ in leaf size, texture, and coloration. All are quite elegant additions to shade settings and can be increased through division in spring or, preferably, fall.

Heart Leaf Ginger *(A. arifolium)*. Recommended as an easy care native by Jeanne Frett of the Mt. Cuba Center in Delaware, heart leaf ginger is distinguished from the two others described here in that its leaves are blotched. Native to: woods from Virginia and Kentucky south to Florida and Louisiana.

Bearberry

Light: Sun
Height: 2 to 12 inches
Bloom Period: White flowers tipped with pink in spring; red berries late summer into fall
Foliage: Dark evergreen, often with red tinge in winter
Zones: 2–9

Heart Leaf Ginger

Light: Part shade to shade
Height: 5 inches
Bloom Period: Small green and maroon flowers in spring
Foliage: Evergreen triangular leaves usually blotched
Zones: 6–8

Canadian Wild Ginger

Light: Part shade to shade
Height: 6 to 10 inches
Bloom Period: Purplish
 brown flowers in spring
Foliage: Large, velvety
 green leaves
Zones: 4–8

Western Wild Ginger

Light: Part shade to shade
Height: 7 to 9 inches
Bloom Period: Insignificant
 brown flowers in spring
Foliage: Shiny dark green
Zones: 4–9

Coyote Bush

Light: Sun
Height: 1 to 2 feet
Bloom Period: Insignificant
 flowers
Foliage: Dark evergreen
Zones: 7–9

Marsh Marigold

Light: Part shade to shade
Height: 1 to 2 feet
Bloom Period: Bright yel-
 low flowers in early
 spring
Foliage: Rich, glossy green
Zones: 3–10

Canadian Wild Ginger *(A. canadense)*. This is the most widely and easily grown species. It spreads slowly by rhizomes (which have been used as a ginger substitute) and has large heart-shaped leaves. Unfortunately, slugs find this groundcover quite tasty and it is not suitable in places where these creatures nest. Mine is situated amidst tree roots in a relatively dry shade area and looks lovely. When I placed a clump in a cool, moist area, slugs devoured it within two days. Native to: New Brunswick to North Carolina, west to Missouri.

Western Wild Ginger *(A. caudatum)*. This handsome Pacific coast native has glossy, evergreen, kidney-shaped leaves and is the best member of the genus for this area of the country. It is so adaptable in its native haunts that it can be grown in dry as well as moist situations—truly a lovely, easy care plant. Native to: Alaska to California.

Coyote Bush *(Baccharis pilularis)*

This handsome evergreen groundcover has thick, glossy leaves. It is not only exceptionally drought-tolerant but can even thrive under slightly boggy conditions. Pigeon Point is a superior and widely used cultivar. Native to: coastal California.

Marsh Marigold *(Caltha palustris)*

Marsh marigolds brighten up moist, early spring settings throughout the northern hemisphere. Because they are among the first perennials to appear, their bright yellow flowers and glossy green leaves look especially handsome as carpets for bare, brown grounds. When trees leaf out, however, these plants go dormant and summer visitors to woods that glowed with their golden spring blossoms have no sign of their underground presence. Native to: moist, shady habitats from Newfoundland to Alaska, south to North Carolina and Tennessee. *(Pictured on page 5)*

Ceanothus *(Ceanothus)*

Native to: California, the following low-growing shrubs are beautiful, low-maintenance groundcovers, particularly in dry and drought-plagued areas.

Maritime Ceanothus *(C. maritimus)*. This very neat, undemanding shrub is a handsome, drought-tolerant groundcover in California landscapes and, according to Bert Wilson of Las Pilitas Nursery, would serve a similar function further north along the Pacific coast and in many areas of the East Coast as well. Though its dark green leaves almost glisten in sunny sea breezes, maritime ceanothus does not like sandy soils; indeed, it is native to thick adobe areas along the California coast. The lovely flowers are a colorful bonus in spring. Native to: California. *(Pictured on page 90)*

Yankee Point *(C. griseus horizontalis* 'Yankee Point'). The flowers on this shrub open later than those on maritime ceanothus; in pairing the two, you can obtain a long flowering period. This plant is not as adaptable and is suited only to gardens and landscapes within its native range. Native to: California. *(Pictured on page 90)*

Goldenstar, Green-and-Gold *(Chrysogonum virginianum)*

The popular names provide an apt description of this plant: its starlike flowers look like gold jewelry placed on a setting of rich green foliage. Just give this groundcover moist, humusy soil to get it started and then you can sit back and never have to do a thing with it except admire its long blooming period. Though selfsowing freely, it cannot be described as invasive because it is so easy to pull out of any unwanted places. The farther south you find it, the more low growing—indeed, almost prostrate—are the forms; conversely, the plants are taller when found in the northern areas of its natural range. Native to: moist but well-drained woodland edges from Pennsylvania to Florida panhandle and Louisiana.

Seaside Daisy *(Erigeron glaucus* 'Wayne Roderick')

West Coast gardeners treasure this plant for many reasons: it is almost everflowering; its green foliage forms a handsome mat that beautifully sets off the lavender flowers; it is unaffected by salt air and breezes; and—perhaps most important of all—deer do not like it. Without ocean breezes, however, it wilts in the heat of high sun and needs either extra watering or some shade protection. Alas for gardeners along much of the East Coast, seaside daisy cannot take the stifling

Maritime Ceanothus

Light: Sun to part shade
Height: 2 to 3 feet
Bloom Period: Pale to dark blue flowers in spring
Foliage: Glossy, dark green, hollylike leaves
Zones: 7–9

Yankee Point

Light: Sun to part shade
Height: 3 feet
Bloom Period: Blue flowers in spring
Foliage: Glossy, dark green
Zones: 8–9

Goldenstar, Green-and-Gold

Light: Part shade to shade
Height: 4 to 10 inches
Bloom Period: Long, heavy bloom of yellow flowers in spring; sporadic bloom to fall in cool areas and frequent rebloom in fall in warm ones
Foliage: Warm green
Zones: 4–10

Seaside Daisy

Light: Sun to part shade
Height: 10 inches
Bloom Period: Lavender flowers from snow melt through light frosts
Foliage: Dark green
Zones: 5–10

Red Buckwheat

Light: Sun
Height: 1 to 2 feet
Bloom Period: Pink flowers
late spring to late sum-
mer
Foliage: Grayish green
Zones: 8–10

Sulfur Flower

Light: Sun to part shade
Height: 1 to 3 feet
Bloom Period: Pale yellow
to creamy green flowers
late spring through sum-
mer
Foliage: Blue green
Zones: 6–10

Golden Yarrow

Light: Sun
Height: 8 to 24 inches
Bloom Period: Yellow daisylike flowers spring
throughout summer
Foliage: Wispy, grayish
green
Zones: Various according
to subspecies and variety;
range is 5–8

humidity that is so often a part of summer gardening in that part of the country. Native to: Pacific coast from Oregon to California. *(Pictured on page 90)*

Buckwheat *(Eriogonum)*

Buckwheats are native to the West Coast and, as such, are drought-tolerant plants. The following two are often used as handsome groundcovers in gardens and landscapes.

Red Buckwheat *(E. grande* var. *rubescens).* This very attractive, low-growing plant is valued for its long bloom time as well as its nice-looking foliage. It's a perfect groundcover for hot, dry sunny areas. Note that, despite its popular name, the flowers are actually a rich pink. Native to: southern California. *(Foliage pictured on page 90)*

Sulfur Flower *(E. umbellatum* var. *polyanthum).* This is one of the few drought-tolerant California natives that can also do well along the humid East Coast. Recommended by Dr. Mike Baad at California State University in Sacramento, sulfur flower has handsome blue green foliage and is covered with lemon yellow blossoms throughout the summer. These are excellent candidates for dried flower arrangements, as are the plant's fluffy seedpods. Native to: British Columbia to California.

Golden Yarrow *(Eriophyllum lanatum)*

This lovely groundcover is decked with yellow, daisylike flowers from spring throughout summer. All it basically requires is a warm, sunny site with excellent drainage. To grow it, however, you should be aware that there are different varieties and subspecies. Though the species is listed in many gardening books as being hardy to zone 5, this reference applies only to the var. *grandiflorum*. The plant native to the West Coast and recommended by Robert T. Ogilvie of the Royal British Columbia Museum is, botanically speaking, subspecies *arachnoideum*. "It needs a mild climate with warm, sunny, dry summers and mild winters," he reports, "and these are the conditions we have in Victoria and which also exist in Vancouver, Seattle, and Portland. The plants do especially well in full sun on rocks or open ground." Native to: dry areas from Montana to British Columbia, south to California.

Salal *(Gaultheria shallon)*

This native shrub has long been grown in British gardens. It was the first plant encountered by explorer David Douglas after an eight-month journey to the West Coast in 1825 and he praised both its ornamental qualities and its fruit when he sent seed to England. With its leathery, red-stalked foliage, lovely flower clusters, and edible purple fruit it was quickly rated as both a classic garden plant and a valued woodland undercover for game reserves. Today, knowledgeable plantspeople in its home continent also stress its virtues; it is recommended by the Royal British Columbia Museum. Furthermore, WYMAN'S GARDENING ENCYCLOPEDIA, a reference work with a decidedly East Coast orientation, describes salal as the showiest of the genus and a good groundcover. Native to: Alaska to southern California.

Canada Waterleaf *(Hydrophyllum canadense)*

This plant is dismissed by many, including WYMAN'S GARDENING ENCYCLOPEDIA, as being basically uninteresting and of little garden

Salal

Light: Part shade to shade
Height: 1 foot in poor soils to 5 feet in fertile soils in sheltered locations
Bloom Period: Pale pink flower clusters in June; edible purple fruit in August
Foliage: Evergreen
Zones: 5–8

Canada Waterleaf

Light: Part shade to shade
Height: 1 to 2 feet
Bloom Period: White flowers in early summer
Foliage: Striking blue green foliage spotted with gray in early spring; matures to solid warm green by summer
Zones: 4–8

After seeing the early spring foliage of Canada waterleaf (Hydrophyllum canadense), *most shade gardeners decide to incorporate this truly undemanding plant in their borders. In early summer, there's a bonus: white flowers tucked under leaves that have turned a warm green.*

value. How anyone could come to such a conclusion after seeing its spring foliage is hard for me to understand. Emerging early in a dark shaded area on my property, the foliage resembles that of maple leaves and is initially a beautiful blue green and heavily marked with gray. It presents a striking picture against the bare brown earth of that time of year. As they age, the leaves on this truly undemanding plant turn a warm green and, in early summer, have white flowers tucked in among them. This is a wonderful medium-height groundcover for dark, shady—but not bone dry—places where little else will grow. Native to: moist woods from Vermont to Wisconsin and Missouri, south to Georgia and Alabama.

Crested Iris *(I. cristata)*

"We treasure this diminutive iris," writes Richard L. Johnson of the Caroline Dormon Nature Preserve in Louisiana. And so do I. Its flowers, which look just like the much larger and more popular garden iris,

A clump of wild lily-of-the-valley (Maianthemum canadense) *in early May looks like a convention of miniature hostas. They are pictured here with pink creeping phlox (P.* stolonifera), *white foamflower* (Tiarella cordifolia)*, and what looks like lipstick smears but which are actually the tiny red petals of fire pink (Silene virginica). The emerging fronds of Christmas fern (Polystichum acrostichoides) add a vertical dimension to this Pennsylvania woodland planting.*

bloom for less than two weeks and are worth every minute of that short period. I have the white form and it glistens in both green shady settings and in sunny areas. Unlike the foliage of its taller relatives, that of crested iris foliage never flops (slugs do like it, however, so I never plant it in a consistently moist area). The rhizomes creep about steadily but not invasively, and are excellent on sloped areas where they hold soil in place. Native to: Maryland to Missouri, south to Georgia and Oklahoma.

Creeping Holly Grape *(Mahonia repens)*

This tough, stoloniferous shrub is often used in land reclamation projects within its native range. Bert Wilson of California's Las Pilitas Nursery reports that it is almost deer-proof and recommends it as a drought-tolerant groundcover well outside its native area; he believes it would be suitable for mountain gardens and those on the East Coast. With its all-season interest, it would not only be suitable but also quite attractive. Native to: North Dakota to British Columbia, south to Colorado and California.

Wild Lily-of-the-Valley *(Maianthemum canadense)*

This charming little groundcover slowly forms a mat that resembles a gathering of teeny hostas. Its rounded leaves reflect the light of its surroundings: rich, dark green in deep shade and a warm green in sun dappled areas. Slugs do not devastate this plant (always a plus in my garden) and in May little spikes of white flowers appear as an added decoration. Native to: moist woods from Newfoundland to South Dakota, south through mountains into northern Georgia and Tennessee.

Partridge Berry *(Mitchella repens)*

Pennsylvania's David Benner claims he has the largest partridge berry patch in the country—a beautiful mat that measures 18 by 25 feet after three decades. Obviously this is not a quickly established groundcover. It is a treasure, however, as it is a plant for all seasons: evergreen foliage with whitish veins in spring, fragrant flowers in summer, bright red berries in fall, and a wonderful Christmas decoration in winter. Note

Crested Iris
Light: Sun to shade
Height: 4 to 9 inches
Bloom Period: Light blue, lilac, purple, or white flowers in spring
Foliage: Diminutive, light green iris leaves
Zones: 4–9

Creeping Holly Grape
Light: Part shade to shade
Height: 1 to 3 feet
Bloom Period: Yellow flowers in late spring; dark blue berries in late summer
Foliage: Evergreen, often with purple bronze tint in winter
Zones: 5–9

Wild Lily-of-the-Valley
Light: Part shade to shade
Height: 2 to 5 inches
Bloom Period: Tiny white flower spikes in spring
Foliage: Shiny, warm green arched leaves
Zones: 3–7

Partridge Berry
Light: Part shade to shade
Height: 6 to 12 inches
Bloom Period: Pinkish white flowers in spring in southern areas and early summer in North; bright red berries throughout winter in most areas
Foliage: Dark evergreen
Zones: 3–9

Redwood Sorrel

Light: Part shade to shade
Height: 10 inches
Bloom Period: White, pink, or rose flowers in spring
Foliage: Rich green
Zones: 4–9

Allegheny Pachysandra

Light: Part shade
Height: 6 to 12 inches
Bloom Period: Fragrant, purplish white flowers in spring
Foliage: Green, heavily mottled with purple, in spring; evergreen in South and deciduous in North
Zones: 4–9

Bush Penstemon

Light: Sun
Height: 6 to 18 inches
Bloom Period: Large purple to lavender blue flowers in early summer
Foliage: Evergreen
Zones: 5–8

Blue Bedder

Light: Sun
Height: 18 to 24 inches
Bloom Period: Rich blue, striking purple flowers spring, well into summer
Foliage: Dark green
Zones: 7–10

that this must be kept clear over winter; thick wet layers of maple and oak leaves will fatally smother the plant. Native to: Nova Scotia to Minnesota, south to Florida and Texas.

Redwood Sorrel *(Oxalis oregana)*

This Northwest native is recommended as an elegant, easy care addition to shady areas by the Leach Botanical Garden in Oregon. Its rich green leaves are similar to those of clover and pair beautifully with the fronds of the western sword fern *(Polystichum munitum)*. Native to: Washington to northern California.

Allegheny Pachysandra *(P. procumbens)*

In southern gardens especially, this is a far superior plant to the ubiquitous Japanese pachysandra and the only reason that it cannot fully claim such distinction in the northern parts of its range is that it is not evergreen. Northern gardeners, for their part, might want to explore its beauty and ease of care by placing it in areas where its absence in winter will not be effectively noticed. They will be rewarded with a handsome groundcover that Jeanne Frett of the Mt. Cuba Center in Delaware describes as being remarkably durable and noninvasive. Native to: Kentucky to Florida and Louisiana.

Penstemon *(Penstemon)*

While members of this diverse genus are classified as annuals, perennials, or shrubs, the following are recommended as groundcovers.

Bush Penstemon *(P. fruticosus).* This Northwest subshrub forms a spreading mounded mat that is ideal for cascading over walls or in xeriscapes. That last situation exemplifies the fact that it must have good drainage and cannot take constantly wet situations. The cultivar Purple Haze was so named because its flowering period is supposed to remind viewers of the haze over distant mountains. Native to: Wyoming to British Columbia, south to Oregon.

Blue Bedder *(P. heterophyllus* var. *purdyi).* Best for areas with annual rainfall above 30 inches, this low-growing plant is exceptionally showy. Cut it back after its first rich flush of bloom and it will flower again. Even if it doesn't, its handsome dark green foliage acts as a wonderful filler in the border. As with all West Coast penstemons, blue bedder requires good drainage. Native to: California.

Pygmaeus Penstemon (*P. hirsutus* 'Pygmaeus'). Scott Woodbury of the Shaw Arboretum in Missouri uses this easy care perennial as a decorative groundcover in a dry shade setting. Looking lovely in the humid heat of the East Coast as well, this plant is rather long-lived for a penstemon (up to ten years in some areas). Its rosettes of green summer leaves turn bronze in winter. Native to: Maine to Wisconsin, south to Virginia. *(Pictured on page 68)*

Phlox *(Phlox)*

From early spring to late summer, members of the phlox genus contribute flowers to garden settings. They are an extremely varied lot, with some growing up to 5 feet tall and others forming spreading mats. In general, the low-growing phlox bloom in spring and in this book and elsewhere are classified as groundcovers. The following are especially recommended.

Sand Phlox (*P. bifida*). This tough little phlox—it can handle both poor soils and drought—forms mounds and spreads very slowly. I have Mina Colvin, also known as Colvin's White, and its white flowers are absolutely stunning in early spring, particularly because they are next to the reddish purple foliage of Montrose Ruby heuchera. The heuchera not only sets off the sand phlox's brilliant white flowers in spring but also conceals much of its ratty foliage in humid summer heat. Native to: southwest Michigan to Tennessee, west to Kansas and Arkansas. *(Pictured on page 254)*

Blue Woodland Phlox (*P. divaricata*). I've subjected this lovely plant to the wrong kind of growing conditions for ten years now and it has nevertheless survived, although it has not spread as rapidly as it does in natural woodland settings. Indeed, its fragrant light blue flowers are blooming in a sunny, rather thick clay spot as I write these words on a May morning and I wish I was outside admiring their beauty and fragrance rather than sitting in front of a computer! In summer, the

Pygmaeus Penstemon

Light: Sun to bright shade
Height: 6 inches
Bloom Period: Violet flowers late spring into summer
Foliage: Green summer rosettes turn bronze in winter
Zones: 3–9

Sand Phlox

Light: Sun to part shade
Height: 10 inches
Bloom Period: Violet purple or white flowers in spring
Foliage: Green needlelike leaves often brown and go dormant in hot, humid summers
Zones: 4–8

Blue Woodland Phlox

Light: Part shade to shade
Height: 8 to 12 inches
Bloom Period: Fragrant blue to white flowers in spring
Foliage: Dark green; goes dormant during hot dry periods in summer
Zones: 4–9

Prairie Phlox

Light: Sun
Height: 1 to 2 feet
Bloom Period: Reddish purple flowers in late spring
Foliage: Green
Zones: 3–9

Creeping Phlox

Light: Part shade to shade
Height: 6 to 12 inches
Bloom Period: Purple violet, blue, pink, or white flowers in spring
Foliage: Warm green
Zones: 3–9

Moss Phlox

Light: Sun to part shade
Height: 2 to 6 inches
Bloom Period: Thick coverings of white through pink to purple flowers in spring
Foliage: Green, needlelike mats; evergreen in southern range and rather ratty by fall farther north
Zones: 3–8

foliage often goes dormant in the heat of a too-sunny location; in shady woods, the dark green leaves blend handsomely with other groundcovers. Native to: Quebec to Michigan, south to Georgia, Florida panhandle, and Texas. *(Pictured on page 87)*

Prairie Phlox (*P. pilosa*). This is one of the plants Bonnie Harper-Lore chose for her front yard prairie in Minnesota. Given its wide native range, it is obviously an adaptable plant. It is also a pretty one, with mildew-resistant, slightly fragrant flowers that bloom for almost a month. A southern variety, sometimes called Ozark phlox (*P. pilosa* var. *ozarkana*), is recommended by Scott Woodbury of the Shaw Arboretum in Missouri and is hardy only to zone 5. "Unlike the species," he reports, "this one suckers and its flowers have a deeper rose color." Native to: dry soils from Connecticut to North Dakota, south to Florida and Texas. *(Pictured on pages 68 and 77)*

Creeping Phlox (*P. stolonifera*). When the Perennial Plant Association began a program to honor outstanding plants in 1990, creeping phlox was the first to be designated Plant of the Year. It's easy to see why. It requires no maintenance, produces a beautiful spring display of flowers, and features thick, mat-forming warm green foliage. Native to: Appalachian mountains from Pennsylvania to Georgia. *(Pictured on pages 98 and 172)*

Moss Phlox (*P. subulata*). This ubiquitous phlox forms bright—some would say jarring—mats of spring color and can be found draped over stone walls or covering hills and slopes across much of the country. Its ease of growth and its commonness have led to the creation of many different cultivars by breeders and to disdain on the part of sophisticated horticulturists. Plantsman Pierre Bennerup thinks the latter group should reconsider their stance toward this easy care native, particularly with regard to several new cultivars developed in Europe. While there is some question as to the true parentage of these groundcovers (do they, for example, have *P. douglasii* genes?), the consensus seems to be that they are forms of moss phlox. Bennerup especially recommends the sensational red pink flowers of Crackerjack. Native to: well-drained soils from New York to Michigan, south to mountains of North Carolina and Tennessee. *(Pictured on page 51)*

May Apple *(Podophyllum peltatum)*

This is a wonderful groundcover to carpet large areas of deciduous woods. Since it spreads rapidly by underground stolons, it is definitely not a plant for small spaces. In early spring, its large, green, umbrella-like foliage pushes up through brown leaves; underneath each is a lovely white flower. Native to: open woods from Quebec to Minnesota, south Florida and Texas.

Creeping Sage *(Salvia sonomensis)*

Recommended by Dr. Mike Baad at California State University in Sacramento, this groundcover can cover a 10-foot-square area when grown in the dry, sloping conditions duplicating its natural habitat. It has pretty gray green leaves and is outstanding in spring, when it is covered with blue violet flowers. Native to: dry slopes in California coast ranges and Sierra Nevada foothills.

Mexican Sedum *(S. mexicanum)*

This is a nice little sprawler for a sunny stone wall. Its warm green, needlelike foliage and cheerful yellow flowers contrast beautifully with the grayish blues or brownish reds of stones. As a further bonus, it is not an invasive plant and spreads slowly. Since this is so little known and because I've only grown it for one year at this writing, I cannot vouch for the hardiness reported in the Plant Delights Nursery catalog and recorded at right. Native to: Mexico.

Ragwort *(Senecio [Packera])*

The following two plants grow over wide areas on our continent, yet are little known. You might want to try one or both.

Golden Ragwort *(S. aureus)*. This is a very showy spring plant with purple stems and buds followed by a large flush of yellow, asterlike flowers. Cut these for bouquets and they will last for almost a week. During the remainder of the growing season, the 6-inch-tall rich green foliage makes an attractive, trouble-free groundcover. Be aware,

---

May Apple

Light: Dappled, deciduous shade
Height: 12 to 18 inches
Bloom Period: White flowers hide under large leaf cover in spring
Foliage: Deeply lobed green leaves
Zones: 3–9

Creeping Sage

Light: Sun
Height: 4 to 16 inches
Bloom Period: Blue violet flowers in spring
Foliage: Gray green
Zones: 7/8–9

Mexican Sedum

Light: Sun to part shade
Height: Prostrate to 6 inches
Bloom Period: Yellow flowers spring into early summer
Foliage: Light green needles
Zones: 4–8

Golden Ragwort

Light: Sun to part shade
Height: 1 to 2 feet
Bloom Period: Yellow flowers in spring
Foliage: Dark green; purple undersides on new leaves
Zones: 4–8

Round-leaf Ragwort

Light: Sun to part shade
Height: 18 to 24 inches
Bloom Period: Yellow
 flowers in spring
Foliage: Dark green
Zones: 4–8

Blue-eyed Grass

Light: Sun to part shade
Height: 6 to 18 inches
Bloom Period: Warm blue
 flowers in early spring in
 south and late in north
Foliage: Green, grasslike
Zones: 3–10 (winter
 mulch required 3–4)

Fringe Cups

Light: Sun to shade
Height: 12 to 18 inches
Color: Creamy white
Bloom Period: Spring
Foliage: Scalloped, rich
 green leaves
Zones: 5–9

Allegheny Foamflower

Light: Part shade to shade
Height: 6 to 12 inches
Bloom Period: White to
 blush pink flowers in
 spring
Foliage: Fuzzy green
 leaves, sometimes marked
 with maroon, evergreen
 in southern range and
 deciduous in North
Zones: 3–9

Prairie Verbena

Light: Sun
Height: 3 to 5 inches

however, that while golden ragwort is not rapid in its spread, it does tend to overwhelm any plants in its path. Native to: damp, fertile habitats from Newfoundland to Minnesota, south to Florida and Texas. *(Pictured on page 166)*

Round-leaf Ragwort *(S. obovatus).* With 3-inch green foliage rosettes and lovely yellow spring flowers, this has proven to be a tough groundcover surviving in Michigan's roadside plantings and a charming addition to home gardens. Native to: Massachusetts to Michigan, south to northern Florida and eastern Texas.

Blue-eyed Grass *(Sisyrinchium angustifolium)*

Thriving in moist situations, this member of the iris family has also flourished through many dry summers in my gardens. It selfsows quite freely and since I use it as a specimen plant rather than as a groundcover, I am constantly (but easily) pulling out seedlings. Peter Hatch at Monticello recommends it as a groundcover and when you see drifts of its warm blue flowers flooding through moist areas you will quickly understand why. Native to: open woods, meadows, and prairies from Newfoundland to Minnesota, south to Florida and Louisiana.

Fringe Cups *(Tellima grandiflora)*

I always thought this was a specimen perennial for a shade setting and have treated it as such in my native plant garden, where its creamy white flowers on wiry stalks appear in early spring. (Though its foliage is attacked by chewing insects later in the season, this does not cause great disfigurement in the overall garden scheme.) What a surprise then to see a whole bank of these flowers blooming in bright sun at the Leiden Botanical Garden in the Netherlands. This obviously adaptable plant is easy care under many situations, which is among the reasons why it was recommended by Danish plantswoman Grethe B. Petersen. Native to: Alaska to California.

Allegheny Foamflower *(Tiarella cordifolia [var. cordifolia])*

Systemic botanists are still working on foamflower nomenclature. In this book, the above designation is used for the plant spreading by underground stolons and the clump forming pink foamflower *(T. wherryi)* is described as a perennial in Chapter 12. While there might be confusion about its botanical classification, there is no doubt as to its excellence as a woodland groundcover. Indeed, the mail-order nursery Primrose Path goes so far as to say, "In our opinion, this is the finest and easiest native groundcover for shade, succeeding even in fairly dense shade under evergreens." Native to: woods from Nova Scotia to Wisconsin, south through Appalachians to Georgia and Mississippi. *(Pictured on pages 98 and 172)*

Prairie Verbena *(V. bipinnatifida)*

One of the stars of the formal native garden at the National Wildflower Research Center in Texas, this groundcover features season-long flowers and handsome foliage. While it is easy care throughout its growing range, it struggles in the humidity of East Coast gardens. Native to: South Dakota to Alaska, south to Mexico and Arizona. *(Pictured on page 19)*

Violet *(Viola)*

Violets draw mixed reactions from many gardeners. There are the invasive kinds that plague chemical-free lawns such as mine and then there are the more refined, colorful versions. Both the following meet the last two criteria and qualify as excellent shade groundcovers.

Appalachian Violet *(V. appalachiensis).* This little-known violet is a true garden treasure. It is not in the least invasive—indeed some may wish it to spread a bit faster—and features dainty foliage and small purple blossoms that appear for over four weeks in my garden. It is perfect for small areas and, given its ground-hugging tendency and mat-forming way of spreading, it would probably be a good choice for shaded spots on slopes. Rarely

Appalachian violet (Viola appalachiensis) *is a well-behaved, mat-forming groundcover with flowers appearing for up to four weeks, starting in mid April in Princeton. It is pictured here on April 27 with the first creamy white flowers on the wiry stems of miterwort* (Mitella diphylla). *Bridget Bloom* (X Heucherella 'Bridget Bloom') *sends up its first pink buds to the right and will continue to do so for as long as eight weeks.*

Bloom Period: Pink, purple, or lavender flowers
spring to frost
Foliage: Deeply lobed,
dark green leaves
Zones: 3–9

Appalachian Violet

Light: Part shade to shade
Height: 1 to 2 inches
Bloom Period: Purple flow-
ers in spring
Foliage: Green
Zones: 5–8

Labrador Violet

Light: Part shade to shade
Height: 1 to 4 inches
Bloom Period: Violet flow-
ers in spring
Foliage: Purple tinged,
especially new growth in
spring
Zones: 3–8

Barren Strawberry

Light: Sun to part shade
Height: 4 to 6 inches
Bloom Period: Yellow
flowers late spring to
early summer
Foliage: Shiny green leaves
resembling those on
strawberry plants
Zones: 4–7

Yellowroot

Light: Sun to shade
Height: 2 to 3 feet
Bloom Period: Purple flow-
ers in spring

offered commercially, plants can be obtained from the Wildwood
Flower. Native to: Pennsylvania to West Virginia.

Labrador violet (*V. labradorica*). Another little-known violet, this
plant is valued for its purple-tinged foliage, which is especially prominent in spring. Though its native range proclaims that this is a plant for
northern gardens, Georgia-based Allan Armitage reports in HERBA-
CEOUS PERENNIAL PLANTS that this charming groundcover does
equally well in the South. Spreading by slender, creeping rhizomes, it
can become invasive in some situations but has yet to do so after five
years in my native plant garden. Native to: Greenland, Newfoundland
to Alaska, south to New Hampshire and Minnesota. *(Pictured on page
51)*

Barren Strawberry *(Waldsteinia fragaroides)*

Doing well on barrens—poor, dry, sunny soils—this pretty little plant
forms nice mats of greenery in places where it is sometimes hard to
have swaths of this color. While both its foliage and flowers resemble
those on strawberry plants, its fruits are not edible. Native to: New
Brunswick to Minnesota, south to Georgia, Tennessee, and Missouri.

Yellowroot *(Xanthoriza simplicissima)*

A relatively tall groundcover, this deciduous shrub is a particularly
good choice for informal woodland settings. Recommended by the
Bernheim Arboretum in Kentucky, yellowroot provides all-season
interest with colorful flowers in spring and foliage in fall. The popular
name derives from its yellow roots; its stems, underneath a covering of
gray bark, are also the same color. Native to: New York to West Virginia, south to Florida panhandle and Mississippi.

VINES AND OTHER WALL CLIMBERS

The following plants look striking on walls or trellises; many also like
to clamber on other plants. All are recommended as easy care and
attractive.

Allegheny Vine *(Adlumia fungosa)*

Technically a biennial, Allegheny vine produces a rosette of leaves the first year from seeding and waits until the following spring, to twine up nearby shrubs or small trees. The foliage is a lovely blue green and the flowers, resembling delicate bleeding hearts that are on a diet, appear all summer to frost. Popular in Europe, this is another native that North American gardeners should better scrutinize, according to plantsman Pierre Bennerup. If you have slugs, as I do, you will not be able to grow this plant because they find it irresistible. Native to: moist wooded areas from Ontario to Michigan, south to North Carolina.

Climbing Aster *(A. carolinianus)*

This native aster quietly twined its way through wild shrubs in a most unremarked way until it caught the attention of Nancy Goodwin, noted North Carolina plantswoman and former proprietor of the now-closed Montrose Nursery. At Montrose, the plant was never cut back; in my garden, however, I notice that its ends die back in winter and do need to be trimmed. Since the plant blooms on new wood, this is no problem, but it does mean that it might not get as tall in northern areas as it does farther south. And just what is its range? This plant is so new to cultivation that no one knows for sure. There might be some question about its bloom period as well. In my garden, it doesn't start to flower until late October, well past the late summer notation in several garden catalogs. Native to: coastal plains and swamps from southern North Carolina to Florida.

Tangerine Beauty *(Bignonia capreolata* 'Tangerine Beauty')

Described as a handsome vine for outdoor use in Bailey's 1914 edition of the CYCLOPEDIA OF HORTICULTURE, bignonia is finally getting some horticultural attention with the development of Tangerine Beauty. Perfect for wooden trellises or stone walls, it features a thick covering of shiny, dark green foliage and profuse flowers in late spring. Native to: Virginia to Illinois, south to Florida and east Texas.

Foliage: Green turning to yellow then red or purple in fall
Zones: 4–9

Allegheny Vine

Light: Part shade to shade
Height: 6 to 12 feet
Color: White to rosy pink
Bloom Period: Summer to frost
Zones: 5–8

Climbing Aster

Light: Sun to part shade
Height: 8 to 12 feet
Color: Fragrant pink flowers
Bloom Period: Late summer into fall
Zones: 6/7–9 (hardiness not fully established; may well survive farther north)

Tangerine Beauty

Light: Full sun to part shade
Height: 30 feet
Color: Peachy apricot flowers
Bloom Period: Late spring into early summer
Zones: 6–10

Trumpet Creeper

Light: Sun to part shade
Height: 20 to 35 feet
Color: Orange to scarlet
Bloom Period: All summer
Zones: 4–10

Balloon vines (Cardiospermum halicacabum) *are among the hardest-working plants in the garden. They flower and set seed in balloonlike capsules all summer to frost. This picture was taken in late September, just as the white, fluffy seedheads on groundsel bush* (Baccharis halimifolia) *are about to open.*

Trumpet Creeper *(Campsis radicans)*

This vigorous, colorful vine is great for covering trellises and arbors. While certainly easy to grow, it is not always easy to root out. If you don't want it popping up about your property, place it in a contained area or cut back new shoots whenever you see them. Besides providing lush thick foliage and summer-long displays of colorful flowers, this vine adds another dimension to a garden setting with the numerous hummingbirds that it attracts. Native to: New Jersey to Nebraska, south to Florida and Texas.

Balloon Vine *(Cardiospermum halicacabum)*

One of the fun things about writing a book such as this is that I get to try a lot of new plants. This is one of my favorite finds, ranking high with me because I successfully direct seeded it into my backyard (few plants have survived this ordeal). Its delicate green foliage obligingly

twined about our trellis fence and within two months the first of the tiny white flowers bloomed. And then the real bonus came: within two or three weeks, 1- to 2-inch green seedpods appeared and did indeed look like balloons. Soon many of these were dangling about, intermingling with the continued opening of more white flowers. If you're looking for a refined vine with visual interest, this one is hard to beat. Native to: Bermuda, Florida to Texas, Mexico.

American Bittersweet *(Celastrus scandens)*

This vine is bittersweet indeed. It is exceptionally hardy—tolerating air pollution, poor soil, and assorted other ills—and is spectacularly beautiful in the fall when its orange fruits open to reveal red coated seeds. For this reason, it is recommended as an easy care native by the Royal Botanical Gardens in Ontario, where cold winters keep it well behaved. Farther south, however, the bitterness associated with the vine becomes apparent as it runs rampant in warmer areas and often strangles the trees and shrubs on which it climbs. Hence this is a very good plant for some and a horrid one for others. Native to: Quebec south to North Carolina and New Mexico.

Clematis *(Clematis)*

At last count, this large genus had over two hundred species spread throughout the northern hemisphere. In general, they all like to have their roots protected from scorching sun and to be placed in good, loamy soil that is well drained and consistently moist in summer but not in winter (snow cover is fine as long as it drains quickly when melting). Most clematis appearing in gardens today are large-flowered cultivars developed from exotic species. American plants, not nearly as numerous as their Asian counterparts, tend to have small flowers but compensate for this with attractive seedheads. In the 1914 edition of his CYCLOPEDIA OF HORTICULTURE, L. H. Bailey recommended both blue jasmine and scarlet clematis for their pretty, bell-shaped flowers and the fact that they are easily grown in a variety of situations. I think today's gardeners would agree with this assessment. The three other varieties described below are also worthy of consideration. Since all bloom on new wood, they can be cut back anytime from fall through midspring; indeed, even if you forget this chore, they will still flower.

Balloon Vine

Light: Sun
Height: 8 to 10 feet
Color: Small white flowers; larger green balloon-like seedpods
Bloom Period: Plants direct seeded in May flower from July to frost; continually following seedpods age from warm green to decorative brown
Zones: Annual

American Bittersweet

Light: Sun to shade
Height: 20 feet
Color: Greenish yellow flowers; bright orange fruits
Bloom Period: Inconspicuous flowers in early summer; long-lasting fruits throughout fall
Zones: 3–9

❋

COLORFUL CLEMATIS

As do their Asian counterparts, North American clematises feature colorful flowers and clamber up shrubs and trellises. While the blossoms on these little-known plants are not as large as those on the exotics, they provide a charming effect in the garden. The following are recommended for both their attractiveness and ease of care by Susan G. Austin, one of the few nursery proprietors specializing in clematis. Austin not only writes and lectures widely about the genus, she also grows the plants she promotes, including those listed here. For a copy of her mail-order catalog, send a $3 check or money order to The Compleat Garden Clematis Nursery, 217 Argilla Road, Ipswich, Massachusetts 01938-2614.

Addison's Clematis *(C. addisonii)*. Purple red flowers in summer.
Blue Jasmine *(C. crispa)*. Bluish purple flowers with pale margins June through August.
Pitcher's Clematis *(C. pitcheri)*. Purplish blue flowers all summer.
Scarlet Clematis *(C. texensis)*. Red or purple red flowers summer to frost.
Virgin's Bower *(C. virginiana)*. Off-white flowers from mid July to late September.

Addison's Clematis

Light: Sun to part shade
Height: 3 to 8 feet
Color: Purple red
Bloom Period: Summer
Zones: 5–8

Blue Jasmine

Light: Sun to part shade
Height: 5 to 9 feet
Color: Bluish purple, pale at margins
Bloom Period: June to August
Zones: 6–9

Addison's Clematis *(C. addisonii [viorna])*. Covered with urn-shaped flowers in summer, this relatively diminutive clematis is a good candidate for small garden spaces. Clematis expert Susan G. Austin likes the creamy stamens and the distinctive, heart-shaped solitary leaves, which have a thick texture and bluish green color. Native to: West Virginia.

Blue Jasmine *(C. crispa)*. Also known as marsh clematis, which indicates its tolerance of damp situations, blue jasmine is one of the parents of the award-winning Betty Corning cultivar and has been grown in England for over 250 years. Its flaring, bell-shaped flowers are valued for both their color and fragrance. Native to: Virginia to Missouri, south to Florida and Texas.

Pitcher's Clematis *(C. pitcheri [simsii])*. One of the few clematis species to do well in the dry, hot climate of the Midwest, this plant features pitcher-shaped flowers that flare slightly and attractive seed clusters. Native to: southern Indiana to Nebraska, south to Tennessee and Texas.

Scarlet Clematis *(C. texensis).* Another clematis for hot, dry weather, this plant makes an excellent screen with its dense foliage; bears profuse numbers of nodding, bell-shaped flowers; and then tops off the garden year with feathery seedheads. However, according to clematis expert Susan G. Austin, there is a drawback: flower color from seed is often muddy and nondescript. Austin carefully controls production at her nursery so that only flowers with the most brilliant colors are offered; for this reason, her supply is often quite limited. Native to: Texas.

Virgin's Bower *(C. virginiana).* "This is a true monster," warns clematis expert Susan G. Austin. "It roots every time it touches the soil and once you have it, you can't get rid of it." Austin offers it through her catalog for that very reason—she can't eradicate it from her property. And it is, she admits, a great plant for extremely harsh growing environments that would look attractive when covered with its green foliage, numerous flowers, and fluffy fruits. Native to: Nova Scotia to Manitoba, south to Florida panhandle and Louisiana.

Fremontia *(Fremontodendron californicum* **X** *F. mexicanum* 'California Glory')

This is a handsome climbing shrub with dark green leaves and large, golden flowers. To me, it is odd that this native from the dry sunny Southwest should be so popular in England. Indeed, my only acquaintance with fremontia—heartily endorsed by noted British horticulturists Will Ingwersen and Graham Stuart Thomas—is admiring it on a late September brick wall in the garden of Amoret and Ralph Tanner near Reading. Though it is supposedly hardy only to zone 9, the Tanners report that winter temperatures in their area drop down to 5° below zero. "We place items of questionable tenderness," they report, "against walls, which act as radiators. And we never have prolonged low temperatures as in New England." In the United States, this plant is often rated difficult to propagate and transplant. In England, however, nursery people easily reproduce it from tip cuttings taken in early summer and have no trouble placing the container-grown plants in

Pitcher's Clematis

Light: Sun to part shade
Height: 6 to 10 feet
Color: Purplish blue with darker interiors and yellow stamens
Bloom Period: Summer
Zones: 4–8

Scarlet Clematis

Light: Sun to part shade
Height: 6 to 15 feet
Color: Red, purple
Bloom Period: Midsummer to frost
Zones: 5–9

Virgin's Bower

Light: Sun to part shade
Height: 10 to 20 feet
Color: Dull white
Bloom Period: Mid July to late September
Zones: 4–8

Fremontia

Light: Sun to part shade
Height: 15 to 20 feet
Color: Golden yellow
Bloom Period: All spring in California; all summer in Great Britain
Zones: 9–10; worth trying in protected areas farther north

Cypress Vine

Light: Sun to part shade
Height: 10 to 20 feet
Color: Crimson red; white
  cultivar sometimes
  offered
Bloom Period: August to
  October
Zones: 8–10; annual else-
  where

Morning Glory

Light: Sun to part shade
Height: 12 feet
Color: Blue, white, ruby,
  or crimson rose
Bloom Period: About two
  months after seeding to
  frost
Zones: Annual

Trumpet Honeysuckle

Light: Sun to dappled
  shade
Height: 12 to 20 feet
Color: Red, orange, or
  yellow
Bloom Period: Heavy
  bloom for five weeks in
  early summer; sporadic
  rebloom until frost
Zones: 4–9

gardens the following year. The key to survival outside its native area is not so much dryness (England is much too wet) but excellent drainage. Native to: California to western Arizona and Baja California. *(Pictured on page 7)*

Ipomea *(Ipomea)*

The vagaries of botanical classification are exemplified in this genus. To the uneducated eye, there is absolutely no resemblance between the following two species except for the fact that both are twiners that easily scramble up shrubs and trellises.

Cypress Vine *(I. quamoclit).* Cypress vine has an elegant, almost fernlike foliage that clearly distinguishes it from morning glories. This foliage alone makes a handsome screen or shrub decoration. While the tubular flowers are much smaller than morning glories, they stand out with the brilliancy of their red color. Supposedly originating in the tropical part of Mexico and Central America, cypress vine has spread steadily northward and is now naturalized throughout the Southeast and into Texas. Native to: tropical Mexico.

Morning Glory *(I. tricolor).* Once used in Aztec religious ceremonies for its hallucinogenic properties, morning glory is now worshipped for its beautiful flowers, which twine about fences, telephone poles, street lamp posts, trellises, or shrubs. Heavenly Blue, discovered in the 1920s by amateur seedsavers, is probably the most popular cultivar; it lives up to its name with a sky blue color and a white neck inside. Pearly Gates, an AAS winner, is a popular all-white mutation. Crimson Rambler is actually misnamed; its flowers are more a ruby color. Native to: Mexico.

Trumpet Honeysuckle *(Lonicera sempervirens)*

Covered with colorful flowers in summer, this carefree native vine also features long-lasting fruits that attract many birds, including hummingbirds. It's an old-fashioned plant, one that was grown by George Washington at Mt. Vernon. Aphids have discovered it in modern times, however. If these pests plague your garden, plant the trumpet honeysuckle in a shaded area; aphids generally do not appreciate the coolness of such a setting. Alabama Crimson is a beautiful, consistent red; yellow fans will want the soft yellow flowers of Sulphurea. Native to: Connecticut south to Florida and Texas. *(Pictured on page 109)*

Climbing Hempweed *(Mikania scandens)*

This fragrant, end-of-summer vine is a recommendation of Sue Vrooman of the Atlanta History Center, who describes it as follows: "My plants grow up through shrubs by loosely twining around their trunks and branches. Once they reach the top, they spread out and bloom. The beautifully fragrant clusters of tiny white flowers, often with a pink blush, remind me of seafoam and are produced over a long period in late summer and fall. I think this would be a great vine for fences or trellises, particularly those on seashores as it resists salt spray. My plants seem unbothered by pests and do not seed around." Climbing hempweed was commercially unavailable at the time Vrooman wrote this description. To rectify this situation, she collected seed and sent it to Niche Gardens. Gardeners across the country owe her a big thanks for her generosity and time in ensuring climbing hempweed's entrance into commercial trade. Native to: salt marshes and wet dune hollows from Ontario through the Atlantic Coast to Florida, and west to Texas and Arkansas.

Mina *(M. lobata)*

This terrific vine is so little known that I decided to name it with its easily pronounced and readily identified genus name. Romantics might want to call it "Crimson Star-Glory" or "Exotic Love," names that are sometimes used in books and seed catalogs. Its handsome dense covering of green leaves alone would make it a desired vine for fences or trellises. By mid August, however, it becomes a star performer in the garden with a profuse bloom of what must rank as among the oddest of vine flowers: banana shaped, with up to four colors at the height of their maturity. They then shrivel up neatly and are followed by many more. Native to: Mexico. *(Pictured on page 188)*

Virginia Creeper *(Parthenocissus quinquefolia)*

Virginia creeper was one of the first plants sent back to Great Britain and now covers stone walls and buildings throughout that nation. It is

Climbing Hempweed

Light: Sun to part shade
Height: 10 feet
Color: Fragrant white to blush pink
Bloom Period: Late summer into fall
Zones: Not established. Native range is 6–8; may thrive in areas above and below these zones

Mina

Light: Sun
Height: 6 to 20 feet
Color: Unusual banana-shaped flowers start red, then age to orange, yellow, and finally white; both buds and mature flowers appear on same stem
Bloom Period: Late summer to frost when direct seeded in midspring
Zones: 10–11; annual elsewhere

Virginia Creeper

Light: Sun to shade
Height: 35 feet
Color: Inconspicuous whitish green flowers; pinkish to crimson red foliage
Bloom Period: Flowers, early summer; foliage, late summer into fall
Zones: 2–10

The fiery fall color of flowering dogwood (Cornus florida) *and highbush blueberries* (Vaccinium corymbusum) *is heightened by the dark green foliage and unusual, multicolored, banana-shaped flowers of mina* (M. lobata).

often featured in fall tourist promotion shots because of the beauty of its brilliant red foliage draped over old structures. Here in Princeton, New Jersey, my friend Owen Shteir uses Virginia creeper as a groundcover in his lovely wooded shade setting and lets it clamber over fallen trunks and scroll about large rocks. In such darkness, the plant is not as rampant as it is in full sun and its foliage turns a light pink. Native to: New England to Florida, eastern Minnesota to Texas.

SOURCES. Mail-order nurseries listed in the chapters on shrubs, annuals, and perennials also carry the above plants.

Chapter 9

Bulbs, Corms, and Tubers

The North American continent, so rich in woody ornamentals, offers a paucity of bulbous plants when compared with other areas of the world. And of the bulbous material available, little has been done to explore its horticultural potential. With the increased interest in American flora, however, this situation is changing. Several small West Coast nurseries and one or two Dutch bulb experts are doing breeding work on native lilies, fritillarias, and erythroniums. On the East Coast, allium expert Mark McDonough is working with a stunning selection of native allium species and cultivars. One can only hope that a greater range of these beautiful plants will soon be available. Currently, however, the following are offered commercially and are great easy care plants for gardens and landscapes.

Though in layperson language, these plants are all "bulbs"—that is, plants with underground food-storage capacities—botanists use distinct terms to differentiate among the kinds of food-storing mechanisms.

The creamy white flower stalks of great camass (C. leichtlinii 'Alba') stand tall in my mid May native plant border as the similarly colored buds on the wiry stems of the nearby prairie heuchera (H. richardsonii) are about to open. Blue Jacob's ladders (Polemonium reptans) and pink bleeding hearts (Dicentra eximia) add quiet color to this setting.

Magic Flower

Light: Light shade
Height: 15 inches
Color: Violet blue
Bloom Period: Summer
Zones: Annual

Nodding Onion

Light: Sun to part shade
Height: 7 to 24 inches
Color: Purplish pink to
  pink to pure white
Bloom Period: Early July to
  mid August
Zones: 4–8

Chives

Light: Sun to part shade
Height: 10 to 14 inches
Color: Purple pink
Bloom Period: Spring, with
  some sporadic rebloom-
  ing
Zones: 3–9

Prairie Onion

Light: Sun to part shade
Height: 10 to 18 inches
Color: Pink
Bloom Period: August
  through October
Zones: 4–9

True bulbs, such as camassias, tend to be round and to have their food stored in meaty scales. Corms, such as liatris, are flatter in shape and have their food stored in an enlarged basal plate. And tubers, such as jack-in-the-pulpits, are enlarged stems or root tissue and come in a variety of shapes. Though tubers are often classified as perennials, many are marketed through bulb catalogs and are thus included in this chapter.

Magic Flower (*Achimenes longiflora* 'Paul Arnold')

Bulb expert John E. Bryan recommends this container bulb as being one of the finest and longest flowering. Named for an *Achimenes* specialist from Binghamton, New York, it has stood the test of time with regard to ease of care and beauty. As with all magic flowers, it requires light shade and is absolutely stunning when placed in hanging baskets. Care is minimal: do not let them dry out, and spray with cold water to discourage red spiders or thrips. Native to: Mexico to Panama.

Flowering Onion (*Allium*)

This genus is one of my favorites. I like it because of its variety in flower color, size, shape, and season of bloom as well as for its ease of care. As a further bonus, insects and animal pests—including deer—avoid its members when they reach mature size (tiny, selfsown seedlings are sometimes eaten). Among the approximately one thousand species within this worldwide genus, the following are not only native Americans but also easy care.

Nodding Onion (*A. cernuum*). Widely distributed throughout the North American continent, nodding onions appear in many sizes and shapes. In my gardens, for example, I have nodding onions that vary in height from 7 to 24 inches; in color from purple pink to white; and in bloom period from early July to mid August. I really think you can't go wrong with any of form of this plant. Native to: well drained sites throughout North America from southern Canada to northern Mexico. *(Pictured on page 203)*

Chives (*A. schoenoprasum*). This circumboreal plant—found throughout cool areas in the northern hemisphere—can be grown in pots or borders and is widely offered at garden centers. Though it has long been used as a culinary herb, its ornamental qualities are now also coming to be admired. Native to: North America.

Prairie Onion *(A. stellatum).* This little-known prairie flower adds freshness to gardens toward the close of the growing season. While you may not admire it in early summer—its foliage is a bit ratty and often dormant in summer heat—you will certainly do so in late summer when its beautiful flowers open. Note that this plant does not do well in acidic soil; add lime if necessary. Prairie onion can be obtained through Forestfarm. Native to: central Canada to northern Mexico.

One-leafed Onion *(A. unifolium).* This lovely allium is topped with long-lasting pompons of delicate pink in late spring. It is really a pretty plant and—perhaps best of all—a very inexpensive one as well. Place it among groundcovers so that its subsequent dormant state will not be noticeable. Native to: coastal ranges of California.

Jack-in-the-Pulpit *(Arisaema triphyllum)*

This magnificent tuber requires a close relationship in order to be appreciated in spring. You need to bend over and peep under its cover of large, leafy foliage in order to see its exquisitely shaped flower. Come fall, however, you can stand tall while admiring the brilliant red berries, for they linger long after the foliage goes dormant. The berries selfseed and, over time, you should have quite a nice colony, which can be easily pulled out if it becomes too widespread. Plants are available from Prairie Nursery. Native to: New Brunswick and Nova Scotia to Minnesota, south to Florida and Texas.

Brodiaea *(Brodiaea [Triteleia])*

Though easy care and definitely attractive, this genus has yet to acquire a popular name. And, in another sense, it has yet to acquire a definite botanical name as botanists switch back and forth (with catalogs and garden centers following suit) between *Brodiaea* and *Triteleia*. At this writing, the following have been assigned to the *Brodiaea* genus.

White Brodiaea *(B. lactea [hyacinthia]).* This brodiaea is the first of the genus to bloom in my garden. Its white flowers, rising amidst a

One-leafed Onion
Light: Sun to part shade
Height: 12 to 18 inches
Color: Rose pink
Bloom Period: Late spring
Zones: Open to debate: some say hardy only to 8 and others zone 5; it has survived for three years in a protected area in my southern zone 6 garden, and, given its native area, should be fine at least from there to zone 9.

Jack-in-the-Pulpit
Light: Shade
Height: 12 to 30 inches
Color: Light green flowers, often magnificently striped with purple, protect the "jack" inside; scarlet berries
Bloom Period: Flowers, spring; berries, late summer into fall
Zones: 4–9

White Brodiaea
Light: Sun
Height: 18 inches
Color: Milky white
Bloom Period: Late spring
Zones: Not completely established; definitely 6–8

Blue Brodiaea

Light: Sun
Height: 20 to 24 inches;
  Queen Fabiola, 10 to 12
  inches
Color: Deep blue
Bloom Period: Early sum-
  mer
Zones: 5–10

Cusick Camass

Light: Sun to part shade
Height: 18 to 30 inches
Color: Pale blue
Bloom Period: Midspring
Zones: 3–8

Great Camass

Light: Sun to part shade
Height: 24 to 38 inches
Color: Lavender blue,
  blue; cultivars in creamy
  white
Bloom Period: Midspring
Zones: 5–9

planting of pink native bleeding hearts, are quite lovely and trouble-free for up to three weeks in late spring. The flowers resemble those of an allium and are long-lasting in arrangements. Native to: Idaho to British Columbia, south to Nevada and California.

Blue Brodiaea *(B. laxa).* With the introduction of Queen Fabiola, this corm has become a popular offering. Since its leaves are unattractive and then go dormant after flowering, I have it planted among the wispy foliage of Moonbeam coreopsis. The early summer combination of sky blue and pale yellow is just lovely. In competing with the coreopsis roots, however, the clumps do not get as thick as I have seen them elsewhere. Native to: southwest Oregon to southern California.

Camassia *(Camassia)*

These wonderful, widely adaptable West Coast bulbs can be grown throughout much of the country. The flower spikes of the cusick and great camass stand tall in spring borders and need not be staked. In my garden, these two bulbs bloom sequentially and are then followed by the striking semidouble form Semiplena. This gives me a solid month of stunning flowers and lots of admiring comments from passersby. The common camass, on the other hand, is shorter and flops but redeems itself with its more floriferous bloom.

Cusick Camass *(C. cusickii).* The spikes on this bulb are a bit shorter and bloom earlier than those on the great camass. Bulb expert John E. Bryan, who highly recommends them, says they make great cut flowers. Native to: northeast Oregon.

Great Camass *(C. leichtlinii).* This is probably the most widely bred camass. Throughout the Pacific northwest, it decorates meadows and woodland edges with spikes of violet or dark blue flowers in late spring. According to Robert T. Ogilvie, curator of botany at the Royal British Columbia Museum, white forms occur naturally at a rate of about 1 in 10,000 plants. Breeders, however, have located these highly recessive color genes and have developed two popular white-flowered cultivars: Alba, as its name implies, has creamy white flowers; Semiplena, which has just recently entered commercial trade, has similarly colored flowers but in a semidouble form. Native to: British Columbia to California. *(Pictured on page 189)*

Common Camass (C. quamash). In contrast to the above two species, the flowers on this bulb tend to sprawl. They are exceptionally easy to grow, however, and increase at a faster rate. I have clumps placed near the front of a border and pair them with the beautiful foliage of Montrose Ruby heuchera. Native to: southern Alberta to southern British Columbia, south to western Montana and northern Oregon. *(Pictured on page 254)*

Soap Plant *(Chlorogalum pomeridianum)*

I admit, given the criteria I've set for inclusion in this book, that soap plant should not be listed. Authors, however, are free to break their rules and that's what I've done here because this plant has an interesting history and was grown in gardens at the beginning of this century. According to Bailey's 1914 CYCLOPEDIA OF HORTICULTURE, this is an easy care bulb, one that is closely related to camassia. Its species name reflects the fact that it bears numerous, starlike white flowers in the afternoon (post meridian); its common name comes from the bulb being used by Indians and Mexicans for making soap. I obtained my plants from Forestfarm in the fall and, at this writing, they have come through two winters. While the foliage is a nice blue green and—unlike the camassias—has not gone dormant, there has yet to appear one flower. I'm willing to be patient with this one and you may be too. Native to: southern Oregon to southern California.

Spring Beauty *(Claytonia virginica)*

This is such a common roadside, meadow, and woodland plant that few recognize its garden potential. Its lovely blush pink flowers, each inwardly etched with dark pink stripes, are perfect for bare areas in early spring gardens. As later-blooming plants emerge, these obliging corms go dormant and remain undetected until the following spring. Though the diminutive flowers will decorate sunny spots in spring, they must be located in areas that receive shade in summer; this shade can be provided by the protective covering of large-foliaged plants baking in full sun or by nearby trees or shrubs. Sunlight Gardens offers

---

Common Camass

Light: Sun to part shade
Height: 1 to 2 feet
Color: Blue, violet blue, white
Bloom Period: Late spring
Zones: 3–8

Soap Plant

Light: Sun
Height: 2 to 6 feet
Color: White
Bloom Period: Summer
Zones: 6–9

Spring Beauty

Light: Sun to shade in spring; part shade to shade thereafter
Height: 3 to 6 inches
Color: Blush pink veined with dark pink
Bloom Period: Spring
Zone: 3–8

❁

BEAUTIFUL BULBS

The following North American natives are recommended for their beauty and ease of culture by world-renowned bulb expert John E. Bryan, the only American to be elected a Fellow of the Institute of Horticulture in London, and president of the Sausalito, California, horticultural consulting firm John E. Bryan, Inc. Whether you garden on the East Coast or the West Coast, on a patio, a sunny open area, or a shady woodland, there is at least one bulb here for you. Further information and colored photographs of these plants appear in the Burpee expert gardener series book JOHN E. BRYAN ON BULBS (Macmillan).

Magic Flower *(Achimenes longiflora* 'Paul Arnold'*)*. Violet blue flowers all summer.
Queen Fabiola *(Brodiaea laxa* 'Queen Fabiola'*)*. Deep blue flowers in early summer.
Cusick Camass *(Camassia cusickii)*. Spikes of pale blue flowers in late spring.
Anemone-flowered Dahlia *(D.* 'Honey'*)*. Flowers comprised of bronze petals and golden yellow centers from midsummer to frost.
Single-flowered Dahlia *(D.* 'Siemen Doorenbosch'*)*. Light magenta flowers from midsummer to frost.
White Beauty Fawn Lily *(Erythronium revolutum* 'White Beauty'*)*. Large white flowers in early spring.
Pagoda Trout Lily *(Erythronium tuolumnense* 'Pagoda'*)*. Soft yellow flowers in spring.
Mt. Hood Fritillaria *(F. recurva* 'Mt. Hood'*)*. Scarlet flowers in spring.
Canada Lily *(L. canadense)*. Crimson-spotted lemon yellow flowers in summer.
Leopard Lily *(L. pardalinum)*. Brown-spotted orange red flowers in July.
Mexican Shell Flower *(Tigridia pavonia)*. White, yellow, orange, or red petals and densely spotted, usually purplish, centers in summer.

these wonderful spring ephermerals. Native to: moist woods and meadows from Nova Scotia to Minnesota, south to Georgia and Texas. *(Pictured on pages 51 and 197)*

Dahlia *(Dahlia)*

This elegant tuber is quite highly bred: over twenty thousand cultivars, grouped by flower shape and size, appear in the INTERNATIONAL REG-

ISTER OF DAHLIA NAMES. While noted bulb expert John E. Bryan thinks that all dahlias are great garden plants, he did select the following widely available cultivars for readers of this book. They are representative of two flower categories that have the easy care attribute of not needing to be staked. As with all dahlias, they should be planted in rich, well-drained soil and regularly watered. Should you wish to save them for the next garden year—a chore I never assign myself—you need to dig the tubers, clean them carefully, and then store them in builder's sand in a cool but not freezing area. Native to: hybrids of species found in Mexico and Central America.

Anemone-flowered Dahlia: 'Honey.' These dahlias have textured flowers and this particular one is bicolored as well. The wide bronze petals surround a densely packed golden yellow center.

Single-flowered Dahlia: 'Siemen Doorenbosch.' These plants bear a faint resemblance to coreopsis and are particularly floriferous. This cultivar has lovely light magenta flowers.

Dutchman's Breeches (*Dicentra cucullaria*)

These charming early spring tubers are in the same genus as bleeding hearts. They have small white flowers that are supposed to resemble the pantaloons on a Dutchman—hence the popular name—and blue green foliage that is dormant by summer. Though woodland natives, Dutchman's breeches dislike highly acidic soil and will not thrive where pine trees are present. Plants are available from Prairie Moon Nursery in limited quantities. Native to: Nova Scotia to North Carolina, west to Kansas. *(Pictured on page 196)*

Ookow (*Dichelostemma congestum [Brodiaea pulchella]*)

Though this West Coast bulb was brought into cultivation as early as 1806, it is difficult to find any current praise for its unassuming yet exceptionally easy care attributes. Its purplish blue flowers top slim stems in late spring in my garden and look quite pretty bobbing among pink bleeding hearts. They are also attractive, long-lasting additions to cut flower arrangements. Native to: grassy places and scrub from Washington to central California.

Dahlias

Light: Sun
Height: 18 inches
Bloom Period: Midsummer to frost
Zones: 9–11; annual elsewhere

Dutchman's Breeches

Light: Part shade to shade
Height: 8 to 12 inches
Color: White
Bloom Period: Spring
Zones: 3–8

Ookow

Light: Sun
Height: 18 to 24 inches
Color: Purplish blue
Bloom Period: Late spring to early summer, depending on location
Zones: Not established; at least 6–9

In late April, a clump of Dutchman's breeches (Dicentra cucullaria) are backed by glistening white bloodroot flowers (Sanguinaria canadensis) at Garden in the Woods in Massachusetts.

Giant Fawn Lily

Light: Part shade to shade
Height: 12 inches
Color: Lage white petals with broad yellow band at inside base
Bloom Period: Early spring
Zones: 5–8

Coast Fawn Lily

Light: Part shade to shade
Height: 7 to 12 inches
Color: Pink or lavender; cultivars in white or rose
Bloom Period: Early spring
Zones: 3–8

Fawn Lily *(Erythronium)*

These superb corms are not only pretty but also rodent-proof. What more could low-maintenance gardeners ask for? Fawn lilies do, however, like the moisture that April showers bring and if rainfall should be absent at this time of year, you'll need to step in and water frequently during this month. Put away your watering can or hose afterward if you have planted them in well-drained woodland soil; in this environment, they can take dryness the remainder of the year.

Giant Fawn Lily *(E. oregonum)*. This beautiful plant is recommended by the Leach Botanical Garden in Portland, Oregon. It is one of the harbingers of spring and is lovely emerging in settings that are just starting to acquire greenery. Giant fawn lily can be obtained through Plants of the Wild. Native to: British Columbia to southwestern Oregon.

Coast Fawn Lily *(E. revolutum)*. Another early spring bloomer recommended by the Leach Botanical Garden in Portland, Oregon, this corm features lovely pink or lavender flowers. Breeders have been busy teasing other colors out of the plant's genes and one resulting cultivar,

The flaring yellow flowers of Pagoda trout lily (E. tuolumnense 'Pagoda') arise from bulbs that were divided and replanted the previous fall. In another five years, they will be divided again. By then, the tiny white spring beauty (Claytonia virginica) in the bottom left corner should have multiplied and spread. Virginia bluebells (Mertensia virginica) hover over this mid April setting and the dainty white flowers in the background are rue anemones (Anemonella thalictroides).

Pagoda Trout Lily

Light: Part shade to shade
Height: 7 to 8 inches;
  species to 12 inches
Color: Soft yellow; species,
  golden yellow
Bloom Period: Spring
Zones: 4–8

White Beauty, is recommended as a fine form by bulb expert John E. Bryan. Native to: Vancouver Island to northern California.

Pagoda Trout Lily *(E. **tuolumnense** 'Pagoda').* This is one of my favorite early spring bulbs. It has flared blossoms that look like minature lilies and handsome, lightly speckled foliage that goes dormant without suffering the lingering agonies so visible with daffodil leaves. After three or four years, you can divide the clumps, as I did, and cheaply increase the supply on your property. Dutch bulbman Frans M. Roozen prefers the species plant, which is taller and has deeper yellow flowers. Native to: species found at base of Sierra Nevada mountains in eastern California.

Fritillaria *(Fritillaria)*

The North American members of this genus all hail from the northwest and generally require growing conditions found in this area of the world: moist winters and springs and a good two months of dry, baking sun. There is also one other essential growing requirement: excellent drainage.

As an East Coast gardener, I have only been able to grow Martha

Martha Roderick

Light: Sun to part shade
Height: 8 to 12 inches
Color: Purplish flowers
  edged in cream
Bloom Period: Spring
Zones: 3–8

Black Lily

Light: Shade
Height: 9 to 18 inches
Color: Dark maroon to
  black
Bloom Period: Midspring
  in warmer areas; mid-
  summer in Alaska
Zones: 4–9

Checker Lily

Light: Sun to part shade
Height: 12 to 20 inches
Color: Checkered purple
  and greenish yellow
Bloom Period: Spring
Zones: 6–9

Scarlet Fritillaria

Light: Dappled shade
Height: 3 feet
Color: Scarlet, checkered
  with yellow inside and
  tinged with purple out-
  side; Mt. Hood, intense
  scarlet
Bloom Period: Spring
Zones: 5–9

Roderick and the checker lily. The scarlet fritillaria is just now being widely propagated and according to bulb expert John E. Bryan this beautiful plant should be suitable for my gardens; I eagerly look forward to planting it. And then there is the black lily—the name alone is enticing and, as you will see from the material below, so too is the description of the flower. I've tried it once and failed but will give it at least two more fall plantings; according to Dutch bulbman Frans M. Roozen, this is an easy care bulb once established.

Martha Roderick *(F. biflora [roderickii] 'Martha Roderick')*. This charming little flower is also sold as Mission Bells. Whatever it's called, it has proven a stalwart performer in my garden. Take care placing it, however, as its diminutive size and muted coloring can get lost among the lushness of other spring plants. Native to: southern Oregon to northern California.

Black Lily *(F. camschatcensis)*. Unlike the other fritillarias listed here, the elegant black lily requires moisture throughout the year. When given such a situation, plus woodsy soil rich in organic matter, it will reward you with maroon purple to black flower bells that dangle from slightly arching stems. Native to: Alaska to Oregon.

Checker Lily *(F. lanceolata)*. To me, this fritillaria is the American equivalent of the guinea-hen fritillaria that is so often seen naturalized with daffodils in England. While I have not been growing checker lily long enough to see if it will naturalize in my garden, I would be pleased if it did so. Native to: Idaho to British Columbia, south to northern California.

Scarlet Fritillaria *(F. recurva)*. Bulb expert John E. Bryan considers this the best species in the genus and—good news for gardeners outside its West Coast habitat—one that would do well in many areas of the country. He says the plant's striking flowers and clean, whorled foliage are not only beautiful but also very reliable. He especially recommends Mt. Hood because of the intensity of its scarlet coloring. Native to: dry hillsides, brush, and woods from southern Oregon through northern California to northwest Nevada.

Liatris *(Liatris)*

Though sold as a perennial, this prairie native is actually a corm and, as such, is included in this chapter. Within the past two decades, the Dutch have discovered the cut flower qualities of its long-lasting flower spikes and have contract growers in Africa and Europe producing staggering quantities for both formal and informal arrangements. You may want to try one or more in your borders as well as in your vases. Liatris species and cultivars are sold by many retail centers and mail order firms. Except where noted, Praire Nursery offers all of the following.

Rough Blazingstar *(L. aspera)*. Though this is a short-lived plant in my garden—rarely surviving more than two years—it contributes spectacular looks during the time it does spend there. In contrast to many other liatris species, this one has puffs of exotic pinkish purple flowers that decorate elegant spikes. Native to: southern Ontario to South Dakota, south to South Carolina and Texas. *(Pictured on page 223)*

Meadow Blazingstar *(L. ligulistylis)*. One of Neil Diboll's favorite late-season plants in his Wisconsin landscape, this liatris is unsurpassed for attracting monarch butterflies. Even without these beautiful creatures hovering about, it is a handsome plant with crimson red buds and profuse purple flowers. Native to: Wisconsin to Alberta, south to Colorado and northern New Mexico.

Dwarf Liatris *(L. microcephala)*. This is one of the easy care natives grown in the outcrop setting at the Atlanta History Center. It forms clumps of fine grassy foliage and bears numerous flower spikes. This plant is offered by Crownsville Nursery. Native to: southern Appalachians.

Kansas Gayfeather *(L. pycnostachya)*. This tough, adaptable native can be found in moist prairies, many wildflower landscapes, and miles of roadside plantings installed by the Iowa Department of Transportation. Its flowers' spikes are dramatic—up to 2 feet in length—and tend to tumble in striking sculptural twists. Native to: moist sites from Indiana to South Dakota, south to Florida and Texas. *(Pictured on page 57)*

Rough Blazingstar

Light: Sun
Height: 3 to 6 feet
Color: Pinkish purple
Bloom Period: Late summer
Zones: 4–8

Meadow Blazingstar

Light: Sun
Height: 30 to 36 inches
Color: Crimson red buds open to brilliant purple flowers
Bloom Period: July and August
Zones: 3–8

Dwarf Liatris

Light: Sun
Height: 18 to 24 inches
Color: Rosy purple
Bloom Period: Late summer into fall
Zones: Not established; at least 6–8

Kansas Gayfeather

Light: Sun
Height: 3 to 4 feet
Color: Purple
Bloom Period: Summer
Zones: 3–10

A DUTCH BULBMAN'S FAVORITES

As technical director of the Dutch bulb industry's promotional institute, Internationaal Bloembollen Centrum, Frans M. Roozen travels throughout the world promoting and studying bulbous plants. The following are among his favorite North American natives—all beautiful, all easy care, and all being propagated by Dutch growers.

Nodding Onion *(Allium cernuum)*. Sprays of white, pink, rose, or lilac flowers in summer.

Queen Fabiola *(Brodiaea laxa* 'Queen Fabiola'*)*. Deep blue flowers in early summer.

Cusick Camass *(Camassia cusickii)*. Spikes of pale blue flowers in late spring.

Great Camass *(Camassia leichtlinii)*. Tall spikes of violet or dark blue flowers in late spring.

Ookow *(Dichelostemma congestum)*. Purplish blue flowers late spring to early summer, depending on location.

Coast Fawn Lily *(Erythronium revolutum)*. Deep pink flowers and mottled leaves in early spring.

Trout Lily *(Erythronium tuolumnense)*. Golden yellow flowers in spring.

Martha Roderick Fritillaria *(F. biflora* 'Martha Roderick'*)*. Brownish flowers edged in cream in spring.

Black Lily *(Fritillaria camschatcensis)*. Maroon purple to black flower bells midspring to midsummer, depending on location.

Gayfeather *(Liatris spicata)*. Lavender pink flower spikes in summer.

Mexican Shell Flower *(Tigridia pavonia)*. White, yellow, orange, or red petals and densely spotted, usually purplish, centers in summer.

Tall Gayfeather

Light: Sun to part shade
Height: 3 to 4 feet
Color: Purple; cultivar in white
Bloom Period: Summer
Zones: 3–8

Dense Blazingstar

Light: Sun
Height: 2 to 5 feet

Tall Gayfeather (*L. scariosa*). I am really hard put to tell the difference between tall gayfeather and dense blazingstar. Supposedly the foliage on the former is a darker green. I have the White Spires cultivar, which has elegantly lived up to its name in my July gardens for five years without any help from me. You should be able to obtain this plant at your local garden center since it is offered through the wholesale firm Sunny Border Nurseries. Native to: mountains of southern Pennsylvania to South Carolina and northern Georgia.

Dense Blazingstar (*L. spicata*). Though this is among the tallest of the blazingstars in the wild, cultivated forms—particularly Kobold—

tend to be more compact. This does make for a neater plant, one that usually does not fall over. Native to: moist areas from Long Island to Michigan, south to Florida and Louisiana. *(Pictured on page 1)*

Lily *(Lilium)*

Dubbed the "aristocrats of the garden" by bulb expert John E. Bryan, lilies constitute a giant genus, literally and figuratively, among bulbous plants. There are close to a hundred species and breeders have crossed, backtracked, and tinkered with them to create thousands more hybrids. While most lilies prefer full sun, the following three native American bulbs actually do best in partially shaded situations. As with other members of the genus, plant them 6 to 8 inches deep in well-drained soil.

Canada Lily *(L. canadense).* One of the early plants shipped back to Europe by explorers, this bulb somehow never made a big hit despite the fact that its blossoms dangle like cheery little bells on an ornate candelabra. Now rarely grown in gardens on either side of the ocean, the colorful charms of this lily are highly recommended by John E. Bryan. To appreciate them fully, however, you must place the bulb in an appropriate situation—a cool location with consistently moist, heavily organic soil. Given its light requirements, the ideal spot would be one that receives early morning and late afternoon sun and bright shade during the height of the day. This hard-to-find bulb is offered by White Flower Farm. Native to: Nova Scotia to Minnesota, south to Virginia and Alabama.

Leopard Lily *(L. pardalinum).* This strikingly colored plant is exceptionally prolific, spreading by a rhizomelike growth on which new bulbs form; Wyman's Gardening Encyclopedia reports a colony of five hundred bulbs originating from just one leopard lily. While there is some question as to the parentage of Giganteum—is it a variety or is it a hybrid with another California native, *L. humboldtii?*—

Color: Purple
Bloom Period: Summer
Zones: 3–10

Canada Lily
Light: Part shade
Height: 3 to 6 feet
Color: Lemon yellow
  petals with crimson spots

In late June, my Princeton garden is aglow with the fluffy, intensely pink flowers of queen-of-the-prairie (Filipendula rubra) and the luminous red petals of leopard lily (Lilium pardalinum 'Giganteum').

Bloom Period: Summer
Zones: 3–8

Leopard Lily

Light: Sun to part shade
Height: 4 to 7 feet; Giganteum to 8 feet
Color: Orange red with numerous brown spots
Bloom Period: July
Zones: 4–8

Turk's Cap Lily

Light: Sun to part shade
Height: 6 to 10 feet
Color: Orange with maroon spots
Bloom Period: Midsummer
Zones: 4–8

Mexican Shell Flower

Light: Sun
Height: 18 to 20 inches
Color: White, yellow, orange, red petals and densely spotted usually purplish centers
Bloom Period: All summer
Zones: 9–10; annual elsewhere

all agree it is just as easy care as the species. Both prefer consistently moist but not waterlogged soil but are adaptable enough to flourish in ordinary garden situations as well. These West Coast bulbs are reputed to be short-lived on the East Coast, despite their tolerance of zone 4 winter temperatures. They are so beautiful, however, that I think they are worth planting if even for only one season. Mine have survived two winters at this writing and are increasing in number. I obtained my bulbs from Dr. Joseph C. Halinar. Native to: coastal ranges from southwest Oregon to southern California. *(Pictured on page 201)*

Turk's Cap Lily *(L. superbum).* Sometimes called Swamp Lily, which indicates where it is found and the constantly moist growing conditions it requires to thrive, this East Coast native is a literal standout in midsummer gardens. Its blazing orange colors are striking whether combined with meadow corms such as purple liatris or when emerging from summer green groundcovers such as foamflowers *(Tiarella)*. Plants are available from Prairie Nursery. Native to: wet areas from New Brunswick to Minnesota, south to Florida and Alabama.

Mexican Shell Flower *(Tigridia pavonia)*

These colorful annual bulbs brighten summer gardens for up to two months with their free-flowering blossoms. They are perfect for patio containers as well as mixed borders as long as they are given good drainage. In July or August, depending on the area where they are grown, the three-petaled flowers will begin to open and reveal their densely spotted centers. While the petal colors vary (and are usually offered in mixed selections), all look their best when placed against a dark background. Native to: Mexico and Guatemala.

SOURCES. Unless noted otherwise in a specific description, the above plants can be obtained from either The Daffodil Mart or McClure & Zimmerman. Addresses for all firms are given in the Appendix.

Chapter 10

Annuals and Biennials

Technically speaking, annuals are plants that complete their life cycle within one growing season: they germinate, flower, set seed, and then die. California poppies, marigolds, and zinnias all meet these specifications. In this book, however, an annual is any plant that does not overwinter in Princeton, New Jersey. Thus plants such as mealycup sage, which are perennial to zone 7, are discussed in this chapter and listed as hardy annuals in plant recommendation lists. Biennials, on the other hand, are usually on a two-year cycle. They set seed that germinates by the end of the first year; the small seedlings winter over and flower the following season. No matter what the classification, however, one or more of the following will add color and charm to your borders.

In early August, the annual flowers of pinkish blue ageratums (A. houstonianum), red cosmos (C. sulphureus), and white lisianthus (Eustoma grandiflorum) surround the delicate white sprays of nodding onion (Allium cernuum).

Light: Sun
Height: 3 feet
Color: Light purple, white
Bloom Period: All summer
Zones: Annual or biennial
that selfseeds to zone 3

Spikes of tall bellflower (Campanula americana) are covered with blue flowers throughout summer and can be found decorating both sun and bright shade borders throughout much of the North American continent.

Fragrant Hyssop *(Agastache foeniculum)*

Though sometimes described as a perennial hardy to zone 3, fragrant hyssop is best treated as a prolific selfseeding annual or biennial. I like this plant for its colorful spikes of flowers, alive with bees that quietly work their way among the fragrant blossoms and foliage. Native to: central North America. *(Pictured on page 209)*

Ageratum *(A. houstonianum)*

The compact, long-blooming mounds of this widely used annual are staples in bedding plant schemes. Look for Blue Danube, which is one of the best in the market and holder of a "highly commended" citation from the Royal Horticultural Society. Native to: central and southern Mexico. *(Pictured on pages 50 and 203)*

Tall Bellflower *(Campanula americana)*

Exemplifying its popular name, this plant forms a slim spire that stands erect in the garden. Clumps are very effective in formal garden settings and are equally attractive when found growing wild along country lanes. Though not well known in commercial circles, tall bellflower does have its fans and these tout its ability to thrive in either hot, dry roadside areas or cool, moist woodlands. They also describe the long-blooming flowers as a pure sky blue; perhaps this reflects conditions in unpolluted areas. Here in smoggy central New Jersey, the flowers are a pale blue. My only complaint about this plant is that it does not selfsow freely in my borders; all the literature says it does so elsewhere. Fortunately for me, and perhaps for you, the Wildwood Flower offers potted seedlings through the mail. Native to: moist woods from New York to Florida, west to Mississippi.

Partridge Pea *(Cassia fasciculata)*

One of the few American annuals native to zone 4 climates, this cheery, often selfsowing plant flourishes in sandy soils. The bright yellow flowers decorate the stems and appear amidst dark green, compound leaves. It tends to flop when left on its own and gratefully leans on other plants when their nearby support is provided. Native to: Maine to Florida, west to South Dakota, Texas, and Mexico.

Coreopsis *(Coreopsis)*

The following two annual members of the genus are exceptionally easy to grow and provide cheery splashes of color. Both have daisylike flowers and finely cut foliage.

Plains Coreopsis *(C. tinctoria).* One of the key and few authentically native ingredients in the "meadow-in-a-can" approach to gardening, this colorful annual is easily grown from seed and will decorate hillsides and sunny meadows throughout summer with its colorful flowers. If given bare ground, it will selfsow and return yearly. Native to: Minnesota to Saskatchewan and Washington, south to Louisiana and California.

Atlantic Coreopsis *(C. tripteris).* This tough, sturdy, reliable annual is determined to bloom in late summer no matter what. Leave it on its own and it will reach a towering height. Cut it down repeatedly—as roadside crews do throughout central New Jersey—and it will flower at a demure 1-foot height. Though a prolific selfseeder, it is very easily yanked out or smothered with mulch. For fresh, new, easy care yellow flowers in late summer gardens, this is hard to beat. Native to: Massachusetts through Ontario to Wisconsin, south to Georgia, Louisiana, and Kansas.

Harlequin Flower *(Corydalis sempervirens)*

Perceived wisdom holds that this is not a good garden flower; indeed, many view it as a pesky weed. And yet it is so pretty: blue green foliage, trailing habit, and tiny deep pink and yellow flowers for a long bloom period. While I have yet to work out a way to incorporate it effectively in a pastel-and-gray garden bed (it keeps selfseeding in the back and can't be seen from the front), I think the Thomas & Morgan seed catalog has come up with an excellent idea: grow it as a container

Ageratum

Light: Sun to part shade
Height: 5 to 30 inches
Color: Blue, purple, pink, or white
Bloom Period: Late spring through frost, if watered and deadheaded
Zones: Annual

Tall Bellflower

Light: Sun to bright shade
Height: 5 to 6 feet
Color: Blue
Bloom Period: Summer
Zones: Annual

Partridge Pea

Light: Sun
Height: 1 to 3 feet
Color: Yellow
Bloom Period: Summer to frost
Zones: Annual

Plains Coreopsis

Light: Sun
Height: 1 to 3 feet
Color: Yellow with dark red centers
Bloom Period: All summer
Zones: Annual

Atlantic Coreopsis

Light: Sun
Height: 7 to 9 feet; can be cut back to less than 1 foot
Color: Sunny yellow
Bloom Period: Late summer
Zones: Annual

Harlequin Flower

Light: Sun to part shade
Height: 2 feet
Color: Tiny deep pink and
yellow flowers on blue
green foliage

*In mid June, a tide of orange
California poppies* (Eschschol-
zia californica) *washes into the
pale yellow flowers of Missouri
primrose* (Oenothera missouriensis 'Lemon Court') *in one of
the spectacular gardens at Wave
Hill in New York City.*

plant, particularly a hanging one that will allow the draping, almost vinelike foliage to be seen at a better angle. Native to: Newfoundland to Georgia, west to Minnesota, Alaska, and British Columbia.

Cosmos *(Cosmos)*

The two garden members of this genus are strikingly different. The common cosmos is a tall plant with feathery foliage and lovely pastel flowers; the yellow cosmos is considerably shorter and has deeply cut leaves and fiery flower colors.

Common Cosmos *(C. bipinnatus).* Given its great ease of care, this has become a popular and beautiful highway planting flower in the Northeast. Tightly massed together and growing in full sun, the flowers present a lovely carpet of color to motorists driving by. In the home garden, particularly mine, these plants are not quite as pretty because they flop over if not staked. Thus, I was pleased to discover Sonata White, a dwarf

cultivar that won the Fleuroselect Award in Europe. This is one of the few flowers that I successfully direct seed. Native to: Mexico.

Yellow Cosmos *(C. sulphureus).* For summer red, orange, or yellow, this is a hard plant to beat. It has dark green, deeply cut foliage and cheerful flowers that just keep on coming as long as seedheads are pinched off. Cultivars, such as Ladybird Scarlet and AAS winner Sunny Red, eliminate any need for staking and thrive in summer heat and humidity. Native to: Mexico. *(Pictured on pages 53 and 203)*

Mexican Daisy *(Erigeron karvinskianus [mucronatus])*

Naturalized throughout Spain, this carefree plant spreads about on green, trailing stems and is great for rock gardens or dry stone walls. When placed in such settings, Mexican daisy selfseeds and comes back year after year. Given its dainty stature and quiet good looks, British horticulturist and author Will Ingwersen ranked it as a classic garden plant. I think you will too. Native to: Mexico.

California Poppy *(Eschscholzia californica)*

When I think of my San Francisco years, I often remember the delightful spring charm of a morning hillside bursting with these flowers. I admired not only the elegant blossoms but also the ferny, blue green foliage. When I seeded California poppies in my Princeton beds, they just never performed as well and I thought it must be the eastern climate. What a treat then, to see them blooming profusely among the sun-drenched rocks in Mary Stambaugh's Newtown, Connecticut, garden, where they selfsow with beautiful abandon. The secret, then, to having these colorful flowers in many areas of the continent is not so much climate as good drainage and lots of light. Native to: well-drained, sandy soils in California.

Poinsettia *(Euphorbia pulcherrima)*

The most widely sold flowering potted plant in the United States, poinsettia has long been a symbol of Christmas celebrations. Brought into cultivation in the 1830s by Joel Poinsett, our first ambassador to Mexico, poinsettias were grown as greenhouse plants until they fell into

Bloom Period: Spring into summer
Zones: Annual

Common Cosmos

Light: Sun
Height: 10 feet; cultivars to 20 inches or more
Color: White, light pink through deep magenta
Bloom Period: About two months from seeding to fall frost
Zones: Annual

Yellow Cosmos

Light: Sun
Height: 7 feet; cultivars to 2 feet or more
Color: Red, orange, yellow
Bloom Period: About two months from seeding through summer
Zones: Annual

Mexican Daisy

Light: Sun
Height: 4 to 6 inches
Color: Tiny white daisy-like flowers fade to pink
Bloom Period: Late spring to frost
Zones: 7–10; annual elsewhere

California Poppy

Light: Sun
Height: 8 to 24 inches
Color: Primarily orange; cultivars in cream, yellow, pink, or red

Bloom Period: Spring into
summer
Zones: 8–10; annual elsewhere

Poinsettia

Light: Sun
Height: 2 to 12 feet
Color: Red, pink, white
Bloom Period: December
for species; up to 6
months for cultivars
Zones: 9–10; annual else-
where

Lisianthus

Light: Sun
Height: 10 to 36 inches
Color: White through pink
to purple blue
Bloom Period: Summer
Zones: Annual

Annual Gaillardia

Light: Sun
Height: 12 to 20 inches
Color: Bicolored with red
and yellow; single color
in red or yellow
Bloom Period: 9 to 12
weeks from seeding
through early fall frost
Zones: Annual

Texas Bluebonnet

Light: Sun
Height: 4 to 16 inches
Color: Blue
Bloom Period: Spring
Zones: 7–9; annual else-
where

the breeding hands of the Ecke family in southern California. In 1920, Paul Ecke developed the first cultivar that could be grown as an indoor potted plant and Christmas has never been the same since. Today, the many poinsettia cultivars are almost unrecognizable when compared with their native forebears: plants have been developed to hold their flowers for up to six months and to range in color from white through pink to red. Because my poinsettias so resolutely refuse to die under my policy of benign neglect, I often transplant them outdoors in June to serve as a green backdrop until killed by frost. Native to: Mexico.

Lisianthus (*Eustoma grandiflorum*)

A prairie pest transformed into an elegant container plant by Japanese breeders, this now well-bred biennial can be difficult in garden settings but is lovely when left in the pot in which it was bought. With a beautiful blue green foliage and flowers that are almost roselike in appearance, it is a handsome plant with a long bloom period if given the sunny, dry conditions of its prairie heritage. I have had mixed results; one year a white flower form was absolutely stunning in my native plant garden and the next year a blue one died about two weeks after transplanting. Native to: Colorado and Nebraska, south to Texas and northern Mexico. *(Pictured on page 203)*

Annual Gaillardia (*G. pulchella*)

Valued for its tolerance to blistering heat and drought, this brightly flowered, selfsowing annual is a standout in sunbleached gardens. AAS winner Red Plume was selected for its uniform dwarf habit, superior length of blooming season, and beautiful, rounded, double brick red flowers. In addition, Red Plume appears immune to most diseases and insects. To be most effective in a garden setting, AAS recommends planting this flower in groups of five or more. Native to: coastal Virginia to Florida; Missouri, Nebraska, and Colorado to New Mexico and Mexico.

Texas Bluebonnet (*Lupinus texensis*)

This is one of five species that are called Texas bluebonnets and collectively designated as the state flower of Texas. It is also a species that likes to stay at home, where it is an exceptionally beautiful, easy care plant that blankets open spaces with sheets of brilliant blues in spring. Elsewhere, however, this flower struggles. Native to: Texas.

Turk's Cap *(Malvaviscus arboreus var. drummondii)*

An old-fashioned plant, the small bright red flowers of this carefree native can be seen thriving under live oaks and magnolias in its native range. Both Denise Delaney of the National Wildflower Research Center in Texas and Sue Vrooman of the Atlanta History Center recommend it for home gardens as well. Vrooman cites Turk's cap for its long bloom period and ability to attract hummingbirds and butterflies. "My plants look like very full shrubs," she says, "and don't need staking." And once you obtain a Turk's cap, you can quickly pass it on since it transplants readily and is easily propagated by seed, cuttings, or division. Obtaining it, however, can be a problem for those outside its

Joyce Anderson's mixed border in Hopewell, New Jersey, contains a preponderance of native plants, including annuals such as short yellow zinnias and red gaillardias along the front edge and, in the middle, spiky fragrant hyssops (Agastache foeniculum). The large clump of perennial ageratums (Eupatorium coelestinum) had been in flower for over three weeks when this picture was taken on September 7. Though the blossoms appear to be lavender, this is a trick of the camera— human eyes view the color as a pale blue.

Turk's Cap

Light: Part shade
Height: 3 to 6 feet
Color: Red
Bloom Period: Midsummer
  to hard frost
Zones: 8–10; annual else-
  where

Purple Butterfly Mint

Light: Sun
Height: 1 to 2 feet
Color: Pale purple
Bloom Period: July to
  December
Zones: 7–9; annual else-
  where

Evening Primrose

Light: Sun to part shade
Height: 3 to 6 feet
Color: Clear yellow
Bloom Period: All summer
Zones: 4–9

Pavonia

Light: Sun to part shade
Height: 2 to 4 feet
Color: Pink
Bloom Period: Late spring
  to frost
Zones: Annual

native area as it is generally offered through local retail centers and not through the mail. Native to: woods and pinelands from Cuba through Florida to Texas and Mexico.

Purple Butterfly Mint *(Monardella antonina)*

Bearing balled clusters of flowers, these plants are eye-catching additions to the fronts of perennial beds. Penny A. Wilson of Las Pilitas Nursery in California thinks they are even more beautiful when decorated with the many colored butterflies that they continually attract. And there's more: the foliage is a lovely gray green and has a minty fragrance. Native to: central coasts of California.

Evening Primrose *(Oenothera biennis)*

Though many members of the *Oenothera* genus are called evening primrose, this is the real McCoy. Its fragrant, lovely yellow flowers can actually be seen unfolding at dusk or on cloudy days. Grethe B. Petersen of Denmark is among the many in her country who love the beauty of its blossoms on long Danish summer nights. Flower arrangers like its tall, dried stalks with interesting seedpods. Goldfinches feast on the tiny seeds. Pests and diseases completely avoid the plant. So it should not be too surprising that most American garden books currently describe this biennial as a weedy plant with little or no horticultural interest. Native to: eastern half of North America.

Pavonia *(P. lasiopetala)*

Denise Delaney of the National Wildflower Research Center in Texas recommends pavonia for home gardens because of its carefree nature and exceptionally long flowering period. Technically a shrub, it is a profuse selfseeder that features velvety green leaves and rich pink flowers resembling small versions of those on a hibiscus. In full sun, they open in the morning and close by afternoon; in part shade, the daily bloom period is often prolonged. This plant is available at garden centers throughout Texas. Native to: well-drained soils from southern Texas to Mexico. *(Pictured on page 33)*

✳

ALL-AMERICA SELECTIONS

All-America Selections (AAS) is an independent testing organization, founded in 1932, that evaluates new flowers and vegetables propagated from seed. Independent, volunteer judges scrutinize entries submitted by seed companies each year at AAS judging locations across the country. Plants deemed outstanding are designated as AAS winners and can be seen at over a hundred AAS Display Gardens throughout the United States and Canada, and bought as seed or bedding plants through catalogs or at local garden centers. For further information, write All-America Selections, 1311 Butterfield Road, Suite 310, Downers Grove, Illinois 60515.

AAS floral winners are chosen for their attractiveness, long blooming period, resistance to disease and insects, and ease of care in home gardens. In addition to meeting all these criteria, the following recently honored annuals are truly all-American in that they have been developed from plants native to the North American continent.

Sunny Red Cosmos *(C. sulphureus* 'Sunny Red'*)*. Dwarf habit and bright red flowers all summer under diverse weather conditions.

Red Plume Gaillardia *(G. pulchella* 'Red Plume'*)*. Dwarf habit and double brick red flowers over a long bloom period.

Indian Summer *(Rudbeckia hirta* 'Indian Summer'*)*. Exceptionally large black-eyed Susan flowers on bushy plants.

Lady in Red Salvia *(S. coccinea* 'Lady in Red'*)*. Dwarf habit and scarlet red flower spikes.

Strata Salvia *(S. farinacea* 'Strata'*)*. Bicolored white and blue flower spikes all summer.

Mandarin Orange *(Sanvitalia procumbens* 'Mandarin Orange'*)*. Creeper with semidouble, golden orange flowers throughout summer.

Golden Gate Marigold *(Tagetes patula* 'Golden Gate'*)*. Large mahogany flowers edged with gold.

Scarlet Splendor Zinnia *(Z. elegans* 'Scarlet Splendor'*)*. Large semiruffled red flowers on plants that need no staking.

Annual Phlox

Light: Sun
Height: 6 to 18 inches
Color: Red, pink, white, or purple
Bloom Period: 10 weeks from seeding to frost
Zones: Annual

Annual Black-eyed Susan

Light: Sun
Height: 36 to 40 inches
Color: Deep golden yellow with brown centers
Bloom Period: 10 to 14 weeks after seeding to early fall frost
Zones: Annual

Brown-eyed Susan

Light: Sun to part shade
Height: 3 feet
Color: Golden yellow with brown centers
Bloom Period: Late July through September
Zones: 4–9

Annual Phlox *(P. drummondii)*

Sometimes called Texas-pride, this colorful annual is consistently described in books as being easy to grow. It's great as a bedding plant and in containers. Two 6-inch cultivars, Dwarf Beauty Mixed and Dwarf Beauty Scarlet, have received Royal Horticultural Society awards. Unfortunately, for me, annual phlox is not available as a potted seedling at my local garden centers and needs to be direct seeded—an activity at which I am not very adept. Only one plant actually made it the year I tried to grow annual phlox and that experience was enough to discourage me from trying it again. Should I see it at a local garden center, however, I would buy it immediately to enjoy its colorful, long-blooming flowers. Native to: south central Texas.

Rudbeckia *(Rudbeckia)*

A North American genus, rudbeckias are noted for their easy care nature and profuse yellow flowers with dark centers. The following two biennials are sometimes classified as short-lived perennials. They often appear as long-lived perennials, however, since both make their stay in a garden permanent through selfseeding.

Annual Black-eyed Susan *(R. hirta)*. The golden yellow petals emanating from the dark brown disks of this black-eyed Susan populate sunny meadows through much of the eastern half of the continent. In gardens that are rather closed in, such as mine, summer humidity often leads to ugly mildew attacks. When this happens, I simply cut the plant to the ground. The 1995 AAS winner, Indian Summer, has the largest flowers yet seen on this species and branching, bushy plants that neither flop nor need to be staked. Native to: Massachusetts to Illinois, south to Georgia and Alabama. *(Pictured on page 64)*

Brown-eyed Susan *(R. triloba)*. "I love this plant," declares Sue Vrooman of the Atlanta History Center. "In groups, its bright golden yellow flowers look like pools of sunlight. Most of its selfsown seedlings appear within a cozy distance of parent plants rather than romping off across the garden—and they're very easy to pull out if you don't want them." While brown-eyed Susans flower prolifically in sun or part shade, they tend to flop in the latter situation. Vrooman places them in front of a border in her shady quarry garden and because they flop gracefully, "I let them go—just cutting off awkward flower spikes when they truly offend me." Native to: moist areas from southern New England to Minnesota, south to Georgia, Louisiana, and Texas.

Salvia *(Salvia)*

Salvia is a huge genus, with over 750 species of annuals, perennials, or shrubs found throughout the world. Many of these are aromatic; indeed the culinary sage is a member. The following North American annuals, however, are grown for their looks and ease of care rather than their flavor.

Texas Sage *(S. coccinea).* Prized for its ability to withstand heat and drought, Texas sage has attracted the attention of breeders in recent years. Lady in Red, for example, is a 1992 AAS selection and features an extended bloom period and a shorter stature, which keeps it from being knocked down in strong winds. As with most salvias, it has spikes of flowers; though not as glaring red as the species, they remain attractive to hummingbirds. Cherry Blossom represents a color break-through because its spikes are a white and salmon pink combination; it too is shorter than the species, which normally reaches 4 feet. Native to: South Carolina to Florida, west to Texas and Mexico. *(Lady in Red pictured on page 244)*

Mealycup Sage *(S. farinacea).* The slim, floriferous spikes of this hardy annual are increasingly seen in gardens, particularly the rich blue of the cultivar Victoria or the dusky white of Victoria White. The 1995 AAS winner, Strata, straddles these two cultivars with striking bicolored white and blue flower spikes. All have nice silvery green foliage, bloom continuously throughout summer, and can be cut repeatedly for flower arrangements. Native to: New Mexico and Texas. *(Pictured on pages 50 and 53)*

Autumn Sage *(S. greggii).* In its native haunts, this shrubby plant blooms from spring through frost and can be found in perennial beds or as colorful, clipped hedges. In northern areas, it is valued for the fresh late summer flowers that give it its popular name. In any area, autumn sage is great in patio pots. Native to: Texas and Mexico. *(Pictured on page 19)*

Texas Sage

Light: Sun
Height: 18 to 48 inches
Color: Scarlet; Cherry Blossom cultivar salmon pink and white
Bloom Period: 12 to 14 weeks from seeding through summer
Zones: 8–10; annual elsewhere

Mealycup Sage

Light: Sun
Height: 18 to 36 inches
Color: Blue; cultivars in dusky white, bicolored blue and white
Bloom Period: Summer to frost
Zones: 7–10; annual elsewhere

Autumn Sage

Light: Sun to part shade
Height: 2 to 3 feet
Color: Red; cultivars in coral, pink, or white
Bloom Period: Late spring to frost
Zones: 8–10; annual elsewhere

Gentian Sage

Light: Sun to part shade
Height: 18 to 30 inches
Color: Azure blue
Bloom Period: Late summer until frost
Zones: 9–10; annual elsewhere

Hummingbird Sage

Light: Sun to open shade
Height: 1 to 2 feet
Color: Magenta
Bloom Period: Summer
Zones: 7–10; annual elsewhere

Sanvitalia

Light: Sun
Height: 5 to 6 inches
Color: Yellow, with dark brown centers; cultivars in golden orange
Bloom Period: 10 to 12 weeks from seeding to early fall frost
Zones: Annual

Marigold

Light: Sun
Height: 8 to 36 inches
Color: Cream white, yellow, orange, or red; many bicolored
Bloom Period: Summer
Zones: Annual

Gentian Sage *(S. patens).* Used by Beatrix Farrand in her landscape designs for Maine estates in the 1920s and 1930s, this annual has recently been reintroduced to gardens through the catalog of White Flower Farm. The copy describing this flower unconsciously reflects that firm's northwest Connecticut base: there it starts to bloom in late July. Here in Princeton, where we often have weeks of humid, 90° readings, this cool temperature plant refuses to put forth one blossom until the end of September. Undoubtedly easy care, it does require patience to appreciate its blue beauty in warm summer areas. Native to: mountains of Mexico.

Hummingbird Sage *(S. spathacea).* Both hummingbirds and passersby adore the summer spikes of deep magenta flowers on this striking plant. On its own, it grows in the dry shade found under live oaks as well as in baked clay by roadsides. In either area, deer avoid the plant. While it can survive with only 15 inches of annual rainfall, it much prefers a minimum of 20. This California native is readily available at retail centers in its home state. Native to: California coast from Napa to Orange counties.

Sanvitalia *(S. procumbens)*

Forming a spreading carpet of dark green and crowned with blossoms resembling miniature sunflowers, this is an exceptionally carefree annual. Mandarin Orange, with blooms that are a golden orange, won both the 1987 AAS award and praise from noted plantsman Allan Armitage of the University of Georgia, who said: "There have been no insect or disease problems; the plants held up in the rain, heat, and humidity. We found sanvitalia to be a very reliable, low maintenance bedding plant for the Southeast." Container gardeners across the country will also appreciate the trailing habit of this colorful plant—it is perfect for hanging baskets or patio urns. Native to: Mexico and Guatemala.

Marigold *(Tagetes)*

Marigolds, I should admit at the start, are not my favorite flower. I will concede, however, that when slugs are not around to devour them overnight, they are an easy care plant. Most of what seems like hundreds of marigolds sold commercially are descended from two species: *T. erecta,* the African marigold, and *T. patula,* the French marigold. How they acquired their popular names is strange, because both plants are native to Mexico. In general, the African marigold is the taller of the two and has larger, often pomponlike flowers. The late David Burpee loved both members of the genus and under his leadership the company that still bears his name produced many award winning cultivars. One of these—First Lady—received an AAS award over twenty-five years ago and, with round masses of clear yellow flowers, has been a top seller ever since its introduction. In recent years, breeders have tapped the potential of yet another Mexican marigold, *T. signata,* and created a line called signet marigolds; these are only 8 inches high and have feathery, lemon-scented foliage. For further information on the many flowers and forms within this genus, contact Marigold Society of America, Inc., P.O. Box 5112, New Britain, Pennsylvania 18901. Native to: Mexico.

Rose Verbena *(V. canadensis)*

Though rose verbena is winter hardy in a large area of the continent, it can't take the soggy soils resulting from snow melt; this is one of the reasons why it is usually grown as an annual. Scott Woodbury, however, grows a local genotype of this plant in a dry shade setting at the Shaw Arboretum and he reports that his rose verbena is a very reliable perennial. I couldn't even grow it as an annual, however, until Allan Armitage and Michael Dirr, two prominent University of Georgia horticulturists, discovered Homestead Purple on a drive through the Georgia countryside. While all my other rose verbenas were lost to humidity or spider mites by early July, this one bloomed straight through summer (its classification is still open at this writing; so perhaps it is not a form of *V. canadensis*). If Homestead Purple doesn't survive this coming winter, I will gladly buy more plants next spring. Native to: Virginia to Florida, west to Iowa, Colorado, and Mexico. *(Homestead Purple pictured on pages 52 and 53)*

Zinnia *(Zinnia)*

While I love seeing cheery summer arrangements of zinnias, I do not enjoy seeing the plants decked with mildew in humid Princeton set-

Rose Verbena

Light: Sun to bright shade
Height: 6 to 18 inches
Color: Purple, red, pink
Bloom Period: Summer, often into early fall
Zones: 6–10; generally treated as annual in most of country

Zinnia

Light: Sun
Height: 4 to 36 inches
Color: All but blue
Bloom Period: 6 to 8 weeks from seeding to early fall frost
Zones: Annual

tings. My thoughts on this matter are obviously irrelevant to the floral trade because zinnias are among the most popular annuals sold in the country. Amenable to tinkering, they come in all sizes, shapes, and colors, with the exception of blue. Scarlet Splendor, a 1990 AAS winner, does not need to be staked and needs less garden space and less care than other large-flowered zinnias. Its flowers are semiruffled and form a beautiful low hedge when planted in a row. Native to: Mexico.

SOURCES. Unless otherwise mentioned under an individual plant description, seed for all of the above can be obtained from one or more of the following: Burpee, Native American Seed, Pinetree, Prairie Moon Nursery, Shepherd's, and Thompson & Morgan. Addresses for these firms are in the Appendix.

Chapter 11

Ferns and Grasses

Since both ferns and grasses are grown primarily for their foliage, they are grouped together in this chapter. They also share one other crucial trait: they are rarely, if ever, eaten by deer.

FERNS

Ferns are among the oldest living life forms on our planet. Fossil records indicate that they have existed for at least three hundred million years and that they have survived both the extinction of dinosaurs and periodic ice ages.

One could create a science fiction world based on their perpetuation. Unlike all other garden plants, ferns reproduce from spores rather than seeds and undergo two cycles to do so. The first stage, when the

A lovely deer-proof planting is among the many garden displays at the Inn on the Common at Craftsbury Common in the northeast corner of Vermont. Ferns in this late July picture, clockwise from lower left, are lady fern (Athyrium filix-femina) and, along the stone wall, ostrich fern (Matteuccia struthiopteris), maidenhair fern (Adiantum pedatum), the thick foliage of sensitive fern (Onoclea sensibilis), and more maidenhair fern. Red baneberry (Actaea rubra) contributes handsome clusters of poisonous color to this setting.

Western Maidenhair Fern

Light: Part shade to shade
Height: 1 to 3 feet
Color: Pale green
Zones: 4–8

Maidenhair Fern

Light: Part shade to shade
Height: 14 to 26 inches
Color: Warm green
Zones: 3–8

Lady Fern

Light: Part shade to shade
Height: 18 to 36 inches
Color: Yellowish to
 medium green
Zones: 3–8

spore germinates, produces a green, heart-shaped intermediate plant, called the prothallium. It is this intermediary that contains what we think of as sexual parts, both male and female. Though tiny—usually ¼ inch in size—the prothallium sprouts rootlets to supply nourishment and an independent life form. When its sexual organs are formed, it fertilizes itself. This act provides the death knell for the prothallium. A new fern, rising as a phoenix among its ashes, grows and assumes its place in nature. More than ten thousand plant species throughout the world grow this way.

The following then, give but a flavor of the great wonder and diversity of ferns. All are easy care and at least one should be suitable for your garden, whether it be in sun or shade, dry or moist.

Maidenhair *(Adiantum)*

Among the most beautiful and elegant of the hardy ferns, maidenhairs require moist, shady conditions to look their best. They spread slowly by rhizomes and are easily divided and transplanted.

Western Maidenhair Fern (*A. aleuticum* [*A. pedatum* ssp. *aleuticum* or f. *imbricatum*]). Sometimes called five finger fern, this plant is recommended by the Leach Botanical Garden in Oregon and is particularly suited to plantings by waterfalls or ponds. Its stems are a blue black to reddish brown and the fronds are a pale green. Native to: Montana to Alaska, south to New Mexico and California.

Maidenhair Fern (*A. pedatum*). The beautiful maidenhair fern has black purple stems and delicate green fronds. It is a refined addition to any moist, well-drained shade setting. Native to: woods throughout North America. *(Pictured on page 217)*

Lady Fern *(Athyrium filix-femina)*

One of the easiest ferns to grow, lady ferns are staple foliage plants in shade gardens—they do especially well in constantly moist, slightly acidic soil. Their intensity of green varies by location and growing conditions. Native to: North America from Atlantic coast to Rocky Mountains. *(Pictured on page 217)*

Deer Fern *(Blechnum spicant)*

Recommended by the Leach Botanical Garden in Oregon for its neat, compact growth, this fern is evergreen in its native area. Its fronds have a very even pinnate arrangement, much like the teeth in a comb. The garden's staff suggest using deer fern as a specimen plant in moist, acidic situations. Native to: Alaska to California.

Walking Fern *(Camptosorus rhizophyllus)*

This is the fern, mentioned in Chapter 1, that was completely denuded from a habitat when Henry Francis DuPont sought to obtain it in the 1930s. He must have planned to place it in his quarry garden, for walking fern does not like the acid soil so prevalent in the north-east. It is not only an exquisite miniature fern for rock gardens, but also an extremely unusual one: it propagates not only through spores

Deer Fern

Light: Part shade to shade
Height: 1 to 3 feet
Color: Dark green
Zones: 5–9

Walking Fern

Light: Part shade
Height: 4 to 12 inches
Color: Green
Zones: 3–8

✤

STARTER FERNS

According to fern authority F. Gorden Foster, the following are among the easiest to incorporate in garden settings. For further information about these plants, as well as detailed sketches showing their crosiers, mature leaf, and spores, see Foster's highly praised FERNS TO KNOW AND GROW, third edition (Timber Press).

Maidenhair Fern *(Adiantum pedatum)*. Black purple stems and delicate green fronds.
Lady Fern *(Athyrium filix-femina)*. Fans of feathery green pinnae.
Marginal Shield Fern *(Dryopteris marginalis)*. Specimen clumps of evergreen fronds.
Ostrich Fern *(Matteuccia struthiopteris)*. Tall, dramatic, and with a potential to be invasive.
Cinnamon Fern *(Osmunda cinnamomea)*. Fertile fronds shoot up as "cinnammon sticks" among rich green foliage.
Interrupted Fern *(Osmunda claytoniana)*. Rich green, leathery fronds.
Rock Polypody *(Polypodium virginianum)*. Beautiful specimen plant for rock gardens.
Christmas Fern *(Polystichum acrostichoides)*. Dark, upright evergreen fronds.

Male Fern

Light: Part shade to shade
Height: 3 to 4 feet
Color: Evergreen on mild
  Pacific coast; deciduous
  elsewhere
Zones: 5–8

Marginal Shield Fern

Light: Part shade to shade
Height: 15 to 20 inches
Color: Dark blue green
Zones: 3–8

Ostrich Fern

Light: Part shade to shade
Height: 40 to 60 inches
Color: Rich green
Zones: 3–8

but also vegetatively. In the latter activity, its long tips root where they touch ground. Native to: bare or moss-covered limestone cliffs from Quebec to Minnesota, south to Georgia and Oklahoma.

Dryopteris *(Dryopteris)*

Give either one of the following two ferns cool shade and moist, rich soil and you will have a handsome, trouble-free specimen plant in your garden or landscape.

Male Fern *(D. filix-mas).* "With large, firm, dark green fronds, this is one of our finest ferns," writes Robert T. Ogilvie of the Royal British Columbia Museum. "It is less susceptible to wind and other minor physical damage, so it does not discolor or become tattered and scraggly during the growing season. In my opinion, this is a superior garden fern than the lady fern, ostrich fern, and most of the other species of Dryopteris." Native to: Newfoundland to Michigan, South Dakota to Texas, British Columbia to California.

Marginal Shield Fern *(D. marginalis).* This fern forms a non-spreading evergreen clump and is a handsome addition to shade gardens. Its leaf color slowly matures from yellow green in spring to a dark blue green by early summer. The leaves eventually become matted over winter and are useful in erosion control on shady slopes. In spring, new crosiers unfurl, starting the cycle once again. Native to: Nova Scotia to Minnesota, south to northern Alabama and Oklahoma.

Ostrich Fern *(Matteuccia struthiopteris)*

To me, this is the most regal of ferns; it reminds me of the fans waved by servants to cool rajahs and potentates. Though it generally reaches no more than 4 feet in garden settings, it can often be seen topping 5 feet in its natural habitats. Be warned, however, that its underground runners, spreading in every direction, can be invasive in optimum growing conditions. Native to: moist areas from Newfoundland to Alaska, south to Virginia and Missouri. *(Pictured on pages 156 and 217)*

Sensitive Fern *(Onoclea sensibilis)*

Though it looks best in moist, bright shade, this fern grows just about anywhere except dry, sunny spots. With its thick, warm green leaves sensitive fern is a great filler in garden settings. It can also become a rampant filler; to control this aspect, just make sure to cut the dark brown "bead sticks" that rise toward the end of the growing season. These are loaded with spores that will ensure the spread of the plant; make use of them indoors in dried arrangements. Native to: Newfoundland to Saskatchewan, south to Florida panhandle and Texas. *(Pictured on page 217)*

Osmunda *(Osmunda)*

Osmunda ferns are good-looking, noninvasive plants that add style and elegance to garden settings.

Cinnamon Fern *(O. cinnamomea).* Found growing in damp acidic soils throughout much of the world, this fern is noted for its dramatic fertile fronds, which appear as "cinammon sticks" shooting up amidst the rich greenery of the foliage. The height of this plant varies considerably according to growing conditions. Native to: Newfoundland to Minnesota, south to Florida and New Mexico.

Interrupted Fern *(O. claytoniana).* One of the first ferns to emerge in spring, the white cottonball crosiers of interrupted fern are a treat for northern gardeners hungry for new growth. The leathery green leaves on this fern contrast nicely with more delicately foliaged plants, such as maidenhair ferns. Native to: Newfoundland to Manitoba, south to Georgia and Arkansas.

Rock Polypody *(Polypodium virginianum)*

As its popular name implies, this leathery evergreen fern loves to cover rocks and cliffs. It spreads by partially exposed rhizomes (polypodium translates to "many feet") that form dense mats and are often seen covering large boulders. This is a great plant for shady rock gardens. Native to: Newfoundland to eastern Alberta, south to northern Georgia and Arkansas.

Sensitive Fern

Light: Sun to shade
Height: 12 to 30 inches
Color: Warm green
Zones: 3–9

Cinnamon Fern

Light: Sun (if kept moist)
  to shade
Height: 2 to 5 feet
Color: Warm to deep
  green
Zones: 3–9

Interrupted Fern

Light: Sun to part shade
Height: 3 to 5 feet
Color: Warm to dark
  green
Zones: 3–8

Rock Polypody

Light: Part to open shade
Height: 10 inches
Color: Warm green
Zones: 4–7

Christmas Fern

Light: Part shade to shade
Height: 2 feet
Color: Rich dark green
Zones: 3–8

Western Sword Fern

Light: Part shade to shade
Height: 2 to 4 feet
Color: Dark evergreen
Zones: 7–9

Broad Beech Fern

Light: Part shade
Height: 10 to 24 inches
Color: Green throughout
summer; yellow and
bronze in fall
Zones: 3–8

Polystichum *(Polystichum)*

In botanical terms, members of this genus are among the most highly evolved ferns. Their appearance certainly confirms this fact, as they are quite elegant—one is tempted to say sophisticated. Though both of the following can be grown throughout much of the continent, each thrives best within its native range. Because this range is so broad, however, you will find that individual members of each species vary considerably in size and leaf color as a result of adaptation to local growing conditions and temperatures.

Christmas Fern (*P. acrostichoides*). This truly elegant fern, with its rich dark green fronds, can be grown in containers as well as sunny areas as long as it receives a good deal of water in both situations. Jeanne Frett of the Mt. Cuba Center in Delaware says it is almost indestructible and I agree. Nothing—slugs, chewing insects, tree roots, 2 feet of hard-packed snow, drought—seems to faze it. My only complaint is that its clump increases very slowly and in order to obtain a greater supply, I have to buy additional plants. Native to: moist, well-drained woodlands from Nova Scotia to Wisconsin, south to Florida and Texas. *(Pictured on page 172)*

Western Sword Fern (*P. munitum*). With evergreen fronds spraying out majestically from a tightly centered clump, it's hard to disagree with the observation made by Bert Wilson of Las Pilitas Nursery in California that western sword fern looks like the cut-off top of a palm tree. Recommended by both the Leach Botanical Garden in Oregon and the Royal British Columbia Museum, this fern can take drier situations than most (indicating its need for good drainage) and is magnificent as a specimen plant. Native to: Alaska to California.

Broad Beech Fern *(Thelypteris hexagonoptera)*

Recommended as a finer-textured alternative to sensitive fern by Scott Woodbury of the Shaw Arboretum in Missouri, broad beech fern has clean, crisp leaves throughout summer and yellow to brown coloring in the fall. Given the right growing conditions—moist, loamy soil—it spreads rapidly by rhizomes. When the situation is less than ideal, such as dry shade in a root infested area, broad beech fern is much more restrained. Native to: Quebec to Minnesota, south to Florida panhandle and eastern Texas.

GRASSES

Thanks to the splendid efforts and examples of nurserymen Kurt Bluemel and Richard Simon and landscape designer Wolfgang Oehme, the word "grass" is now beginning to conjure up images of sculptural plants in different forms and colors rather than flat expanses of endlessly mowed greenery. Though many have championed these beautiful pest- and disease-resistant plants for decades, these three men were among the first in this country not only to propagate, breed, and sell them but also to create stunning displays. Their designs showed how grasses can be used to extend the concept of a garden scene from one lasting just a season or two to an artistic presentation that evolves and changes throughout the entire year.

You may wish to join the many reevaluating their concept of grasses and include one or more of the following in your beds or borders. Unlike the widespread lawn grasses, these need to be mowed once a year at the most. And unlike many of the ornamental exotics that were first used in gardens here, the following natives are noninvasive.

It should be noted that in this book, as in most popular literature, the grass category is a broad one and applies to plants botanically classified as grasses as well as to others, such as sedges, that have grasslike characteristics.

Bluestem *(Andropogon)*

A major component of the North American prairies of long ago, bluestems are now being reevaluated for both their horticultural potential in gardens and their great durability and beauty in roadside plantings.

The Chicago Botanic Garden presents magnificent displays, all carefully labeled, of plants grouped by settings and themes. In late August in the naturalistic garden, the purple spikes of rough blazing star (Liatris aspera) add just a hint of color to a grouping that features the statuesque foliage of big bluestem (Andropogon gerardii) towering over a spray of rich green prairie dropseed (Sporobalus heterolepis). By early October, both grasses will have matured into a spectrum of colors ranging from rich orange gold to reddish bronze.

Big Bluestem

Light: Sun
Height: 4 to 7 feet
Color: Blue green foliage
matures to bronze tones
in fall and through much
of winter
Zones: 4–10

Split Beard Bluestem

Light: Sun
Height: 4 to 5 feet
Color: Deciduous blue
green foliage; fluffy white
flower plumes
Zones: 6–9

Broom Sedge

Light: Sun
Height: 4 to 5 feet
Color: Purplish green
foliage turns orange in
fall and lasts through
winter; silvery flower
heads
Zones: 6–9

Sideoats Grama

Light: Sun
Height: 18 to 30 inches
Color: Gray green leaves
mature to golden brown
and then light straw over
winter; flower heads con-
tain purple and orange
colors
Zones: 4–9

Buffalo Grass

Light: Sun
Height: 4 to 6 inches

Big Bluestem *(A. gerardii)*. An easy care recommendation from the Iowa Department of Transportation, blue bluestem lives up to its name with statuesque blue green foliage that softly waves in hot summer breezes. In fall, it turns a rich bronze and often holds its color into early winter. The distinctive, three-branched seedhead is responsible for another of its common names: turkey foot. Native to: tall grass prairies from Canada to Mexico.

Split Beard Bluestem *(A. ternarius)*. Among the tall grasses planted at the entryway to the Atlanta History Center in Georgia, split beard bluestem is valued as an erosion control plant and for its fluffy white flower plumes. These last are striking in the landscape and stunning in arrangements. Native to: dry sandy soils in eastern United States.

Broom Sedge *(A. virginicus)*. Featured in the Granite Outcrop garden in front of the museum at the Atlanta History Center, broom sedge is a beautiful plant with multiseason color and interest. Native to: rocky outcrops in eastern U.S.

Sideoats Grama *(Bouteloua curtipendula)*

Recommended as a superb plant for gardens by the Dyck Arboretum of the Plains in Kansas and routinely incorporated in highway plantings by the Iowa Department of Transportation, this small to medium-size grass is excellent in both loamy and dry soils. Its flower stalks—gleaming in summer sun with purple and orange colors—are among the most attractive of all the grasses and pair beautifully with prairie flowers. Native to: prairies and rocky hills from Maine to Montana, south to Virginia, Arizona, and southern California.

Buffalo Grass *(Buchloe dactyloides)*

The National Wildflower Research Center in Texas chose this grass for the lawn area in its formal native plant landscape. It is a tough plant that tolerates heat, cold, and drought, but not excessive moisture. Indeed, if you spend time watering and fertilizing this grass, you will be creating all sorts of pest and disease problems. Because it is so short, it rarely if ever needs to be mowed. As a warm season grass, it overwinters as beige and does not turn green again until late spring. Its winter color and the fact that it is slow to spread are its only negative qualities. Native to: plains from Canada to Texas. *(Pictured on page 19)*

Sedge *(Carex)*

Sedges are grasslike plants that are usually noted for their foliage clumps rather than their flowers. Those described below are good candidates for moist, bright shade gardens.

Palm Sedge (*C. muskingumensis*). The arching, warm green leaves of this relatively short ornamental grass contribute to its beauty as a specimen plant in containers or small gardens. It is also useful—and decorative—as erosion control material on moist banks. Native to: Great Lakes region. *(Pictured on page 55)*

Tussock Sedge (*C. stricta*). Scott Woodbury of the Shaw Arboretum in Missouri describes this as the wetland counterpart to prairie dropseed and recommends it as a perfect landscape plant for both wet and average soils. Its arching, light green foliage forms graceful, fountainlike clumps that hold their color throughout the growing season. In the winter garden, tussock sedge appears as a light tan sculpture. Native to: wet meadows from Nova Scotia, Quebec, and Minnesota, south to North Carolina, Tennessee, and Iowa.

Berkeley Sedge (*C. tumulicola*). Recommended as an attractive groundcover for large areas by grass expert John Greenlee, this evergreen clumper is also handsome as a specimen plant in a small garden. And it is perfect for moist, root-infested areas under trees where little else will grow. Indeed, according to Greenlee, its toughness and attractiveness makes it is a great choice for yards shared with dogs. Native to: northern California.

Northern Sea Oats *(Chasmanthium latifolium)*

This grass is especially valued in winter landscapes, where its ivory-colored, drooping seedheads sway in cold winds and cast intricate shadows on white snow. It looks good in summer borders as well, including those in bright shade; at that time of year it forms thick

---

Color: Gray green foliage becomes beige over winter
Zones: 3–9

Palm Sedge

Light: Sun to shade
Height: 2 to 3 feet
Color: Warm green; deciduous in northern range
Zones: 4–9

Tussock Sedge

Light: Sun to part shade
Height: 30 inches
Color: Light green
Zones: 3–7

Berkeley Sedge

Light: Sun to shade
Height: 1 to 2 feet
Color: Dark green all year
Zones: 8–10

Northern Sea Oats

Light: Sun to part shade
Height: 2 to 4 feet
Color: Green in spring and summer, copper in fall, tan in winter
Zones: 5–10

In late June, the foliage and flowers of bottlebrush grass (Elymus hystrix) *provide cooling color and airy form to a shaded setting at the Shaw Arboretum in Missouri. [Photo: Scott Woodbury]*

Bottlebrush Grass

Light: Part shade to shade
Height: 1 to 2 feet
Color: Green leaves and
    flowers throughout sum-
    mer mature to brown by
    early fall
Zones: 5–9

green clumps and is often used as an accent plant. City and shade gardeners take note: this plant can be grown in containers and tolerates salt spray. Native to: eastern half of United States and northern Mexico.

Elymus *(Elymus)*

Both of the following grasses are shade-tolerant. Other than that, they have little else in common save their ease of care.

Bottlebrush Grass (*E. hystrix [Hystrix patula]*). This is one of the few grasses grown for its flowers rather than its foliage, which does indeed resemble brushes used to scrub bottles. It is especially attractive when naturalized or planted in large swaths in woodland gardens, as can be seen at the Shaw Arboretum in Missouri. Native to: moist, rocky woodlands in eastern United States.

Beardless Wild Rye (*Elymus [Leymus] tritichoides*). This relatively new introduction to the horticultural scene is attracting a lot of attention from breeders; new cultivars bred for color, height, and tolerance for salt spray or drought should be entering the market soon. All on its own, however, the fast spreading species plant is a beautiful green groundcover in summer months. Unlike bottlebrush grass, its flowers are nondescript. Native to: western United States.

June Grass *(Koeleria macrantha [cristata])*

As its popular name implies, this is an early emerging grass, one of the few prairie grasses to green up spring settings. It's perfect for dry, sandy soils and pairs well with spring flowers. Native to: prairies throughout southern Canada and United States.

Muhly *(Muhlenbergia)*

Muhly hails from the southwest and Mexico and as such is a grass that can take hot, dry weather. The genus is valued for more than these

❁

GREAT GRASSES

John Greenlee, one of the most knowledgeable and enthusiastic promoters of American grasses, has compiled the following representative list so that every reader of this book will have at least one easy care ornamental grass that is suitable for their garden or landscape. For further information about native grasses as well as hundreds of colored photographs, see Greenlee's THE ENCYCLOPEDIA OF ORNAMENTAL GRASSES (Rodale Press).

Berkeley Sedge *(Carex tumulicola)*. Lush clumps of evergreen sprays of foliage.
Northern Sea Oats *(Chasmanthium latifolium)*. Green foliage and arching flower heads turn copper in fall and then tan in winter.
Bottlebrush Grass *(Elymus hystrix)*. Warm green leaves and brushlike flowers throughout summer mature to brown by early fall.
Beardless Wild Rye *(Elymus tritichoides)*. Green to blue green summer foliage matures to wheat and then bleaches to gray.
Deer Grass *(Muhlenbergia rigens)*. Upright gray green leaves emerge in spring and fan out as they mature to buff by fall.
Switch Grass *(Panicum virgatum)*. Gray to blue green leaves and airy panicles with dark red and purple tones mature first to yellows and then to warm beiges.
Little Bluestem *(Schizachyrium scoparium)*. Stalks in blue to green hues turn brilliant bronze red to orange in fall.
Indian Grass *(Sorghastrum nutans)*. Soft, golden brown fall seedheads become burnt orange over winter.
Prairie Dropseed *(Sporobalus heterolepis)*. Spraying mounds of emerald green leaves turn orange gold in fall and then a rich rust brown in winter.
Gamma Grass *(Tripsicum dactyloides)*. Magnificent fountains of dark evergreen foliage.

traits, however, as individual species are beautiful plants with sculptural forms and striking flowers.

Lindheimer Muhly (*M. lindheimeri*). An easy care recommendation from the National Wildflower Research Center in Texas, this grass features fountains of blue green foliage in summer and striking silvery plumes throughout fall. Native to: Texas and northern Mexico.

Beardless Wild Rye

Light: Sun to part shade
Height: 2 to 4 feet
Color: Green to blue green summer foliage matures to wheat and

The colorful foliage on little bluestem (Schizachyrium sco- parium) has attracted the atten- tion of breeders. At Prairie Nursery in Wisconsin, where this picture was taken in late August, Neil Diboll has filled a nursery bed displaying the many hues of this plant. No matter what the summer color, however, all of these short, exceptionally handsome prairie grasses feature fluffy white seedheads and burnt orange foliage in fall.

Deer Grass *(M. rigens).* This exceptionally drought-tolerant plant is an easy care recommendation from grass expert John Greenlee, who says it is also appropriate for wet conditions and can grow in sun or shade. It's also a favorite of Bert Wilson of California's Las Pilitas Nurs- ery. "It looks like a small pampas grass," Wilson says, "but is more use- ful because of its shorter stature." Western gardeners yearning for green especially appreciate this plant because it holds its color throughout much of summer. Native to: California to Texas and northern Mexico.

Switch Grass *(Panicum virgatum)*

This very adaptable plant—it can be grown in a wide range of soils and even tolerates salt spray—is a current favorite among grass breed-

ers, who have been busy introducing cultivars where reds or blues predomi- nate. The Dawes Arboretum in Ohio thinks the species plant alone is a worthy candidate for gardens. I have Heavy Metal, a blue-toned cultivar introduced by Kurt Bluemel, and it forms an elegant pairing with the sim- ilarly colored foliage of boltonia in a perennial border. Native to: prairies in eastern half of North American conti- nent.

Little Bluestem *(Schizachyrium scoparium [Andropogon scoparius])*

The most highly recommended of all grasses in this book, tough and relatively short little bluestem is a beautiful addi- tion to highway plantings, prairie land- scapes, and home gardens. It features exceptionally colorful foliage as well as fluffy white seedheads. The former attribute has caught the eyes of breeders and many new colored forms should be entering the market soon. Look for the one that is an almost solid robin's egg blue and offered by Neil Diboll of Prairie nursery (this cultivar is not pictured). Whether you grow a cultivar or a species, you will find this drought-tolerant grass easy care in all but consistently wet soils. Native to: Quebec to Alberta, south to Florida and Arizona.

Indian Grass *(Sorghastrum nutans)*.

A major component of tall grass prairies of long ago, Indian grass can serve a similar function in landscapes today. It is extensively used by the Iowa Department of Transportation and one of the standouts in Neil Diboll's prairie landscape. Grass expert John Greenlee, who also recommends this widely adaptable plant, further suggests that it would make a stunning specimen plant. Its seedheads look lovely in either winter landscapes or dried arrangements. Native to: tall grass prairies in eastern half of North American continent.

Prairie Dropseed *(Sporobalus heterolepis)*

This elegant grass has many uses in gardens and landscapes. Because of its height, color, and form, it makes an excellent front-of-the-border edging when planted 18 to 24 inches apart. In larger, open settings, its beautiful spraying mounds form sculptural groundcovers. No wonder that many consider this to be the most handsome of the prairie grasses. Native to: prairies from Canada to Texas. *(Pictured on page 223)*

Gamma Grass *(Tripsicum dactyloides)*

Gamma grass contributes scupltural form to moist shade gardens. Its lush, spraying arches of green foliage appear as fountains amidst underplanting of ferns and purple-foliaged heucheras. This easily adaptable plant can also be a featured attraction in containers. Native to: moist areas from Massachusetts to Michigan, south to Florida and Texas.

Bear Grass *(Xerophyllum tenax)*

I love the silver color of this plant's new foliage, which slowly but steadily emerges in the center of the clump throughout summer. The

then bleaches to gray over winter
Zones: 7–10

June Grass

Light: Sun
Height: 12 to 18 inches
Color: Blue green spring foliage dries to golden brown before dormancy in midsummer
Zones: 4–9

Lindheimer Muhly

Light: Sun
Height: 18 to 30 inches
Color: Blue green foliage ages to silvery gray
Zones: 7–9

Deer Grass

Light: Sun to part shade
Height: 3 to 4 feet
Color: Gray green leaves in spring and mature to buff
Zones: 6–9

Switch Grass

Light: Sun
Height: 4 to 7 feet
Color: Species, green to gray green leaves mature to various shades of yellow and then beige; Heavy Metal, blue green leaves mature to bright yellow
Zones: 5–9

Little Bluestem

Light: Sun to part shade
Height: 2 to 3 feet

Color: Blue and green
hues turn bronze red to
orange
Zones: 3–9

Indian Grass

Light: Sun
Height: 2 to 5 feet
Color: Light to medium
green foliage turns yel-
lowish in fall and then
burnt orange through
winter
Zones: 4–9

Prairie Dropseed

Light: Sun
Height: 18 to 36 inches
Color: Emerald green
foliage turns orange gold
in fall and then a rich
rust brown in winter
Zones: 3–9

Gamma Grass

Light: Sun to part shade
Height: 3 to 5 feet
Color: Medium to dark
evergreen in southern
range; deciduous in frost
areas
Zones: 5–10

Bear Grass

Light: Sun to part shade
Height: 1 to 2 feet
Color: Silver green new
foliage; white flower
plumes
Zones: 5–9

effect is that of a small, quiet fountain in the garden. Toward the end of summer, flower plumes up to 4 feet tall create a striking splash. Native to: British Columbia to central California.

SOURCES: Many of the plants described in this chapter can be obtained at local garden centers. Others, however, will probably have to be purchased through the mail. Check with Forestfarm or Varga's Nursery for ferns and Kurt Bluemel, Inc., Greenlee Nursery, Native American Seed, or Prairie Moon Nursery for grasses. Addresses for these mail-order firms are in the Appendix.

Chapter 12

Perennials

Easy care perennials are wonderful plants. They provide a changing stream of flower and foliage color, shape, and texture throughout the growing season. And then, they all come back and do the same thing the next year! As you will read below, the North American continent is rich in the number and variety of such plants. No matter where you live, there are many great plants here for your gardens or landscapes.

Mountain Yarrow *(Achillea millefolium var. lanuosa)*

A very adaptable and handsome perennial, the lacy white flowers and feathery foliage of this plant can be found decorating snow fields, rocky outcrops, and live oak bases throughout the West Coast. Penny A. Wilson of Las Pilitas Nursery in California suggests that it would be a wonderful addition to flower gardens as well. As long as it has good

In late July, the white spires of black cohosh (Cimicifuga racemosa) and the blue blossoms on the grasslike clump of spiderwort (Tradescantia virginiana) are among the many native flowers in the borders of the Inn on the Common at Craftsbury Common in northeastern Vermont.

Mountain Yarrow

Light: Sun to part shade
Height: 12 to 18 inches
Color: White
Bloom Period: Summer
Zones: 3–8

Doll's Eyes

Light: Shade
Height: 2 to 4 feet
Color: Flowers, white;
  berries, white with black
  dots (the "eyes") in center
Bloom Period: Flowers, late
  spring; berries, summer
Zones: 3–8

Red Baneberry

Light: Shade
Height: 18 to 24 inches
Color: Flowers, white;
  berries, bright red
Bloom Period: Flowers, late
  spring; berries, summer
Zones: 3–7

Dwarf Amsonia

Light: Sun to part shade
Height: 12 to 15 inches
Color: Flowers, light blue;
  foliage, golden yellow
Bloom Period: Flowers,
  spring; foliage, fall
Zones: 3–9

drainage, it can grow in either dry or wet climates. Native to: Quebec to Yukon, south to Oklahoma and California.

Actaea *(Actaea)*

A must for deep shade gardens plagued by deer, the poisonous members of this genus need moisture to look their best. They are treasured not only for their imperviousness to pests but also for their beautiful berries.

Doll's Eyes *(A. pachypoda [alba]).* The rich green, elegant foliage on this plant resembles that of the more popular astilbes. While the white flowers are small and quite transitory, the resulting white berries are handsome additions to dark scenes. Native to: moist woods from Quebec to Minnesota, south to Florida and Missouri.

Red Baneberry *(A. rubra).* This is a shorter member of the genus with thick summer clusters of bright red berries. It is a true mystery to me why this exceptionally handsome and equally disease- and pest-resistant plant is so little seen in gardens and landscapes. Native to: Nova Scotia to South Dakota, south to New Jersey and Nebraska. *(Pictured on page 217)*

Amsonia *(Amsonia)*

Amsonia is among the many neglected genera now being brought to the gardening fore with the upsurge in interest in American plants. Indeed, this genus is so little known that it's not even grown in Europe. What Europeans are missing but what American gardeners are discovering is that amsonias are valued more for their fall foliage, which is a beautiful golden tan, than for their equally nice if less dramatic blue flowers in spring. Should you feel any of the following are too floppy after flowering, simply cut them back to half their height and you'll be rewarded with not only shorter but also bushier plants.

Dwarf Amsonia *(A. montana).* While botanists insist this is a variety of willow amsonia *(A. tabernaemonta)*, nursery people sell it as a distinct species. It is a shorter, neater plant than its close relative and has glossy green leaves. Native to: southeastern United States.

Arkansas Amsonia *(A. hubrectii)*. The wispy, elegant foliage on this plant resembles that on the common cosmos and provides a lovely contrast with thicker-leaved plants such as butterfly weeds *(Asclepias tuberosa)* during summer months. In fall, it turns a golden tan and appears as if painted in the garden by a French Impressionist. Native to: dry or well-drained areas in southern and southeastern United States.

Willow Amsonia *(A. tabernaemontana)*. Currently the most popular amsonia species, this wide-ranging easy care perennial thrives in many climates and soils. As it ages, it becomes quite large and bushy and forms a beautiful accent plant from spring through fall in the garden. Those with dry, sandy areas should choose var. *salicifolia*. Native to: New Jersey west to Kansas, south to Louisiana. *(Pictured on page 29)*

Anemone *(Anemone)*

This genus contains about 120 diverse species, ranging from 2 inches to 5 feet and blooming from early spring to late fall. The following easy care natives, however, are quite similar.

Windflower *(A. multifida)*. A recommendation of Danish nurserywoman Grethe B. Petersen, this widespread plant is little known and grown in its home continent. Native to: Newfoundland to Alaska, south to northern border states, New Mexico, and California.

Thimbleweed *(A. virginiana)*. An unassuming plant for easy care shade gardens, this native has attractive divided leaves and a slim form, which is accented by its thin flower stalks. I have grown it for four years at this writing and find it to be a demure, noninvasive presence in a site reserved for moisture-loving plants. Native to: Nova Scotia to South Carolina, west to Kansas.

Rue Anemone *(Anemonella [Thalictrum] thalictroides)*

Noted American landscape architect A. J. Downing recommended this charming native, to no avail, in the mid-nineteenth century. It's time his advice was heeded. It bears white to pale pink flowers that resemble miniature versions of fall anemones and has wiry but

---

Arkansas Amsonia

Light: Sun to part shade
Height: 2 to 4 feet
Color: Flowers, light blue; foliage, golden tan
Bloom Period: Flowers, spring; foliage, fall
Zones: 6–8

Willow Amsonia

Light: Sun to part shade
Height: 2 to 4 feet
Color: Flowers, pale blue; foliage, golden yellow
Bloom Period: Flowers, spring; foliage, fall
Zones: 3–9

Windflower

Light: Sun to part shade
Height: 18 to 24 inches
Color: White
Bloom Period: Early summer
Zones: 4–9

Thimbleweed

Light: Part shade to shade
Height: 30 to 45 inches
Color: Creamy white
Bloom Period: Early summer
Zones: 4–9

Rue Anemone

Light: Part shade to shade
Height: 4 to 8 inches
Color: White, pale pink
Bloom Period: Early to midspring
Zones: 3–8

American Columbine

Light: Part shade to shade
under deciduous trees
Height: 15 to 24 inches
Color: Red and yellow
Bloom Period: Spring
Zones: 3–9

Golden Columbine

Light: Sun to part shade
Height: 30 to 40 inches
Color: Pale yellow
Bloom Period: Spring into
early summer
Zones: 3–10

upright stems that allow it to fit delicately into many spring settings. It selfsows slowly; you really can't have too many of these diminutive plants. Under the stress of dry summer heat in my gardens, the foliage often turns purple and then goes dormant; this does not appear to affect the following year's performance. Native to: woodlands from New Hampshire to Minnesota, south to Florida and Kansas. *(Pictured on page 197)*

Columbine *(Aquilegia)*

Columbines are lovely perennials with pretty foliage and exquisite flowers. They thrive in well-drained, ordinary garden soil and, though short-lived, selfseed so satisfactorily that you never have the opportunity to miss the parent plant. There is a hitch, however, and it is called leaf miner. Perhaps there are areas in this continent where this pest is absent; Princeton, New Jersey, is not one of them. It tunnels ("mines") its way through foliage, disfiguring and often killing the plant. Since leaf miner foraging usually starts after flowering is underway, I enjoy the blossoms, let one or two go to seed, and cut the remaining plant to the ground. Infected leaves are not composted for my vegetable garden, but bagged and taken to the town dump.

American Columbine *(A. canadensis).* Probably the easiest and most widely grown columbine species, this plant bears delicate red and yellow flowers that are stalwarts in spring shade gardens. Thomas Jefferson grew it at Monticello and the Dyck Arboretum of the Plains in Kansas recommends it for gardeners today. At the warmer edge of its range, the foliage is evergreen; further north, it is deciduous. Native to: Nova Scotia to Florida, west to Minnesota and Kansas. *(Pictured on page 77)*

Golden Columbine *(A. chrysantha).* When I saw this plant looking absolutely elegant in a hot July display at Rockefeller Center in the heart of Manhattan, I decided it could do the same in my gardens and promptly ordered some. Though golden columbine is one of the parents contributing beauty and grace to many hybrid columbines, I like it just for itself. Its spurs are long and lovely and its petals the palest yellow. Native to: New Mexico, Arizona, and northwest Mexico.

Western Columbine (A. formosa). The western counterpart of the American columbine, this perennial is a favorite of hummingbirds. If you grow it in full sun, you will need to water once or twice a week; in the coolness of part shade, it requires less water. Though not long-lived, western columbine selfseeds nicely so that once you plant it, you should have its dainty red and yellow flowers in your garden for years. Native to: Alaska south to Montana, Utah, and northern California.

Spikenard *(Aralia racemosa)*

This perennial is valued by designers and horticulturists for its beautiful structure and is a recommendation of plantsman Pierre Bennerup. It has an arching form with large rich green foliage, panicles of white flowers in spring, and—best of all to many—clusters of deep purple berries at the end of the growing season. Native to: rich, moist woods from New Brunswick to North Carolina, west to Utah and Mexico.

Artemisia *(Artemisia)*

Artemisias are valued by gardeners for their soft gray foliage and detested by both deer and slugs for the same reason. The following are not invasive and are excellent choices for easy care gardens. Just make sure that they have good drainage and lots of sun.

White Sage (A. ludoviciana). Utilized by Gertrude Jekyll at the beginning of this century and popular in midwestern gardens today, white sage is not as invasive as the Silver King cultivar. As its name implies, it has silver gray foliage and it contributes a cool touch to prairie settings known for hot colors. Native to: Michigan to Washington, south to Arkansas, Texas, and Mexico.

David's Choice (A. pycnocephala 'David's Choice'). This is the artemisia for native plant purists who covet but cannot admit the Silver Mound cultivar from Japan. It is also for those who have difficulty growing Silver Mound, because David's Choice is sturdier and more adaptable to soils that are either heavy or sandy. Its habit is slightly more open, its foliage is a whiter gray, and its flowers appear earlier than those of Silver Mound. Neither plant, it should be noted, likes humidity. Native to: Oregon to California.

Western Columbine
Light: Sun to part shade
Height: 3 feet
Color: Red and yellow
Bloom Period: May to August
Zones: 3–9

Spikenard
Light: Part shade to shade
Height: 4 to 6 feet
Color: Flowers, white; berries, deep purple
Bloom Period: Flowers, late spring; berries, late summer into fall
Zones: 4–8

White Sage
Light: Sun
Height: 2 to 3 feet
Color: Silver gray
Bloom Period: Late summer
Zones: 4–9

David's Choice
Light: Sun to part shade
Height: 10 to 14 inches
Color: Whitish gray
Bloom Period: Summer
Zones: Species, 9–10; cultivar, 6–9 (and possibly zone 5)

White Woodland Milk-weed

Light: Bright or dappled shade of woodland edges
Height: 3 to 5 feet
Color: White
Bloom Period: Summer
Zones: 4–8

Swamp Milkweed

Light: Sun
Height: 3 to 5 feet
Color: Pink, white
Bloom Period: Early summer
Zones: 3–9

Purple Silkweed

Light: Sun to part shade
Height: 2 to 3 feet
Color: Deep rose to purple
Bloom Period: Late spring
Zones: Not established; definitely 5–7 and probably 4–8

Butterfly Weed

Light: Sun
Height: 18 to 30 inches
Color: Orange flowers; tan, canoe-shaped seedpods
Bloom Period: Flowers repeat bloom in summer; seedpods in September and October
Zones: 3–10

Asclepias *(Asclepias)*

This genus is certainly a diverse one. There are plants for sun or shade, plants for front of the border or back of the border, and plants with showy or quiet flowers. What all share, however, is ease of care.

White Woodland Milkweed *(A. exaltata).* Offered by Prairie Nursery, this plant features large umbels of white flowers in shaded summer gardens. It's a well-behaved plant that also provides a fall bonus: upright pods that are handsome additions to dried arrangements. Native to: Maine to Minnesota, south to Georgia and Iowa.

Swamp Milkweed *(A. incarnata).* Despite its popular name—which reflects its natural habitat—swamp milkweed is an excellent candidate for all sunny borders. I have the Ice Ballet cultivar and love its gleaming white flowers in early summer and its striking seedpods in August. I like even more the fact that it doesn't need to be staked. Native to: moist areas from Nova Scotia to Utah, south to Florida.

Purple Silkweed *(A. purpurascens).* This beautiful native is an easy care recommendation of Scott Woodbury, horticulturist at the Shaw Arboretum in Missouri. It has glossy dark green foliage that is hairy underneath and—unusual for an asclepias—handsome globose, rose purple flowers, which bloom for three to four weeks in late spring. Woodbury has combined this plant with poppy mallows *(Callirhoe involucrata)* and pale purple coneflowers *(Echinacea pallida)* to create a stunning display in a sunny setting and reports that purple silkweed is also an excellent candidate for dry shade areas. Native to: thickets and open woods from New Hampshire through southern Ontario, south to Virginia and eastern Kansas.

Butterfly Weed *(A. tuberosa).* This tried-and-true perennial should be a staple of every sun garden. I love it for the monarch butterflies that swarm about, for its repeat-blooming orange flowers, and for its handsome fall seedpods that open to feathery white seed plumes. With its deep taproot, butterfly weed resists drought—and rots in constantly moist areas (give it good drainage). Though butterfly weed was previously thought unsuitable for thick clay soils, Prairie Nursery is now offering a strain that does well in such situations. Native to: New

England to North Dakota, south to Florida and Arizona. *(Pictured above and on page 53)*

Aster *(Aster)*

One or more of the following easy care asters will star in your late summer and fall borders. Unlike the many finicky hybrids that dominate the market, these resist mildew and disease. Most eventually form thick, woody clumps and should be divided every three or four years. If you share my dislike for staking plants, cut back the taller ones to about 2 feet in June.

Sky Blue Aster *(A. azureus).* Despite its popular name, the flowers on this aster are a pale rather than robust sky blue. They are lovely though, and, when given good drainage, they bloom for a long time. You might want to pair them, as I do, with white boltonias for a lovely pastel effect at a garden time of year noted for fiery colors. Native to:

The blue flowers of American alpine speedwell (Veronica wormskjoldii) *bloom for up to four weeks in midsummer. They look particularly colorful with orange butterfly weed* (Asclepias tuberosa) *and pale yellow Moonbeam coreopsis.*

Sky Blue Aster

Light: Sun
Height: 2 to 4 feet
Color: Blue
Bloom Period: Late summer
Zones: 4–8

❋

OVERLOOKED AMERICAN PLANTS

As owner of the East Coast's largest perennial wholesale operation, Sunny Border Nurseries, Inc., Pierre Bennerup offers a selection from around the world. He loves plants for their attributes, not for where they come from. As a plant enthusiast then, rather than as a champion of American flora, he feels the following easy care natives have been overlooked by American gardeners. Wholesale (indeed, only wholesale) buyers such as garden centers, landscapers, and landscape architects can order any of these by calling 800/732-1627.

Allegheny Vine *(Adlumia fungosa)*. Climber with white to rosy pink flowers summer to frost.
Spikenard *(Aralia racemosa)*. Perennial with white flowers in late spring and deep purple berries late summer into fall.
False Goatsbeard *(Astilbe biternata)*. Perennial with creamy white plumes in summer.
Boltonia *(B. asteroides)*. Perennial with white, daisylike flowers late summer into fall.
Soapwort *(Gentiana saponaria)*. Perennial with blue flowers in late summer.
Bowman's Root *(Gillenia trifoliata)*. Perennial with white flowers on reddish stems in summer.
Barbara's Buttons *(Marshallia grandiflora)*. Perennial with pink flowers in summer.
Prickly Pear *(Opuntia humifusa)*. Perennial with large yellow flowers in early summer.
Crackerjack Phlox *(P. subulata* hybrid 'Crackerjack'). Groundcover with glowing red pink flowers in spring.
Red Mexican Hat *(Ratibida columnifera* var. *pulcherrima)*. Perennial with rich red petals that skirt dark cones all summer into fall.
Indian Pink *(Spigelia marilandica)*. Perennial with red and yellow tubular flowers late spring through early summer.

White Wood Aster

Light: Part shade to shade
Height: 12 to 30 inches
Color: White
Bloom Period: Late summer into fall
Zones: 3–9

southern Ontario and western New York to Minnesota, south to Alabama and Texas.

White Wood Aster *(A. divaricatus).* This is yet another native derided as a weed in its home territory and honored abroad. A century ago, for example, noted British plantswoman Gertrude Jekyll routinely incorporated white wood asters in her fall borders. I think you will enjoy their late season white flower sprays as much as I do if you have dry shade situations. True, white wood asters spread, but not invasively. "Just don't combine them with plants having finicky or fragile dispositions," suggests Sue Vrooman of the Atlanta History Center. Native to: mountain woodlands from New Hampshire to Ohio, south to northern Georgia and eastern Alabama.

Dwarf Aster (*A. dumosus*). Here's another plant with mixed-up nomenclature. Though the species is rarely offered commercially, many short, front-of-the-border cultivars are. I have two: Alice Haslam with rosy pink flowers and Prof. Kippenberg with lavender blue flowers. Many insist that these cultivars are hybrids and list them as *A. X dumosus*. Whatever they are called botanically, they are wonderful plants for late season front borders. Native to: southwest Maine to Florida and Louisiana.

Heath Aster (*A. ericoides*). This bushy aster looks like it has been heavily dusted with white snow when its flowers open in late summer. The plant is absolutely spectacular in full sun and even does well (though with diminished blooms) in dry shade. The cultivar Blue Star is on my list for new plants to incorporate in my gardens. Native to: Maine to Minnesota and South Dakota, south to Georgia, New Mexico, and adjacent Mexico.

Smooth Aster (*A. laevis*). Highly recommended by three contributors to this book for its ease of care and beauty, this adaptable aster can be grown in both moist and dry soils. In late summer, it is covered with a striking display of showy flowers. I think it wins the "aster with the most beautiful foliage" award. The leaves are blue green and blend beautifully with the similarly tinted foliage of boltonia and Heavy Metal switchgrass *(Panicum virgatum)*. Native to: Maine to Georgia, west to Yukon, northeast Oregon, and New Mexico.

Calico Aster (*A. lateriflorus* var. *horizontalis*). It seems as if every time I go out to inspect my spring and summer borders, I have to reconfirm this plant's label to make sure it is indeed an aster. At this time of year, it is quite unaster like—a lovely, upright, bushy plant with purple-tinged older leaves and pale, creamy green tips on new foliage. I would grow it for its appearance in just these seasons. Then, starting mid September, tiny pale lilac flowers with centers of rosy red stamens cover the plant for a good four weeks. What a bonus! What a plant!

Dwarf Aster

Light: Sun
Height: 1 to 3 feet; cultivars 6 to 18 inches
Color: Blue, pale lavender, white; cultivars in many shades of pink
Bloom Period: Late summer
Zones: 3–8

Heath Aster

Light: Sun to part shade
Height: 1 to 3 feet
Color: White
Bloom Period: Late summer into fall
Zones: 3–10

Smooth Aster

Light: Sun
Height: 2 to 4 feet
Color: Light bluish purple, white
Bloom Period: Late summer
Zones: 3–8

Calico Aster

Light: Sun
Height: 24 to 40 inches
Color: Pale lilac petals and rosy red stamens
Bloom Period: Late summer into early fall
Zones: 3–9

New England Aster

Light: Sun to part shade
Height: 4 to 6 feet; culti-
vars 2 to 5 feet
Color: Bluish purple; culti-
vars pink to deep purple
Bloom Period: Late summer
into fall
Zones: 4–8

*When cut back in June, umbel-
latus aster (A. umbellatus) is
almost hedgelike when its white
flowers start their eight-week
bloom period in mid August.*

Native to: southeastern Canada to Florida, west to Minnesota, Missouri, and Texas

New England Aster *(A. novae-angliae).* While the unadorned New
England aster is a great plant for highways and roadsides, I prefer two
cultivars for garden settings: Alma Potchke features an unusual reddish
pink color, short stature, and resistance to mildew; Harrington's Pink
does not need to be divided as frequently as the species and is covered
with pretty pink flowers for many weeks. Honeysong Pink, recommended by Scott Woodbury at the Shaw Arboretum in Missouri, is
another short cultivar (3 to 4 feet) and is covered with clear pink flowers from August to September. Native to: New England to Alabama,
west to Wyoming, and New Mexico. *(Alma Potchke cultivar pictured on
page 242)*

Umbellatus Aster *(A. umbellatus).* This is often referred to as flat-
topped aster, an atrocious common name that doesn't begin to convey

the striking appearance of this aster. Left unpinched, it can reach a towering 8 feet; pinched heavily in June, it is only 4 feet when its white flowers start to open and begin their eight-week-long bloom period. In the seven years that I have grown this aster, I have yet to find any pests or diseases blatantly disfiguring it. Though it grows in moist areas in the wild, it has done supremely well in my gardens with only twice weekly watering during dry spells. Native to: moist areas from Newfoundland to Georgia, west to Minnesota and Illinois.

False Goatsbeard *(Astilbe biternata)*

Though the American astilbe's plumes are not as colorful as those of its many Asian relatives, they are larger, showier, and longer-lasting. They are also more heat-tolerant, according to perennial plantsman Pierre Bennerup. A superb plant for the back of a border or in a dramatic grouping of its own, it does nevertheless take its time to settle in; mine dawdled three years before finally flowering. Native to: moist woodlands from Virginia to Kentucky, south to Georgia. *(Pictured on page 6)*

Baptisia *(Baptisia)*

Baptisias are wonderful easy care plants that have tidy, blue green foliage; colorful pealike spring flowers; and handsome, decorative seed pods summer into fall. All are long-lived, deep-rooted, drought-tolerant, and require good drainage.

Wild Blue Indigo *(B. australis)*. The most popular of the baptisias, this plant features gorgeous blue flowers in late spring gardens. The subsequent striking black seedpods are often used in dried flower arrangements. When grown in partial shade, this will need to be staked. Native to: woodland borders from Pennsylvania and Indiana south to Georgia and Tennessee.

Prairie Indigo *(B. leucantha [lactea])*. This perennial—recommended by Neil Diboll in Wisconsin for its creamy white flowers and strikingly black end-of-season pods—makes a rapid appearance in spring borders: it often reaches 4 feet in a matter of days. Native to: Ohio to Minnesota, south to Mississippi and Texas. *(Pictured on page 29)*

Umbellatus Aster

Light: Sun to part shade
Height: 8 feet unpinched
Color: White
Bloom Period: Mid August to mid October
Zones: 3–8

False Goatsbeard

Light: Part shade to shade
Height: 3 to 6 feet
Color: Creamy white
Bloom Period: Summer
Zones: 4–8

Wild Blue Indigo

Light: Sun to part shade
Height: 3 to 4 feet
Color: Indigo blue
Bloom Period: Late spring
Zones: 3–9

Prairie Indigo

Light: Sun
Height: 3 to 6 feet
Color: Creamy white
Bloom Period: Late spring to early summer, depending on location
Zones: 4–8

Boltonia

Light: Sun to part shade
Height: 4 to 7 feet
Color: White; cultivar in
  pink
Bloom Period: Late summer
  into fall

Poppy Mallow

Light: Sun to part shade
Height: 6 to 18 inches
Color: Wine red
Bloom Period: Late spring
  well into summer
Zones: 4–8

Boltonia *(B. asteroides)*

This perennial really does have it all: fabulous good looks and amazing ease of care. With clean, cool blue green foliage, it survives summer heat, insects, humidity, diseases, and drought with understated elegance. In late August, it caps all these attributes with the opening of its white daisylike flowers for up to five weeks. Most literature recommends the shorter, sturdier Snowbank cultivar. Unfortunately, not all plants sold under that name are the real thing; thus, though I bought Snowbank, it appears that I actually have the species plant. To eliminate any need for staking, I cut the stems down to 2 feet in late June and have a bushy plant covered with white flowers in late summer. I also have Pink Beauty, and while its foliage and flowers are quite lovely, the latter are not as long-blooming as the species. Native to: slightly moist soils from New Jersey to North Dakota, south to Florida and Texas. *(Pictured below and on page 27)*

Poppy Mallow *(Callirhoe involucrata)*

I grew this perennial for two years before I finally discovered what it was—I had bought a young plant through the mail and had promptly lost the name tag after placing it in a raised, bright shade garden

For a colorful fall foursome, combine cerise red Alma Potchke (A. novae-angliae 'Alma Potchke'), *white boltonia* (B. asteroides), *Maryland golden aster* (Chrysopsis mariana), *and blue sage* (Salvia azurea).

infested with chewing insects. While its dark green, deeply lobed foliage reminded me of our native geranium *(G. maculatum)*, it flopped rather than stood erect. What an absolute treat, then, when its beautiful wine red flowers opened in late June and lasted for a good four weeks. This is a really tough, elegant plant that should find its way into more gardens, with or without name tags. It tolerates poor or dry soils, selfsows moderately (alas, it has yet to do so in my garden), and can be increased by division. Native to: Missouri to Wyoming, south to Texas. *(Pictured on page 272)*

Wild Senna *(Cassia [Senna] marilandica)*

A member of the pea family, this is a tough, sturdy plant with yellow flowers in summer and clean, smooth green compound leaflets. It will grow all on its own in thick clay soil as well as in loamy garden borders. Though generally recommended for informal plantings, there is a formal row of these plants behind a partially shaded teak beach at the U.S. Arboretum in Washington, D.C.—the effect is quite elegant. Native to: Pennsylvania to Florida, west to Iowa, Kansas, and Texas. *(Foliage pictured on page 50)*

Turtlehead *(Chelone)*

The popular name for this genus is supposed to describe the odd-shaped flowers, which cluster about the top of the stem and resemble the heads of turtles. Like turtles, the plants demand cool, moist conditions. Indeed, they are often found growing in bogs or by stream banks in the wild.

White Turtlehead *(C. glabra).* WYMAN'S GARDENING ENCYCLOPEDIA cites the attractive foliage of this plant. Alas, I thought it was that of an uninvited weed that had crept into my border and I yanked it out in an afternoon frenzy of tidying the garden. Up until that drastic moment, its really nice late summer flowers had bloomed for three years in a shaded border that I water regularly. Native to: Newfoundland to Minnesota, south to Georgia and Missouri.

Pink Turtlehead *(C. lyonii).* This is the preferred species for gardens because of its glossy green foliage; its attractiveness when planted en

Wild Senna
Light: Sun to part shade
Height: 3 to 6 feet
Color: Yellow
Bloom Period: Summer
Zones: 3–10

White Turtlehead
Light: Part shade
Height: 2 to 3 feet
Color: Creamy white
Bloom Period: Late summer
Zones: 4–8

Pink Turtlehead
Light: Part shade
Height: 16 to 40 inches
Color: Pink, rosy purple
Bloom Period: Late summer
Zones: 4–9

In late August, the naturalistic garden at the Chicago Botanic Garden features a stunning presentation of pink turtleheads (Chelone lyonii). Lady in Red salvia (S. coccinea 'Lady in Red') provides a red accent in the bottom left corner and the foliage and last blossoms of obedient plants (Physostegia virginiana) create a texture and color interlude between the two large turtlehead plantings.

Maryland Golden Aster

Light: Sun to part shade
Height: 1 to 3 feet
Color: Yellow

masse; and its flower color. It is an easy care recommendation of both Garden in the Woods and the New York Botanical Garden. Native to: Appalachian mountains in North and South Carolina and Tennessee.

Maryland Golden Aster *(Chrysopsis mariana)*

Typically described as a roadside weed, the bright yellow flowers and fluffy seedheads of this perennial are beautiful additions to my fall gardens. Though naturally found in dry, well-drained sunny sites, it has thrived in a partially shaded location in one of my gardens. As I do with asters, I often cut this plant back in late June so that it need not be staked. Native to: sandy soils from New York to Ohio, south to Florida and east Texas. *(Pictured on page 242)*

Bugbane *(Cimicifuga)*

With deeply lobed, dark green foliage and soaring spires of summer flowers, these are striking plants. While preferring rich, humusy soil, they can also be grown in drier, leaner situations, but will be shorter and less floriferous. In either situation, water at least twice a week during dry spells.

Black Cohosh *(C. racemosa).* This is the most popular and widely grown species. Its flowers are lovely when grouped naturally at woodland edges or when incorporated into more formal plantings. Native to: Massachusetts to Ontario, south to Georgia, Tennessee, and Missouri. *(Pictured on page 231)*

Fairy Candles *(C. racemosa* **var.** *cordifolia).* Recommended by Danish plantswoman Grethe B. Petersen, this form differs from the species in that it is shorter, has creamier flowers, and is later blooming. Native to: Virginia, North Carolina, and Tennessee.

Stoneroot *(Collinsonia canadensis)*

Sue Vrooman of the Atlanta History Center likes this plant for its bold foliage and the fragrance of its late season blossoms. "In our gardens," she reports, "the pale yellow flowers seem to offer two odors—one reminds me of lemon and the other of anise." Stoneroot is an easy care natural for the center's Quarry Garden since its native habitat is moist, rocky woodlands. Native to: Quebec to Wisconsin, south to Florida panhandle, Alabama, and Arkansas.

Coreopsis *(Coreopsis)*

Daisylike coreopsis flowers add cheerful yellow to summer gardens outdoors and are charming components of informal arrangements indoors. While all are long-blooming, some need to be deadheaded to live up to that reputation.

Goldfink *(C. grandiflora* **'Goldfink').** This is the dwarf version of big-flower coreopsis. It's best planted in a hot, relatively dry area to discourage slugs, who love to hide among its thick foliage clumps and to chew away at them. I like this plant because it is perfect for a summer border edge; it does, however, need to be deadheaded almost daily to prolong its flowering period. Native to: species found in Missouri and Kansas, south to Florida and New Mexico.

Bloom Period: Late summer
  into fall
Zones: 4–9

Black Cohosh

Light: Part shade to shade
  in South; sun to part
  shade in North
Height: 5 to 7 feet
Color: White
Bloom Period: Midsummer
Zones: 3–9

Fairy Candles

Light: Part shade to shade
  in south; sun to part
  shade in north
Height: 4 to 6 feet
Color: Greenish white
Bloom Period: Late summer
Zones: 3–9

Stoneroot

Light: Part shade
Height: 3 to 5 feet
Color: Yellow
Bloom Period: Late summer
Zones: 3–8

Goldfink

Light: Sun
Height: 6 to 8 inches
Color: Golden yellow
Bloom Period: All summer
  if deadheaded; otherwise,
  early summer
Zones: 5–10

Lance Coreopsis

Light: Sun
Height: 1 to 2 feet
Color: Golden yellow
Bloom Period: Late spring
through much of sum-
mer if deadheaded
Zones: 3–9

Moonbeam Coreopsis

Light: Sun
Height: 18 to 24 inches
Color: Pale yellow
Bloom Period: Late spring
throughout summer and
sometimes into early fall
Zones: 3–10

Stiff Coreopsis

Light: Sun
Height: 18 to 36 inches
Color: Yellow
Bloom Period: Late spring
into summer
Zones: 3–8

Threadleaf Coreopsis

Light: Sun
Height: 1 to 3 feet
Color: Golden yellow
Bloom Period: Summer;
rebloom in early fall if
cut back
Zones: 3–10

Fringed Bleeding Heart

Light: Partial shade to
shade
Height: 12 to 18 inches
Color: Pink; cultivars in
white

Lance Coreopsis *(C. lanceolata).* This is a floppy plant that's great in an informal border. While it too needs to be deadheaded to prolong its flowering period, it requires absolutely no other care. Native to: Michigan south to Florida and New Mexio.

Moonbeam Coreopsis *(C. 'Moonbeam').* This is one of the workhorses of any sunny garden—formal, informal, native, nonnative. Its pale yellow flowers bloom away for months and do not need dead-heading. Its wispy foliage takes on an almost ethereal form as it floats among larger-leaved plants. There is much discussion as to the true botanical name for this plant. While some say it is a form of threadleaf coreopsis, it has none of that plant's invasive tendencies. Though it tolerates some shade, this is really best grown in full sun. Native to: cultivated variety with American parents. *(Pictured on pages 53 and 237)*

Stiff Coreopsis *(C. palmata).* Forming dense patches through spreading rhizomes, stiff coreopsis was a major component in the prairies of long ago. Today it is a staple in the intersection and overpass plantings of the Iowa Department of Transportation. This is a good candidate for dry soils and will even grow in sand. Native to: central United States.

Threadleaf Coreopsis *(C. verticillata).* With a long bloom period of golden yellow flowers and fine, feathery green foliage, this is a very attractive plant. It is also a very invasive one, if given the opportunity. Scott Woodbury at the Shaw Arboretum in Missouri keeps it well behaved by placing it among the dry shade roots of a large tree. You can also enjoy this plant if you have dry, difficult spots or need to cover a large planting area. Do not, as I did, place it in a small garden with good soil; in that situation, it becomes a takeover plant. Native to: Maryland to Florida, west to Arkansas. *(Pictured on page 50)*

Fringed Bleeding Heart *(Dicentra eximia)*

I love this plant. It has pretty teardrop-shaped flowers and good-looking, feathery, blue green foliage; it decorates border edges and flower arrangements for long periods; and it requires no care. It is the kind of perennial I call a garden workhorse. And it is a highly adaptable one at that, as evidenced by contributors to this book recommending it for woodland gardens, European borders, and city containers and balconies. Native to: mountains from New York to Georgia. *(Pictured on pages 55 and 189)*

Coneflower *(Echinacea)*

If there is one genus that typifies the native plant movement, this would be it. Its exceptionally durable members bear colorful flowers throughout the summer and can be grown in many different situations and circumstances. All have prominent disks (the "cones") and colorful petals.

Western Coneflower (E. angustifolia). Larry G. Vickerman, director of the Dyck Arboretum of the Plains in Hesston, Kansas, recommends this species because it is "shorter and more drought-tolerant than purple coneflower." Native to: Minnesota to Saskatchewan, south to Tennessee and Texas.

Pale Purple Coneflower (E. pallida). To me, this plant looks like a purple coneflower on a diet. Its color is a softer purple and its petals are not only thinner but hang from the central cone much as a pageboy hairdo. While purple coneflowers can be incorporated into a formal border, this plant is more suitable for roadway sites or informal, prairie settings. In these last situations, it is a tough, long-lived perennial. Native to: midwestern United States, south to Georgia, Alabama, and Louisiana. *(Pictured on page 64)*

Purple Coneflower (E. purpurea). The most popular of the coneflowers, this plant has been taken over by breeders and now appears in many colors and forms. All are colorful, easy care additions to garden borders. The species plant, however, remains the best candidate for highway plantings. Native to: prairies from Ohio to Iowa, south to Georgia and Louisiana. *(Pictured on pages 1, 57, 104, and 263)*

Rattlesnake Master *(Eryngium yuccifolium)*

With its gray foliage and off-white flowers, this is a prairie plant on the verge of discovery by garden designers. Pair it with other pastels, as garden writer Peter Loewer does in his Asheville, North Carolina, garden for an easy care plant in a humid setting. Plant it in dry areas

Bloom Period: Profuse flowers in spring; sporadic rebloom through rest of growing season with ample water and cool temperatures
Zones: 3–10

Western Coneflower
Light: Sun
Height: 18 to 24 inches
Color: Rose purple, white
Bloom Period: Summer
Zones: 3–7

Pale Purple Coneflower
Light: Sun
Height: 2 to 4 feet
Color: Pale purple
Bloom Period: Early summer
Zones: 4–8

Purple Coneflower
Light: Sun to bright shade
Height: 3 to 4 feet; cultivars 18 to 48 inches
Color: Many purples and pinks, white
Bloom Period: All summer; often into fall with deadheading
Zones: 3–9

Rattlesnake Master
Light: Sun
Height: 4 feet
Color: Off-white
Bloom Period: Summer
Zones: 3–10

The white buttonlike flowers and grayish green foliage of rattlesnake master (Eryngium yuccifolium) *are handsome in both dry Kansas gardens—it is a recommendation of the Dyck Arboretum of the Plains—and humid North Carolina borders. Garden writer Peter Loewer uses it in the latter situation and in so doing demonstrates what a handsome contribution this prairie plant makes to pastel plantings.*

with a skirt of wine red poppy mallows *(Callirhoe involucrata).* Use your imagination and try it! Native to: Connecticut to Florida, west to Minnesota, Kansas, and Texas.

Eupatorium *(Eupatorium)*

European breeders have done a lot of work with this genus and are producing towering plants that make dramatic statements in garden borders. Both species and cultivars are valued for their late season bloom and ease of care.

Hardy Ageratum *(E. coelestinum).* "It's true that this is invasive," Sue Vrooman of the Atlanta History Center admits and then quickly adds, "but what a wonderful color and what a long, late bloom season. Besides, it isn't that hard to pull out anyway." Well, maybe so. I spend a good hour or more every spring cursing hardy ageratum as I yank out its white underground stolons. And then I love it every August when its numerous fuzzy blue flowers start to open and add a cool, fresh dimension to the garden border. If you want more love than hate in your relationship with this plant, place it in a contained growing area. Native to: New Jersey to Kansas, south to West Indies, Florida and Texas. *(Pictured on page 209)*

Hollow Joe-Pye Weed *(E. fistulosum).* Left to its own devices, this can be a garden giant. In my garden, however, it's whacked back to 3 feet in early June so that it's bushier and doesn't top 6 feet. Its large, dusty rose flowers are alive with bees; generally, I can only cut flowers for arrangements in the evening. Though its natural habitat is moist soils, it does fine in my beds with a good weekly watering during dry spells. A short (less than 5 feet) white form, Album, has just entered the trade and is a handsome addition to gardens with white or pastel themes. Native to: Maine south to Florida and Texas.

White Snakeroot *(E. rugosum).* Talk about ruggedness: last year, I saw this plant growing out of a crack in a second-floor balcony on the grounds of Rockefeller University in Manhattan. Actually, its bright white flowers were quite decorative, showing once again that nature can create splendid displays all on its own. In my gardens, I have placed this plant in the back of a small, dry shade border and treasure its fresh blooms from early September to mid October. What is truly remarkable about both settings is that this plant is supposed to need constant moisture in order to perform well. Native to: eastern North America.

Flowering Spurge *(Euphorbia corollata)*

Here's a mystery: not even an effusive copy treatment and lush photograph in Wayside catalogue can convince gardeners to incorporate this wonderful plant in their borders; it was dropped from Wayside due to lack of demand. This drought-tolerant perennial with elegant bluish green foliage is covered with swarms of tiny white flowers throughout July and August. If you think it's too tall, you can whack it back to 6 inches or more and it will just get bushier and more floriferous. It even adds interest to a fall garden, as its foliage turns a nice red. All this and a constitution as tough as nails: the Michigan Department of Transportation routinely uses it in its highway plantings. Native to: Ontario to Minnesota, south to Florida and Texas. *(Pictured on page 53)*

Hardy Ageratum

Light: Sun to part shade
Height: 1 to 3 feet
Color: Blue
Bloom Period: Late summer
 into fall
Zones: 6–10

Hollow Joe-Pye Weed

Light: Sun to part shade
Height: 6 to 10 feet
Color: Dusty rose
Bloom Period: Summer
 into fall
Zones: 3–10

White Snakeroot

Light: Sun to shade
Height: 30 to 50 inches
Color: White
Bloom Period: Late summer
 into fall
Zones: 3–10

Flowering Spurge

Light: Sun to part shade
Height: 1 to 3 feet
Color: White
Bloom Period: Summer;
 rebloom into fall if cut
 back
Zones: 3–10

Queen-of-the-Prairie

Light: Sun
Height: 6 to 7 feet
Color: Pink
Bloom Period: Early summer
Zones: 4–8

Bottle Gentian

Light: Sun to shade
Height: 1 to 2 feet
Color: Blue
Bloom Period: Fall
Zones: 3–9

Soapwort Gentian

Light: Light shade
Height: 10 to 28 inches
Color: Blue
Bloom Period: Late summer into fall
Zones: 5–9

Wild Geranium

Light: Part shade
Height: 18 to 24 inches
Color: Blue-violet
Bloom Period: Spring
Zones: 3–9

Queen-of-the-Prairie *(Filipendula rubra)*

There's only one reason why I grow and list this plant: the two to three weeks in July when its cotton candy plumes of pink flowers are in bloom. These flowers are so luscious that I forgive the plant its invasiveness (indeed, I've moved it to a place where it's safely hemmed in) and its susceptibility to Japanese beetles. When beetle attacks are severe, I cut the stalks to the ground, with no apparent detriment to next year's growth. Native to: Pennsylvania to Michigan, south to Georgia and Missouri. *(Pictured on page 201)*

Gentian *(Gentiana)*

These natives are grown for the fresh blue color they add to borders at the end of the garden year.

Bottle Gentian *(G. andrewsii).* This is supposed to be a somewhat difficult plant to grow, one preferring moist areas. For some reason, it has done very well in my native plant bed. It is in a sunny area but receives cooling shade from larger, nearby plants. The site is well drained, so I don't think one can call it moist, particularly during the dry spells Princeton has experienced the past couple of summers. For three years now, it has produced blue flowers from early October into the first or second week of November. In my garden at least, this is an exceptionally easy care plant. Native to: eastern North America.

Soapwort Gentian *(G. saponaria).* Perennial plantsman Pierre Bennerup says this is the most heat-tolerant gentian and easily raised from seed. He received his first batch as a gift from noted plantsman and author Allen Lacy. As with all gentians, its lovely blue flowers are a beautiful complement in late season borders filled with yellows. Native to: Pennsylvania to Illinois, south to Florida panhandle and Louisiana.

Wild Geranium *(G. maculatum)*

This eastern woodland plant is a charming addition to spring borders. L. H. Bailey was telling gardeners this at the beginning of the century and now, toward its close, Heather McCargo at Garden in the Woods in Massachusetts and Robert Bartolomei at the New York Botanical Garden are repeating his message. All cite its ease of care, colorful spring flowers, and large, deeply lobed green leaves. Native to: woodlands from Maine to Georgia and Mississippi.

Prairie Smoke *(Geum triflorum)*

Prairie smoke, as the popular name implies, is native to the middle part of North America. It is valued not only for its colorful flowers and exotic seed plumes—which do indeed resemble low smoke wisps—but also its bloom time, since it is one of the few such plants to decorate spring settings. Native to: dry woods and prairies from Ontario to Alberta, south to Illinois, Nebraska, and Montana. *(Pictured on pages 29 and 95)*

Bowman's Root *(Gillenia [Porteranthus] trifoliata)*

Long admired in Europe for its glossy, cut leaf foliage, mahogony red stems, and summer-long swarms of dainty white flowers, this plant is rarely found in borders in its home continent. Perhaps part of the problem is that it is touted as being trouble-free and this is not always the case. Something does eat the foliage of mine in late spring but eventually the plant grows big enough to overcome it. In addition, bowman's root requires good drainage, which is why I killed two plants in some unamended heavy clay soil in one section of my property. Treat it right, however—good soil and good drainage—and you will be rewarded, as I finally am, with an elegant plant that adds a touch of class to garden settings. Native to: New York, Ontario, and Michigan, south to Georgia and Alabama. *(Pictured on page 55)*

Helenium *(H. autumnale)*

Sometimes called Helen's flower, this American native has been transformed under the careful attention of European breeders. Moorheim Beauty, a popular cultivar, has rich red blossoms that fade to a bronze orange from July to mid September. I have this plant plus the species, which is yellow and blooms from mid August through September.

Prairie Smoke

Light: Sun to part shade
Height: 8 to 12 inches
Color: Rose red flowers, silver pink seed plumes
Bloom Period: Spring
Zones: 3–8

Bowman's Root

Light: Light shade
Height: 2 to 4 feet
Color: White
Bloom Period: Summer
Zones: 4–8

Helenium

Light: Sun
Height: 4 to 5 feet; cultivars 2 to 6 feet
Color: Yellow; cultivars in reds, oranges, coppers, and bronzes
Bloom Period: Late summer into fall; cultivars often start earlier
Zones: 3–9

Swamp Sunflower

Light: Sun
Height: 4 to 8 feet
Color: Golden yellow
Bloom Period: Late summer
  to early fall
Zones: 6–8

Sheila's Sunshine

Light: Sun
Height: 7 to 9 feet
Color: Pale yellow
Bloom Period: Early fall
Zones: Not established;
  probably 6–9

Downy Sunflower

Light: Sun
Height: 4 to 5 feet
Color: Butter yellow
Bloom Period: Summer
Zones: 4–8

Willowleaf Sunflower

Light: Sun
Height: 6 to 8 feet
Color: Yellow
Bloom Period: Late summer
  into fall
Zones: 4–10

Both are handsome, easy care perennials and wonderful additions to borders. Check garden catalogs for even more luscious cultivars to try. Native to: Quebec to Florida, west to British Columbia and Arizona. *(Pictured on pages 3, 27, and 268)*

Sunflower *(Helianthus)*

Members of this North American genus are valued for their cheerful yellow flowers and great ease of care.

Swamp Sunflower *(H. angustifolius).* "Nothing can beat this one for mass display," writes Richard L. Johnson of the Caroline Dormon Nature Preserve in Louisiana. "Indeed," he adds, "it forms a very cheerful sight on a grand scale." Swamp sunflower features both large leaves that accent early gardens and then 2- to 3-inch flowers in late summer gardens. Through fall and much of winter, birds are attracted to the seedheads. Native to: open woods, meadows, and wetlands from Long Island to Florida, west to southern Missouri, southeastern Oklahoma, and Texas.

Sheila's Sunshine *(H. giganteus* 'Sheila's Sunshine'). Brought into commercial trade by Niche Gardens, this sunflower is unique in that it has pale yellow flowers. Native to: cultivar found growing in fields near Chapel Hill, North Carolina; species found Virginia to Tennessee, south to South Carolina and Mississippi.

Downy Sunflower *(H. mollis).* The popular name for this plant reflects the white hairs that cover its foliage. Thriving in many garden situations, including those with poor, dry soils, this sunflower features an abundance of large flowers and is an easy care recommendation of Robert Bartolomei, curator of the native plant garden at the New York Botanical Garden. Native to: Massachusetts to northern Georgia, west to Wisconsin, Kansas, Oklahoma, and Texas.

Willowleaf Sunflower *(H. salicifolius).* With good upright habit and great flowers, this is an easy care favorite of both the Dyck Arboretum of the Plains in Kansas and the New York Botanical Garden. It features airy, willowlike foliage and numerous flowers with purplish brown disks and yellow petals. Native to: dry or limestone areas from western Missouri and eastern Kansas, south to Oklahoma and northern Texas.

Woodland Sunflower *(H. strumosus).* Even shade gardeners can have a sunflower in their beds! As with all sunflowers, this one has large yellow flowers that bloom for almost a month. Though it does need to be staked to stand tall (I just let it flop), it is easy care in every other aspect. Be warned, however, that it can become invasive in optimum growing conditions. Native to: Maine through Ontario to Minnesota, south to Florida and Texas.

Ox-Eye Sunflower *(Heliopsis helianthoides)*

Featuring a continuous supply of orange yellow flowers resembling large chrysanthemum blossoms, ox-eye sunflower is a wonderful staple of the summer garden. I have the cultivar Summer Sun; it is a double form that has selfseeded true over the years. Its flowers are a standout in the garden and long-lasting in arrangements. Native to: New York to Michigan and northern Illinois, south to Georgia and New Mexico. *(Pictured on page 50)*

Hepatica *(H. acutiloba)*

This diminutive perennial is a treasure in early season woodland gardens, when its blush purple flowers brighten up bare settings. Sometimes called sharp-lobed hepatica, its leaves have three sharp points. If your soil is heavily acidic, try the closely related *H. americana*, which has more rounded leaves and greater tolerance for such soils. Native to: Quebec to Manitoba, south to Georgia, Alabama, and Missouri.

Red Yucca *(Hesperaloe parviflora)*

Denise Delaney of the National Wildflower Research Center in Texas introduced me to this plant and I am looking forward to testing it in the humidity of a New Jersey summer. It sounds just wonderful. In its native areas, its slim, arching flower stalks spray out to over 5 feet and are covered with tiny tubular flowers from March through July. Its only drawback—and this is a serious obstacle to many gardeners—is that deer love it. Native to: Texas. *(Pictured on page 19)*

Woodland Sunflower

Light: Part shade
Height: 4 feet
Color: Yellow
Bloom Period: Mid to late summer
Zones: 4–8

Ox-Eye Sunflower

Light: Sun
Height: 40 to 60 inches
Color: Yellow, orange yellow
Bloom Period: All summer, if deadheaded
Zones: 4–9

Hepatica

Light: Light shade
Height: 3 to 5 inches
Color: Blush purple, pale pinkish white
Bloom Period: Late winter in southern range; early spring farther north
Zones: 3–8

Red Yucca

Light: Sun to bright shade
Height: Foliage, 2 feet; flower stalks, 5 feet
Color: Coral to salmon pink
Bloom Period: Spring into early summer; some rebloom
Zones: 6–10

Heuchera *(Heuchera)*

This is one of my favorite genera. I love its members for their handsome foliage, attractive flowers, and great ease of care. They are, it must be admitted, a promiscuous lot and interbreed among themselves with abandon. This has led to the creation of stunning hybrids and cultivars and a good deal of confusion within the gardening public, for what you read about is not always what you get.

Palace Purple is a classic example. This cultivar was found growing on the grounds of Kew Gardens and reintroduced to its homeland by plantsman Allen Bush. When Palace Purple was named 1991 Plant of the Year by the Perennial Plant Association, the garden public clamored for it. Many breeders inexpensively obliged by propagating thousands of plants from seed, and the result was more often than not plants with dark green leaves rather than rich purple ones. I believe I am among the many who are disappointed with this plant.

Dan Heims of the wholesale firm Terra Nova Nursery in Portland, Oregon, had a better idea. He not only propagates heucheras, he also patents them, which means he controls the result and profits from it. Under his truly creative approach, a range of stunning cultivars have appeared on the market. Heims, as I have written in magazine articles, must have kissed the Blarney Stone in his youth because he is the most

The rich purple foliage of Montrose Ruby (Heuchera americana X H. 'Palace Purple') provides color in the garden from early spring through frost. It is pictured here in mid May as the last white blossoms of sand phlox (P. bifida) appear and the blue buds of common camass (Camassia quamash) prepare to open.

persuasive plant seller I have ever come across. To read his descriptions of his plants or, even better, to hear him talk about them is to become his immediate customer. Here, for example, is what he wrote about the metallic sheen on the 7-inch-wide, ruffled leaves of Stormy Seas: "Visions of dark gray waves smashing into the seashore evoked this name." Thanks to lack of room on my property, I have been pretty good at resisting Heims; however, I have completely succumbed to his Pewter Veil, described on page 256.

Heucheras require good drainage and should probably be divided every three or four years. Just break up a clump with a trowel and replant rooted sections elsewhere or give them to friends. Where summer heat is humid, give them shade and good air circulation. One sad note: heucheras are subject to attack from vine weevils. Happily, however, these pests—which are quite prevalent on my property—do at most minor damage to the following.

Dale's Strain *(H. americana* **'Dale's Strain')**. This is among the most beautiful shade foliage plants to be found. It has large leaves mottled with silver; in winter, those that remain turn purple with the cold. Its greenish white flowers, appearing on top of stems that can reach 4 feet in height, are dramatic in dried arrangements. There's also a rather sad story to this plant. The original was found and named by Dale Hendricks of Northcreek Nursery and was known as Dale's Selection (I have this plant). Breeders started producing it from seed and the resulting plants were not always as beautiful as those produced vegetatively, which is why plants offered today are called Dale's Strain. Native to: dry woods from Connecticut to Ontario and Minnesota, south to Georgia and Louisiana.

Montrose Ruby *(H. americana* **X** *H.* **'Palace Purple')**. To me, writing about heucheras is a challenge because it is so difficult to come up with new superlatives. Montrose Ruby is yet another garden treasure. I bought this plant four years ago when I read the following description in Nancy Goodwin's Montrose Nursery catalog: "We were terribly excited when we noticed a flat of heucheras with dark purple leaves, mottled with silver. . . . Flowers appear in summer rather than spring and are similar to those of *H. villosa.* The best feature of this plant is that it does not lose its dark foliage color even in mid-summer." When Goodwin later decided to close her nursery,

---

Dale's Strain

Light: Part shade to shade
Height: Basal foliage, 6 to 8 inches; wiry flower stems 2 to 4 feet
Color: Greenish white
Bloom Period: Late spring to early summer
Zones: 4–9

Montrose Ruby

Light: Part shade
Height: 22 to 26 inches
Color: Blush pink
Bloom Period: Summer
Zones: Not established; probably 4–9

Pewter Veil

Light: Part shade
Height: Basal foliage, 6 to
  8 inches; wiry flower
  stems to 3 feet
Color: Pinkish white
Bloom Period: Late spring
  to early summer
Zones: Not established;
  probably 4–9

Cylindrica Heuchera

Light: Sun to part shade
Height: 2 to 3 feet
Color: Cream; occasional
  intense coral pink
Bloom Period: Spring
Zones: 3–10

Prairie Heuchera

Light: Sun to part shade
Height: 2 to 3 feet
Color: Creamy tan, tinged
  with green
Bloom Period: Spring
Zones: Not established; at
  least 3–6 and possibly
  farther south

Coral Bells

Light: Sun to shade
Height: 12 to 18 inches
Color: Red, pink, white
Bloom Period: Spring well
  into summer
Zones: 3–10

other mail-order nurseries bought and propagated the plant. In addition to shorter, later-blooming flowers, Montrose Ruby has more red in its purple coloring than Pewter Veil. Native to: hybrid with American parents. *(Pictured on page 254)*

Pewter Veil (H. americana 'Pewter Veil'). In essence, this is the purple version of Dale's Strain. It is hard to find any green on this plant. Its leaves are purple underneath and then strikingly mottled purple and silver on top. The long, wiry stems are purple also and the flowers are a pinkish white. This is an absolutely stunning, easy care plant. Native to: cultivar with American parents.

Cylindrica Heuchera (H. cylindrica). This heuchera is primarily grown for its large, lush green clumps of foliage. In good growing conditions—such as those at the New York Botanical Garden—cylindrica heuchera rivals hosta as a foliage plant. The soil in my garden, however, does not rival that in the New York Botanical Garden; as a result, the foliage clump is quite restrained, but nice nevertheless. There are also those who praise the creamy flowers; the cultivar Greenfinch is reputed to be a favorite among flower arrangers. What a surprise then when my seed-propagated cylindrica heuchera bore intense coral pink flowers, the kind that appear on the cultivar Hyperion. It would seem then that this color is a spontaneous as well as a cultivated one. Native to: Alberta to British Columbia, south to Wyoming, Nevada, and northern California.

Prairie Heuchera (H. richardsonii). While the flowers on this heuchera are definitely not as colorful as those on others, they are upright and have an airy grace about them. Simply by chance, I planted prairie heuchera next to a creamy white form of great camass *(Camassia leichtlinii 'Alba')* and the two paired together beautifully. Unlike great camass, which goes dormant, prairie heuchera contributes continued interest to the garden with its handsome clump of green foliage. Native to: eastern side of Rocky Mountains from Manitoba and Saskatchewan south to Indiana and Minnesota. *(Pictured on page 189)*

Coral Bells (H. sanguinea). This is the very first heuchera I grew and it remains a favorite twenty years later. My neighbor, Jean Woodward, gave me my original clump when we moved into our house; her plants had already been growing for twenty-five years on her property. These are truly tough, adaptable, and beautiful perennials. In full sun they will bear coral pink flowers on wiry stems for up to four months; in full shade their mottled foliage provides texture and contrast. These plants are also parents to a group of hybrids known as *H. X brizoides*. I've tried several and the only one that has proved as satisfactory as the species is Chatterbox, which has larger flowers. Native to: New Mexico and Arizona, south to Mexico. *(Pictured on pages 52 and 53)*

Hairy Alumroot (*H. villosa*). This species has large, maplelike leaves that are very variable with regard to foliage color. I am a fan of two named offerings. Royal Red was chosen by Eleanor Saur for its deep purple coloring. I have this plant in dark shade and it looks stunning. At the other light extreme—full sun—is Purpurea (Crownsville Nursery is the only mail order source I know of for this selection). As its name implies, it has beautiful purple foliage and is lovely paired with the silver gray of David's Choice artemisia *(A. pycnocephala)* and many other plants as well. Native to: Virginia to Tennessee, south to Georgia.

Bridget Bloom (X *Heucherella* 'Bridget Bloom')

A gift to the gardening world from noted British plantsman Alan Bloom, this wonderful hybrid is an elegant addition to shade gardens. It has lobed, marked foliage and dainty flower spikes that bloom up to eight weeks. It increases slowly—to my great frustration because I would love to have plants scattered in abundance throughout my property—by forming clumps that can be divided. Native to: an intergeneric hybrid created from American *Heuchera* and *Tiarella* plants. *(Pictured on page 179)*

Rose Mallow *(Hibiscus moscheutos)*

Featured in the wetland area at the National Garden in Washington, D.C., this colorful late summer native can also be seen decorating marshes throughout the eastern half of the country. Its large flowers with dark, crimson centers are elegant in both natural and more formal settings. Breeders have been busy working on this species, often crossing it with closely related *H. coccineus* and *H. militaris,* and have listed the resulting hybrids as cultivars of *H. moscheutos.* Among the

Hairy Alumroot

Light: Sun to shade
Height: 1 to 3 feet
Color: White
Bloom Period: Late summer
Zones: 5–9

Bridget Bloom

Light: Part shade
Height: 18 inches
Color: Pink touched with white
Bloom Period: Late spring into summer
Zones: 3–10

Rose Mallow

Light: Sun to part shade
Height: 3 to 5 feet
Color: Red, pink, or white
Bloom Period: Late summer to midfall
Zones: 5–9

Copper Iris

Light: Sun to part shade
Height: 2 to 3 feet
Color: Reddish brick
 petals and apricot centers
Bloom Period: Late May to
 early June
Zones: 6–9

Louisiana Iris

Light: Sun to part shade
Height: 6 to 48 inches
Color: The entire rainbow
 spectrum, plus white
Bloom Period: Spring to
 summer
Zones: 4–9

Contraband Girl

Light: Sun to part shade
Height: 20 inches
Color: Blue purple
Bloom Period: Spring
Zones: 6–10

more popular of these is the dwarf Disco Belle strains, often used as standards in pot plants, and the Lord Baltimore series, which feature brilliant red flowers. Native to: salt and fresh water marshes from Massachusetts to Michigan, south to Florida panhandle and Alabama.

Iris *(Iris)*

Unlike the popular German irises, American irises are not top-heavy with flowers and tend to have more beautiful foliage.

Copper Iris *(I. fulva)*. This handsome iris with strikingly colored spring flowers is one of the parents contributing to the hybrid group known as Louisiana irises. Scott Woodbury of the Shaw Arboretum in Missouri recommends pairing it with Husker Red *(Penstemon digitalis* 'Husker Red'*)* and rose verbena *(V. canadensis)* for an interesting and bold color scheme. Native to: swamps from Illinois to Georgia, west to Missouri and Texas.

Louisiana Iris *(I. X 'Louisiana', a group of native species that interbreed).* "Unique to our state and grown worldwide now—these natural hybrids of south Louisiana extract ooh's and aah's by all who see them in bloom," writes Richard L. Johnson of the Caroline Dormon Nature Preserve in Louisiana. The preserve hosts a superb display of these irises, all descendants of those collected by Caroline Dormon during the 1920s and 1930s. "They constitute one of the great botanical mysteries," she wrote. "The unbelievable variations in size, form and color make classifying extremely difficult." Among the many hybrids and forms available, the purplish red Dorothea K. Williamson is widely recognized as the hardiest, though certainly not the prettiest. Native to: all meet in Louisiana; various species found from Ohio to Illinois, south to Florida and west to Kansas and Texas.

Contraband Girl *(I. virginica 'Contraband Girl')*. This southern version of the popular blue flag bears much larger flowers than the species plant and is a beautiful addition to spring borders. Scott Woodbury of the Shaw Arboretum in Missouri says that it grows well in swamps or in regular garden soil and that its robust foliage is truly outstanding in the garden throughout the growing season. Native to: wet areas on coastal plains from southeastern Virginia to Texas.

Twinleaf

Light: Woodland shade
Height: 10 to 12 inches
Color: White
Bloom Period: Early spring
Zones: 5–8

Lewisia

Light: Sun
Height: 6 to 8 inches
Color: White, orange,
  salmon, and pink
Bloom Period: Spring to
  early summer
Zones: 6–8

Twinleaf *(Jeffersonia diphylla)*

Named for Thomas Jefferson, the gleaming white flowers on this perennial are among the first to emerge in the spring garden. David Benner, however, recommends and grows this easy care plant in his Pennsylvania woodland garden because of its handsome, almost sculptural foliage. The leaves not only rival those of medium-sized hostas but also have greater resistance to disfigurement by slugs and insects. Native to: Ontario to Wisconsin, south to Georgia and Alabama.

Lewisia *(L. cotyledon hybrids)*

When given perfect drainage—not an easily attained situation in many gardens—these are beautiful spring plants. Though native to the West Coast, they can be grown in humid East Coast gardens, as evidenced by Helen Benedict's stunning display of these flowers in Rocky Hill, New Jersey. Lewisias are among the easy care natives recommended by Danish plantswoman Grethe B. Petersen. Native to: species found in rocky mountain areas in southern Oregon and northern California.

Blue Flax

Light: Sun
Height: Arching 3 feet
Color: Sky blue
Bloom Period: For up to three months after snow melts
Zones: 3–8

Cardinal Flower

Light: Sun to shade
Height: 2 to 4 feet
Color: Scarlet
Bloom Period: Late summer
Zones: 2–9

Hybrid Lobelias

Light: Sun to shade, with part shade the most suitable for all
Height: 2 to 5 feet
Color: The entire red-blue-white spectrum
Bloom Period: Various times from July through September
Zones: 4–9

Blue Flax *(Linum perenne var. lewisii)*

"Petite blue flowers perched on long, swaying stems," is how Penny A. Wilson of Las Pilitas Nursery in California describes this charming plant. Exceptionally drought-tolerant, blue flax can be grown in gardens located in mountains or deserts; it does, however, need water in the latter situation. In both areas and particularly in ordinary garden settings, it is exceptionally long-blooming. Native to: middle to high elevations from Alaska to southern California.

Lobelia *(Lobelia)*

In the wild, lobelias are found growing in moist soils. Thus, not surprisingly, this kind of garden setting ensures the greatest success with these plants. Big blue lobelia is so tough, however, that it can grow in just about any kind of nondesert situation. Thurman Maness, proprietor of the Wildwood Flower, has been working with the genus for over a decade now and has created some absolutely stunning cultivars. Most have the toughness of big blue lobelia and all exhibit the elegance of red cardinal flower. My favorite among his many hybrids is Ruby Slippers, which is described in greater detail below.

Cardinal Flower *(L. cardinalis).* The scarlet red spikes of cardinal flowers are magnets for hummingbirds and always pop up when I ask horticulturists to name their favorite easy care plants. They are, then, an excellent example of my tenet that what is easy care for some is not necessarily so for all. I killed this plant. This does not upset me, because there are hundreds of other wonderful flowers to take its place. I probably killed it because I placed it in a dry rather than a moist area. This leads to a second tenet: if a plant is to be truly easy care, it must be planted in suitable growing conditions. Native to: New Brunswick to Minnesota, south to Florida and east Texas.

Hybrid Lobelias *(L. X hybrida).* The tall grace of lobelias, their many colors, and their strong constitutions have attracted the eyes of plant breeders and the result is many stunning and wonderful cultivars. I like Rose Beacon, a pretty rose pink that blooms in midsummer, and I adore Ruby Slippers, which blooms late summer into fall. The color on this plant is a real breakthrough—a luscious ruby red. Native to: parents native to eastern United States. *(Rose Beacon pictured on page 53; Ruby Slippers picutred on page 27)*

Big Blue Lobelia *(L siphilitica).* This is a tough-as-nails plant: I once saw it growing out of a curbstone crack. I'd rather, however, see its flower spires rising in late summer garden beds. While I have both the blue and the white forms, I much prefer the latter because I think the flowers stand out more. Native to: Maine to South Dakota, south to North Carolina, Mississippi, and Kansas.

Lupine *(Lupinus)*

Members of this genus are valued for their exquisite flower spires that decorate spring gardens.

Wild Lupine *(L. perennis).* With its colorful blue spikes, this is one of the most successful plants in Bonnie Harper-Lore's front yard garden in Minnesota. It also thrives in many other areas as well—as long as the soil is sandy. Native to: dry sandy soils from Maine to Minnesota, south to Florida and Louisiana.

Streamside Lupine *(L. polyphyllus* hybrids). Recommended by Danish plantswoman Grethe B. Petersen, this northwest native has large, beautiful green leaves and handsome flower spikes. According to noted American author and University of Georgia horticultural professor Allan Armitage, the species plant survives well outside its cool, moist habitat and can take the cold, heat, and humidity of the East Coast. Native to: species found in meadows and by mountain streams from British Columbia to California.

Fringed Loosestrife *(Lysimachia ciliata* var. *purpurea)*

Valued for its purple foliage, fringed loosestrife also features pale yellow flowers in summer. While not as invasive as Asian loosestrifes, this plant can travel rampantly when given room and placed in rich garden soil. At the New York Botanical Garden, curator Bob Bartolomei pairs it with the reddish hues of bowman's root *(Gillenia trifoliata)* and keeps it

Big Blue Lobelia

Light: Sun to shade
Height: 2 to 4 feet
Color: Blue, white
Bloom Period: Late summer into fall
Zones: 4–9

Wild Lupine

Light: Sun
Height: 1 to 2 feet
Color: Blue
Bloom Period: Spring
Zones: 3–8

Streamside Lupine

Light: Sun to part shade
Height: 15 to 48 inches
Color: Yellow, white, blue through red, pink
Bloom Period: Spring
Zones: 5–8

Fringed Loosestrife

Light: Sun to partial shade
Height: 36 to 40 inches
Color: Pale yellow flowers; purple-tinged foliage
Bloom Period: Summer
Zones: 3–10

Barbara's Buttons

Light: Sun to part shade
Height: 1 to 2 feet
Color: Pink
Bloom Period: Summer
Zones: 5–9

Virginia Bluebell

Light: Dappled shade to
　shade
Height: 1 to 2 feet
Color: Pink buds opening
　to sky blue flowers
Bloom Period: Early spring
Zones: 3–9

**Allegheny Monkey
Flower**

Light: Part shade
Height: 2 to 3 feet
Color: Purple splotched
　with yellow
Bloom Period: All summer
Zones: 3–9

Miterwort

Light: Shade
Height: 10 to 16 inches
Color: Creamy white
Bloom Period: Spring
Zones: 3–8

Bee Balm

Light: Sun to part shade
Height: 18 to 40 inches
Color: Purple, red, pink,
　white
Bloom Period: Early to
　midsummer
Zones: 4–9

beautifully hemmed in with guardian clumps of other easy care natives. Native to: streambanks from Nova Scotia to British Columbia, south to Florida and New Mexico. *(Pictured on page 55)*

Barbara's Buttons *(Marshallia grandiflora)*

This rarely grown native is a recommendation of perennial plantsman Pierre Bennerup. "It's easy to propagate from seeds, cuttings, or divisions," he reports. A compact plant with neat basal rosettes of 7-inch leaves and pretty summer flowers, it is best placed in front of the border where it can get the attention it deserves. Native to: moist soils from Pennsylvania to North Carolina and Tennessee.

Virginia Bluebell *(Mertensia virginica)*

Blue, balmy skies seem to touch down upon the ground when the Virginia bluebells bloom in early spring. They are a lovely sight at that time of year, but a rather messy one later on as they take their time in going dormant. Either cut back the sprawling foliage when it gets truly unsightly or place these beautiful harbingers of spring in an area where the upright flowers can be admired from a distance and the decaying leaves will not be noticed. Native to: rich, moist woodlands from New York to Michigan, south to Georgia, Alabama, and Kansas. *(Pictured on pages 51 and 197)*

Allegheny Monkey Flower *(Mimulus ringens)*

A moisture-loving perennial, this otherwise undemanding plant bears small, colorful flowers on upright, unstaked stalks for over two months. Perhaps it's time this plant, grown in gardens at the beginning of this century, is returned to beds and borders at the end of the century. Native to: moist areas from Nova Scotia to Manitoba and North Dakota, south to Virginia, Texas, and Colorado.

Miterwort *(Mitella diphylla)*

This is a dainty plant for a small shade setting. In spring, its wiry stems bear tiny, creamy white flowers and throughout the remainder of the growing year its foliage contrasts nicely with that of other diminutive shade flowers. Though its native habitat consists of neutral soils, it has survived in my rather acidic shade border. Native to: neutral soils from Quebec to Minnesota, south to Georgia and Missouri. *(Pictured on page 179)*

Monarda *(Monarda)*

Members of the mint family, these plants have exotic flowers and aromatic foliage. While they like to spread about, they are shallow-rooted and can easily be pulled out.

Bee Balm *(M. didyma)*. Also called Oswego Tea in reference to its role as a tea substitute during the American Revolution, bee balm attracts hummingbirds, butterflies, bees, and mildew. To reduce the last, make sure the plant does not dry out and cut back some stems to ensure good air circulation. Breeders are working on developing mildew-resistant plants; Raspberry Wine, a White Flower Farm introduction, is an excellent example of this work. Native to: rich, moist woodlands and mountain slopes from Maine to Michigan, south to Georgia and Tennessee. *(Pictured on page 1 and at right)*

Wild Bergamot *(M. fistulosa)*. Used extensively by the Michigan Department of Transportation in its highway plantings, wild bergamot is less colorful than bee balm but more than compensates for this with its greater hardiness and resistance to both mildew and drought. Native to: eastern North America.

Horsemint *(M. punctata)*. This exceptionally colorful plant is recommended by Garden in the Woods in Massachusetts. While it was easy care in my garden, it only lasted one season; perhaps this is why HORTUS THIRD says it can also be classified as an annual or biennial. Native to: Long Island south to Florida and Louisiana.

Hot, humid August gardens can be colorful displays when filled with native plants, as Mickey Eggers demonstrates in her Princeton, New Jersey, borders. Pictured here are—clockwise from bottom left—yellow black-eyed Susans (Rudbeckia fulgida *var.* sullivantii *'Goldsturm') and Golden Glow* (Rudbeckia laciniata *'Golden Glow'), white garden phlox* (P. paniculata *'David'), purple coneflowers* (Echinacea purpurea), *and red bee balm* (Monarda didyma).

Wild Bergamot

Light: Sun to part shade
Height: 3 to 5 feet
Color: Lavender
Bloom Period: Mid to late
  summer
Zones: 3–9

Horsemint

Light: Sun to part shade
Height: 18 to 24 inches
Color: Purple-spotted yel-
  low flowers with pink
  bracts
Bloom Period: Summer
Zones: 5–10

Well-behaved Sundrops

Light: Sun to shade
Height: 18 to 30 inches
Color: Yellow
Bloom Period: Late spring
  into summer
Zones: 4–9

Missouri Primrose

Light: Sun to partial shade
Height: 6 to 18 inches
Color: Yellow
Bloom Period: Summer
Zones: 4–9

Pilosella Sundrops

Light: Sun to part shade
Height: 24 to 28 inches
Color: Yellow
Bloom Period: Heavy in
  spring, some sporadic
  rebloom thereafter
Zones: Not established;
  probably 4–8

Oenothera *(Oenothera)*

If you want color in your gardens—be they in sun or in shade—you will want at least one oenothera in them. Those with flowers opening all day are usually called sundrops and those whose blossoms open late afternoon are called evening primroses. All range in height from short to medium tall and reliably produce lovely flowers for a good three weeks and generally much longer. Japanese beetles like these plants and when their depredations are too ugly, I just cut the plants back after flowering to their basal foliage.

Well-behaved Sundrops *(O. fruticosa).* To my nonscientific eye, the chief differences between this plant and its rampant relative are that its foliage is a bit finer and it does not spread. Another difference—one that requires no scientific background to realize—is that it is rarely offered, despite being named 1989 "Wildflower of the Year" by the North Carolina Botanical Garden. You can buy it through the mail, as I did, from the Primrose Path. Native to: eastern United States. *(Pictured on page 52)*

Missouri Primrose *(O. missouriensis).* An exceptionally drought-tolerant plant, Missouri primrose has somehow managed to do well in the damp of England. It finds it rougher going in our southeast, however, when high humidity is combined with brutal heat. To make sure this is an easy care plant for you, give it excellent drainage and provide it with some shade in warm areas. I have Greencourt Lemon, a lovely pale yellow cultivar. Native to: Missouri and Kansas to Texas. *(Pictured on page 206)*

Pilosella Sundrops *(O. pilosella).* This is another noninvasive sundrop, one that is shorter and earlier blooming than its rampant relative. According to Charles and Martha Oliver of the Primrose Path, it was grown in nineteenth-century gardens and is the best of the eastern species for general garden use. Native to: central United States.

Pink Sundrops *(O. speciosa).* This is probably the most aggressive sundrop to be found in gardens. It definitely has a siren quality about it: beguiling, pale pink flowers and wicked underground stolons that spread about in every direction. Try placing it, as did Scott Woodbury at the Shaw Arboretum in Missouri, among the open shade and shallow roots of trees. The plant flowers in such challenging conditions, but its aggressiveness is contained. Native to: Kansas to Texas. *(Pictured on page 68)*

Rampant Sundrops (*O. tetragona [fruticosa* ssp. *glauca]*). This is the sundrop most commonly found in mail-order catalogs and at garden centers. It's one of the first perennials I ever grew and I always give it to those who are just starting to garden: it blooms the first year, has foliage that often turns red by late summer, and can be grown in many conditions. It does spread, however, and once you start adding other easy care perennials you may decide, as I have, that it's time to clear this plant out of your borders. Try placing it in a container; I've had one planting in a pot for seven years now and only need to water it during dry spells and thin it out at the end of the growing season. Native to: eastern United States.

Prickly Pear (*Opuntia humifusa [compressa]*)

This colorful plant, a wonderful easy care recommendation made by perennial plantsman Pierre Bennerup, is a standout in sandy seashore gardens or in shale barrens habitats. But once you plant this cactus, keep your distance—it is thorny. Native to: dry sandy sites from Massachusetts to Montana, south to Florida and eastern Texas. *(Foliage pictured on page 29)*

Golden Club (*Orontium aquaticum*)

In recommending this plant as an easy care native, Richard L. Johnson of the Caroline Dormon Nature Preserve in Louisiana wrote that it is "a fine plant for the bog garden." As a further bonus for southern gardeners, he noted that it is "evergreen for us." Native to: Massachusetts to Florida and Louisiana.

Wild Quinine (*Parthenium integrifolium*)

Though it has pure white flowers for a good 3 to 4 weeks from midsummer on, this plant has just never caught a horticulturist's fancy. While its leaves are rather coarse, they are a nice dark green. As long

---

Pink Sundrops

Light: Sun to bright shade
Height: 6 to 20 inches
Color: Pink
Bloom Period: Late spring
 to early summer
Zones: 5–10

Rampant Sundrops

Light: Sun to shade
Height: 2 to 3 feet
Color: Yellow
Bloom Period: Late spring
 into summer
Zones: 4–10

Prickly Pear

Light: Sun
Height: 6 to 10 inches
Color: Yellow
Bloom Period: Early summer
Zones: 5–9

Golden Club

Light: Sun
Height: Aquatic plant;
 spadix 3 to 4 inches
 above water
Color: Golden yellow
Bloom Period: Early spring
Zones: 6–8

Wild Quinine

Light: Sun to part shade
Height: 2 to 4 feet
Color: White
Bloom Period: Summer
Zones: 4–8

Cobaea Penstemon

Light: Sun
Height: 2 feet
Color: Purple, lavender,
 white
Bloom Period: Late spring
Zones: 5–9

White Penstemon

Light: Sun to part shade
Height: 2 to 4 feet
Color: White; cultivar in
 blush pink
Bloom Period: Late spring
 to early summer
Zones: 3–9

Shell-leaf Penstemon

Light: Sun
Height: 3 to 4 feet
Color: Lavender
Bloom Period: Late spring
Zones: 3–8

as you give wild quinine fertile soil and good drainage (or, alternatively, place it in a dry setting), you will find it completely maintenance free. Native to: Massachusetts to Minnesota, south to Georgia and Texas.

Penstemon *(Penstemon)*

Penstemons, for the most part, know their place. They tend to grow well in their native haunts and poorly elsewhere. Fortunately, there are about 250 species indigenous to the North American continent and there is at least one easy care penstemon for every garden. To further explore the beauty and diversity of this genus, send a self-addressed, stamped envelope to American Penstemon Society, 1569 Holland Court, Lakewood, Colorado 80232.

Cobaea Penstemon (*P. cobaea*). Larry G. Vickerman, director of the Dyck Arboretum of the Plains in Hesston, Kansas, recommends this plant for its large flowers and waxy, dark green foliage. "It blooms for almost a month in spring," he reports, "and grows in poor soils and dry conditions." While this is definitely easy care, it is also—as are so many penstemons—often short-lived, disappearing from the garden after three or four years. Native to: southeastern Nebraska to southern Texas. *(Pictured on page 77)*

White Penstemon (*P. digitalis*). This is really a pretty flower, a fact often forgotten because it is so common. In June, its white flowers drift among open fields throughout the eastern part of our continent and create a lovely scene for those driving by in cars or riding in trains. To keep it from spreading too much in my garden, I cut the flower heads after blooming has finished. Husker Red, a selection made by the University of Nebraska, has reddish purple foliage and blush pink flowers. The Perennial Plant Association thought so much of this flower that it named it 1996 Perennial Plant of the Year. I must be doing something wrong for though Husker Red is undoubtedly a more handsome plant, it is not as robust in my gardens as the white-flowered species. Native to: eastern and central United States.

Shell-leaf Penstemon (*P. grandiflorus*). Another penstemon recommendation from Larry G. Vickerman, director of the Dyck Arboretum of the Plains in Hesston, Kansas, this plant features lovely blue green foliage, a true asset in gardens situated in hot, dry areas. It self-seeds readily, Vickerman reports, so you are always assured of a good supply. Native to: Illinois to North Dakota and Wyoming, south to Texas. *(Pictured on page 77)*

Small's Beard Tongue (*P. smallii*). This is a charming penstemon, one that I've only grown in shaded situations, where its lovely pink and white flowers stand out. While not supposed to be long-lived, my plants are now five years old. My gardens are too crowded for them to selfseed; you might want to leave space in yours for them to do so. Native to: North Carolina and Tennessee.

Purple Prairie Clover *(Petalostemon purpureum [Dalea purpurea])*

Covered with small rose purple flower cones in summer, this prairie plant is a wonderful addition to small borders. It has a long bloom period and rich green, fine-textured foliage. It's also a nice easy care plant in larger situations, as evidenced by its use in roadside plantings by the Iowa Department of Transportation. Native to: dry hillsides from Indiana to Saskatchewan, south to Texas and New Mexico.

Phlox *(Phlox)*

These taller members of the phlox genus provide lovely color in the garden as well as in flower arrangements.

Smooth Phlox (*P. glaberrima*). Recommended by Scott Woodbury of the Shaw Arboretum in Missouri, this is one of the few tall phlox to bloom in spring. And then it keeps right on flowering through much of the summer, though not with quite the exuberance that it demonstrates in spring. Strong color, ease of care, long flowering time—this is a great plant for gardens! Native to: meadows, woodland edges, and swamps from southeastern Virginia to Ohio, south to Georgia and Texas.

Old Garden Phlox (*P. paniculata [decussata])*. Where there is no summer humidity, there is the old garden phlox in all its magnificent

---

Small's Beard Tongue

Light: Sun to part shade
Height: 18 to 24 inches
Color: Pink and white
Bloom Period: Late spring into summer
Zones: 4–10

Purple Prairie Clover

Light: Sun
Height: 1 to 3 feet
Color: Rose Purple
Bloom Period: Summer
Zones: 3–8

Smooth Phlox

Light: Sun to part shade
Height: 2 to 4 feet
Color: Reddish purple to pink
Bloom Period: Midspring well into summer
Zones: 3–8

Old Garden Phlox

Light: Sun to shade
Height: 2 to 5 feet
Color: Magenta, white
Bloom Period: Late summer into fall
Zones: 4–9

Obedient Plant

Light: Sun to part shade
Height: 2 to 3 feet
Color: Rose, pink, or
  white
Bloom Period: Varies by
  form and cultivar from
  midsummer to early fall
Zones: 3–10

At the University of Liverpool's Ness Gardens in England, orange red heleniums (H. autumnale) *and intense pink obedient plant* (Physostegia virginiana) *create a stunning color combination in late September.*

floral glory. Where there is summer humidity, there is a messy-looking plant covered with mildew and often attacked by spider mites. I have the species plant that selfseeds to produce a range of flower color from pure white to a rich magenta. In early spring, I cut out flower stalks among the clumps so that there is room for air to circulate. This eliminates much, if not all, of the mildew from these tough, unimproved plants. When spider mites strike—as they generally do when springs are hot and dry—I just cut the plants completely to the ground and either have a really late bloom or just forego flowers for the year (the shadier the location, I have found, the less likely the appearance of mites). The cultivar David, discovered growing in a parking lot of the Brandywine Conservancy in southeastern Pennsylvania, not only has exceptionally beautiful white flowers but also a lot of built-in resistance to mildew. Native to: fertile, moist soil from New York to Georgia, west to Illinois, Missouri, and Arkansas. *(Pictured on pages 1 and 263)*

Obedient Plant *(Physostegia virginiana)*

Toward the end of summer, the species form of this plant sends up slim, elegant flower spikes that provide a clean, refreshing color at a hot time of year. My obedient plants are crammed in clay soil packed with many other easy care perennials and do not have an opportunity to demonstrate their invasive tendencies. When given an opportunity, however, this characteristic manifests itself. I learned this when my neighbor, Jean Woodward, gave me the Summer Snow cultivar, which has white flowers and blooms as early as July. I planted this in a small front bed filled with good loamy soil; within just a year, it had started to take over and I quickly pulled out all vestiges of the plant. The moral of this story: without question, obedient plant is a colorful, easy care native just as long as it's placed in a setting where it can't roam rampantly. Native to: New Brunswick to Alberta, south to Georgia and Texas. *(Pictured at left and on page 244)*

American Jacob's Ladder *(Polemonium reptans)*

The dainty blue flowers on this rather neglected perennial are a wonderful springtime treat and the dark green, fernlike foliage makes a handsome front-of-the-border decoration. The flowers are long-lasting in arrangements—up to two weeks—and as they age, they turn a soft white. Deer, for some strange, wonderful reason, do not like this plant and neither does any other pest as long as it's grown in shade. Since clumps get thick and woody over time, you might want to cut them in half or quarters every five or six years, or just pull them out and let new, selfsown seedlings take their place. This is also a great pot plant, suitable for both city balconies and suburban decks. Native to: moist woodlands from New Hampshire to Georgia and Alabama, west to Minnesota and Oklahoma. *(Pictured on pages 51, 166, and 189)*

Ratibida *(Ratibida)*

The colorful flowers in this genus thrive in dry soils and blistering summer heat.

Mexican Hat *(R. columnifera).* An easy care recommendation of the Dyck Arboretum of the Plains in Kansas, the flowers on this perennial do indeed resemble Mexican sombreros with their dark cones and "rims" of yellow or red and yellow petals. Given a relatively dry situation, they will bob above airy green foliage for up to four months. The variety *pulcherrima*, a recommendation of perennial plantsman Pierre Bennerup, has dark red petals from July into October. Native to: well-drained soils from Minnesota to southwestern Canada, south to Texas and northern Mexico.

Prairie Coneflower *(Ratibida pinnata).* Considerably taller and with larger, more dramatic flowers than those on the closely related Mexican hat, this perennial is a standout in summer prairies. It is a proven—and highly recommended—performer in decorating roadsides and a must for gardens with almost solid clay soils. Native to: Ontario to Minnesota, south to Georgia and Oklahoma. *(Pictured on page 50)*

Matilija Poppy *(Romneya coulteri)*

Handle this perennial with care and with awe. With care, because it can become highly invasive when grown in unbounded, sandy, well-drained soil. With awe because its large, fragrant white flowers are

---

American Jacob's Ladder

Light: Part shade to shade
Height: 8 to 20 inches
Color: Blue
Bloom Period: Spring
Zones: 3–8

Mexican Hat

Light: Sun
Height: 1 to 3 feet
Color: Red, yellow; bicolored red and yellow
Bloom Period: Summer
Zones: 3–9

Prairie Coneflower

Light: Sun
Height: 4 to 6 feet
Color: Yellow petals hang from dark cones
Bloom Period: Summer
Zones: 4–8

Matilija Poppy

Light: Sun
Height: 3 to 8 feet
Color: White with yellow centers
Bloom Period: All summer
Zones: 6/7–10

Goldsturm Black-eyed Susan

Light: Sun to part shade
Height: 40 to 48 inches;
  shorter in shade
Color: Golden yellow
  flowers with almost black
  centers
Bloom Period: Summer
  into fall
Zones: 3–10

Cutleaf Coneflower

Light: Sun to part shade
Height: 30 to 72 inches
Color: Yellow
Bloom Period: Late summer
  into fall
Zones: 3–9

exquisite copies of those found on poppies (hence the popular name) and the blue green foliage is stunning. It is somewhat ironic that such a fast-spreading plant can be difficult to transplant. If you decide you can't resist it, buy young, container-grown plants. Native to: California and Baja California. *(Pictured on page 75)*

Rudbeckia *(Rudbeckia)*

Home to black-eyed Susans, this is among the more popular of the American genera. It features easy care, colorful flowers that usually bloom toward the end of the garden season.

Goldsturm Black-eyed Susan *(Rudbeckia fulgida* var. *sullivantii* 'Goldsturm'). This is probably the most widely grown rudbeckia. It was bred in eastern Germany prior to World War II and then supposedly smuggled out to the West in the late 1940s. Between then and now a lot of confusion has arisen as to what is really the true Goldsturm. Many feel that what is sold under this name is the variety and not the cultivar. While the cultivar is more compact and floriferous than the species, both are highly regarded for their dark green foliage, long-blooming colorful flowers (the German cultivar name translates to "gold storm"), and ease of maintenance. Native to: Connecticut to West Virginia; west to Michigan and Missouri. *(Pictured on pages 1, 50, and 263)*

Cutleaf Coneflower *(R. laciniata).* Sue Vrooman of the Atlanta History Center recommends this for its cheerful yellow flowers at the end of summer. In her Quarry Garden, they have all-winter interest as well, with evergreen rosettes of leaves. I have Golden Glow, which was introduced a century ago with the special botanical nomenclature of var. *hortensia.* Unlike the species, this is an invasive plant. It also needs to be staked in my border so that its double, lemon yellow flowers will not smother plants in front of it. I am at the point now where I don't know if the flowers are worth my effort. I gave a clump—with appropriate warnings—to Mickey Eggers, a neighbor down the street, and she has placed it in the back of a tightly packed border. Here the plant has no room to spread and looks coolly stunning in muggy August heat. Native to: Quebec to northern Florida, west to Rocky Mountains and beyond. *(Golden Glow pictured on page 263)*

Herbsonne *(R. nitida 'Herbsonne').* This is a fabulous plant in many ways. It is a towering giant that often does not need staking; it bears golden yellow flowers for three uninterrupted months; and it requires no maintenance. It is extremely popular in European gardens (indeed, when sold here its German name is sometimes rendered as Autumn Sun) and should be more widely used in this country. Native to: species found from Georgia and Florida to Texas. *(Pictured on page 3)*

Sweet Black-eyed Susan *(Rudbeckia subtomentosa).* "This truly outstanding plant is destined for future fame!" declares Neil Diboll of Prairie Nursery. He grows it in his own private prairie landscape and feels many others should follow his example. It is taller than the Goldsturm and has reddish brown as opposed to almost black cones. When placed in medium to moist soils, it produces flowers throughout the latter half of summer. Native to: Wisconsin south to Louisiana and Texas. *(Pictured on page 57)*

Ruellia *(Ruellia)*

This wonderful plant grows in dry shade to baking hot sun and is covered for up to two months with lavender blossoms resembling petunias. As petunias do, these plants flop and are best situated where they can drape down a slope or over a wall. The nomenclature is a bit messy; it appears that *R. caroliniensis, R. cilosa,* and *R. humilis* are all closely related to, or forms of, one another. Try any of these plants—I have all three and can't tell the difference—and you'll be in for an easy care summer treat. Native to: New Jersey to Nebraska, south to Florida panhandle and Texas. *(Pictured on pages 53 and 272)*

Blue Sage *(Salvia azurea [var. grandiflora])*

Recommended for midwestern gardens by the Dyck Arboretum of the Plains in Kansas, this has also proven to be an easy care perennial in my New Jersey gardens. I like it for its sky blue flowers at the end of summer. I do not like its floppiness and always cut it back in early June to create a bushier, stouter plant. Native to: Minnesota and Nebraska, south to Kentucky, Tennessee, and Arkansas. *(Pictured on page 242)*

Herbsonne

Light: Sun
Height: 5 to 7 feet
Color: Yellow
Bloom Period: Mid July to mid October
Zones: 4–10

Sweet Black-eyed Susan

Light: Sun
Height: 4 to 6 feet
Color: Yellow
Bloom Period: Mid through late summer
Zones: 4–8

Ruellia

Light: Sun to bright shade
Height: 1 to 2 feet
Color: Lavender
Bloom Period: Summer
Zones: 5–9

Blue Sage

Light: Sun to part shade
Height: 3 to 5 feet
Color: Blue
Bloom Period: Late summer into fall
Zones: 4–9

In the midst of a hot, dry July, lavender ruellias and wine red poppy mallows (Callirhoe involucrata) *provide superb, carefree color on the rocks of Mary Stambaugh's Newtown, Connecticut, garden.*

Bloodroot *(Sanguinaria canadensis)*

This plant provides an elegant introduction to spring—its glistening white flowers are truly aristocrats in shade borders—and then handsome foliage throughout the remainder of the gardening year. During dry spells, the foliage will go dormant but, in my garden at least, this does not affect the following year's performance. Underground, bloodroot forms clumps that can be divided; when you cut the roots they appear to "bleed," hence the popular name. Above ground, it selfseeds in open spaces. "These seedlings," reports Ken Moore, assistant director of the North Carolina Botanical Garden, "eventually display a wide variety of flower forms." I can personally vouch that each and every one is beautiful. Native to: woodlands from Nova Scotia to Manitoba, south to Florida and Oklahoma. *(Pictured on page 196)*

Hoary Skullcap *(Scutellaria incana)*

Recommended by the Bernheim Arboretum in Kentucky, this perennial is valued not only for its exceptional ease of care but also for its pretty blue flowers, which appear throughout most of summer. Native to: dry woods and thickets from Ontario south to Virginia and Missouri.

Fire Pink *(Silene virginica)*

The popular name for this plant should really be fire red, for that more accurately describes its colorful petals. Though a diminutive plant, its crimson color makes it stand out in spring settings. For a striking impact, plant fire pink in clumps rather than as single specimens. Native to: well-drained woodland edges from New Jersey to Minnesota, south to Georgia and Oklahoma. *(Pictured on page 172)*

Silphium *(Silphium)*

Members of this North American genus are usually called structural plants, which means they are big and bold. They are perfect for meadow plantings or situated at the back of sunny borders needing large yellow flowers.

Compass Plant *(S. laciniatum).* Neil Diboll of Prairie Nursery explains that this classic prairie plant gets its name from the north–south orientation of its leaves. He also says it's slow growing and I can certainly second that statement. I think it's worth the wait, however, because at maturity—at least five years—it bears up to a hundred flowers that open for well over a month. Native to: prairies from northern Ohio to South Dakota, south to Alabama and Texas.

Cup Plant *(S. perfoliatum).* This plant gets its popular name from the cuplike formation created at the point where its leaves join the stems. Indeed, water often gathers in this area and provides a drinking source for birds and butterflies. Neil Diboll of Prairie Nursery suggests planting these two feet apart to create a nearly impenetrable summer fence, one that is crowned with summer flowers. I think you would like even one as a specimen plant; the foliage is exceptionally neat and tidy and

Bloodroot
Light: Part shade to shade
Height: 6 to 9 inches
Color: White
Bloom Period: Early spring
Zones: 3–9

Hoary Skullcap
Light: Sun to part shade
Height: 1 to 3 feet
Color: Blue
Bloom Period: All summer
Zones: 3–9

Fire Pink
Light: Sun to part shade
Height: 12 to 18 inches
Color: Red
Bloom Period: Spring
Zones: 3–9

Compass Plant
Light: Sun
Height: 5 to 9 feet
Color: Yellow
Bloom Period: Mid to late summer
Zones: 3–10

Cup Plant
Light: Sun
Height: 4 to 8 feet
Color: Yellow
Bloom Period: Mid to late summer
Zones: 3–10

Prairie Dock

Light: Sun
Height: 3 to 9 feet
Color: Yellow
Bloom Period: Late summer
Zones: 3–10

False Solomon's Seal

Light: Part shade to shade
Height: 18 to 36 inches
Color: Flowers, white;
  berries, red
Bloom Period: Flowers,
  spring; berries, late sum-
  mer
Zones: 3–8

**Western Solomon's
Seal**

Light: Part shade to shade
Height: 3 feet
Color: Flowers, white;
  berries, red
Bloom Period: Flowers,
  spring; berries, late sum-
  mer
Zones: 4–8

Stiff Goldenrod

Light: Sun
Height: 2 to 5 feet
Color: Yellow
Bloom Period: Late summer
  into fall
Zones: 3–8

Seaside Goldenrod

Light: Sun
Height: 4 to 6 feet
Color: Yellow
Bloom Period: Early fall
Zones: 3–10

the lemon yellow flowers are handsome. Native to: southern Ontario to South Dakota, south to Georgia, Mississippi, and Oklahoma . *(Pictured on page 57)*

Prairie Dock *(S. terebinthinaceum).* Recommended for its dramatic foliage by Robert Bartolomei, curator of the native plant garden at the New York Botanical Garden, prairie dock features upright leaves that resemble elephant ears and are as long as 2 feet. This is not a plant for small places! Given a large, well-drained area, however, it is a standout not only with its foliage but also with its mass of yellow flowers crowning tall stems. These last, Bartolomei cautions, may need staking. Native to: prairies from southern Ontario through Ohio to Minnesota, south to Georgia, Louisiana, and Missouri.

Solomon's Seal *(Smilacina)*

The following two members of the *Smilacina* genus are both handsome woodland perennials. Each has elegant, arching foliage; clusters of white spring flowers; and then striking berries at the end of the garden season.

False Solomon's Seal *(S. racemosa).* This plant, popular in Europe as well as among knowledgeable North American gardeners, is the most widely grown member of the genus. Native to: Nova Scotia west to British Columbia, south to Georgia.

Western Solomon's Seal *(S. racemosa* var. *amplexicaulis).* Recommended by the Leach Botanical Garden in Oregon for both its flowers and fruit, this is the preferred form for Pacific coast gardeners. Native to: southern British Columbia and Alberta, south to California, Arizona, and New Mexico.

Goldenrod *(Solidago)*

Goldenrods are an acquired taste that I have yet to adopt. Yes, I know, they do not cause hayfever. And yes, they do have yellow flowers at the end of the year. I think they are on the messy side and I have yet to feel they have a place in my borders. As you read about the following recommended plants, however, you may disagree with me.

Stiff Goldenrod *(S. rigida).* This plant was an outstanding performer in Bonnie Harper-Lore's Minnesota garden and might be in yours as well. It bears flat tops of pretty yellow flowers at summer's end; grows well in many soils from moist clays to dry sands; stands tall without staking; and does not spread by rhizomes. Native to: Massachusetts to Saskatchewan, south to Georgia and Texas. *(Pictured on page 104)*

Seaside Goldenrod *(S. sempervirens).* Another noninvasive goldenrod, this is a recommendation of Garden in the Woods in Massachusetts. As its popular name implies, this is a perfect late season perennial for shore gardens because it resists salt spray. Native to: Atlantic and Gulf Coasts.

Showy Goldenrod *(S. speciosa).* This is the member of the genus that could make me join a goldenrod fan club. It has rather elegant, deep green foliage, neat rounded buds, and a beautiful display of late season flowers that give it its popular name. Native to: southern New Hampshire to Minnesota and Wyoming, south to Georgia, Arkansas, and Texas.

Indian Pink *(Spigelia marilandica)*

Indian pink, named for the color of its roots rather than its flowers, was described as an elegant plant for perennial borders in Bailey's CYCLOPEDIA OF HORTICULTURE at the beginning of this century and is now an easy care recommendation made by plantsman Pierre Bennerup at the end of the century. Even without such illustrious backing, I think shade gardeners would covet this plant once they had seen its unusual deep red flowers and golden yellow centers. Native to: North Carolina through south Indiana to Missouri, south to Florida and Texas.

Showy Goldenrod

Light: Sun
Height: 1 to 3 feet
Color: Yellow
Bloom Period: Midsummer
  into fall
Zones: 5–8

In mid June, the regal beauty of Indian pink (Spigelia marilandica) *is on display in the native plant garden at the New York Botanical Garden.*

Indian Pink

Light: Part shade
Height: 1 to 2 feet
Color: Red and yellow
Bloom Period: Late spring
  through early summer;
  sometimes reblooms in
  late summer
Zones: 5–10

Chadds Ford Orchid

Light: Light to dark shade
Height: 18 to 30 inches
Color: Spires of fragrant
  white flowers
Bloom Period: Fall
Zones: Not established;
  definitely zones 5–7,
  probably 4–9, and worth
  trying 3–10

Stokesia

Light: Sun to bright shade
Height: 1 to 2 feet
Color: Blue, white, pale
  yellow
Bloom Period: Summer
  into fall
Zones: 5–9

Chadds Ford Orchid *(Spiranthes cernua f. odorata* 'Chadds Ford')

Barry Glick of Sunshine Farm & Gardens introduced this plant to me and many others attending the 1994 Perennial Plant Association annual meeting. He explained that it was found in a Delaware roadside ditch in 1956 and, after being pampered in greenhouses across the country, went on to receive the prestigious Certificate of Cultural Merit from the American Orchid Society. "It's really an outdoor plant," Glick said, "and one that is exceptionally easy to grow in any moist, well-drained soil." He then showed a slide illustrating its spires of white flowers blooming in October. It really sounded too good to be true and several knowledgeable gardeners confirmed my gut feeling, saying it was often temperamental. However, I couldn't resist trying the plant and I put it—as Glick emphasized—in a well-drained, shaded location. Despite drought conditions that first year, and periods without water for at least ten days, this tough, gorgeous plant came through in early fall. It's great for me and I hope it will perform as well for you. Native to: cultivar found in Delaware; species found eastern Canada to southern Florida and Texas.

Stokesia *(S. laevis)*

This is a workhorse of the summer garden. It just keeps blooming and blooming as long as you periodically cut or snip off the spent flower heads. European breeders admire it and have created a lot of cultivars in different colors, ranging from purple blue to white. Unbeknownst to them, a naturally occurring pale yellow form flourishes in the South Carolina garden of Mary Gregory. Kim Hawks of Niche Gardens heard about it and introduced it in 1994 as the appropriately named Mary Gregory. This is a lovely color breakthrough for stokesias. Native to: South Carolina to Florida and Louisiana.

Celandine Poppy *(Stylophorum diphyllum)*

This shade garden stalwart gives daffodils a run for their money as far as providing cheery yellow flowers. In my native plant garden, it starts blooming the second week of April and continues right on through

June, long after the daffodils have petered out. In a cooler, shadier border, it periodically reblooms through July. Celandine poppies selfseed and are great for naturalizing in woodland settings. If you don't wish to increase your stock of these plants, mulch them thoroughly. Native to: rich, moist woods from Pennsylvania to Wisconsin, south to Georgia and Arkansas. *(Pictured on pages 51 and 98)*

Pink Foamflower *(Tiarella wherryi [cordifolia var. wherryi])*

This lovely little shade flower was discovered by noted American horticulturist Dr. Edgar T. Wherry in the 1930s. He sent seeds to England in 1939 and in 1948 it received a Royal Horticultural Society Award of Merit for its dainty charm, handsome foliage, and spikes of soft pink spring flowers. At the time, the only way American gardeners could obtain the plant was to import it from England! Fortunately, that situation has changed and pink foamflower and its many cultivars are now widely available on this side of the Atlantic. Native to: Virginia and Tennessee to Georgia, Alabama, and Mississippi.

Virginia Tovara *(T. [Persicaria] virginianum 'Variegata')*

I grow this plant for its colorful foliage and find it particularly valuable in dry shade settings. It is so adaptable, however, that it does equally well in sunny, moist clay areas. For reasons unknown to me, some of the plants—particularly those in wetter situations—get a brown fungus on their foliage. I simply snip off the offending leaves when on garden inspection tours. At the end of the garden season, Virginia tovara provides a bonus with wiry wands covered with tiny but bright red flowers; I cut these back after a week or two to reduce selfseeding. Native to: eastern and central United States.

Tradescantia *(Tradescantia)*

This is another incestuous genus, with members interbreeding among themselves both in the wild and in the breeder's shed. The hybrids, generally designated as *T.* X *andersoniana* and claiming the following

Celandine Poppy

Light: Part shade
Height: 12 to 18 inches
Color: Yellow
Bloom Period: Spring and, if deadheaded, into midsummer
Zones: 4–9

Pink Foamflower

Light: Part shade
Height: 6 to 12 inches
Color: Pale pink, white
Bloom Period: Spring
Zones: 3–9

Virginia Tovara

Light: Sun to shade
Height: 2 to 4 feet
Color: Flower, red; foliage, cream-splashed green
Bloom Period: Late summer into fall
Zones: 4–8

Ohio Spiderwort

Light: Sun to shade
Height: 2 to 3 feet
Color: Deep blue, rose,
 white
Bloom Period: Spring into
 summer
Zones: 4–8

Spiderwort

Light: Sun to shade
Height: 1 to 3 feet
Color: Blue, rose, white,
 bicolored blue and white
Bloom Period: Spring and,
 if cut back, rebloom in
 late summer
Zones: 4–9

Big Merrybells

Light: Part shade to shade
Height: 12 to 30 inches
Color: Yellow
Bloom Period: Spring
Zones: 3–9

Wingstem

Light: Sun to part shade
Height: 6 to 8 feet
Color: Yellow
Bloom Period: July to early
 October
Zones: 5–8

Tall Ironweed

Light: Sun to part shade
Height: 8 to 15 feet
Color: Rose purple
Bloom Period: Late summer
 into fall
Zones: 4–9

two species among their parentage, have larger and more colorful flowers. Whether species or hybrid, however, most spiderworts will rebloom in late summer if cut back after their spring flowering. And, when grown in rich garden soil, all tend to be invasive. To be easy care, these plants should be placed in difficult situations.

Ohio Spiderwort (*T. ohiensis*). This is one of the stalwarts in Bonnie Harper-Lore's sunny front yard prairie garden in Minnesota. It is one of the relatively few prairie plants that bloom in spring and adds color to a scene filled with the green texture of emerging grasses and later-blooming perennials. At the Shaw Arboretum in Missouri, horticulturist Scott Woodbury also considers this a key plant; here, however, Ohio spiderwort blooms in many colors while wandering about surface roots shaded by a large tree. Native to: southern New England to Florida, west to Minnesota and Texas.

Spiderwort (*T. virginiana*). This is an excellent plant for dry shade. I have a clump nestled among tree roots and it bears deep blue flowers throughout May with less than two hours of morning sun. Native to: Connecticut to Georgia, west to Missouri. *(Pictured on page 231)*

Big Merrybells *(Uvularia grandiflora)*

This woodlander contributes a nice yellow to spring garden scenes and then a light green foliage the remainder of the garden year. The only work required is to divide the plant every three or four years. Native to: woodlands from Quebec to Minnesota, south to Georgia and Oklahoma.

Wingstem *(Verbesina alternifolia)*

This undemanding perennial bears a crown of yellow daisies all summer and is recommended by Sue Vrooman of the Atlanta History Center. "Its flower stalks, thick and winged, are very interesting to look at," she reports, "and the birds love the seeds." Native to: moist woods and pastures from southeastern New York through southern Ontario to Illinois, south to Georgia, Louisiana, and Kansas. *(Pictured on page 59)*

Ironweed *(Vernonia)*

Ironweeds add an intense red purple to late summer and early fall landscapes. Their popular name reflects their constitutions: they are exceptionally easy plants and though often attacked by insects in their early season growth, always survive to flower beautifully.

Tall Ironweed *(V. altissima [gigantea]).* This plant really lives up to its popular name. While it usually reaches 6 feet in the wild, it soars to almost three times that height when given good garden soil. As part of the research for this book, I sent this little-known plant to three friends: Lisa Corey in Massachusetts; Betsy Houser in South Dakota; and Judy Jakobsen in California. Jakobsen got rid of hers within a month because it was so eaten by bugs. It has thrived, relatively uneaten, in the other two gardens. In my garden it is severely attacked in spring, but because I put the plants at the back of the border, this low-level degradation is hidden. For some reason unknown to me, all foliage over the 4-foot mark is not eaten by insects. Native to: western New York to Georgia, west to Missouri and Louisiana.

New York Ironweed *(V. noveboracensis).* Lacking the dramatic height of tall ironweed, this plant is a perfect candidate for informal settings such as that of meadow gardens. Its color stands out when mingled with the blues of asters and the deep yellows of goldenrods. Native to: Massachusetts to Ohio, south to Florida and Mississippi.

American Alpine Speedwell *(Veronica wormskjoldii)*

This is among the many uncommon plants promoted by the now-closed Montrose Nursery in central North Carolina. Here's an excerpt from the firm's catalog: "We can all thank Norman Singer for

In late September, the majestic height of tall ironweed (Vernonia altissima) is crowned with gleaming rose purple flowers.

New York Ironweed

Light: Sun to part shade
Height: 5 to 8 feet
Color: Rose purple
Bloom Period: Late summer into fall
Zones: 5–9

American Alpine Speedwell

Light: Sun to part shade
Height: 1 foot
Color: Blue
Bloom Period: Midsummer
Zones: Not established; at the minimum 3–8

Culver's Root

Light: Sun to light shade
Height: 4 to 6 feet
Color: White, light blue
Bloom Period: Mid to late summer
Zones: 3–8

California Fuchsia

Light: Sun to part shade
Height: 1 to 3 feet
Color: Red
Bloom Period: Species, July often into December; subspecies, late summer to early fall
Zones: Species, 8–10; subspecies, 5–10

Heartleaf Alexander

Light: Sun to light shade
Height: 1 to 3 feet
Color: Yellow
Bloom Period: Spring
Zones: 5–8

On a midsummer's morning, the white spires of culver's root (Veronicastrum virginica) *form an etheral display in the Rocky Hill, New Jersey, garden of Helen Benedict.*

sharing seeds of this splendid veronica. . . . It is native to the northern tier of states but hasn't complained a bit about living here in the hot and humid South." It hasn't complained in my garden either, where it has produced lovely blue flowers in midsummer heat for four years at this writing. It has survived dry summers, record-cold winters, and the degradations inflicted by a gas utility repair crew. This is a great easy care plant. Native to: mountains of North America. *(Pictured on page 237)*

Culver's Root *(Veronicastrum virginica [Veronica virginiana])*

Culver's root is among the many plants that belie the popular conception of native plants being coarse and lacking elegance. At 2- to 3-inch intervals, five thin dark green leaves form star-shaped circles around the upright stems and are then topped with spires of summer flowers. This dependable perennial stands tall when given soil rich in organic matter and regular watering; while it will still perform well in leaner, drier conditions, it will probably need to be staked. Native to: Massachusetts, Ontario, and Manitoba, south to Florida and Texas.

California Fuchsia *(Zauschneria californica [Epilobium canum])*

Both the nomenclature and classification of this plant are hopelessly confusing for nonbotanists. What matters, I think, is that both the species and the subspecies (ssp. *latifolia*) are handsome, drought-tolerant plants. The species plant is hardy only to zone 8 and blooms from July often in December. The subspecies plant, which is hardy to zone 5 and can be grown throughout much of the country if given excellent drainage, waits until September to start producing its warm red tubular flowers. In my garden, it looks quite smashing interspersed among Purple Homestead *(Verbena canadensis* 'Purple Homestead'*)* and the tiny white flowers of Mexican daisies *(Erigeron karvinskianus).* Native to: Oregon to California.

Alexander *(Zizia)*

Alexanders are little-known perennials that provide colorful flowers in spring gardens and clean foliage the remainder of the garden year.

Heartleaf Alexander (Z. aptera). This elegant perennial features golden yellow flowers clustered like Queen Anne's lace in spring and deep green leaves tipped with a hint of yellow all season long. The spent flower heads keep a light green color and look attractive throughout the growing season. Scott Woodbury of the Shaw Arboretum in Missouri reports that though its natural habitat consists of moist soils, heartleaf alexander will tolerate dry situations as well. Native to: moist, well-drained soils from New York to British Columbia, south to Florida and Arkansas. *(Pictured on page 31)*

Golden Alexander (Z. aurea). This tough, attractive spring perennial can be grown in a variety of soils ranging from sandy loam to fairly thick clay. Bonnie Harper-Lore of Minnesota likes it for its cheerful color and attractiveness in flower arrangements. Native to: moist prairies from New Brunswick and Minnesota, south to Florida and Texas.

The scarlet flowers of California fuchsia (Zauschneria californica) *fire up a midsummer planting on the grounds of the C. M. Goethe Arboretum at California State University at Sacramento. [Photo: Judy Jakobsen]*

Golden Alexander

Light: Sun
Height: 30 to 40 inches
Color: Yellow
Bloom Period: Spring
Zones: 3–8

FOR FURTHER INFORMATION about native perennials, read the catalogs of the mail-order nurseries listed below. They are a rich source of admittedly biased descriptions about the above and many other North American plants.

SOURCES. Check your local garden center first, and if they don't have a perennial that you want, have them contact one of the whole-sale suppliers listed in the Appendix. Otherwise, unless noted differently under a specific description, most of the above plants can be obtained from one or more of the following mail-order nurseries: Forestfarm, Las Pilitas Nursery, Niche Gardens, Prairie Nursery, Prairie Moon Nursery, the Primrose Path, Sunlight Gardens, Wood-landers, and Yucca Do Nursery. Addresses for all firms are in the Appendix.

APPENDIX

Master List of Recommended Plants

The following is an alphabetical listing, by botanical name, of plants recommended by contributors to this book.

Vine Maple *(Acer circinatum)* Tree with yellow to vibrant red fall foliage. Loring M. Jones, Idaho Seedman; Leach Botanical Garden, Oregon

Red Maple *(Acer rubrum)* Tree with bright red early spring flower clusters and colorful red or yellow fall foliage. Famous and Historic Trees

    'Red Sunset' (early orange to red foliage)—Mt. Cuba Center, Delaware

    'October Glory' (consistent, long-lasting red foliage)—William Flemer III, Nurseryman

Green Mountain Maple *(Acer saccharum* 'Green Mountain'*)* Tree with brilliantly colored fall foliage. William Flemer III, Nurseryman

Mountain Yarrow *(Achillea millefolium* var. *lanuosa)* Perennial with lacy white blooms in summer. Penny A. Wilson, California

Magic Flower *(Achimenes longiflora* 'Paul Arnold'*)* Tuber with violet blue flowers all summer. John E. Bryan, Bulb Expert

Western Maidenhair Fern *(Adiantum aleuticum)* Fern with graceful green fronds. Leach Botanical Garden, Oregon

Maidenhair Fern *(Adiantum pedatum)* Fern with black purple stems and delicate green fronds. F. Gordon Foster, Fern Expert

Allegheny Vine *(Adlumia fungosa)* Climber with white to rosy pink flowers summer to frost. Pierre Bennerup, Perennial Plantsman

Bottlebrush Buckeye *(Aesculus parviflora)* Shrub with cones of creamy white flowers in midsummer. Greensboro Arboretum, North Carolina; Royal Botanical Gardens, Ontario; National Garden, Washington, D.C.

Red Buckeye *(Aesculus pavia)* Shrub with bright red flowers in spring. Gold Medal Award; Caroline Dormon Nature Preserve, Louisiana

Ageratum *(A. houstonianum)* Annual with fuzzy summer-long flowers in blue, purple, pink, or white. Linda Yang, New York City

Nodding Onion *(Allium cernuum)* Bulb with sprays of white, pink, rose, or lilac flowers in summer. Garden in the Woods, Massachusetts; Frans M. Roozen, Dutch Bulbman

Western Serviceberry *(Amelanchier alnifolia)* Shrub with white spring flowers and edible blue berries in summer. Loring M. Jones, Idaho Seedman

Shadblow *(Amelanchier canadensis)* Tree with white flowers in early spring, handsome slate gray bark, colorful fall foliage, and resistance to road salt. William Flemer III, Nurseryman

Leadplant *(Amorpha canescens)* Shrub with purple and orange flowers in summer. Dyck Arboretum of the Plains, Kansas

Arkansas Amsonia *(A. hubrectii)* Perennial with light blue flowers in spring and striking golden tan fall foliage. Patricia A. Taylor, New Jersey

Big Bluestem *(Andropogon gerardii)* Grass with statuesque blue green leaves that turn a rich bronze in fall. Iowa Department of Transportation

Windflower *(Anemone multifida)* Perennial with white flowers in early summer. Grethe B. Petersen, Denmark

Rue Anemone *(Anemonella thalictroides)* Perennial with white or pale pink flowers early to mid-spring. Patricia A. Taylor, New Jersey

American Columbine *(Aquilegia canadensis)* Perennial with red and yellow flowers in spring. Dyck Arboretum of the Plains, Kansas; Monticello, Virginia

Western Columbine *(Aquilegia formosa)* Perennial with red and yellow flowers May to August. Penny A. Wilson, California

Spikenard *(Aralia racemosa)* Perennial with white flowers in late spring and deep purple berries late summer into fall. Pierre Bennerup, Perennial Plantsman

Bearberry *(Arctostaphylos uva-ursi)* Evergreen groundcover bearing white flowers tipped with pink in spring and red berries late summer through fall. Loring M. Jones, Idaho Seedman

Red Chokeberry *(Aronia arbutifolia)* Shrub with white flowers in spring, orange to red fall foliage, and bright red berries persisting into December. Greensboro Arboretum, North Carolina

Heart Leaf Ginger *(Asarum arifolium)* Groundcover with attractive, evergreen leaves. Mt. Cuba Center, Delaware

Canadian Wild Ginger *(Asarum canadense)* Groundcover with large, velvety green leaves. New York Botanical Garden

Western Wild Ginger *(Asarum caudatum)* Groundcover with shiny, dark green, heart-shaped leaves. Leach Botanical Garden, Oregon

Swamp Milkweed *(Asclepias incarnata)* Perennial with pink or white flowers in early summer. Will Ingwersen, Great Britain; Garden in the Woods, Massachusetts

Purple Milkweed *(Asclepias purpurascens)* Perennial with deep rose to purple flowers in late spring. Shaw Arboretum, Missouri

Butterfly Weed *(Asclepias tuberosa)* Perennial with bright orange flowers in summer and striking seedpods in September. Iowa Department of Transportation; Bonnie Harper-Lore, Minnesota; Dawes Arboretum, Ohio; Neil Diboll, Wisconsin

White Wood Aster *(A. divaricatus)* Perennial with white flowers late summer into fall. Atlanta History Center, Georgia; Will Ingwersen, Great Britain

Heath Aster *(A. ericoides)* Perennial with sprays of white flowers late summer into fall. Dyck Arboretum of the Plains, Kansas; Neil Diboll, Wisconsin

Smooth Aster *(A. laevis)* Perennial with white through lavender flowers late summer into fall. Garden in the Woods, Massachusetts; Bonnie Harper-Lore, Minnesota; Neil Diboll, Wisconsin

New England Aster *(A. novae-angliae)* Perennial with bluish purple flowers late summer into fall. Michigan Department of Transportation

Umbellatus Aster *(A. umbellatus)* Perennial with white flowers mid August to mid October. Patricia A. Taylor, New Jersey

False Goatbeard *(Astilbe biternata)* Perennial with creamy white plumes in summer. Pierre Bennerup, Perennial Plantsman

Lady Fern *(Athyrium filix-femina)* Fern with fans of feathery green pinnae. F. Gordon Foster, Fern Expert

Wild Blue Indigo *(Baptisia australis)* Perennial with indigo blue flowers in early summer. Mt. Cuba Center, Delaware; Dawes Arboretum, Ohio

Prairie Indigo *(Baptisia leucantha)* Perennial with creamy white flowers in summer and striking black seedpods fall into winter. Neil Diboll, Wisconsin

River Birch *(Betula nigra)* Tree with reddish brown to light tan bark that exfoliates to reveal a salmon pink to reddish brown inner bark. Famous and Historic Trees; William Flemer III, Nurseryman

      'Heritage' (creamy white bark)—Gold Medal Award

Deer Fern *(Blechnum spicant)* Evergreen fern with neat, compact growth. Leach Botanical Garden, Oregon

Boltonia *(B. asteroides)* Perennial with white, daisylike flowers late summer into fall. Pierre Bennerup, Perennial Plantsman

Sideoats Grama *(Bouteloua curtipendula)* Grass with purple and orange flower parts in summer. Dyck Arboretum of the Plains, Kansas

White Brodiaea *(B. lactea)* Corm with white flowers in spring. Patricia A. Taylor, New Jersey

Queen Fabiola *(Brodiaea laxa 'Queen Fabiola')* Corm with deep blue flowers in early summer. John E. Bryan, Bulb Expert; Frans M. Roozen, Dutch Bulbman

American Beautyberry *(Callicarpa americana)* Shrub with tiny blush pink flowers in spring and purple berries late summer through winter, depending on geographical location. Atlanta History Center, Georgia; National Garden, Washington, D.C.

Poppy Mallow *(Callirhoe involucrata)* Perennial with wine red flowers late spring well into summer. Shaw Arboretum, Missouri

Sweet Shrub *(Calycanthus floridus)* Shrub with highly fragrant, brownish maroon flowers in spring. Monticello, Virginia

California Allspice *(Calycanthus occidentalis)* Shrub with fragrant, reddish brown flowers spring into summer. California State University at Sacramento

Cusick Camass *(Camassia cusickii)* Bulb with spikes of pale blue flowers in late spring. John E. Bryan, Bulb Expert; Frans M. Roozen, Dutch Bulbman

Great Camass *(Camassia leichtlinii)* Bulb with tall spikes of violet or dark blue flowers in late spring. Native Plant Gardens, Royal British Columbia Museum; Frans M. Roozen, Dutch Bulbman

Trumpet Creeper *(Campsis radicans)* Vine with orange to scarlet flowers all summer. National Garden, Washington, D.C.

Tussock Sedge *(Carex stricta)* Grass with arching, light green foliage spring through summer and rustling tan sprays fall through winter. Shaw Arboretum, Missouri

Berkeley Sedge *(Carex tumulicola)* Grass with lush foliage clumps of evergreen sprays. John Greenlee, Grass Expert

Bush Anemone *(Carpenteria californica)* Evergreen shrub with fragrant, glistening white flowers in the first half of summer. California State University at Sacramento

American Hornbeam *(Carpinus caroliniana)* Tree with ash gray bark and orange to deep red fall foliage. Dawes Arboretum, Ohio; Royal Botanical Gardens, Ontario

American Bittersweet *(Celastrus scandens)* Vine with bright orange fruits in fall. Royal Botanical Gardens, Ontario

Hackberry *(Celtis occidentalis)* Tough, low maintenance tree with pale yellow fall foliage. William Flemer III, Nurseryman

Eastern Redbud *(Cercis canadensis)* Small tree with purple pink flowers in spring. Bernheim Arboretum, Kentucky; Dawes Arboretum, Ohio; Royal Botanical Gardens, Ontario

'Forest Pansy' (plum purple foliage)—Greensboro Arboretum, North Carolina

Western Redbud *(Cercis occidentalis)* Small tree with brilliant magenta flowers late winter to spring, reddish purple seed pods throughout fall, and yellow or red fall foliage. Penny A. Wilson, California

Mountain Mahogany *(Cercocarpus betuloides)* Evergreen shrub covered with sprays of silvery seed and fruit in fall. California State University at Sacramento

Curl-leaf Mountain Mahogany *(Cercocarpus ledifolius)* Evergreen shrub with white bark and dark green leaves. Loring M. Jones, Idaho Seedman

Alaska Cedar *(Chamaecyparis nootkatensis* 'Pendula'*)* Conifer with dense, drooping, bluish green foliage. U.S. National Arboretum, Washington, D.C.

Northern Sea Oats *(Chasmanthium latifolium)* Grass with green foliage and arching flower heads that turn copper in fall and then tan in winter. John Greenlee, Grass Expert; National Wildflower Research Center, Texas

Pink Turtlehead *(Chelone lyonii)* Perennial with pink or rosy purple flowers in late summer. Garden in the Woods, Massachusetts; New York Botanical Garden

Desert Willow *(Chilopsis linearis)* Small tree with fragrant, lilac flowers all summer. Penny A. Wilson, California

Fringetree *(Chionanthus virginicus)* Tree with feathery white late spring flowers and bright yellow fall foliage. Royal Botanical Gardens, Ontario

Goldenstar *(Chrysogonum virginianum)* Groundcover with yellow flowers spring into early summer and often reblooming in fall. David Benner, Pennsylvania

Black Cohosh *(Cimicifuga racemosa)* Perennial with candlelike spires of white flowers in summer. Grethe B. Petersen, Denmark; Royal Botanical Gardens, Ontario

Fairy Candles *(Cimicifuga racemosa* **var.** *cordifolia)* Perennial with fragrant, creamy white flowers in late summer. Grethe B. Petersen, Denmark

American Yellowwood *(Cladrastis lutea)* Tree with fragrant white spring flowers and yellow fall foliage. Gold Medal Award; Bernheim Arboretum, Kentucky

Spring Beauty *(Claytonia virginica)* Corm with blush pink flowers veined with dark pink in spring. Patricia A. Taylor, New Jersey

Addison's Clematis *(C. addisonii)* Vine with purple red flowers in summer. Susan G. Austin, Clematis Expert

Blue Jasmine *(Clematis crispa)* Vine with bluish purple flowers with pale margins June through August. Susan G. Austin, Clematis Expert

Pitcher's Clematis *(C. pitcheri)* Vine with purplish blue flowers all summer. Susan G. Austin, Clematis Expert

Scarlet Clematis *(C. texensis)* Vine with red or purple red flowers summer to frost. Susan G. Austin, Clematis Expert

Virgin's Bower *(Clematis virginiana)* Vine with off white flowers from mid July to late September. Susan G. Austin, Clematis Expert

Cinnamon Clethra *(C. acuminata)* Shrub with white flowers in summer and exfoliating, rich cinnamon brown stems in winter. Royal Botanical Gardens, Ontario

Sweet Pepperbush *(Clethra alnifolia)* Shrub with fragrant white or pink flowers in summer. Atlanta History Center, Georgia; Caroline Dormon Nature Preserve, Louisiana; Greensboro Arboretum, North Carolina

'Hummingbird' (dwarf)—Mt. Cuba Center, Delaware; Gold Medal Award

Stoneroot *(Collinsonia canadensis)* Perennial with yellow flowers in late summer. Atlanta History Center, Georgia

Pagoda Dogwood *(Cornus alternifolia)* Tree with creamy white spring flowers and maroon purple fall foliage. Royal Botanical Gardens, Ontario

Flowering Dogwood *(Cornus florida)* Tree with white to pink flowers in spring and brilliant red late summer foliage. Bernheim Arboretum, Kentucky

Red Osier Dogwood *(Cornus sericea)* Shrub with creamy white flowers in spring and colorful bare red bark in winter. Iowa Department of Transportation; Royal Botanical Gardens, Ontario; National Garden, Washington, D.C.

> 'Flaviramea' (yellow bark)—Royal Botanical Gardens, Ontario
> 'Silver and Gold' (variegated foliage)—Gold Medal Award

Sunny Red Cosmos *(C. sulphureus 'Sunny Red')* Annual with dwarf habit and bright red flower all summer under diverse weather conditions. All-America Selection

Princeton Sentry Hawthorn *(Crataegus phaenopyrum 'Princeton Sentry')* Almost thornless tree with billowing white spring flowers, orange to scarlet fall foliage, and striking winter display of red berries. William Flemer III, Nurseryman

Winter King Hawthorn *(Crataegus viridis 'Winter King')* Disease resistant, almost thornless tree with white spring flowers, purple fall foliage, and orange red winter fruit. William Flemer III, Nurseryman; Gold Medal Award

Anemone-flowered Dahlia *(D. 'Honey')* Tuber with flowers composed of bronze petals and golden yellow centers from midsummer to frost. John E. Bryan, Bulb Expert

Single-flowered Dahlia *(D. 'Siemen Doorenbosch')* Tuber with light magenta flowers from midsummer to frost. John E. Bryan, Bulb Expert

Dutchman's Breeches *(Dicentra cucullaria)* Tuber with white flowers in spring. Will Ingwersen, Great Britain

Fringed Bleeding Heart *(Dicentra eximia)* Perennial with pink flowers late spring into fall. Grethe B. Petersen, Denmark; Linda Yang, New York City; David Benner, Pennsylvania

Ookow *(Dichelostemma congestum)* Corm with purplish blue flowers late spring to early summer, depending on location. Frans M. Roozen, Dutch Bulbman

Male Fern *(Dryopteris filix-mas)* Stately fern with large, dark green, twice pinnate fronds. Native Plant Gardens, Royal British Columbia Museum

Marginal Shield Fern *(Dryopteris marginalis)* Fern with specimen clumps of evergreen fronds. F. Gordon Foster, Fern Expert

Western Coneflower *(Echinacea angustifolia)* Perennial with rose purple or white flowers in summer. Dyck Arboretum of the Plains, Kansas

Purple Coneflower *(Echinacea purpurea)* Perennial with purple, rose pink, or white flowers all summer. Grethe B. Petersen, Denmark; Iowa Department of Transportation; Dawes Arboretum, Ohio; National Wildflower Research Center, Texas

Bottlebrush Grass *(Elymus hystrix)* Grass with warm green leaves and brushlike flowers that mature to brown by early fall. John Greenlee, Grass Expert

Beardless Wild Rye *(Elymus tritichoides)* Grass with green to blue green summer foliage that matures to wheat and then bleaches to gray. John Greenlee, Grass Expert

Seaside Daisy *(Erigeron glaucus 'Wayne Roderick')* Groundcover with lavender flowers in spring. Penny A. Wilson, California

Mexican Daisy *(Erigeron karvinskianus)* Annual with white flowers aging to pink spring through frost. Will Ingwersen, Great Britain

Sulfur Flower *(Eriogonum umbellatum* **var.** *polyanthum)* Groundcover with pale yellow flowers late spring through summer. California State University at Sacramento

Golden Yarrow *(Eriophyllum lanatum)* Groundcover with mats of yellow flowers throughout summer. Native Plant Gardens, Royal British Columbia Museum

Rattlesnake Master *(Eryngium yuccifolium)* Perennial with white buttonlike flowers in summer. Dyck Arboretum of the Plains, Kansas

Giant Fawn Lily *(Erythronium oregonum)* Corm with large white flowers and strongly mottled leaves in early spring. Native Plant Gardens, Royal British Columbia Museum; Leach Botanical Garden, Oregon

Coast Fawn Lily *(Erythronium revolutum)* Corm with deep pink flowers and mottled leaves in early spring. Leach Botanical Garden, Oregon; Frans M. Roozen, Dutch Bulbman

    'White Beauty' (pure white)—John E. Bryan, Bulb Expert

Trout Lily *(Erythronium tuolumnense)* Corm with golden yellow flowers in spring. Frans M. Roozen, Dutch Bulbman

    'Pagoda' (soft yellow)—John E. Bryan, Bulb Expert; Will Ingwersen, Great Britain

Eastern Wahoo *(Euonymus atropurpureus)* Tree with reddish purple flowers in early summer and carmine pink to bright red fall foliage. Bernheim Arboretum, Kentucky

Hardy Ageratum *(Eupatorium coelestinum)* Perennial with blue flowers midsummer to early fall. Atlanta History Center, Georgia

White Snakeroot *(Eupatorium rugosum)* Perennial with white flowers late summer to early fall. Atlanta History Center, Georgia

Flowering Spurge *(Euphorbia corollata)* Perennial with sprays of white flowers summer into fall. Michigan Department of Transportation; Bonnie Harper-Lore, Minnesota

American Beech *(Fagus grandifolia)* Magnificent tree with slate gray bark and yellow fall foliage. Bernheim Arboretum, Kentucky

Apache Plume *(Fallugia paradoxa)* Shrub with white roselike flowers in May and feathery plumes of purple fruits late summer into fall. California State University at Sacramento

Dwarf Fothergilla *(F. gardenii)* Shrub with white flowers in spring and flashy orange red foliage in fall. Mt. Cuba Center, Delaware; Greensboro Arboretum, North Carolina; Royal Botanical Gardens, Ontario; National Garden, Washington, D.C.

    'Blue Mist' (blue green foliage)—Gold Medal Award

Large Fothergilla *(F. major)* Shrub with white flowers in spring and fall foliage blended with orange, yellow, red, and purple tints. Greensboro Arboretum, North Carolina

Franklin Tree *(Franklinia alatamaha)* Tree with fragrant white flowers through latter half of summer and orange to scarlet red fall foliage. Famous and Historic Trees

White Ash *(Fraxinus americana)* Strong, upright tree with rich purple or bronze fall foliage. Famous and Historic Trees

'Autumn Purple' (deep purple fall foliage)—William Flemer III, Nurseryman

Green Ash *(Fraxinus pennsylvanica)* Shade tree with golden yellow to orange fall foliage. Famous and Historic Trees; Iowa Department of Transportation

'Patmore' (superb selection)—William Flemer III, Nurseryman

Fremontia *(Fremontodendron californicum* X *F. mexicanum* **'California Glory')** Climber with golden yellow flowers all summer. Will Ingwersen, Great Britain

Martha Roderick Fritillaria *(F. biflora* **'Martha Roderick')** Bulb with brownish flowers edged in cream in spring. Frans M. Roozen, Dutch Bulbman

Black Lily *(Fritillaria camschatcensis)* Bulb with maroon purple to black flower bells midspring to midsummer, depending on location. Frans M. Roozen, Dutch Bulbman

Mt. Hood Fritillaria *(F. recurva* **'Mt. Hood')** Bulb with scarlet flowers in spring. John E. Bryan, Bulb Expert

Red Plume Gaillardia *(G. pulchella* **'Red Plume')** Annual with dwarf habit and double brick red flowers over a long bloom period. All-America Selection

Salal *(Gaultheria shallon)* Evergreen groundcover with pale pink flower clusters in June and edible purple fruit in August. Native Plant Gardens, Royal British Columbia Museum

Bottle Gentian *(Gentiana andrewsii)* Perennial with blue flowers late summer into fall. Neil Diboll, Wisconsin

Soapwort *(Gentiana saponaria)* Perennial with blue flowers in late summer. Pierre Bennerup, Perennial Plantsman

Wild Geranium *(G. maculatum)* Perennial with blue violet flowers in spring. Garden in the Woods, Massachusetts; New York Botanical Garden

Prairie Smoke *(Geum triflorum)* Perennial with rose red flowers and silver pink seed plumes in spring. Bonnie Harper-Lore, Minnesota

Bowman's Root *(Gillenia trifoliata)* Perennial with white flowers on reddish stems in summer. Pierre Bennerup, Perennial Plantsman; Grethe B. Petersen, Denmark; Will Ingwersen, Great Britain; Garden in the Woods, Massachusetts; New York Botanical Garden

Kentucky Coffee Tree *(Gymnocladus dioicus)* Bold tree, especially handsome in winter landscapes, with blue green foliage. Famous and Historic Trees; William Flemer III, Nurseryman

Carolina Silverbell *(Halesia carolina)* Small tree with white bell-shaped flowers in spring and lemon yellow fall foliage. Mt. Cuba Center, Delaware; William Flemer III, Nurseryman; Monticello, Virginia

Florida Silverbell *(Halesia diptera* var. *magniflora)* Tree with large, white bell-shaped flowers in spring and yellow fall foliage. Gold Medal Award

Common Witch Hazel *(Hamamelis virginiana)* Tree with yellow ribbonlike flowers appearing immediately after yellow foliage drop in fall. Dawes Arboretum, Ohio

Swamp Sunflower *(Helianthus angustifolius)* Perennial with golden yellow flowers late summer to early fall. Caroline Dormon Nature Preserve, Louisiana

Downy Sunflower *(Helianthus mollis)* Perennial with butter yellow flowers in summer. New York Botanical Garden

Willowleaf Sunflower *(Helianthus salicifolius)* Perennial with yellow flowers late summer into fall. Dyck Arboretum of the Plains, Kansas; New York Botanical Garden

Red Yucca *(Hesperaloe parviflora)* Perennial with coral to salmon pink flowers on pinkish stems from spring into early summer. National Wildflower Research Center, Texas

Montrose Ruby **(*Heuchera americana* X *H.* 'Palace Purple')** Perennial with reddish maroon foliage and blush pink flowers on reddish maroon stems late spring to early summer. Patricia A. Taylor, New Jersey

Rose Mallow *(Hibiscus moscheutos)* Perennial with dark-eyed red, pink, or white flowers late summer to midfall. National Garden, Washington, D.C.

Ocean Spray *(Holodiscus discolor)* Shrub with creamy white flower clusters in summer and orange fall foliage. Native Plant Gardens, Royal British Columbia Museum; Loring M. Jones, Idaho Seedman

Wild Hydrangea *(H. aborescens)* Shrub with creamy white flowers in summer and huge ball-shaped dried flower heads in fall. Royal Botanical Gardens, Ontario

Oakleaf Hydrangea *(H. quercifolia)* Shrub with white summer flowers aging to pink and rich wine red fall foliage. Linda Yang, New York City; Royal Botanical Gardens, Ontario

> 'Snow Queen' (more floriferous)—Mt. Cuba Center, Delaware; Gold Medal Award

Possumhaw *(Ilex decidua)* Shrub with orange to scarlet red berries lasting through winter. Royal Botanical Gardens, Ontario; National Wildflower Research Center, Texas

> 'Warren's Red' (consistent red berries)—Greensboro Arboretum, North Carolina

Inkberry *(Ilex glabra)* Shrub with handsome jet black berries that often persist through winter. Linda Yang, New York City

> 'Compacta' (rounded habit)—Greensboro Arboretum, North Carolina
> 'Densa' (denser, thicker)—Gold Medal Award

Winterberry *(Ilex verticillata)* Shrub with scarlet red berries persisting through January. Royal Botanical Gardens, Ontario; National Garden, Washington, D.C.

> 'Scarlet O'Hara' (numerous small berries)—Gold Medal Award
> 'Winter Gold' (yellow berries)—Royal Botanical Gardens, Ontario
> 'Winter Red' (long-lasting berries)—Mt. Cuba Center, Delaware; Gold Medal Award

Yaupon Holly *(Ilex vomitoria)* Evergreen shrub decorated with numerous bright red berries in fall. Caroline Dormon Nature Preserve, Louisiana

Florida Anise *(Illicium floridanum)* Shrub with red flowers in spring. Caroline Dormon Nature Preserve, Louisiana

Crested Iris *(I. cristata)* Groundcover with light blue, lilac, purple, or white flowers in spring. Caroline Dormon Nature Preserve, Louisiana

Copper Iris *(I. fulva)* Perennial with reddish brick petals and apricot centers late May to early June. Shaw Arboretum, Missouri

Louisiana Iris *(I. X 'Louisiana', a group of native species that interbreed)* Stunning perennial group with spring to summer flowers in every color of the spectrum, plus white. Caroline Dormon Nature Preserve, Louisiana

Contraband Girl *(Iris virginica 'Contraband Girl')* Perennial with blue purple flowers late May to early June. Shaw Arboretum, Missouri

Virginia Sweetspire *(Itea virginica 'Henry's Garnet')* Shrub with fragrant white flowers late spring to early summer and scarlet to purple red fall foliage. Gold Medal Award

Twinleaf *(Jeffersonia diphylla)* Perennial with white flowers in early spring. David Benner, Pennsylvania

Nova Cedar *(Juniperus virginiana 'Nova')* Narrow, upright conifer with bluish green foliage. U.S. National Arboretum, Washington, D.C.

Silver Spreader Cedar *(Juniperus virginiana 'Silver Spreader')* Conifer with low, greenish silver foliage. U.S. National Arboretum, Washington, D.C.

Mountain Laurel *(Kalmia latifolia)* Evergreen shrub with large, beautiful white to blush pink blossoms in spring. Caroline Dormon Nature Preserve, Louisiana

Box Sandmyrtle *(Leiophyllum buxifolium)* Shrub with pink buds opening to white flowers in spring. Will Ingwersen, Great Britain

Drooping Leucothoe *(L. fontanesiana 'Rainbow')* Shrub with white flowers in spring and glossy green leaves variegated with pink, cream, and yellow tints. Greensboro Arboretum, North Carolina

Lewisia *(L. cotyledon hybrids)* Perennial with white, orange, salmon, or pink flowers in late spring. Grethe B. Petersen, Denmark

Meadow Blazingstar *(Liatris ligulistylus)* Corm with crimson red buds that open to purple flowers midsummer through Labor Day. Neil Diboll, Wisconsin

Kansas Gayfeather *(Liatris pychnostachya)* Corm with spikes of purple flowers in midsummer. Iowa Department of Transportation; Bonnie Harper-Lore, Minnesota

Gayfeather *(Liatris spicata)* Corm with lavender pink flower spikes in summer. Grethe B. Petersen, Denmark; Frans M. Roozen, Dutch Bulbman

Canada Lily *(L. canadense)* Bulb with crimson-spotted lemon yellow flowers in summer. John E. Bryan, Bulb Expert

Leopard Lily *(L. pardalinum)* Bulb with brown-spotted orange red flowers in July. John E. Bryan, Bulb Expert

Spicebush *(Lindera benzoin)* Shrub with fragrant yellow flowers in spring, scarlet red berries in September, and bright yellow fall foliage. Dawes Arboretum, Ohio; David Benner, Pennsylvania

Blue Flax *(Linum perenne* var. *lewisii)* Perennial with petite blue flowers for almost three months, starting when snow melts. Penny A. Wilson, California

Tulip Tree *(Liriodendron tulipifera)* Tree with large creamy flowers in late spring and lemon yellow fall foliage. Famous and Historic Trees

Cardinal Flower *(Lobelia cardinalis)* Perennial with scarlet flowers in late summer. Dawes Arboretum, Ohio; National Wildflower Research Center, Texas

Ruby Slippers *(Lobelia* X *hybrida* 'Ruby Slippers') Perennial with spikes of ruby red flowers late summer into early fall. Patricia A. Taylor, New Jersey

Trumpet Honeysuckle *(Lonicera sempervirens)* Vine with red, orange, or yellow flowers throughout summer. Bernheim Arboretum, Kentucky; Linda Yang, New York City; National Wildflower Research Center, Texas

Wild Lupine *(Lupinus perennis)* Perennial with spires of blue flowers in spring. Bonnie Harper-Lore, Minnesota

Streamside Lupine *(Lupinus polyphyllus* hybrids) Perennial with yellow, white, blue through red, or pink flowers late spring into summer. Grethe B. Petersen, Denmark

Osage Orange *(Maclura pomifera)* Tough tree with yellow fall foliage. Famous and Historic Trees

Cucumbertree Magnolia *(M. acuminata)* Majestic specimen tree with creamy yellow green flowers in late spring and pink to red berried conelike fruits in early fall. William Flemer III, Nurseryman

Southern Magnolia *(M. grandiflora)* Tree with large, fragrant, creamy white flowers in June and July.

> 'Edith Bogue' (extra hardy)—Mt. Cuba Center, Delaware; Gold Medal Award
> 'Little Gem' (dwarf)—Greensboro Arboretum, North Carolina

Bigleaf Magnolia *(M. macrophylla)* Tree with fragrant, creamy white flowers in early summer. Caroline Dormon Nature Preserve, Louisiana

Sweetbay Magnolia *(M. virginiana)* Tree with large creamy white flowers in late spring and sporadic bloom through summer. New York Botanical Garden; Greensboro Arboretum, North Carolina

Oregon Grape *(Mahonia aquifolium)* Shrub with yellow flowers in spring and edible blue berries in summer. Leach Botanical Garden, Oregon

Longleaf Oregon Grape *(Mahonia nervosa)* Evergreen shrub with yellow flowers in late spring and edible dark blue berries in late summer. Native Plant Gardens, Royal British Columbia Museum

Creeping Holly Grape *(Mahonia repens)* Groundcover with yellow flowers in late spring and dark blue berries in late September. Loring M. Jones, Idaho Seedman

Agarito *(Mahonia trifoliata)* Evergreen shrub with yellow flowers in early spring and bright red berries in summer. National Wildflower Research Center, Texas

Turk's Cap *(Malvaviscus arboreus* var. *drummondii)* Hardy annual with red flowers late summer into fall. Atlanta History Center, Georgia; National Wildflower Research Center, Texas

Barbara's Buttons *(Marshallia grandiflora)* Perennial with pink flowers in summer. Pierre Bennerup, Perennial Plantsman

Ostrich Fern *(Matteuccia struthiopteris)* Tall, dramatic fern with a potential to be invasive. F. Gordon Foster, Fern Expert

Virginia Bluebell *(Mertensia virginica)* Perennial with pink buds opening to sky blue flowers in early spring. Monticello, Virginia

Climbing Hempweed *(Mikania scandens)* Vine with fragrant, blush pink flowers late summer into fall. Atlanta History Center, Georgia

Mina *(M. lobata)* Vine with banana-shaped red, orange, yellow, and white flowers late summer to frost. Patricia A. Taylor, New Jersey

Bee Balm *(Monarda didyma)* Perennial with purple, red, pink, or white flowers in summer. National Garden, Washington, D.C.

Wild Bergamot *(Monarda fistulosa)* Perennial with lavender flowers in summer. Michigan Department of Transportation

Horsemint *(Monarda punctata)* Perennial with purple-spotted yellow flowers in summer. Garden in the Woods, Massachusetts

Purple Butterfly Mint *(Monardella antonina)* Hardy annual with pale purple flower balls from July to December. Penny A. Wilson, California

Lindheimer Muhly *(Muhlenbergia lindheimeri)* Grass with fountainlike form and silvery plumes in fall. National Wildflower Research Center, Texas

Deer Grass *(Muhlenbergia rigens)* Grass with upright gray green leaves that emerge in spring and fan out as they mature to buff by fall. John Greenlee, Grass Expert

Wax Myrtle *(Myrica cerifera)* Willowy evergreen shrub with numerous, waxy, pale gray berries. Caroline Dormon Nature Preserve, Louisiana

Bayberry *(Myrica pensylvanica)* Shrub with neat, dark green foliage and grayish white berries over winter. Mt. Cuba Center, Delaware; Royal Botanical Gardens, Ontario

Black Tupelo *(Nyssa sylvatica)* Tree with scarlet red fall foliage. Bernheim Arboretum, Kentucky

Evening Primrose *(Oenothera biennis)* Biennial with yellow flowers all summer. Grethe B. Petersen, Denmark

Missouri Primrose *(Oenothera missouriensis)* Perennial with yellow flowers in summer. Will Ingwersen, Great Britain

Prickly Pear *(Opuntia humifusa)* Perennial with large yellow flowers in early summer. Pierre Bennerup, Perennial Plantsman

Golden Club *(Orontium aquaticum)* Aquatic perennial with golden yellow flowers in early spring. Caroline Dormon Nature Preserve, Louisiana

Cinnamon Fern *(Osmunda cinnamomea)* Fern with fertile fronds that shoot up as "cinammon sticks" among rich green foliage. F. Gordon Foster, Fern Expert

Interrupted Fern *(Osmunda claytoniana)* Fern with rich green, leathery fronds. F. Gordon Foster, Fern Expert

American Hop Hornbeam *(Ostrya virginiana)* Tree with yellow fall foliage. Dawes Arboretum, Ohio

Redwood Sorrel *(Oxalis oregana)* Groundcover with cloverlike leaves and white or rose flowers in spring. Leach Botanical Garden, Oregon

Sourwood *(Oxydendron arboreum)* Tree with sprays of creamy white flowers in July and scarlet red fall foliage. Greensboro Arboretum, North Carolina

Allegheny Pachysandra *(P. procumbens)* Groundcover with mottled purple spring foliage. Mt. Cuba Center, Delaware; New York Botanical Garden

Switch Grass *(Panicum virgatum)* Grass with gray to blue green leaves and airy panicles with dark red to purple tones that mature first to yellows and then to warm beiges. John Greenlee, Grass Expert; Dawes Arboretum, Ohio

Virginia Creeper *(Parthenocissus quinquefolia)* Vine with pinkish to crimson red fall foliage. National Garden, Washington, D.C.

Pavonia *(P. lasiopetala)* Annual with pink flowers from late spring to frost. National Wildflower Research Center, Texas

Cobaea Penstemon *(P. cobaea)* Perennial with purple, lavender, or white flowers in late spring. Dyck Arboretum of the Plains, Kansas

Bush Penstemon *(P. fruticosus)* Groundcover with mats of large purple or lavender blue flowers in summer. Native Plant Gardens, Royal British Columbia Museum

Shell-leaf Penstemon *(P. grandiflorus)* Perennial with lavender flowers in late spring. Dyck Arboretum of the Plains, Kansas

Blue Bedder *(Penstemon heterophyllus var. purdyi)* Groundcover with rich blue or striking purple flowers spring well into summer. Penny A. Wilson, California

Smalls's Beard Tongue *(Penstemon smallii)* Perennial with pink and white flowers late spring into summer. Garden in the Woods, Massachusetts

Wild Mock Orange *(Philadelphus lewisii)* Shrub with fragrant white flowers in early summer and yellow fall foliage. Native Plant Gardens, Royal British Columbia Museum; Loring M. Jones, Idaho Seedman

Blue Woodland Phlox *(P. divaricata)* Groundcover with fragrant light blue flowers in spring. Garden in the Woods, Massachusetts; David Benner, Pennsylvania

Smooth Phlox *(P. glaberrima)* Perennial with reddish purple to pink flowers spring well into summer. Shaw Arboretum, Missouri

Prairie Phlox *(P. pilosa)* Groundcover with reddish purple flowers in late spring. Bonnie Harper-Lore, Minnesota

Ozark Phlox *(P. pilosa var. ozarkana)* Groundcover with deep rose colored flowers in late spring. Shaw Arboretum, Missouri

Creeping Phlox *(P. stolonifera)* Groundcover with blue, pink, white, or purple violet flowers in spring. David Benner, Pennsylvania

Crackerjack Phlox *(P. subulata hybrid 'Crackerjack')* Groundcover with glowing red pink flowers in spring. Pierre Bennerup, Perennial Plantsman

Obedient Plant *(Physostegia virginiana)* Perennial with rose, pink, or white flowers and with bloom times ranging from midsummer to early fall. Atlanta History Center, Georgia

Colorado Blue Spruce *(Picea pungens)* Conifer with blue green foliage. Following cultivars recommended by U.S. National Arboretum, Washington, D.C.

> 'Fat Albert' (shorter and stouter than species)
> 'Hoopsii' (majestic and with magnificent blue foliage)
> 'R. H. Montgomery' (shortest of all)

Mountain Andromeda *(Pieris floribunda)* Shrub with white flowers in spring. Will Ingwersen, Great Britain

Ponderosa Pine *(Pinus ponderosa)* Conifer with dark green, horizontal branches. Loring M. Jones, Idaho Seedman

Dwarf Eastern White Pine *(Pinus strobus 'Nana')* Dwarf conifer with bluish green needles. U.S. National Arboretum, Washington, D.C.

American Jacob's Ladder *(Polemonium reptans)* Perennial with blue flowers early to midspring. Patricia A. Taylor, New Jersey

Rock Polypody *(Polypodium virginianum)* Beautiful specimen fern for rock gardens. F. Gordon Foster, Fern Expert

Christmas Fern *(Polystichum acrostichoides)* Fern with dark, evergreen fronds. Mt. Cuba Center, Delaware; F. Gordon Foster, Fern Expert; Linda Yang, New York City

Western Sword Fern *(Polystichum munitum)* Fern with large, once-pinnate evergreen fronds. Native Plant Gardens, Royal British Columbia Museum; Leach Botanical Garden, Oregon

Cherokee Plum *(Prunus angustifolia)* Shrub with white flowers in spring, edible reddish yellow fruits in summer, and yellow fall foliage. Monticello, Virginia

Douglas Fir *(Pseudotsuga menziesii)* Conifer with dark green needles. Loring M. Jones, Idaho Seedman

Antelope Bitterbush *(Purshia tridentata)* Shrub with yellow flowers in spring and year-round gray foliage. Loring M. Jones, Idaho Seedman

White Oak *(Quercus alba)* State tree of Illinois with burgundy fall foliage. Famous and Historic Trees

Bur Oak *(Quercus macrocarpa)* Massive tree with ridged bark and yellow brown fall foliage. Iowa Department of Transportation

Pin Oak *(Quercus palustris)* Easily transplanted tree with colorful red fall foliage. William Flemer III, Nurseryman

Willow Oak *(Quercus phellos)* Shade tree with neat foliage turning yellow in fall. Monticello, Virginia

Live Oak *(Quercus virginiana)* Great stress-tolerant urban tree for South and Southwest. Famous and Historic Trees

Mexican Hat *(Ratibida columnifera)* Perennial with red and yellow flowers in summer. Dyck Arboretum of the Plains, Kansas

Red Mexican Hat *(Ratibida columnifera var. pulcherrima)* Perennial with rich red petals that skirt dark cones all summer into fall. Pierre Bennerup, Perennial Plantsman

Prairie Coneflower *(Ratibida pinnata)* Perennial with yellow flowers in midsummer. Iowa Department of Transportation; Michigan Department of Transportation; Bonnie Harper-Lore, Minnesota

Carolina Buckthorn *(Rhamnus caroliniana)* Tree with red berries in summer and golden yellow fall foliage. Bernheim Arboretum, Kentucky

Sweet Azalea *(Rhododendron arborescens)* Shrub with unusually fragrant white flowers in spring and rich red fall foliage. A. Richard Brooks, American Rhododendron Society

Coast Azalea *(Rhododendron atlanticum)* Shrub with fragrant pale pink or white flowers in spring and yellow fall foliage. A. Richard Brooks, American Rhododendron Society

Florida Flame Azalea *(Rhododendron austrinum)* Shrub with fragrant yellow to orange red flowers in spring and reddish to golden yellow fall foliage. A. Richard Brooks, American Rhododendron Society; Caroline Dormon Nature Preserve, Louisiana

Flame Azalea *(Rhododendron calendulaceum)* Shrub with yellow orange to reddish orange flowers in late spring and bright yellow fall foliage. A. Richard Brooks, American Rhododendron Society

Rhodora *(Rhododendron canadense)* Dwarf shrub with rose purple or white flowers in spring. A. Richard Brooks, American Rhododendron Society

Carolina Rhododendron *(R. carolinianum)* Compact, evergreen shrub with a profusion of white, blush pink, or rosy purple flowers in spring. A. Richard Brooks, American Rhododendron Society

Catawba Rhododendron *(R. catawbiense)* Hardy evergreen shrub with magenta, lilac, or purple flowers in late spring. A. Richard Brooks, American Rhododendron Society

Rosebay Rhododendron *(R. maximum)* Tall, evergreen shrub with purplish pink to white blossoms in early summer. A. Richard Brooks, American Rhododendron Society; David Benner, Pennsylvania

Western Azalea *(Rhododendron occidentale)* Shrub with fragrant white to blush pink flowers in spring and orange red fall foliage. A. Richard Brooks, American Rhododendron Society; Leach Botanical Garden, Oregon

Pinxterbloom *(Rhododendron periclymenoides)* Shrub with white to light pink flowers in late spring. Monticello, Virginia

Roseshell Azalea *(Rhododendron prinophyllum)* Shrub with fragrant rosy pink or purple flowers in May. A. Richard Brooks, American Rhododendron Society; David Benner, Pennsylvania

Pinkshell Azalea *(Rhododendron vaseyi)* Shrub with rose or white flowers in early May and crimson to purple fall foliage. A. Richard Brooks, American Rhododendron Society

Swamp Azalea *(Rhododendron viscosum)* Shrub with clove-scented white to light pink flowers in early summer and orange to purple fall foliage. A. Richard Brooks, American Rhododendron Society; David Benner, Pennsylvania

Fragrant Sumac *(Rhus aromatica)* Shrub with clusters of yellow flowers in early spring, bright red berries summer into winter, and orange to intense scarlet red fall foliage. Royal Botanical Gardens, Ontario

Staghorn Sumac *(Rhus typhina)* Small tree with yellowish green flower clusters in early summer; bright red berries late summer through winter; and yellow, orange, or bright red fall foliage. National Garden, Washington, D.C.

Golden Currant *(Ribes aureum)* Shrub with scented yellow flowers in spring and yellow, red, or purple fruits in late summer. California State University at Sacramento; Loring M. Jones, Idaho Seedman

Red Flowering Currant *(Ribes sanguineum)* Shrub with crimson red flowers in spring and bluish black fall berries. Native Plant Gardens, Royal British Columbia Museum; Leach Botanical Garden, Oregon

Matilija Poppy *(Romneya coulteri)* Perennial with large, fragrant white flowers all summer. California State University at Sacramento

Goldsturm Black-eyed Susan *(Rudbeckia fulgida* **var.** *sullivantii* **'Goldsturm')** Perennial with black-centered yellow flowers summer into fall. Grethe B. Petersen, Denmark

Black-eyed Susan *(Rudbeckia hirta)* Annual with golden yellow flowers all summer. Iowa Department of Transportation; Michigan Department of Transportation

'Indian Summer' (exceptionally large flowers on bushy plants)—All-America Selection

Cutleaf Coneflower *(Rudbeckia laciniata)* Perennial with yellow flowers late summer into fall. Atlanta History Center, Georgia

Sweet Black-eyed Susan *(Rudbeckia subtomentosa)* Perennial with golden yellow flowers in late summer. Neil Diboll, Wisconsin

Brown-eyed Susan *(Rudbeckia triloba)* Biennial with golden yellow flowers late July through September. Atlanta History Center, Georgia

Blue Sage *(Salvia azurea)* Perennial with blue flowers late summer into fall. Dyck Arboretum of the Plains, Kansas

Pozo Blue Sage *(Salvia clevelandii* **X** *S. leucophylla)* Evergreen shrub with violet blue flowers in summer. Penny A. Wilson, California

Lady in Red Salvia *(Salvia coccinea* **'Lady in Red')** Hardy annual with dwarf habit and scarlet red flower spikes. All-America Selection

Mealycup Sage *(Salvia farinacea)* Hardy annual with white or blue flower spikes all summer. National Wildflower Research Center, Texas

'Strata' (bicolored blue and white spikes)—All-America Selection

Autumn Sage *(Salvia greggii)* Hardy annual with red, coral, pink, or white flowers spring to frost. National Wildflower Research Center, Texas

Creeping Sage *(Salvia sonomensis)* Groundcover with blue violet flowers in spring. California State University at Sacramento

Hummingbird Sage *(Salvia spathacea)* Hardy annual with spikes of deep magenta flowers in summer. California State University at Sacramento; Penny A. Wilson, California

Bloodroot *(Sanguinaria canadensis)* Perennial with white flowers in early spring. National Garden, Washington, D.C.

Mandarin Orange *(Sanvitalia procumbens* **'Mandarin Orange')** Annual creeper with semidouble, golden orange flowers throughout summer. All-America Selection

Little Bluestem *(Schizachyrium scoparium)* Grass with stalks in blue to green hues that turn brilliant bronze red to orange in fall. John Greenlee, Grass Expert; Iowa Department of Transportation; Dyck Arboretum of the Plains, Kansas; Bonnie Harper-Lore, Minnesota; Neil Diboll, Wisconsin

Hoary Skullcap *(Scutellaria incana)* Perennial with blue flowers all summer. Bernheim Arboretum, Kentucky

Round-leaf Ragwort *(Senecio obovatus)* Groundcover with yellow flowers in spring. Michigan Department of Transportation

Prairie Dock *(Silphium terebinthinaceum)* Perennial with yellow flowers in late summer. New York Botanical Garden

Blue-eyed Grass *(Sisyrinchium angustifolium)* Groundcover with blue flowers in spring. Monticello, Virginia

Western Solomon's Seal *(Smilacina racemosa* var. *amplexicaulis)* Perennial with white flowers in spring and red berries in late summer. Leach Botanical Garden, Oregon

Stiff Goldenrod *(Solidago rigida)* Perennial with yellow flowers late summer into fall. Bonnie Harper-Lore, Minnesota

Seaside Goldenrod *(Solidago sempervirens)* Perennial with golden flowerheads in fall. Garden in the Woods, Massachusetts

Showy Goldenrod *(Solidago speciosa)* Perennial with blazing yellow flower clusters in fall. Neil Diboll, Wisconsin

Indian Grass *(Sorghastrum nutans)* Tall grass with soft, golden brown fall seedheads that become burnt orange over winter. John Greenlee, Grass Expert; Iowa Department of Transportation; Neil Diboll, Wisconsin

Indian Pink *(Spigelia marilandica)* Perennial with red and yellow tubular flowers late spring through early summer. Pierre Bennerup, Perennial Plantsman

Prairie Dropseed *(Sporobalus heterolepis)* Grass with spraying mounds of emerald green leaves that turn orange gold in fall and a rich rust brown in winter. John Greenlee, Grass Expert; Bonnie Harper-Lore, Minnesota; Shaw Arboretum, Missouri; Neil Diboll, Wisconsin

Celandine Poppy *(Stylophorum diphyllum)* Perennial with yellow flowers in spring and sometimes into midsummer. Linda Yang, New York City; David Benner, Pennsylvania

Snowdrop Bush *(Styrax officinalis* var. *californica)* Shrub with pendulant white flowers in spring. California State University at Sacramento

Snowberry *(Symphoricarpos albus)* Shrub with small pink flowers in spring and white berries late summer into fall. Will Ingwersen, Great Britain; Loring M. Jones, Idaho Seedman; Monticello, Virginia

Pearlberry *(Symphoricarpos* 'Mother of Pearl' **Doorenbos hybrid***)* Shrub with tiny pink flowers in early summer and iridescent blush pink berries in fall. Patricia A. Taylor, New Jersey

Golden Gate Marigold *(Tagetes patula* 'Golden Gate'*)* Annual with large mahogany flowers edged with gold. All-America Selection

Fringe Cups *(Tellima grandiflora)* Groundcover with small, greenish white bell flowers on wiry stems in late spring. Grethe B. Petersen, Denmark

Broad Beech Fern *(Thelypteris hexagonoptera)* Fern with crisp green leaves in summer and yellow and bronze fall color. Shaw Arboretum, Missouri

American Arborvitae *(Thuja occidentalis)* Conifer with fine textured, yellow green foliage. Linda Yang, New York City

'Emerald Green' (holds green color throughout winter)—U.S. National Arboretum, Washington, D.C.

'Sunkist' (bright gold splashes on tips of green foliage)—U.S. National Arboretum, Washington, D.C.

'Wareana Lutescens' (dense, dark green column flecked with creamy white)—U.S. National Arboretum, Washington, D.C.

Allegheny Foamflower *(Tiarella cordifolia)* Groundcover with white flowers in spring. New York Botanical Garden; Dawes Arboretum, Ohio; Royal Botanical Gardens, Ontario; David Benner, Pennsylvania; National Garden, Washington, D.C.

Mexican Shell Flower *(Tigridia pavonia)* Bulb with white, yellow, orange, or red petals and densely spotted, usually purplish, centers in summer. John E. Bryan, Bulb Expert; Linda Yang, New York City; Frans M. Roozen, Dutch Bulbman

Gamma Grass *(Tripsicum dactyloides)* Grass with magnificent fountains of dark evergreen foliage. John Greenlee, Grass Expert

Canadian Hemlock *(Tsuga canadensis)* Conifer with dark green foliage. Dawes Arboretum, Ohio

'Brandley' (dwarf; globose when young and matures into pyramidal form)—U.S. National Arboretum, Washington, D.C.

'Jeddeloh' (dwarf; low spreader with spiraling branches)—U.S. National Arboretum, Washington, D.C.

Blueberry *(Vaccinium corymbosum)* Shrub with white spring flowers, edible blue summer fruit, and crimson fall foliage. Linda Yang, New York City; David Benner, Pennsylvania

Evergreen Huckleberry *(Vaccinium ovatum)* Evergreen shrub with blush pink flowers in spring and edible dark purple berries in fall. Native Plant Gardens, Royal British Columbia Museum

Rose Verbena *(V. canadensis)* Hardy annual with purple, red, or pink flowers all summer and often into fall. Shaw Arboretum, Missouri

Wingstem *(Verbesina alternifolia)* Perennial with yellow daisylike flowers throughout summer. Atlanta History Center, Georgia

Culver's Root *(Veronicastrum virginica)* Perennial with spires of white or light blue flowers mid to late summer. Will Ingwersen, Great Britain; Royal Botanical Gardens, Ontario

American Alpine Speedwell *(Veronica wormskjoldii)* Perennial with blue flowers in midsummer. Patricia A. Taylor, New Jersey

Nannyberry Viburnum *(V. lentago)* Small tree with creamy white flower clusters in spring and purple red fall foliage. Iowa Department of Transportation

Count Pulaski Viburnum *(V. nudum 'Count Pulaski')* Shrub with creamy white flowers in early summer, salmon pink berries in early fall, and russet orange to earthy red fall foliage. Shaw Arboretum, Missouri

Winterthur Viburnum *(V. nudum 'Winterthur')* Shrub with creamy white flowers in early summer, dusty blue berries in early fall, and red to purple fall foliage. Gold Medal Award

Black Haw *(Viburnum prunifolium)* Shrub with white flowers in late spring, dark blue berries late summer through fall, and wine red fall foliage. Monticello, Virginia

Rusty Black Haw *(Viburnum rufidulum)* Tree with creamy white flowers in late spring and red to purple fall foliage. Bernheim Arboretum, Kentucky

American Cranberry Bush *(Viburnum trilobum)* Shrub with white spring flowers, red to orange berries late summer to late winter, and purplish red fall foliage. Royal Botanical Gardens, Ontario

Appalachian Violet *(Viola appalachiensis)* Groundcover with purple flowers in spring. Patricia A. Taylor, New Jersey

Labrador Violet *(Viola labridorica)* Groundcover with purple flowers in spring and purple-tinged foliage throughout growing season. Garden in the Woods, Massachusetts

Yellowroot *(Xanthoriza simplicissima)* Groundcover with delicate purple flowers in spring and yellow to reddish purple fall foliage. Bernheim Arboretum, Kentucky

Scarlet Splendor Zinnia *(Z. elegans 'Scarlet Splendor')* Annual with large semiruffled red flowers on plants that need no staking. All-America Selection

Heartleaf Alexander *(Zizia aptera)* Perennial with golden yellow flowers clustered like Queen Anne's lace in spring. Garden in the Woods, Massachusetts; Shaw Arboretum, Missouri

Golden Alexander *(Zizia aurea)* Perennial with yellow flowers in spring. Bonnie Harper-Lore, Minnesota

SOURCES

It's weird. Economics is almost a taboo word in horticulture. You can write about plants, you can breed them, you can go to exotic places looking for them, and you can design with them, but somehow you can never talk about making money from them. That's what this last and final text briefly touches on— the firms that sell the plants discussed in this book.

You, the gardener, form a symbiotic relationship with these firms. If you don't ask for high-quality, new plants you will not get them; the owners, after all, cannot afford to stay in business if there is no demand for their products. One of the nurseries below, for example, recently composted thousands of Virginia sweetspires (*Itea virginica*) because the expected demand for these carefree, multiseason shrubs never materialized. Many of these businesses extend their offerings beyond standard, proven money makers and work hard to introduce exceptional plants to gardeners. They supplement this work by writing informative catalogs, publishing articles in garden magazines, and lecturing throughout the country. Their contributions have immeasurably enriched our horticultural scene.

Your local garden center should be a major source of plants for your garden or landscape. It should offer the convenience of buying plants on the day you want to put them in the ground as well as the opportunity to inspect them personally before making a purchase. Too many garden centers, alas, exist in the horticultural equivalent of the Dark Ages. Their staff cannot answer questions beyond where to plant an impatiens or daylily and they will often tell you that the plants you want are not available. To help correct this last situation, I've provided the names of several excellent wholesale firms, chosen primarily to represent geographical diversity. Thus, if your garden center says it cannot obtain a plant for you, suggest that they contact one of the wholesale suppliers listed below.

However, because many of the wonderful plants described in this book are so little known, they can only be obtained through specialty nurseries; this means you will probably want to explore the great possibilities of buying plants through the mail. To make this task as initially easy as possible, I have deliberately limited the number of sources listed here. There are many more superb, knowledgeable nurseries to serve you and the best place to read and learn about many of them is Barbara J. Barton's book SPECIALTY NURSERIES (Houghton Mifflin). If your local library doesn't have it, tell them to get it.

MAIL-ORDER FIRMS

BULBS

The Daffodil Mart
Gloucester, Virginia 23061
800/255-2852
Catalog: Free

Large selection of high-quality bulbs at very low prices; many natives offered under large miscellaneous category

Dr. Joseph C. Halinar
2333 Crooked Finger Road
Scotts Mills, Oregon 97375
Catalog: 2 first-class stamps

Hybridizer of lilies, including several natives; primarily offers seed; does provide bulbs for leopard lily

McClure & Zimmerman
P.O. Box 368
Friesland, Wisconsin 53935
414/326-4220
Catalog: Free

Large offering of miscellaneous and small bulbs; good descriptions of each; native species usually marked as such

SEEDS

W. Atlee Burpee & Co.
Warminster, Pennsylvania 18974
800/888-1447
Catalog: Free

The source of marigold and zinnia seeds; many other popular annuals also offered; catalog does not indicate if a plant is native

Native American Seed
Mail Order Station
610 Main Street
Junction, Texas 76849
915/446-3600
Catalog: Free

Concentrates on seed for plants native to Texas; supplier for National Wildflower Research Center; quantities offered from packet to bulk

New England Wild Flower Society
180 Hemenway Road
Framingham, Massachusetts 01701-2699
Catalog: $2.50 check made out
   to SEEDS

Offers seeds for many hard-to-find perennials and a selection of shrubs and ferns; catalog request must be received by March 1

Northplan
P.O. Box 9107
Moscow, Idaho 83843-1607
Catalog: Long SASE

Offers seeds for woody ornamentals and perennials; see description on page 25

Pinetree Garden Seeds
New Gloucester, Maine 04260
207/926-3400
Catalog: Free

Dedicated to the home gardener, thus offers small seed packets at very reasonable prices; many old-fashioned flowers, including annuals, and perennials; does not indicate if a plant is native

Prairie Moon Nursery
Route 3, Box 163
Winona, Minnesota 55987
507/452-1362
Catalog: $2

Largest selection of native perennials among firms listed here; small selection of woody ornamentals; over four dozen grasses; quantity varies from packet to bulk

Prairie Nursery
P.O. Box 306
Westfield, Wisconsin 53964
608/296-3679
Catalog: $3

Offers only native plants; extensive seed list of perennials, sedges, and grasses; quantities range from 1/8 ounce to 1 pound; data presented on number of seed by weight (such as 800,000 bottle gentian seeds per ounce)

Shepherd's Garden Seeds
Order Department
30 Irene Street
Torrington, Connecticut
203/482-3638
Catalog: Free

Specializes in vegetable seed; offers good selection of vines and old-fashioned flowers, many of which are American natives

Thompson & Morgan
P.O. Box 1308
Jackson, New Jersey 08527-0308
908/363-2225
Catalog: Free

Offers over 100 pages of flower seed in its color-filled catalog; many superior cultivars not found elsewhere; generally does not indicate if a plant is native American

PLANTS

Kurt Bluemel, Inc.
2740 Greene Lane

Wonderful selection of grasses, of which many are native; broad list of perennials as well

Baldwin, Maryland 21013-9523
410/557-7229
Catalog: $3

Compleat Garden Clematis Nursery
217 Argilla Road
Ipswich, Massachusetts 01938-2614
Catalog: $3

Clematis specialist; see description on
page 184

The Crownsville Nursery
P.O. Box 797
Crownsville, Maryland 21032
401/849-3143
Catalog: $2

Offers a wide range of perennials and some
woody ornamentals; native plants highlighted
in catalog copy; excellent packaging

Fairweather Gardens
P.O. Box 330
Greenwich, New Jersey 08323
609/451-6261
Catalog: $3

Specializes in woody ornamentals, with a
good percentage of these being American
species and cultivars

Forestfarm
990 Tetherow Road
Williams, Oregon 97544-9599
514/846-7269
Catalog: $3

Wonderful source for exceptionally
large selection of woody ornamentals
and perennials; indicates whether a plant
is native

Greenlee Nursery
301 East Franklin Avenue
Pomona, California 91766
909/629-9045
Catalog: $5
Price List: Free

Premier source of grasses, particularly
those native to western part of
continent

Lamtree Farm
2323 Copeland Road
Warrensville, North Carolina 28693
910/385-6144
Catalog: $2

Specializes in southeastern native trees and
shrubs

Las Pilitas Nursery
Las Pilitas Road

Premier source of California natives, including
woody ornamentals, perennials, and annuals

Santa Margarita, California 93453
Catalog: $10
Price List: 1 first-class stamp

Niche Gardens
1111 Dawson Road
Chapel Hill, North Carolina 27516
919/967-0078
Catalog: $3

Concentrates on native plants, including perennials and woody ornamentals; good source of many uncommon plants

Plant Delights Nursery
9241 Sauls Road
Raleigh, North Carolina 27603
919/772-4794
Catalog: 10 stamps

Catalog price not a typo—firm enjoys creative responses; when not praising hostas, focuses on native plants deserving wider use

Plants of the Wild
P.O. Box 866
Tekoa, Washington 99033
509/284-2848
Catalog: $1

Specializes in trees, shrubs, perennials, and bulbs native to Pacific Northwest

Prairie Moon Nursery
Route 3, Box 163
Winona, Minnesota 55987
507/452-1362
Catalog: $2

Only offers species plants; good selection of wildflowers (many rare), woody ornamentals, and grasses

Prairie Nursery
P.O. Box 306
Westfield, Wisconsin 53964
608/296-3679
Catalog: $3

Large selection of prairie flowers; selected grasses; many planting suggestions for different habitats and garden settings

The Primrose Path
R.D. 2, Box 110
Scottdale, Pennsylvania 15683
Catalog: $2

Likes to explore genera in depth; noted for breeding work in Tiarellas and Heucheras, and good source for many Oenotheras; indicates whether plant is native

Sunlight Gardens
174 Golden Lane
Andersonville, Tennessee 37705

Primarily offers southeastern natives, with some exotics—clearly marked as such— mixed in; great descriptive catalog with

423/494-8237
Catalog: $3

many design suggestions

Sunshine Farm & Gardens
Route 5EN
Renick, West Virginia 24966
304/497-3163
Catalog: $2

Plant fanatic Barry Glick runs two
businesses; one sells hot tubs and the other a
wide variety of plants, many of them hard-to-
find natives

Varga's Nursery
2631 Pickertown Road
Warrington, Pennsylvania 18976
215/343-0646
Catalog: $1

Fern specialist offering all ferns described
in this book

White Flower Farm
Litchfield, Connecticut 06759-0050
203/496-9600
Catalog: Free

Lushly illustrated catalog; beguiling copy;
many natives—usually not indicated as such
—among plant offerings

The Wildwood Flower
5233 U.S. 64 W
Pittsboro, North Carolina 27312
Catalog: $1

A very small nursery with a selection of
choice plants, the great majority being
native; nationally recognized for breeding
work in lobelias

Woodlanders, Inc.
1128 Colleton Avenue
Aiken, South Carolina 29801
803/648-7522
Catalog: $2

Specializes in native plants hardy from zone
8 north; many superior selections among its
extensive offerings

Yucca Do Nursery
P.O. Box 450
Waller, Texas 77484
Catalog: $4

Specializes in natives from Texas, the
Southwest, and Mexico; tempting selections
of little-known plants

WHOLESALE FIRMS

The following firms **do not sell plants at the retail level.** They are included in this book only as an
aid to help you obtain superb native plants through your local garden center or through the services of

a landscape architect or designer. None concentrate solely on native plants; all offer a good selection and Bowood Farms in Missouri features an outstanding variety.

CONNECTICUT	Sunny Border Nurseries, Inc. P.O. Box 483 1709 Kensington Road Kensington, Connecticut 06037 800/732-1627
GEORGIA	Saul Nurseries, Inc. P.O. Box 190403 Atlanta, Georgia 31119 404/458-0058
MICHIGAN	Walters Gardens, Inc. P.O. Box 137 Zeeland, Michigan 49464 616/772-4697
MISSOURI	Bowood Farms Inc. Foxcreek Lane Clarksville, Missouri 63336-9717 800/246-3840 (Provides separate list featuring all native plant offerings)
NEBRASKA	Bluebird Nursery, Inc. Box 460 Clarkson, Nebraska 68629 402/892-3457
OHIO	Springbrook Gardens P.O. Box 388 6776 Heisley Road Mentor, Ohio 44061 216/255-3059
OREGON	Blooming Nursery, Inc. 3839 Southwest Golf Course Road Cornelius, Oregon 97113 503/357-2904

INDEX